ACCOUNT

manga:SHIZUMU WATANABE

5

CONTENTS

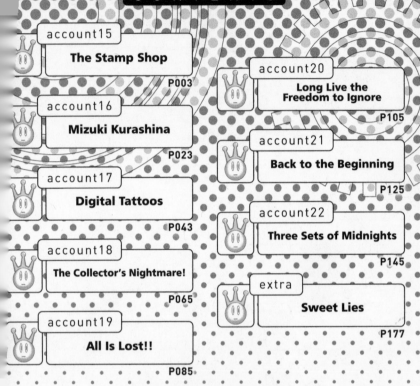

STORY

In April 20XX, shocking events suddenly befall Japan's national social network, Real Account. With no prior warning, 10,000 people are sucked into the Real Account Zone, their bodies left in the real world as they're forced to stake their lives in a series of outrageous and lethal games…

One of the players, Yuma Mukai, is fighting for his life alongside Ayame Kamijo. They've followed each other's accounts, uniting their fates for the rest of their time in the zone. The fourth game, "Operation: Reply or Regret," forces players to immediately reply to all texts—or else get hanged on the spot! The game continues until the player population is cut in half. How will the duo cope with being taken to the brink of exhaustion, as sleep becomes their greatest enemy?

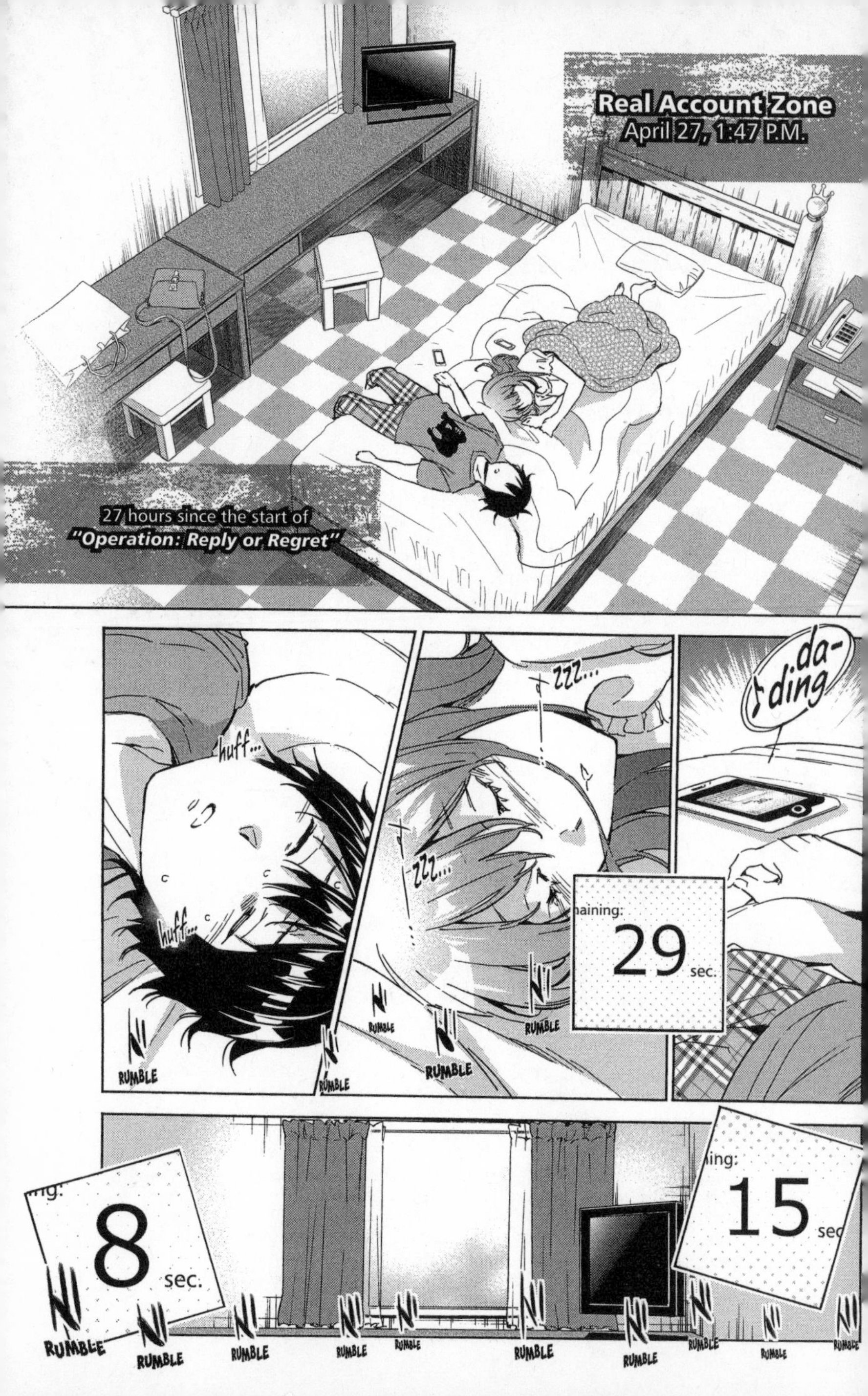
Real Account Zone
April 27, 1:47 P.M.
27 hours since the start of
"Operation: Reply or Regret"
da-ding
aining:
29 sec.
zzz...
zzz...
RUMBLE
RUMBLE
huff...
huff...
RUMBLE
RUMBLE
ing:
15 sec
ng:
8 sec.
RUMBLE RUMBLE RUMBLE RUMBLE RUMBLE RUMBLE RUMBLE RUMBLE RUMBLE RUMBLE

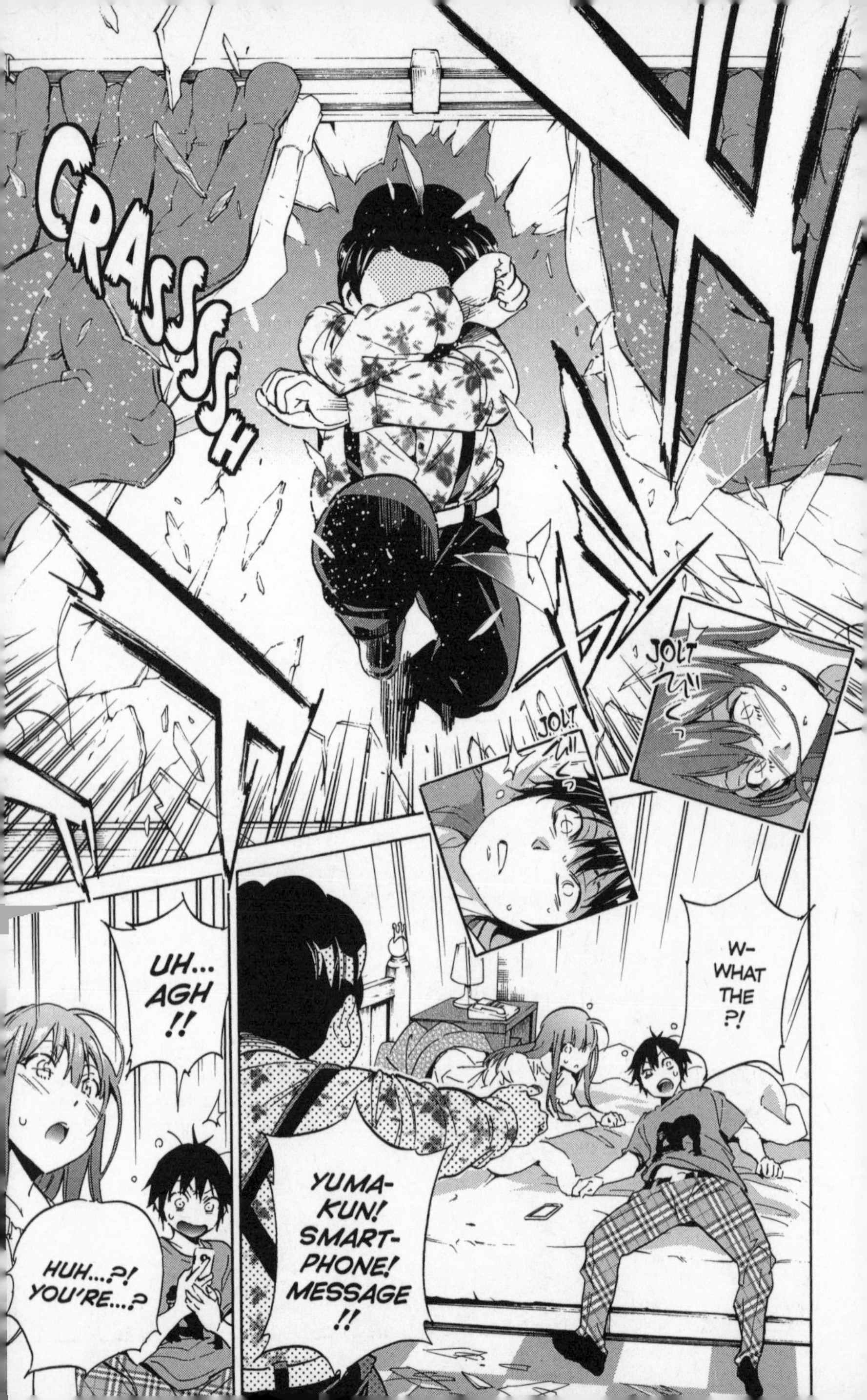
CRASSSSH
JOLT
JOLT
W-
WHAT
THE
?!
YUMA-
KUN!
SMART-
PHONE!
MESSAGE
!!
UH...
AGH
!!
HUH...?!
YOU'RE...?

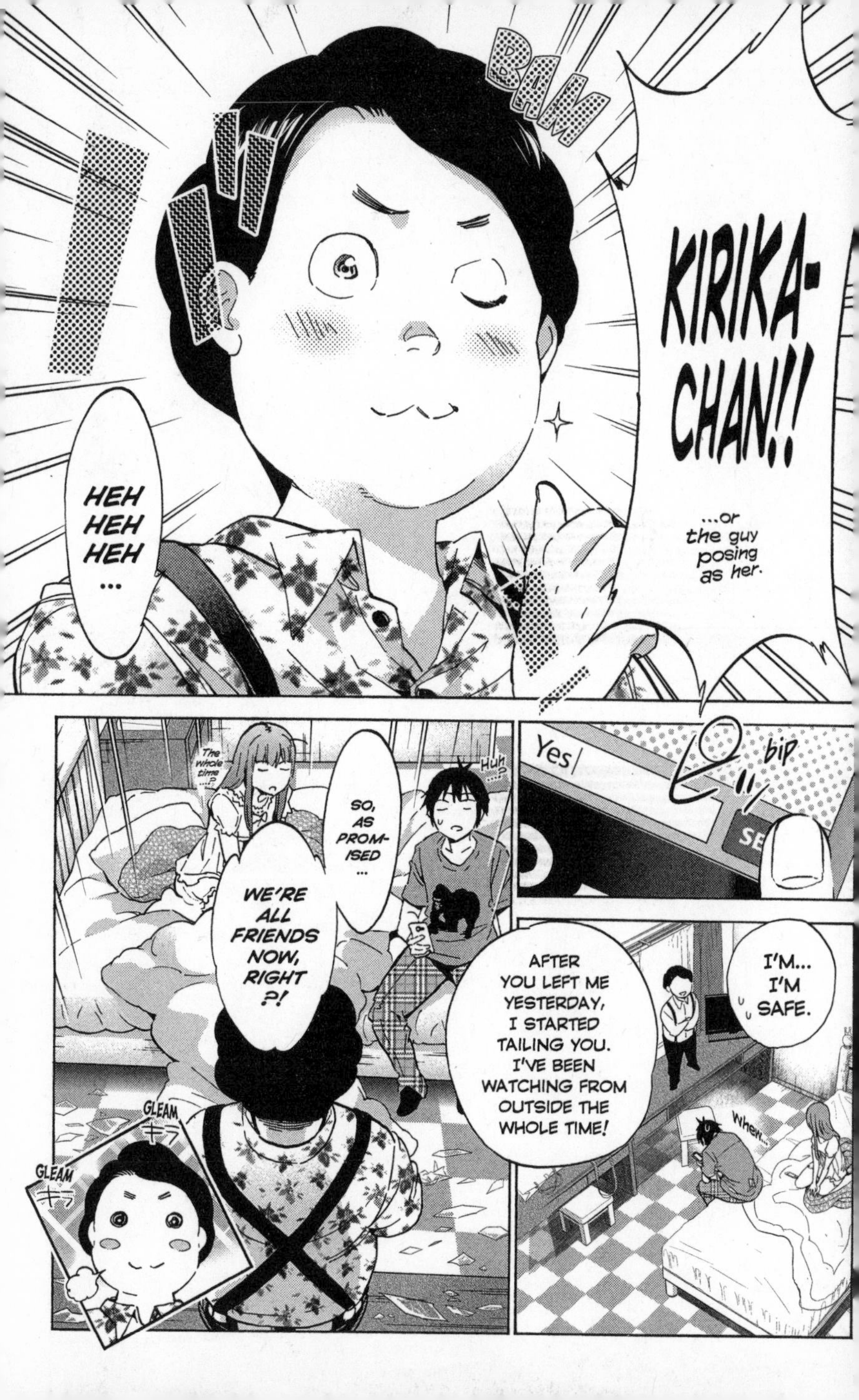
KIRIKA-CHAN!!
...or the guy posing as her.
BAM
HEH HEH HEH...
Yes|
bip
I'M... I'M SAFE.
AFTER YOU LEFT ME YESTERDAY, I STARTED TAILING YOU. I'VE BEEN WATCHING FROM OUTSIDE THE WHOLE TIME!
Whew...
Huh...?
SO, AS PROMISED...
The whole time...?
WE'RE ALL FRIENDS NOW, RIGHT?!
GLEAM
GLEAM

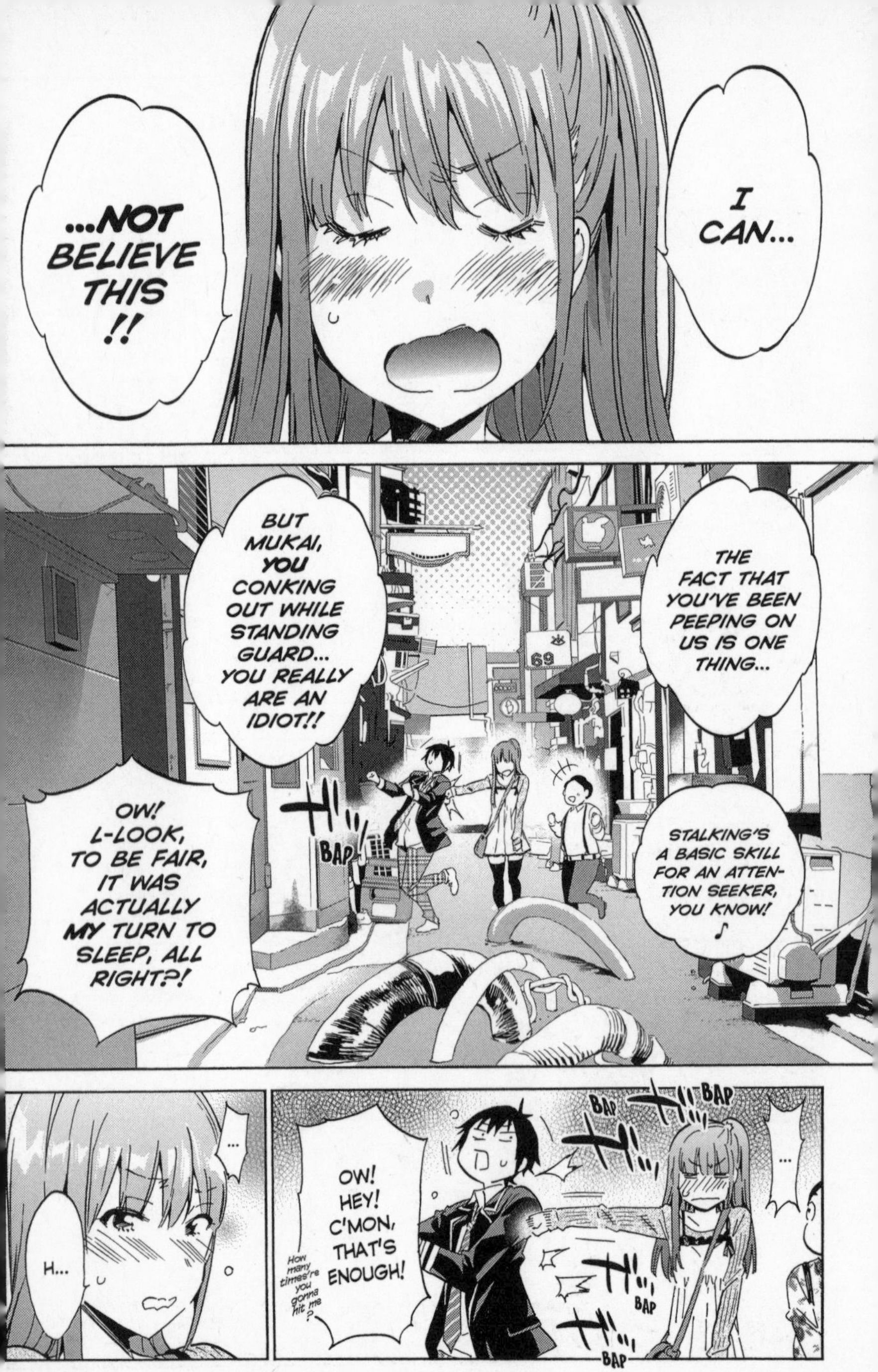
I CAN...
...NOT BELIEVE THIS!!
THE FACT THAT YOU'VE BEEN PEEPING ON US IS ONE THING...
BUT MUKAI, YOU CONKING OUT WHILE STANDING GUARD... YOU REALLY ARE AN IDIOT!!
STALKING'S A BASIC SKILL FOR AN ATTEN-TION SEEKER, YOU KNOW! ♪
BAP
OW! L-LOOK, TO BE FAIR, IT WAS ACTUALLY MY TURN TO SLEEP, ALL RIGHT?!
...
BAP
BAP
OW! HEY! C'MON, THAT'S ENOUGH!
How many times're you gonna hit me?
BAP
BAP
...
H...

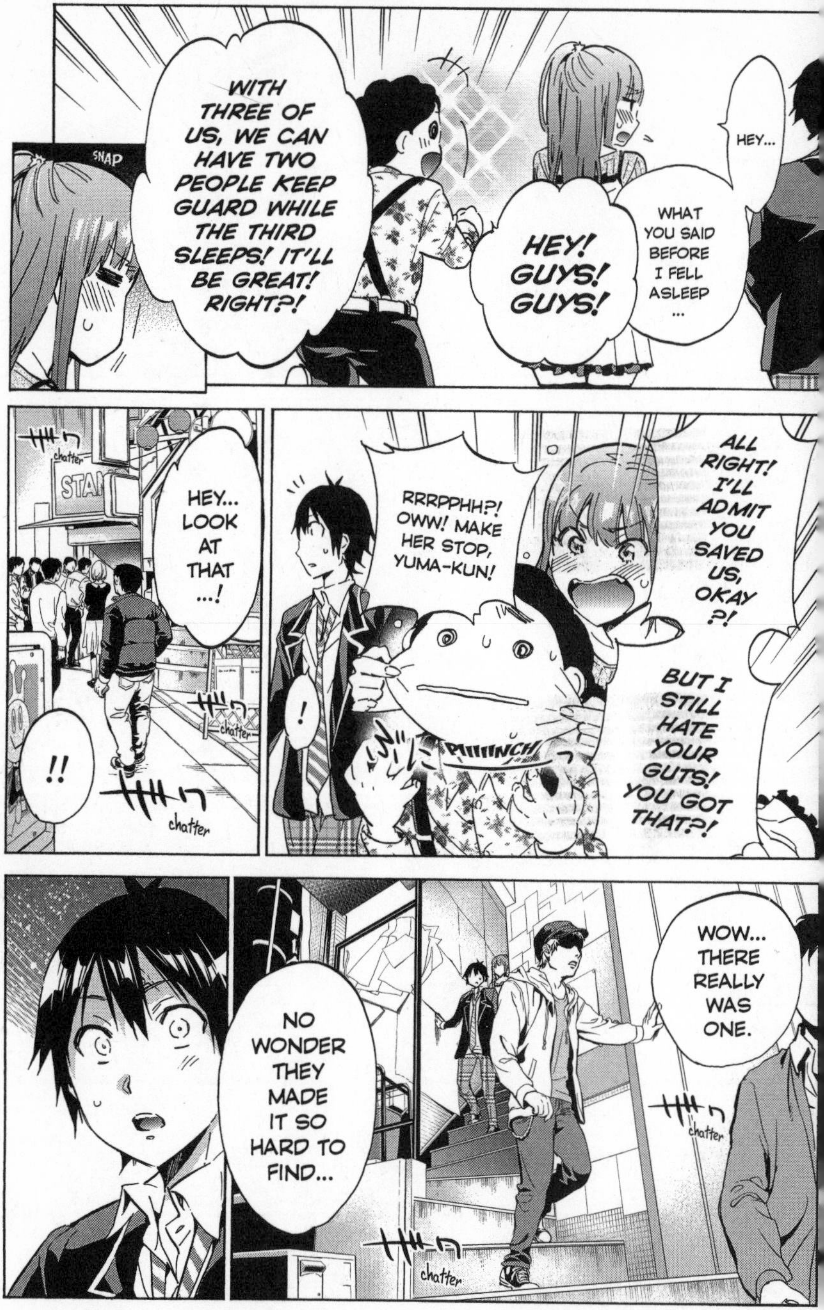
HEY...
WHAT YOU SAID BEFORE I FELL ASLEEP ...
HEY! GUYS! GUYS!
WITH THREE OF US, WE CAN HAVE TWO PEOPLE KEEP GUARD WHILE THE THIRD SLEEPS! IT'LL BE GREAT! RIGHT?!
SNAP
ALL RIGHT! I'LL ADMIT YOU SAVED US, OKAY?!
BUT I STILL HATE YOUR GUTS! YOU GOT THAT?!
RRRPPHH?! OWW! MAKE HER STOP, YUMA-KUN!
PIIIINCH
!
chatter
HEY... LOOK AT THAT ...!
chatter
!!
chatter
WOW... THERE REALLY WAS ONE.
chatter
chatter
NO WONDER THEY MADE IT SO HARD TO FIND...

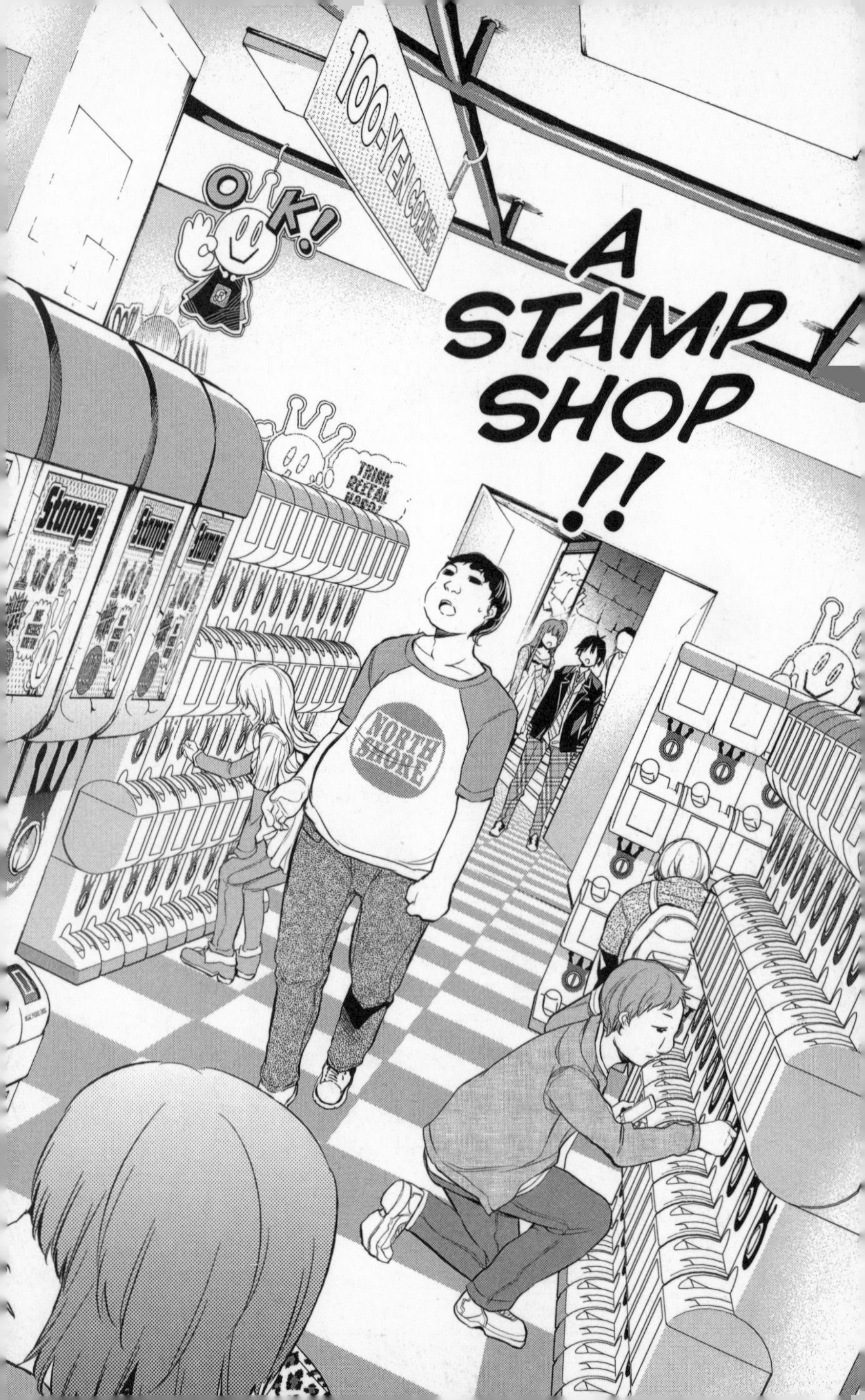
100-YEN CORNER
O K!
A STAMP SHOP!!
Stamps
Stamps
Stamps
NORTH SHORE

ACCOUNT 15
The Stamp Shop

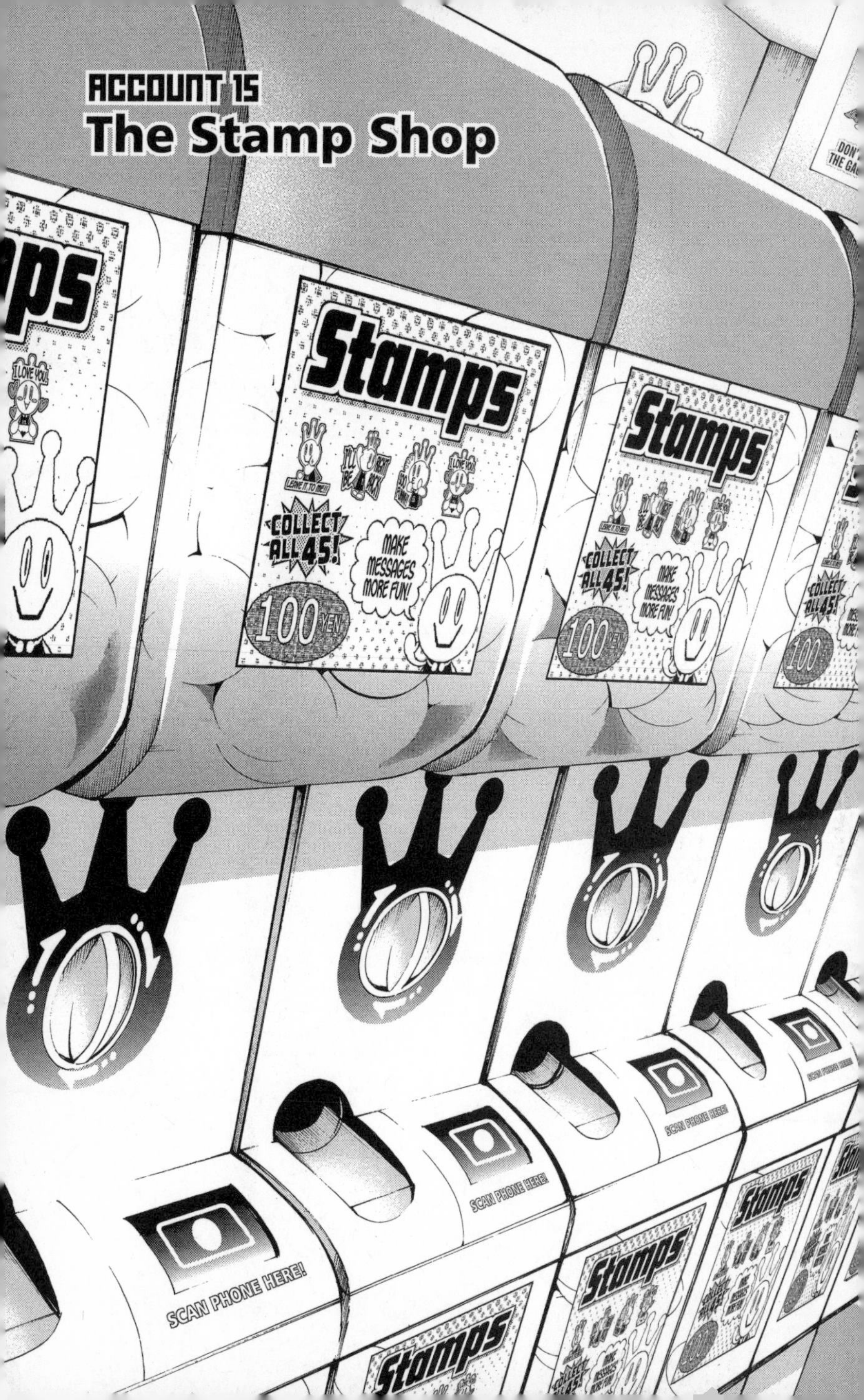
Stamps
I LOVE YOU!
LEAVE IT TO ME!!
I'LL BE RIGHT BACK
I LOVE YOU!
COLLECT ALL 45!
MAKE MESSAGES MORE FUN!
100 YEN
Stamps
COLLECT ALL 45!
MAKE MESSAGES MORE FUN!
100 YEN
SCAN PHONE HERE!
SCAN PHONE HERE!
SCAN PHONE HERE!
Stamps
Stamps
Stamps

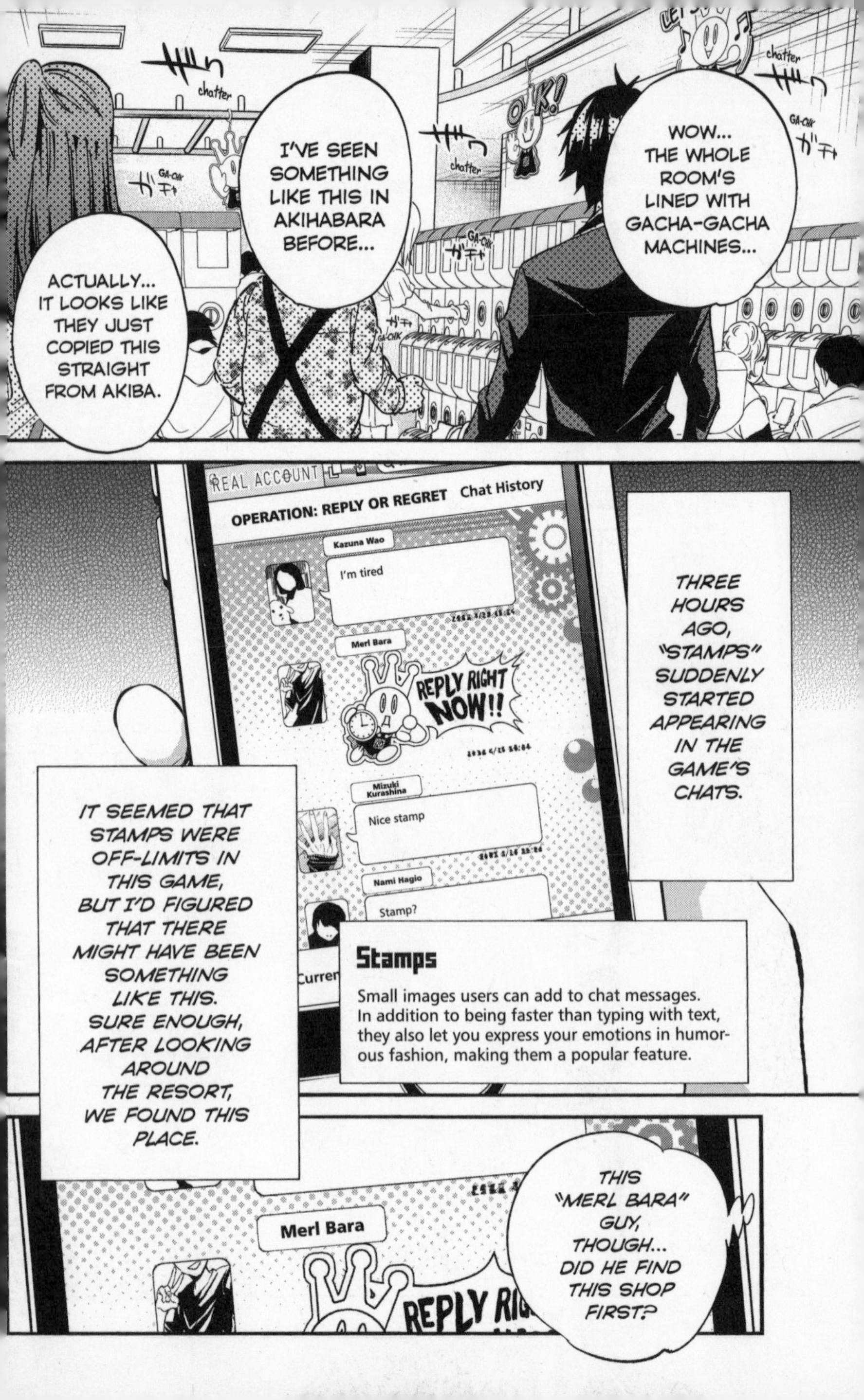
chatter
GA-CHK
WOW... THE WHOLE ROOM'S LINED WITH GACHA-GACHA MACHINES...
chatter
GA-CHK
I'VE SEEN SOMETHING LIKE THIS IN AKIHABARA BEFORE...
chatter
GA-CHK
ACTUALLY... IT LOOKS LIKE THEY JUST COPIED THIS STRAIGHT FROM AKIBA.
THREE HOURS AGO, "STAMPS" SUDDENLY STARTED APPEARING IN THE GAME'S CHATS.
REAL ACCOUNT
OPERATION: REPLY OR REGRET Chat History
Kazuna Wao
I'm tired
Merl Bara
REPLY RIGHT NOW!!
Mizuki Kurashina
Nice stamp
Nami Hagio
Stamp?
IT SEEMED THAT STAMPS WERE OFF-LIMITS IN THIS GAME, BUT I'D FIGURED THAT THERE MIGHT HAVE BEEN SOMETHING LIKE THIS. SURE ENOUGH, AFTER LOOKING AROUND THE RESORT, WE FOUND THIS PLACE.
Stamps
Small images users can add to chat messages. In addition to being faster than typing with text, they also let you express your emotions in humorous fashion, making them a popular feature.
THIS "MERL BARA" GUY, THOUGH... DID HE FIND THIS SHOP FIRST?
Merl Bara
REPLY RIG

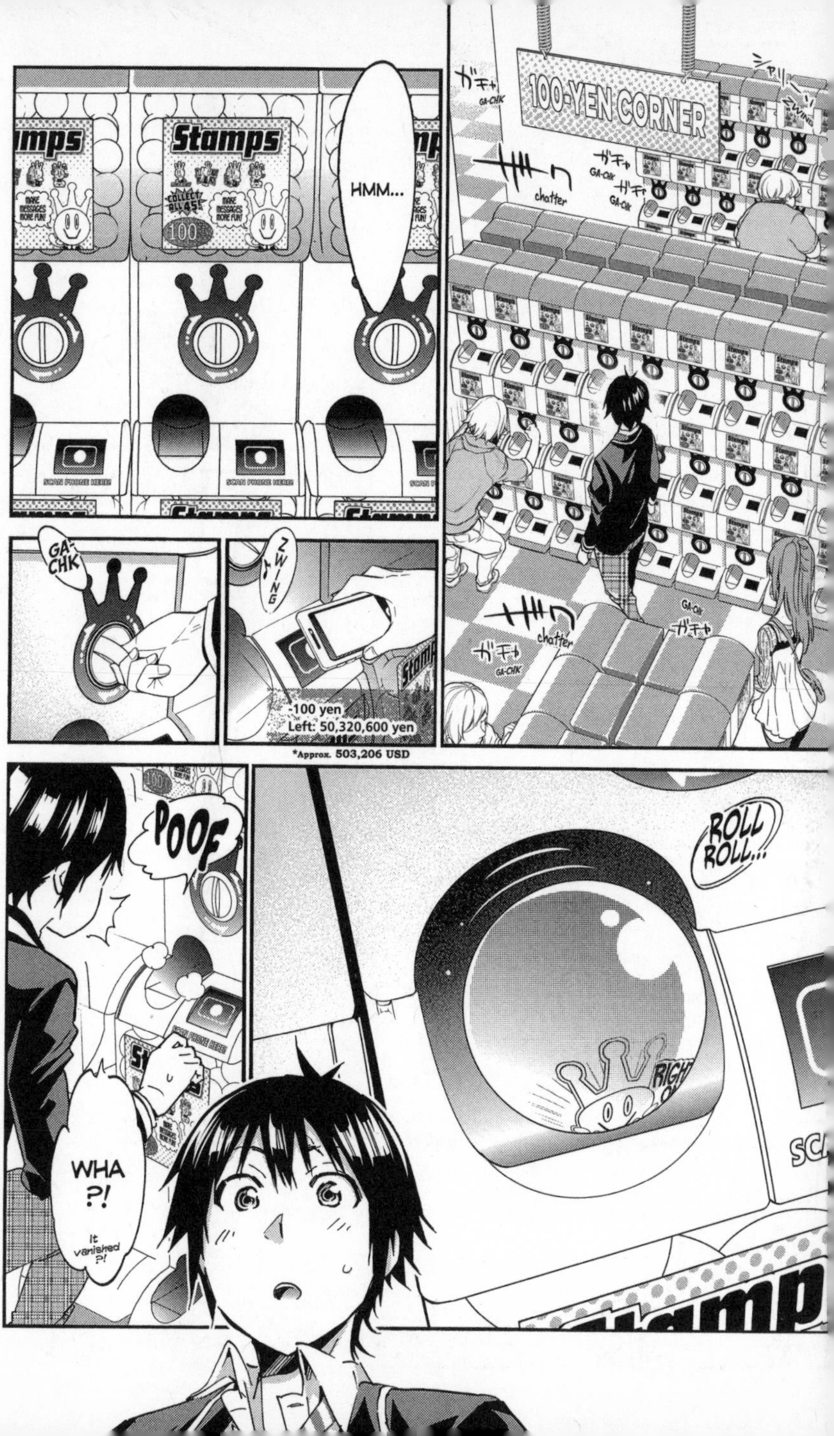
100-YEN CORNER
ZWING
GA-CHK
chatter
GA-CHK
GA-CHK
chatter
GA-CHK
GA-CHK
Stamps
COLLECT ALL 45!
MORE MESSAGES MORE FUN!
100
SCAN PHONE HERE!
HMM...
ZWING
-100 yen
Left: 50,320,600 yen
GA-CHK
*Approx. 503,206 USD
ROLL ROLL...
RIGHT
SCA
POOF
SCAN PHONE HERE!
WHA ?!
It vanished ?!

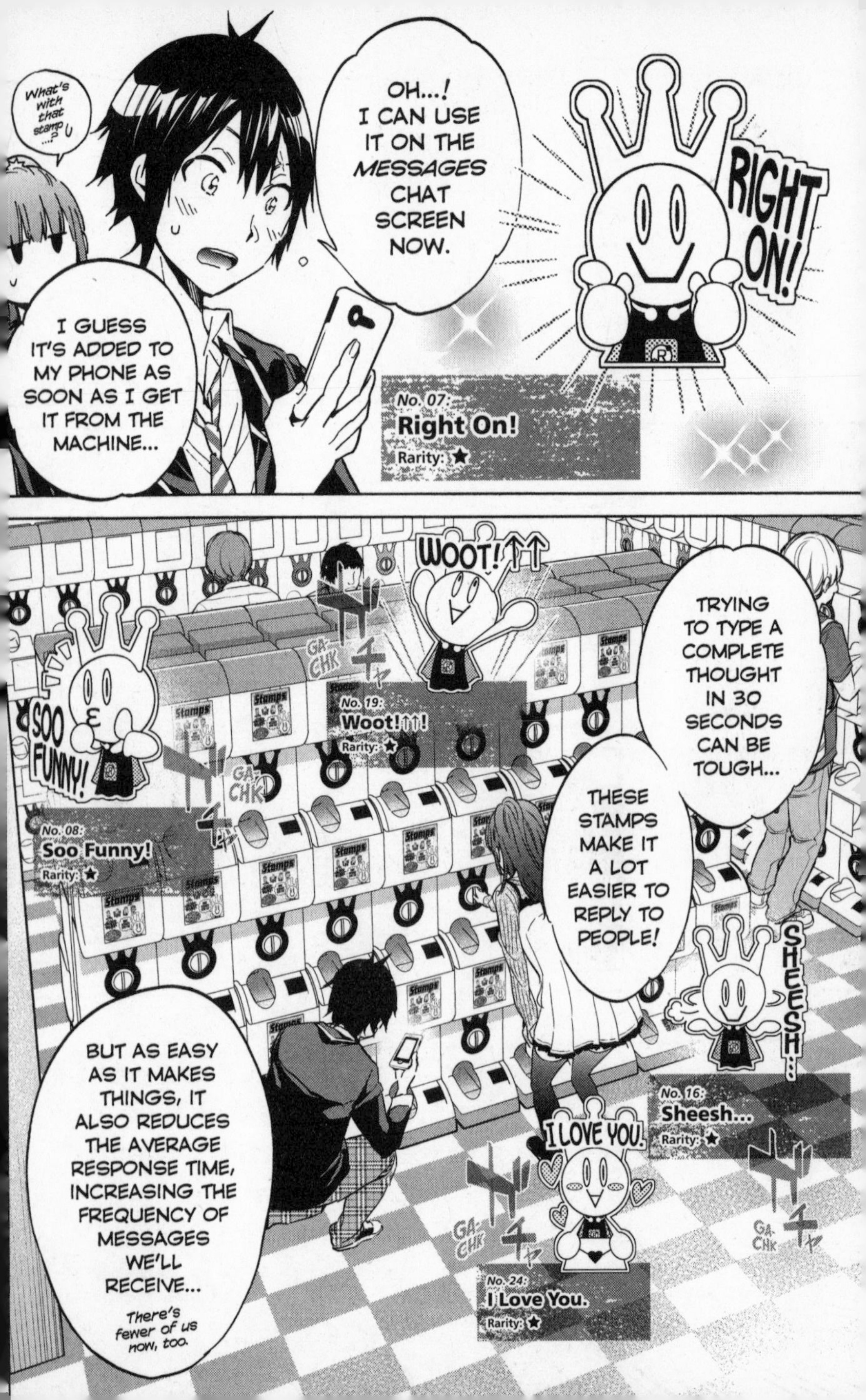
RIGHT ON!
No. 07:
Right On!
Rarity: ★
OH...! I CAN USE IT ON THE MESSAGES CHAT SCREEN NOW.
What's with that stamp ...?
I GUESS IT'S ADDED TO MY PHONE AS SOON AS I GET IT FROM THE MACHINE...
TRYING TO TYPE A COMPLETE THOUGHT IN 30 SECONDS CAN BE TOUGH...
WOOT!↑↑
GA-CHK
No. 19:
Woot!↑↑!
Rarity: ★
THESE STAMPS MAKE IT A LOT EASIER TO REPLY TO PEOPLE!
SOO FUNNY!
GA-CHK
No. 08:
Soo Funny!
Rarity: ★
SHEESH...
No. 16:
Sheesh...
Rarity: ★
GA-CHK
I LOVE YOU.
GA-CHK
No. 24:
I Love You.
Rarity: ★
BUT AS EASY AS IT MAKES THINGS, IT ALSO REDUCES THE AVERAGE RESPONSE TIME, INCREASING THE FREQUENCY OF MESSAGES WE'LL RECEIVE...
There's fewer of us now, too.

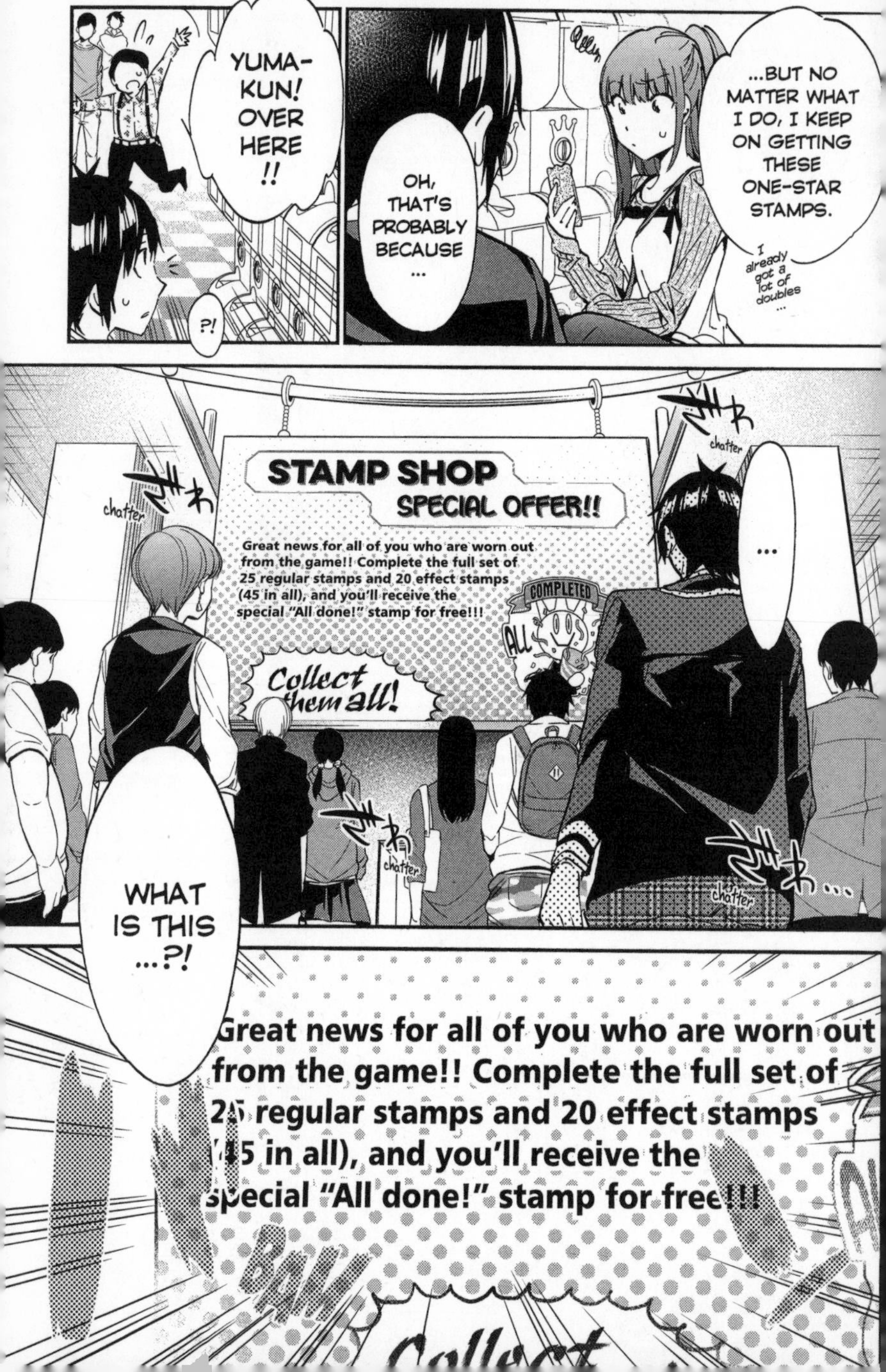
...BUT NO MATTER WHAT I DO, I KEEP ON GETTING THESE ONE-STAR STAMPS.
I already got a lot of doubles ...
OH, THAT'S PROBABLY BECAUSE ...
YUMA-KUN! OVER HERE!!
?!
chatter
...
STAMP SHOP
SPECIAL OFFER!!
Great news for all of you who are worn out from the game!! Complete the full set of 25 regular stamps and 20 effect stamps (45 in all), and you'll receive the special "All done!" stamp for free!!!
COMPLETED
ALL
Collect them all!
chatter
chatter
chatter...
WHAT IS THIS ...?!
Great news for all of you who are worn out from the game!! Complete the full set of 25 regular stamps and 20 effect stamps (45 in all), and you'll receive the special "All done!" stamp for free!!!

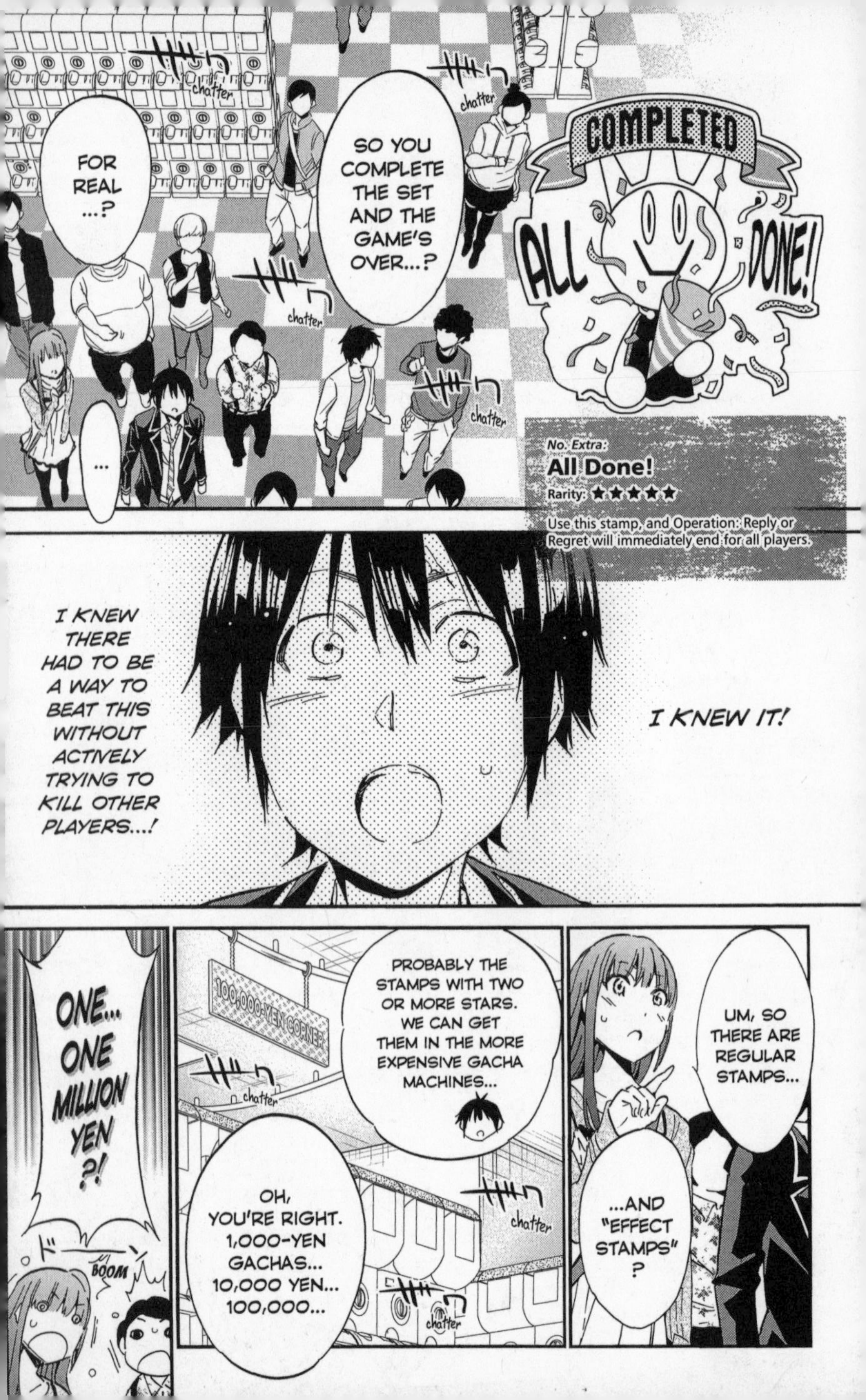
COMPLETED
ALL DONE!
No. Extra:
All Done!
Rarity: ★★★★★
Use this stamp, and Operation: Reply or Regret will immediately end for all players.
chatter
SO YOU COMPLETE THE SET AND THE GAME'S OVER...?
chatter
FOR REAL...?
chatter
chatter
...
I KNEW IT!
I KNEW THERE HAD TO BE A WAY TO BEAT THIS WITHOUT ACTIVELY TRYING TO KILL OTHER PLAYERS...!
UM, SO THERE ARE REGULAR STAMPS...
...AND "EFFECT STAMPS"?
100,000-YEN CORNER
PROBABLY THE STAMPS WITH TWO OR MORE STARS. WE CAN GET THEM IN THE MORE EXPENSIVE GACHA MACHINES...
chatter
chatter
OH, YOU'RE RIGHT. 1,000-YEN GACHAS... 10,000 YEN... 100,000...
chatter
ONE... ONE MILLION YEN?!
BOOM

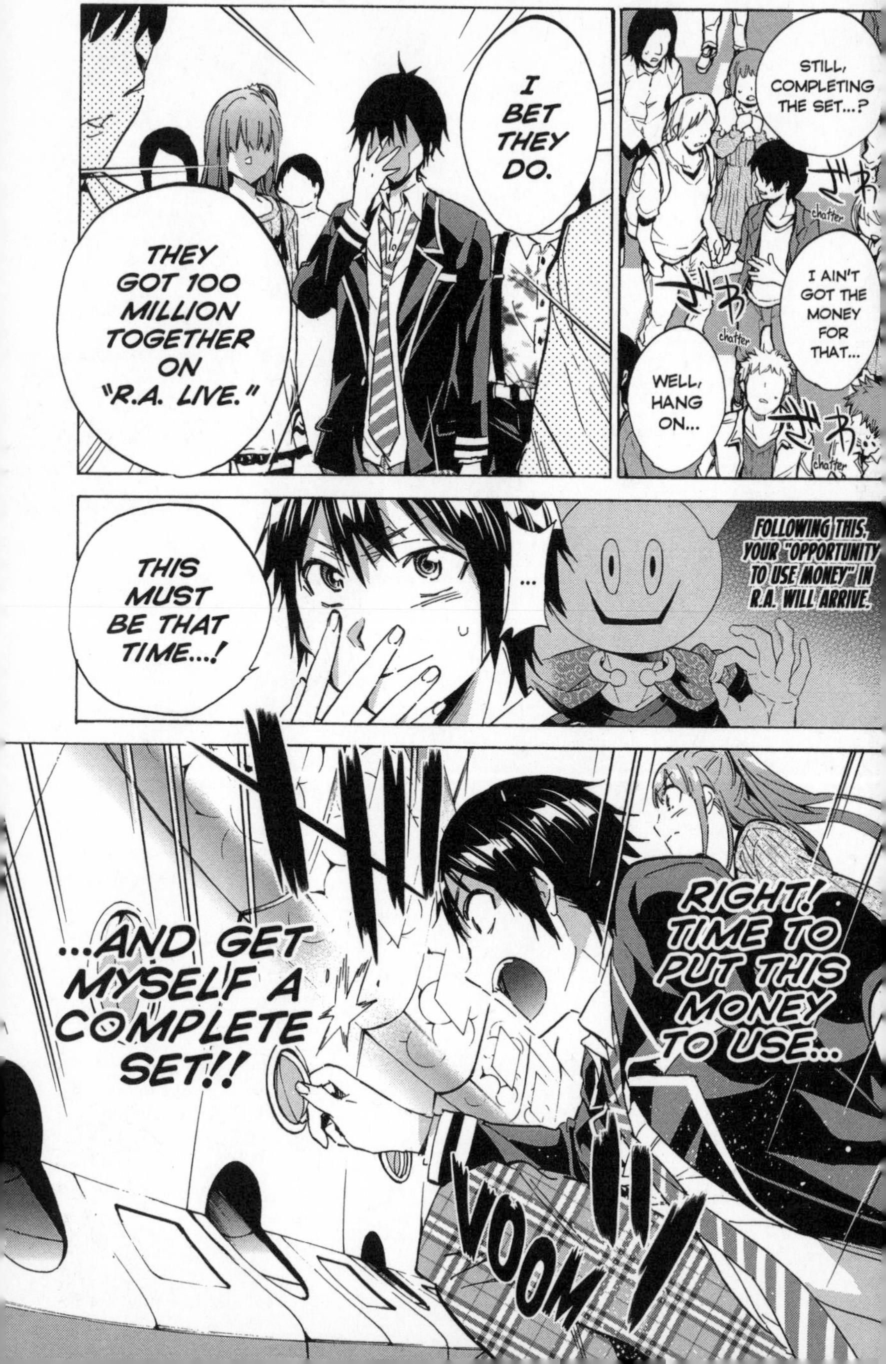
STILL, COMPLETING THE SET...?
chatter
I AIN'T GOT THE MONEY FOR THAT...
chatter
WELL, HANG ON...
chatter
I BET THEY DO.
THEY GOT 100 MILLION TOGETHER ON "R.A. LIVE."
FOLLOWING THIS, YOUR "OPPORTUNITY TO USE MONEY" IN R.A. WILL ARRIVE.
...
THIS MUST BE THAT TIME...!
RIGHT! TIME TO PUT THIS MONEY TO USE...
...AND GET MYSELF A COMPLETE SET!!
VOOM

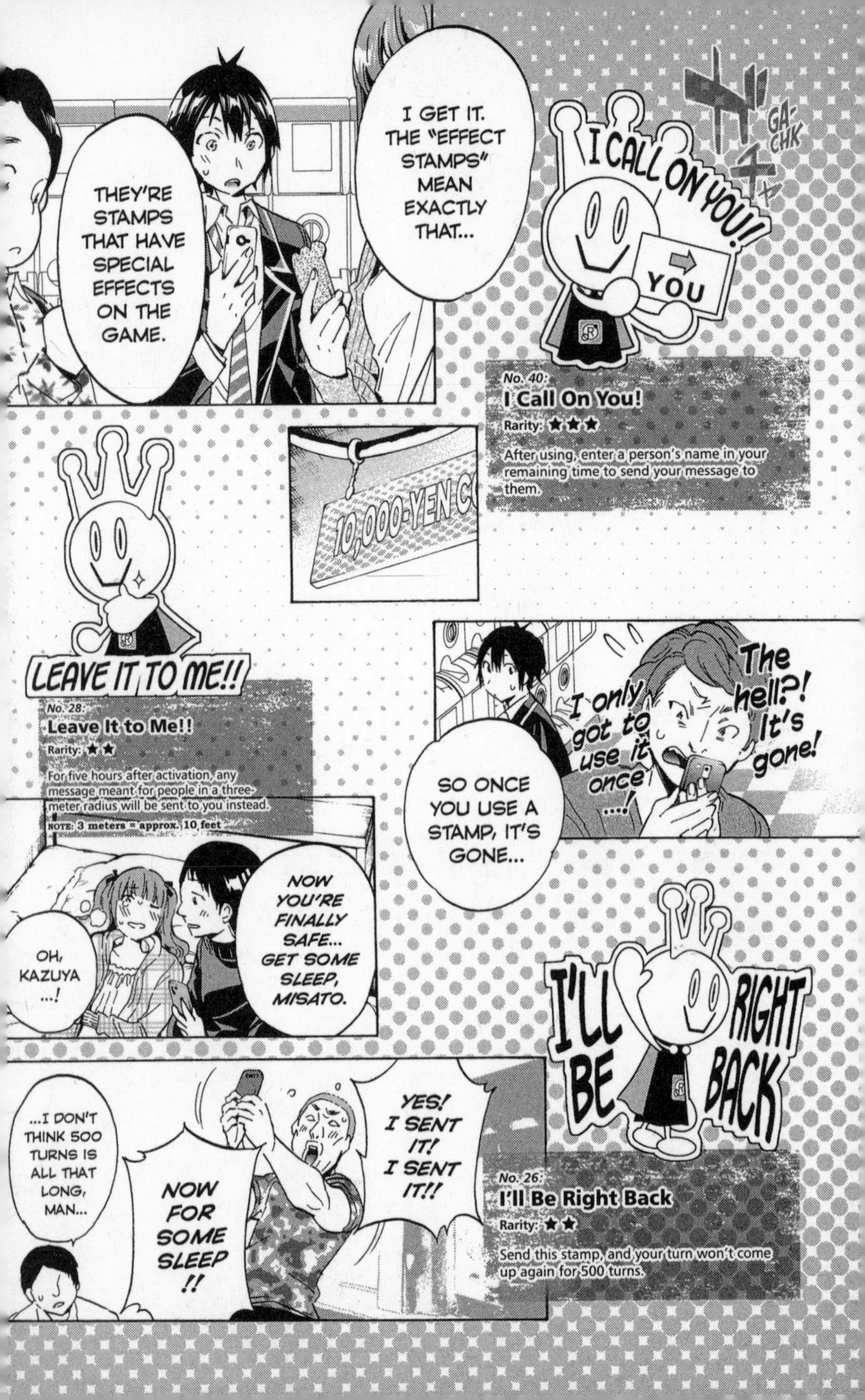
GA-CHK
I CALL ON YOU!!
YOU
No. 40:
I Call On You!
Rarity: ★★★
After using, enter a person's name in your remaining time to send your message to them.
I GET IT. THE "EFFECT STAMPS" MEAN EXACTLY THAT...
THEY'RE STAMPS THAT HAVE SPECIAL EFFECTS ON THE GAME.
10,000-YEN C
The hell?! It's gone!
I only got to use it once ...!
SO ONCE YOU USE A STAMP, IT'S GONE...
LEAVE IT TO ME!!
No. 28:
Leave It to Me!!
Rarity: ★★
For five hours after activation, any message meant for people in a three-meter radius will be sent to you instead.
NOTE: 3 meters = approx. 10 feet
I'LL BE RIGHT BACK
NOW YOU'RE FINALLY SAFE... GET SOME SLEEP, MISATO.
OH, KAZUYA ...!
No. 26:
I'll Be Right Back
Rarity: ★★
Send this stamp, and your turn won't come up again for 500 turns.
YES! I SENT IT! I SENT IT!!
NOW FOR SOME SLEEP!!
...I DON'T THINK 500 TURNS IS ALL THAT LONG, MAN...

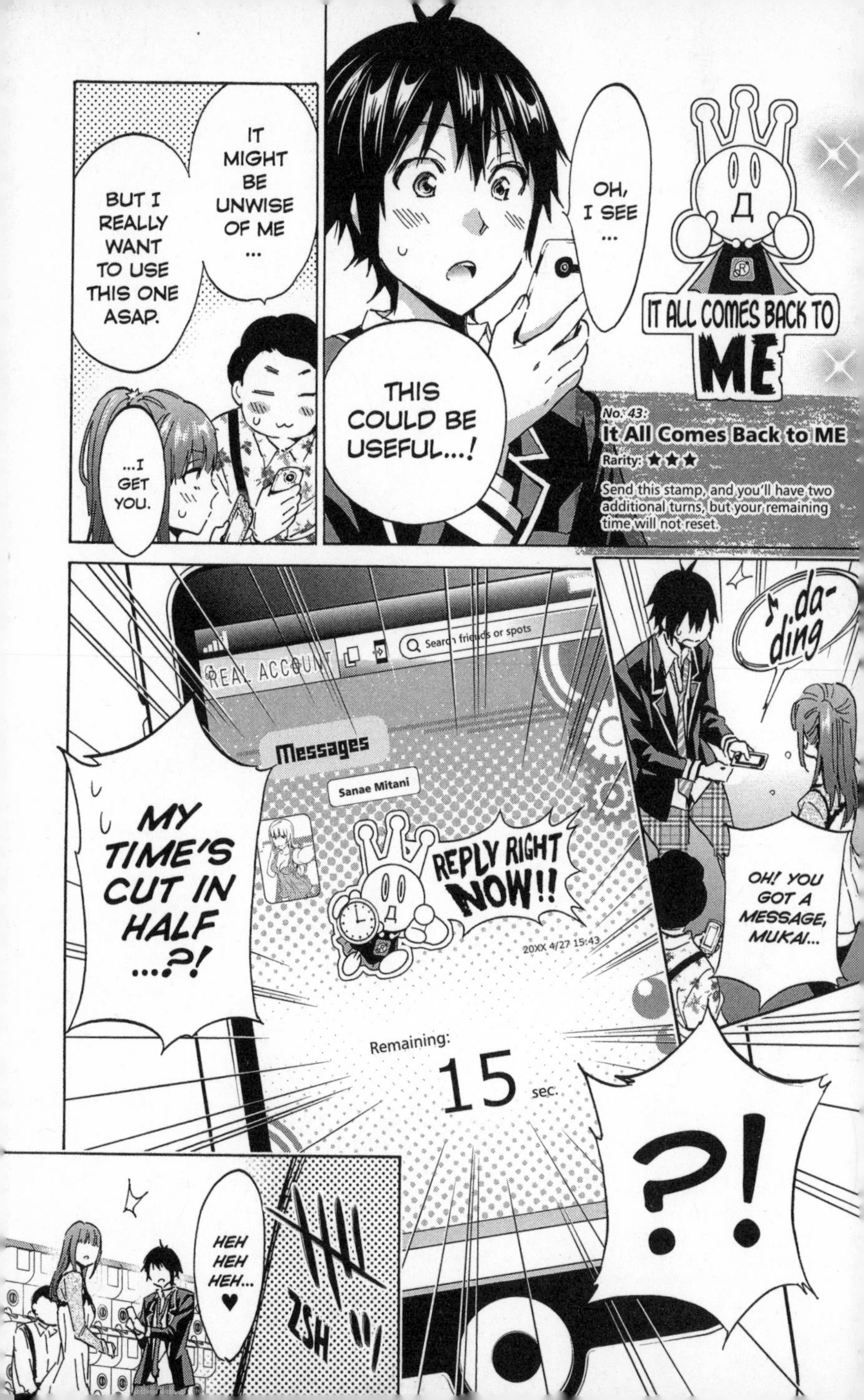
IT ALL COMES BACK TO ME
OH, I SEE ...
No. 43:
It All Comes Back to ME
Rarity: ★★★
Send this stamp, and you'll have two additional turns, but your remaining time will not reset.
THIS COULD BE USEFUL...!
IT MIGHT BE UNWISE OF ME ...
BUT I REALLY WANT TO USE THIS ONE ASAP.
...I GET YOU.
♪da-ding
OH! YOU GOT A MESSAGE, MUKAI...
REAL ACCOUNT
Search friends or spots
Messages
Sanae Mitani
REPLY RIGHT NOW!!
20XX 4/27 15:43
MY TIME'S CUT IN HALF ...?!
Remaining:
15 sec.
?!
HEH HEH HEH... ♥
ZSH

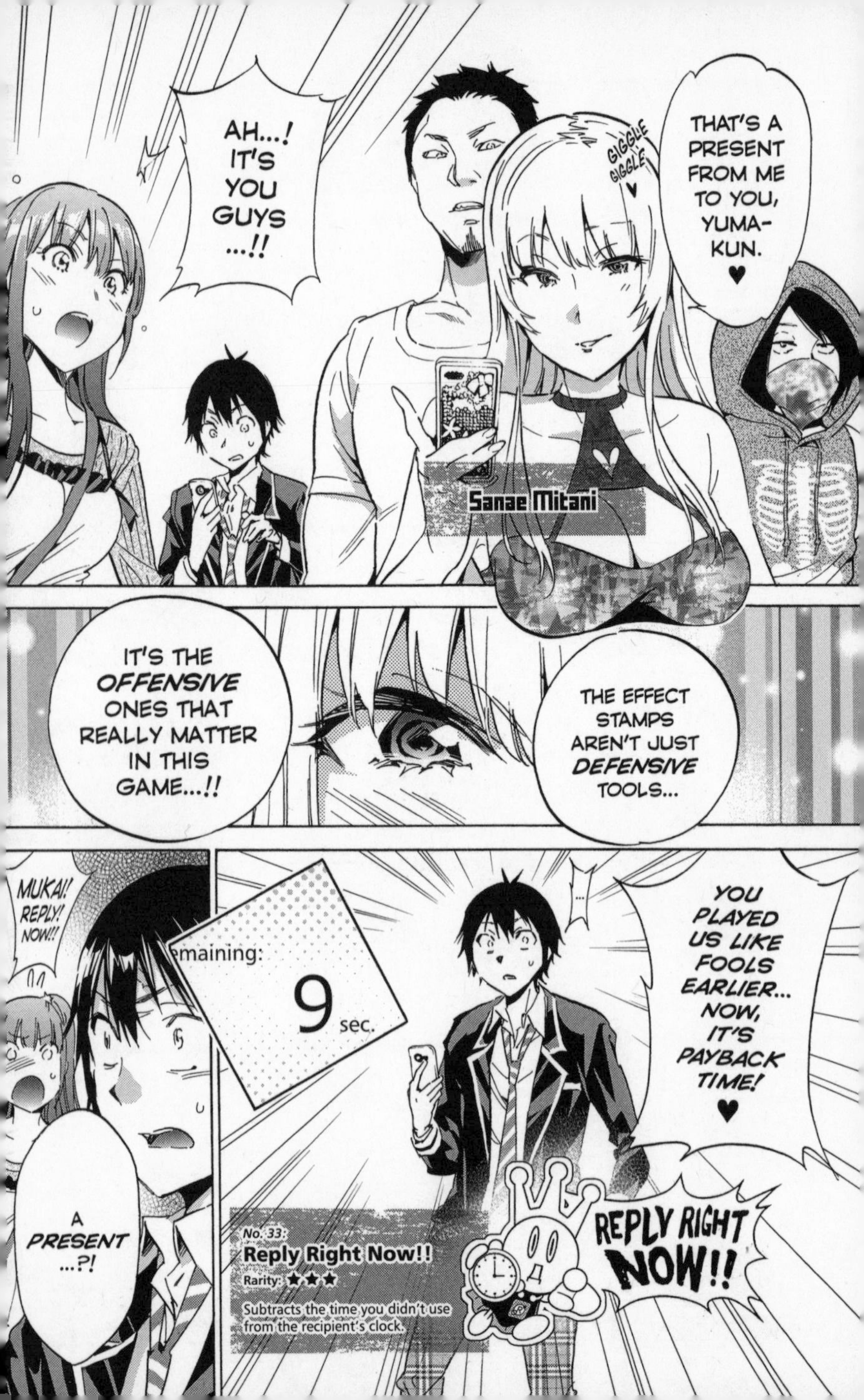
THAT'S A PRESENT FROM ME TO YOU, YUMA-KUN. ♥
GIGGLE GIGGLE ♥
AH...! IT'S YOU GUYS ...!!
Sanae Mitani
THE EFFECT STAMPS AREN'T JUST DEFENSIVE TOOLS...
IT'S THE OFFENSIVE ONES THAT REALLY MATTER IN THIS GAME...!!
...
YOU PLAYED US LIKE FOOLS EARLIER... NOW, IT'S PAYBACK TIME! ♥
REPLY RIGHT NOW!!
No. 33:
Reply Right Now!!
Rarity: ★★★
Subtracts the time you didn't use from the recipient's clock.
emaining:
9 sec.
MUKAI! REPLY! NOW!!
A PRESENT ...?!

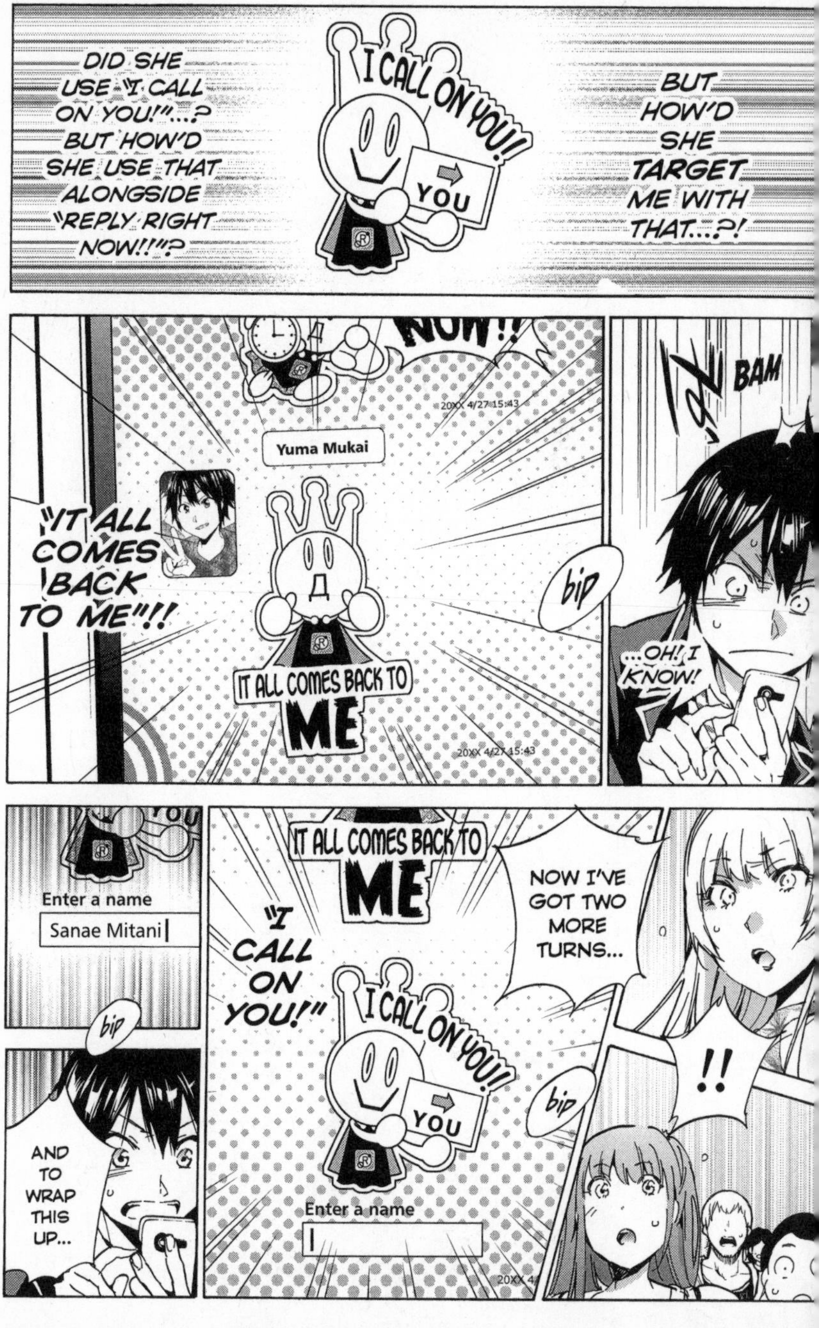
BUT HOW'D SHE TARGET ME WITH THAT...?!
I CALL ON YOU!!
YOU
DID SHE USE "I CALL ON YOU!"...? BUT HOW'D SHE USE THAT ALONGSIDE "REPLY RIGHT NOW!!"?
BAM
...OH! I KNOW!
bip
NOW!!
20XX 4/27 15:43
Yuma Mukai
"IT ALL COMES BACK TO ME"!!
IT ALL COMES BACK TO ME
20XX 4/27 15:43
NOW I'VE GOT TWO MORE TURNS...
!!
IT ALL COMES BACK TO ME
"I CALL ON YOU!"
I CALL ON YOU!!
YOU
bip
Enter a name
YOU
Enter a name
Sanae Mitani
bip
AND TO WRAP THIS UP...

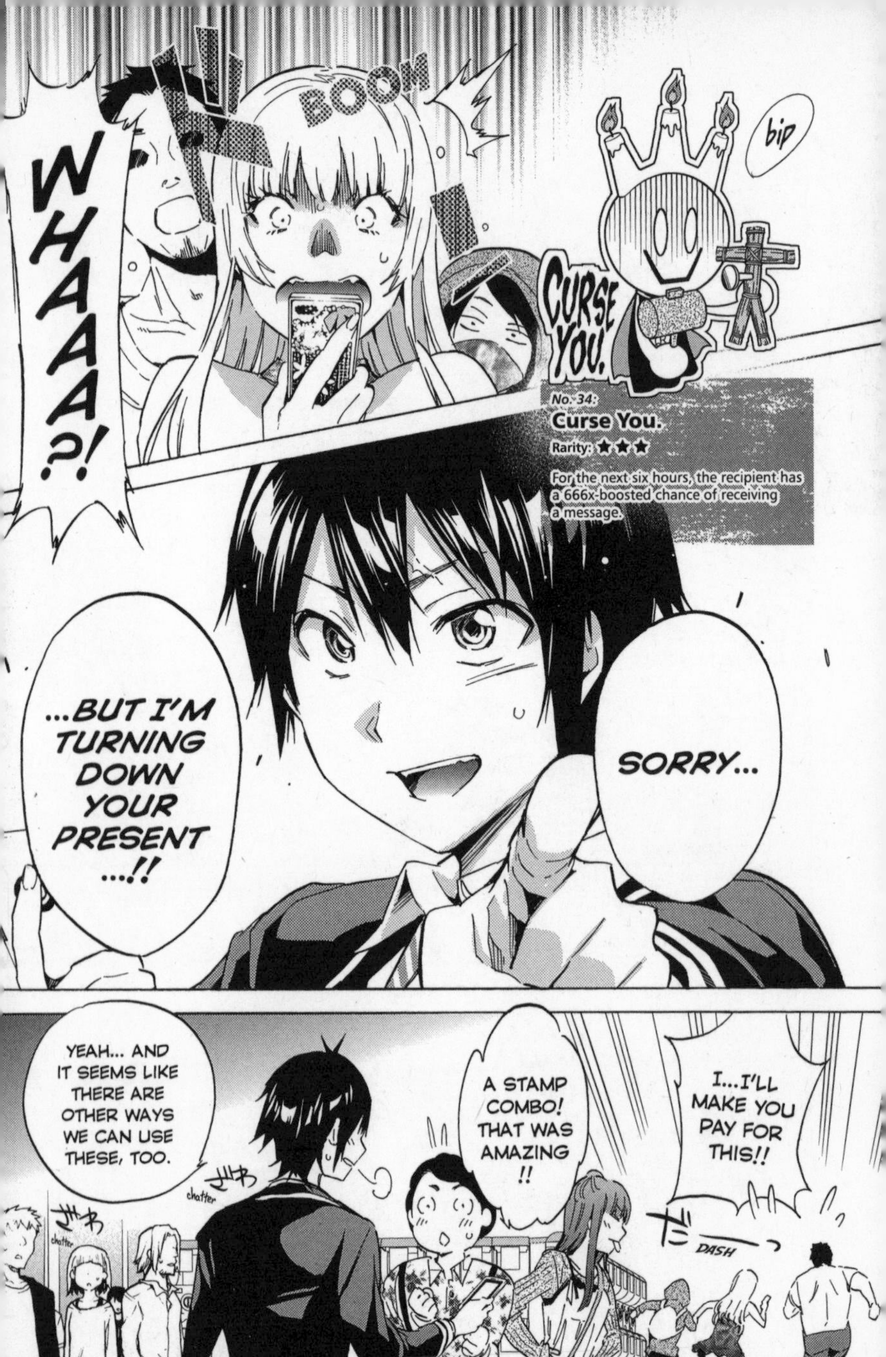
bip
CURSE YOU.
No. 34:
Curse You.
Rarity: ★★★
For the next six hours, the recipient has a 666x-boosted chance of receiving a message.
BOOM
WHAAAA?!
SORRY...
...BUT I'M TURNING DOWN YOUR PRESENT ...!!
I...I'LL MAKE YOU PAY FOR THIS!!
DASH
A STAMP COMBO! THAT WAS AMAZING !!
YEAH... AND IT SEEMS LIKE THERE ARE OTHER WAYS WE CAN USE THESE, TOO.
chatter
chatter

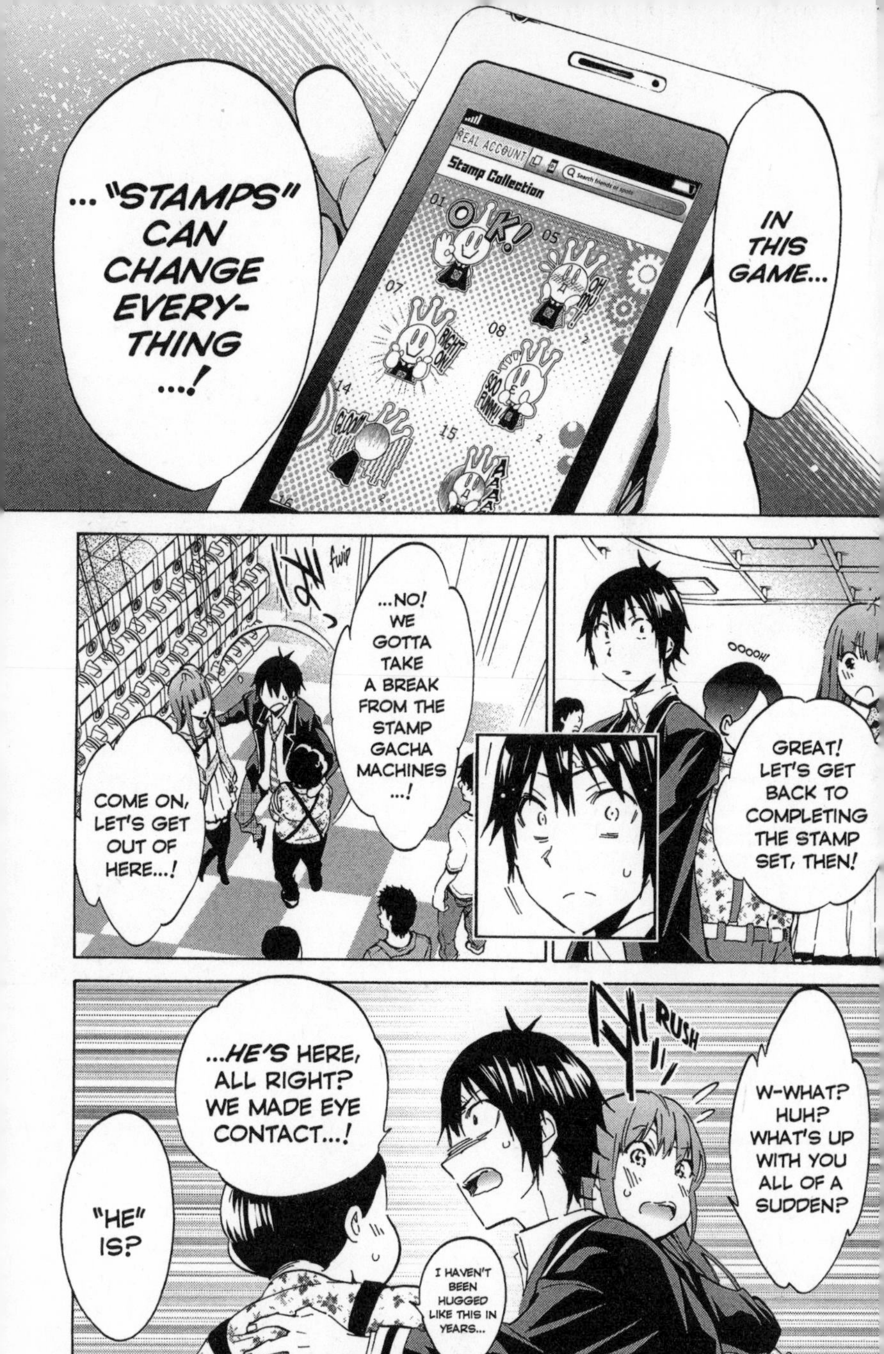
IN THIS GAME...
... "STAMPS" CAN CHANGE EVERY-THING ...!
REAL ACCOUNT
Stamp Collection
OK!
OH MY!
RIGHT ON!
SOO FUNNY!
OOOOH!
GREAT! LET'S GET BACK TO COMPLETING THE STAMP SET, THEN!
fwip
...NO! WE GOTTA TAKE A BREAK FROM THE STAMP GACHA MACHINES ...!
COME ON, LET'S GET OUT OF HERE...!
RUSH
W-WHAT? HUH? WHAT'S UP WITH YOU ALL OF A SUDDEN?
...HE'S HERE, ALL RIGHT? WE MADE EYE CONTACT...!
I HAVEN'T BEEN HUGGED LIKE THIS IN YEARS...
"HE" IS?

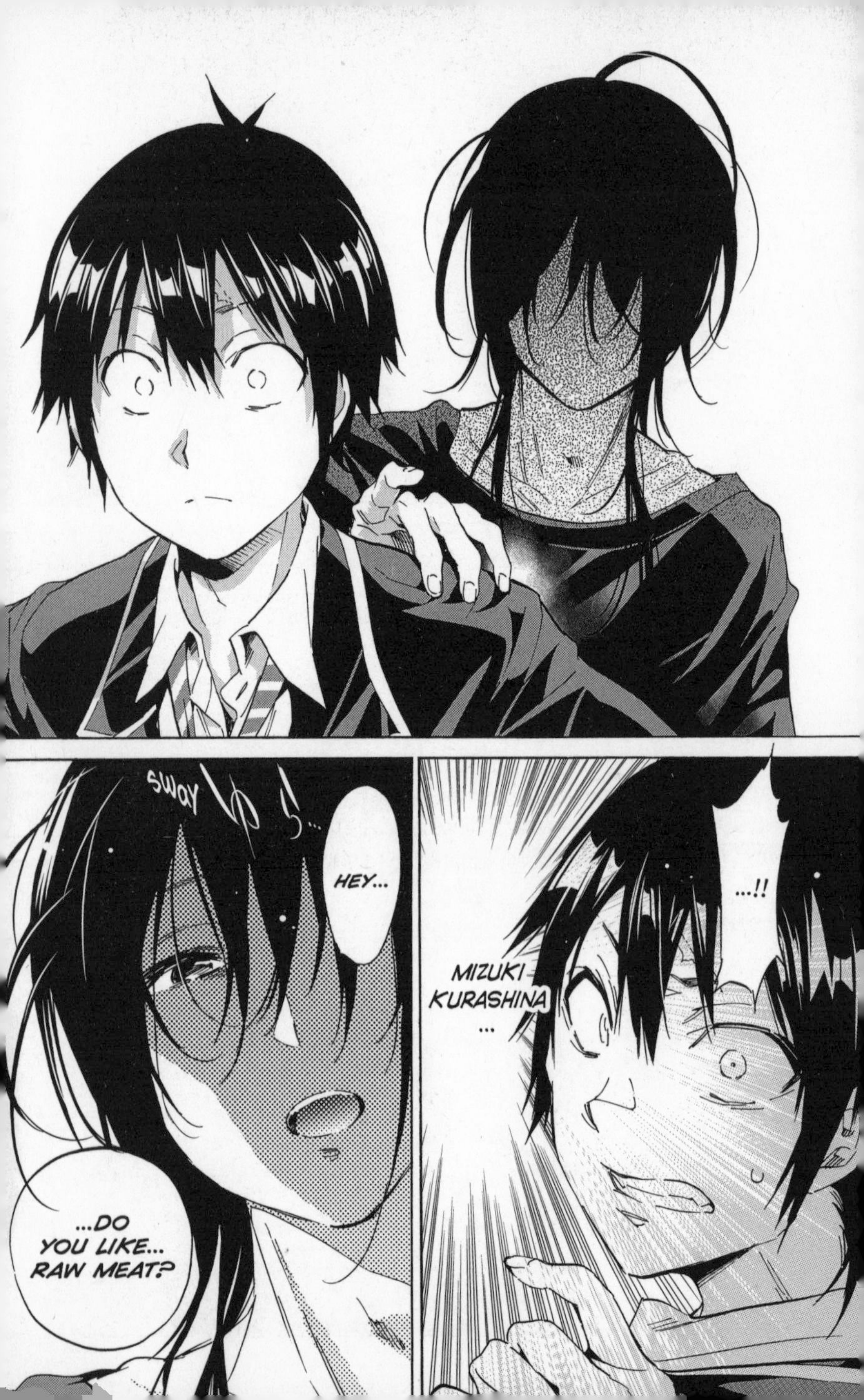
...!!
MIZUKI KURASHINA ...
sway
HEY...
...DO YOU LIKE... RAW MEAT?

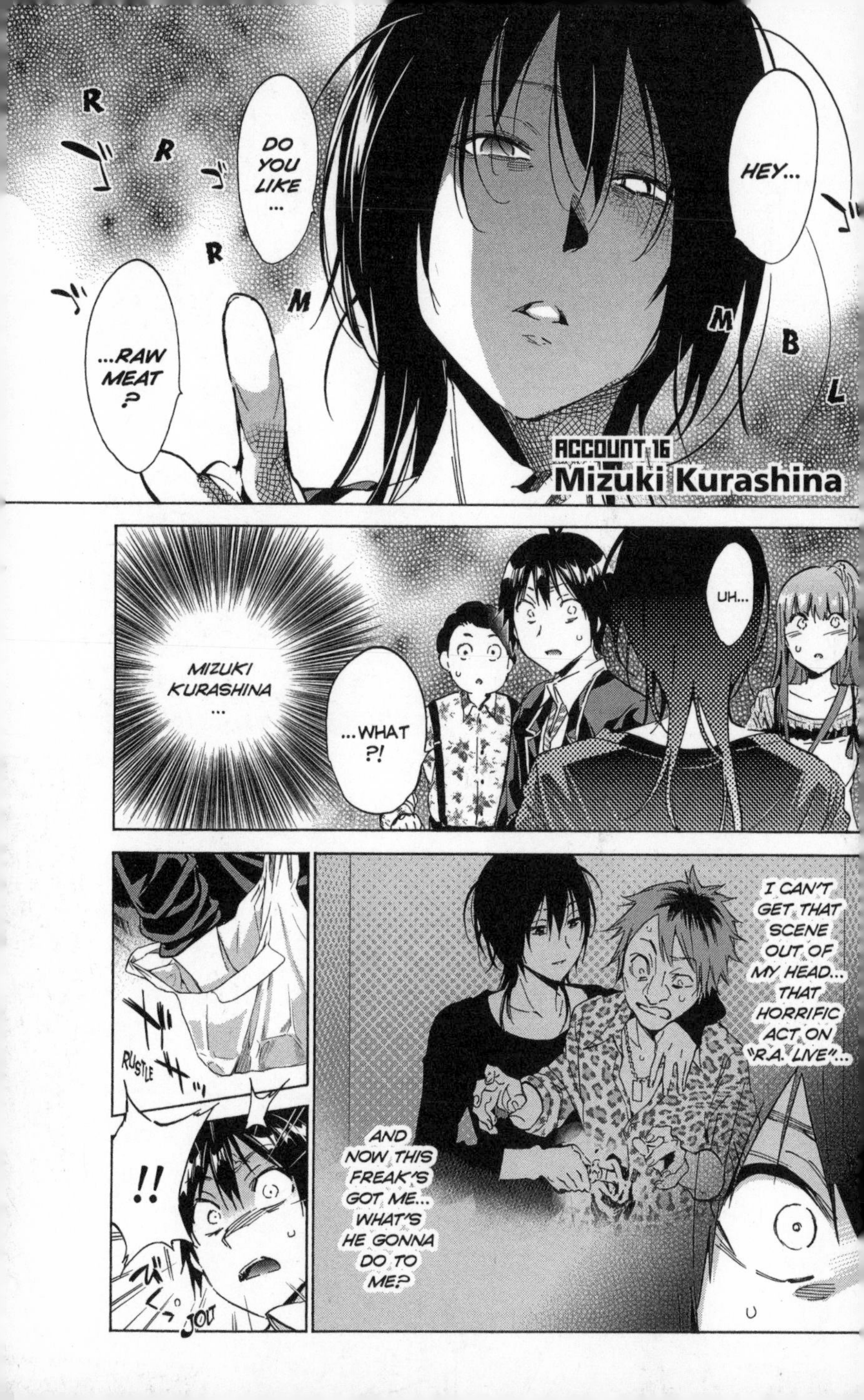
HEY...
R R R M M B L
DO YOU LIKE ...
...RAW MEAT?
ACCOUNT 16
Mizuki Kurashina
UH...
...WHAT?!
MIZUKI KURASHINA ...
I CAN'T GET THAT SCENE OUT OF MY HEAD... THAT HORRIFIC ACT ON "R.A. LIVE"...
AND NOW THIS FREAK'S GOT ME... WHAT'S HE GONNA DO TO ME?
RUSTLE
!!
JOLT

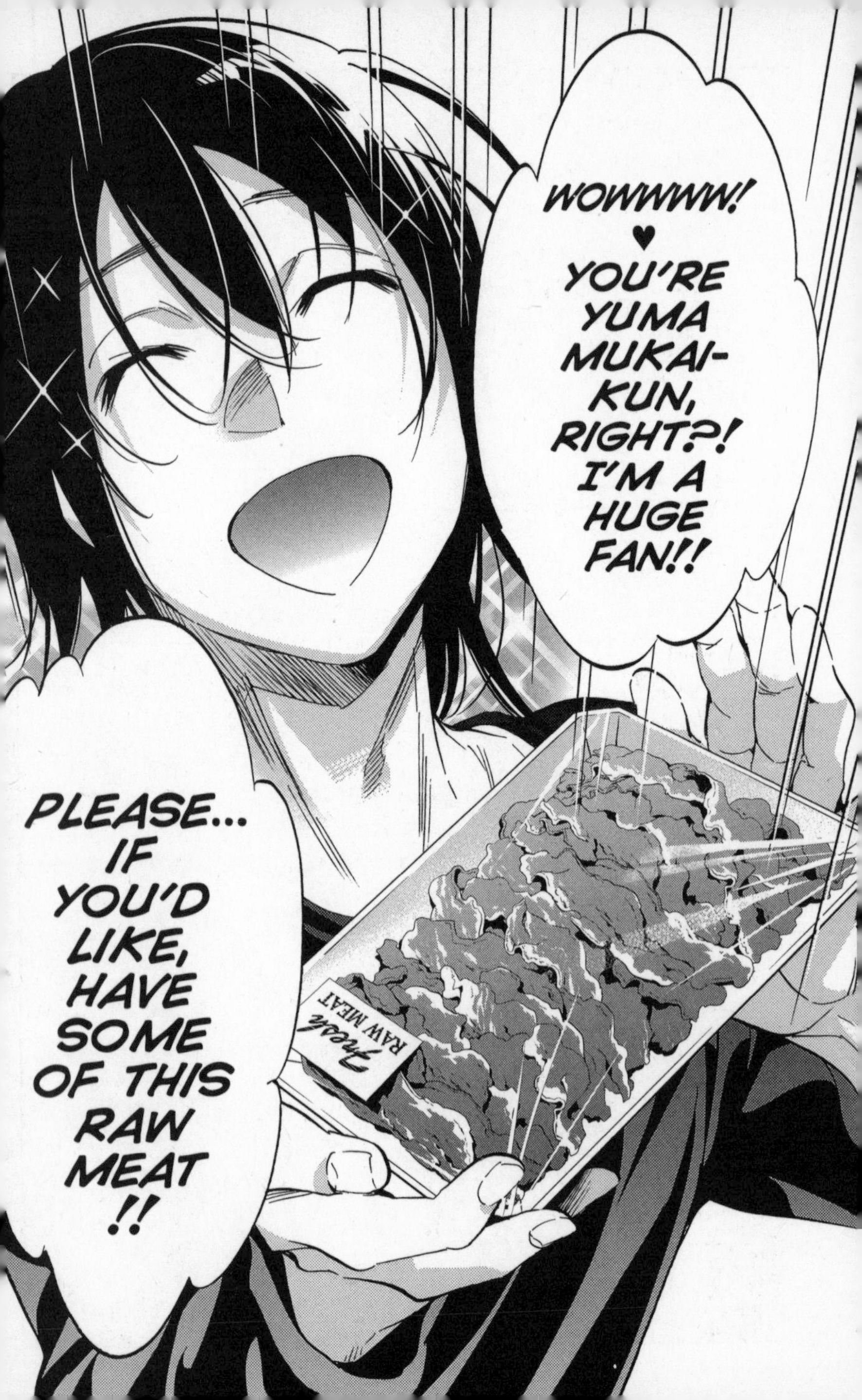
WOWWWW! ♥ YOU'RE YUMA MUKAI-KUN, RIGHT?! I'M A HUGE FAN!!
PLEASE... IF YOU'D LIKE, HAVE SOME OF THIS RAW MEAT!!
Fresh RAW MEAT

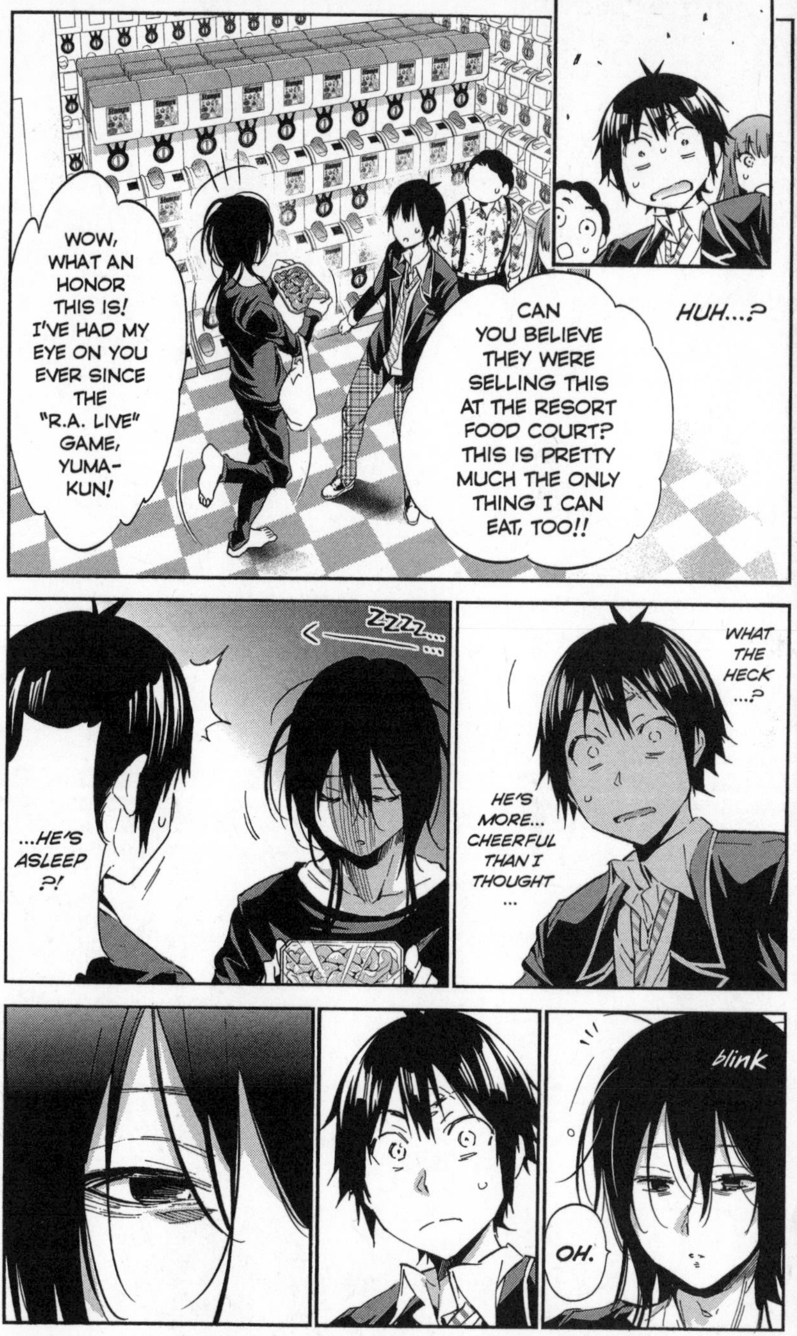
HUH...?
CAN YOU BELIEVE THEY WERE SELLING THIS AT THE RESORT FOOD COURT? THIS IS PRETTY MUCH THE ONLY THING I CAN EAT, TOO!!
WOW, WHAT AN HONOR THIS IS! I'VE HAD MY EYE ON YOU EVER SINCE THE "R.A. LIVE" GAME, YUMA-KUN!
WHAT THE HECK ...?
HE'S MORE... CHEERFUL THAN I THOUGHT ...
Z-Z-Z...
...HE'S ASLEEP ?!
blink
OH.

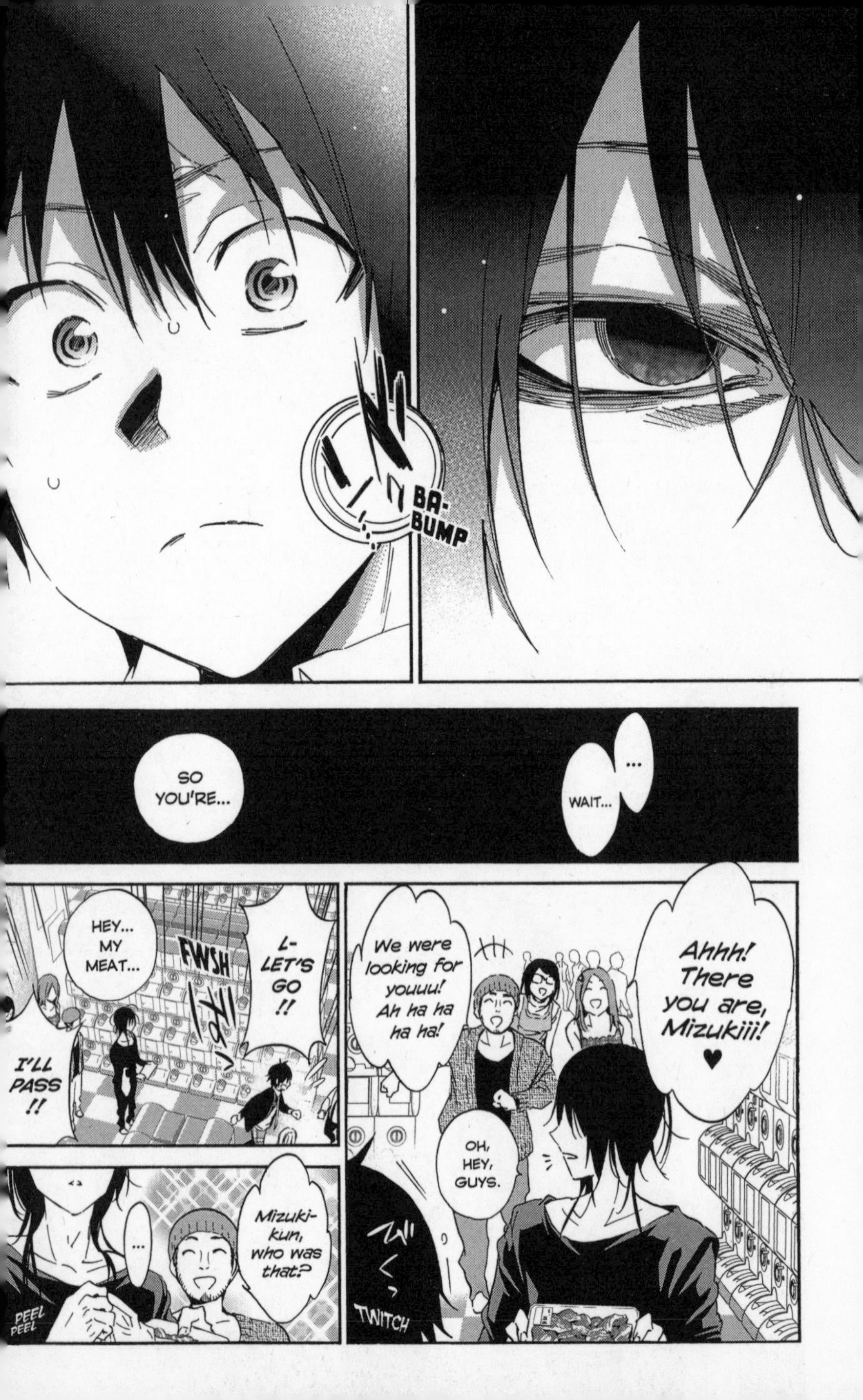
BA-BUMP
...
WAIT...
SO YOU'RE...
Ahhh! There you are, Mizukiii! ♥
We were looking for youuu! Ah ha ha ha!
OH, HEY, GUYS.
TWITCH
L-LET'S GO!!
FWSH
HEY... MY MEAT...
I'LL PASS!!
Mizuki-kun, who was that?
...
PEEL PEEL

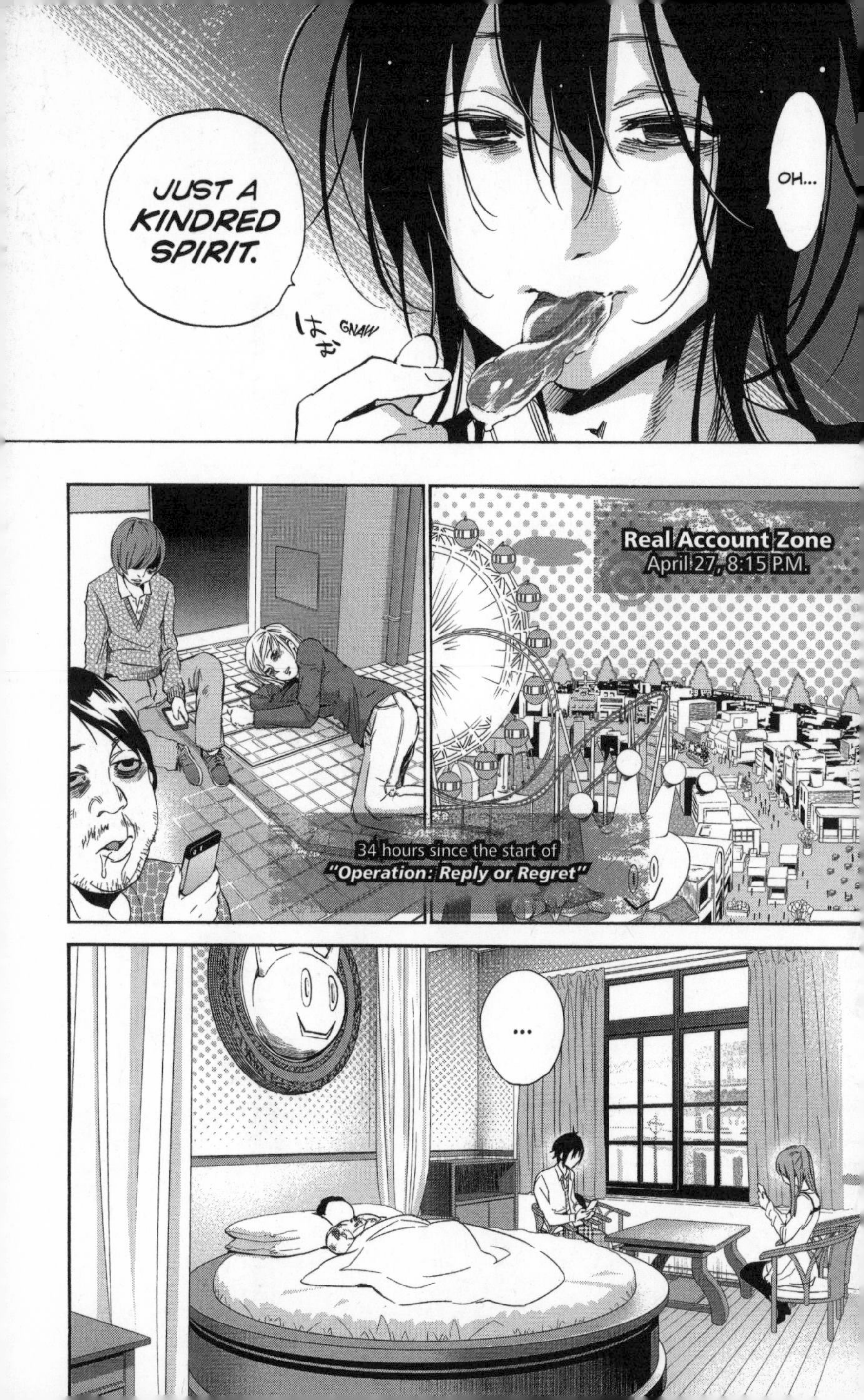
OH...
JUST A KINDRED SPIRIT.
はむ
GNAW
Real Account Zone
April 27, 8:15 P.M.
34 hours since the start of
"Operation: Reply or Regret"
...

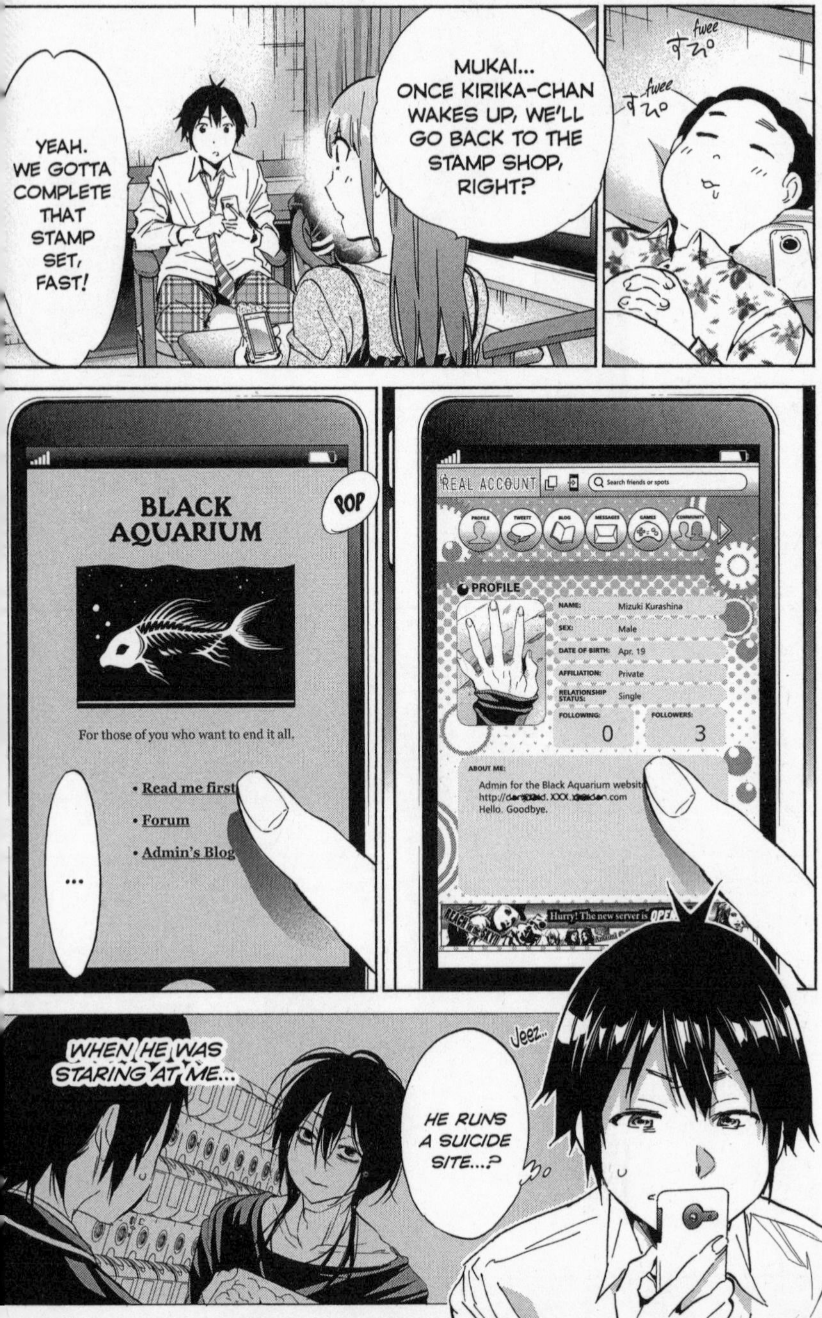
fwee
fwee
MUKAI... ONCE KIRIKA-CHAN WAKES UP, WE'LL GO BACK TO THE STAMP SHOP, RIGHT?
YEAH. WE GOTTA COMPLETE THAT STAMP SET, FAST!
REAL ACCOUNT
Search friends or spots
PROFILE
NAME: Mizuki Kurashina
SEX: Male
DATE OF BIRTH: Apr. 19
AFFILIATION: Private
RELATIONSHIP STATUS: Single
FOLLOWING: 0
FOLLOWERS: 3
ABOUT ME:
Admin for the Black Aquarium website
http://[redacted].XXX.[redacted].com
Hello. Goodbye.
Hurry! The new server is OPE
POP
BLACK AQUARIUM
For those of you who want to end it all.
• Read me first
• Forum
• Admin's Blog
...
Jeez...
HE RUNS A SUICIDE SITE...?
WHEN HE WAS STARING AT ME...

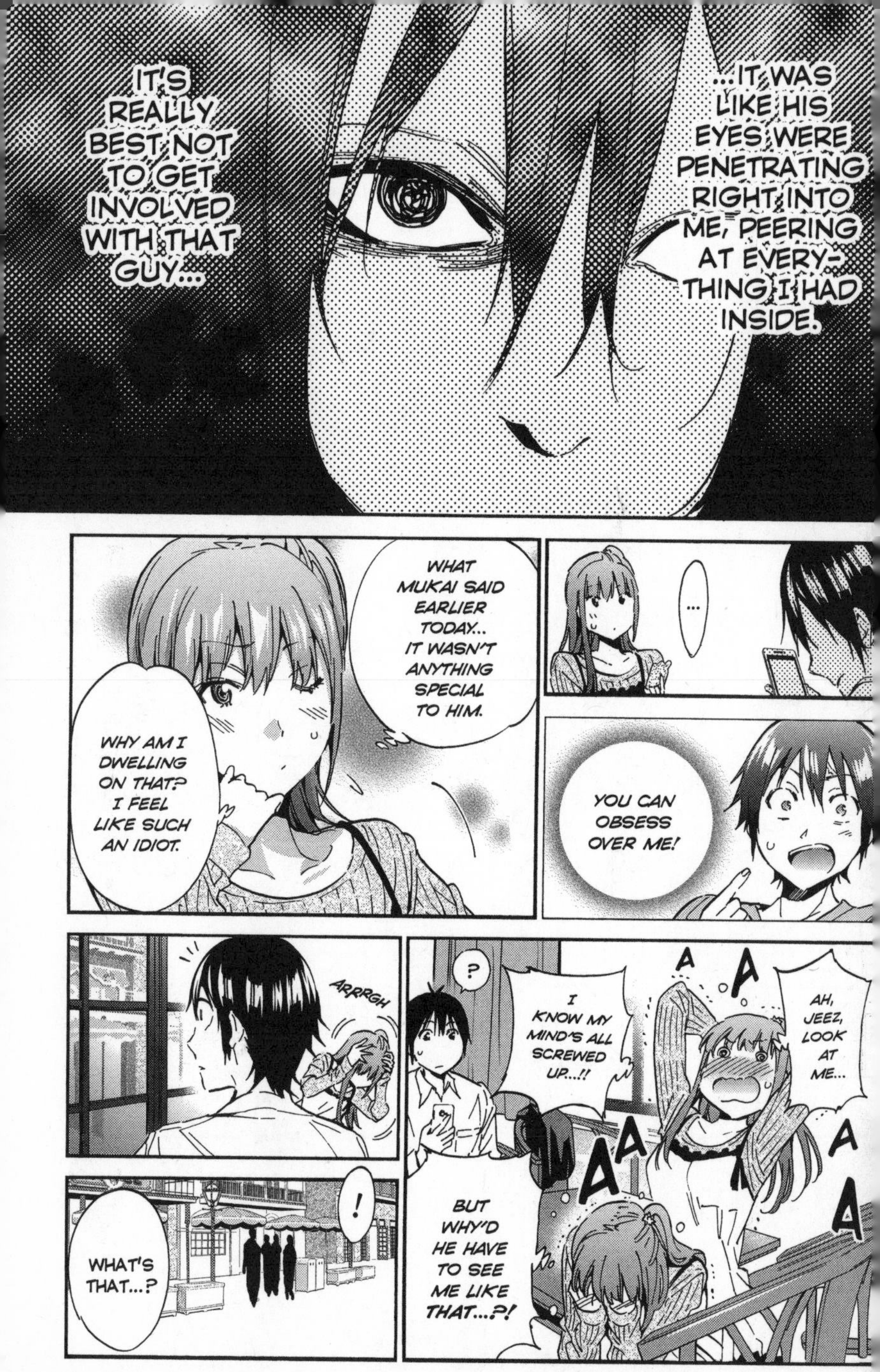
...IT WAS LIKE HIS EYES WERE PENETRATING RIGHT INTO ME, PEERING AT EVERY-THING I HAD INSIDE.
IT'S REALLY BEST NOT TO GET INVOLVED WITH THAT GUY...
...
YOU CAN OBSESS OVER ME!
WHAT MUKAI SAID EARLIER TODAY... IT WASN'T ANYTHING SPECIAL TO HIM.
WHY AM I DWELLING ON THAT? I FEEL LIKE SUCH AN IDIOT.
AH, JEEZ, LOOK AT ME...
A A
I KNOW MY MIND'S ALL SCREWED UP...!!
?
A A A A
BUT WHY'D HE HAVE TO SEE ME LIKE THAT...?!
ARRRGH
!
WHAT'S THAT...?

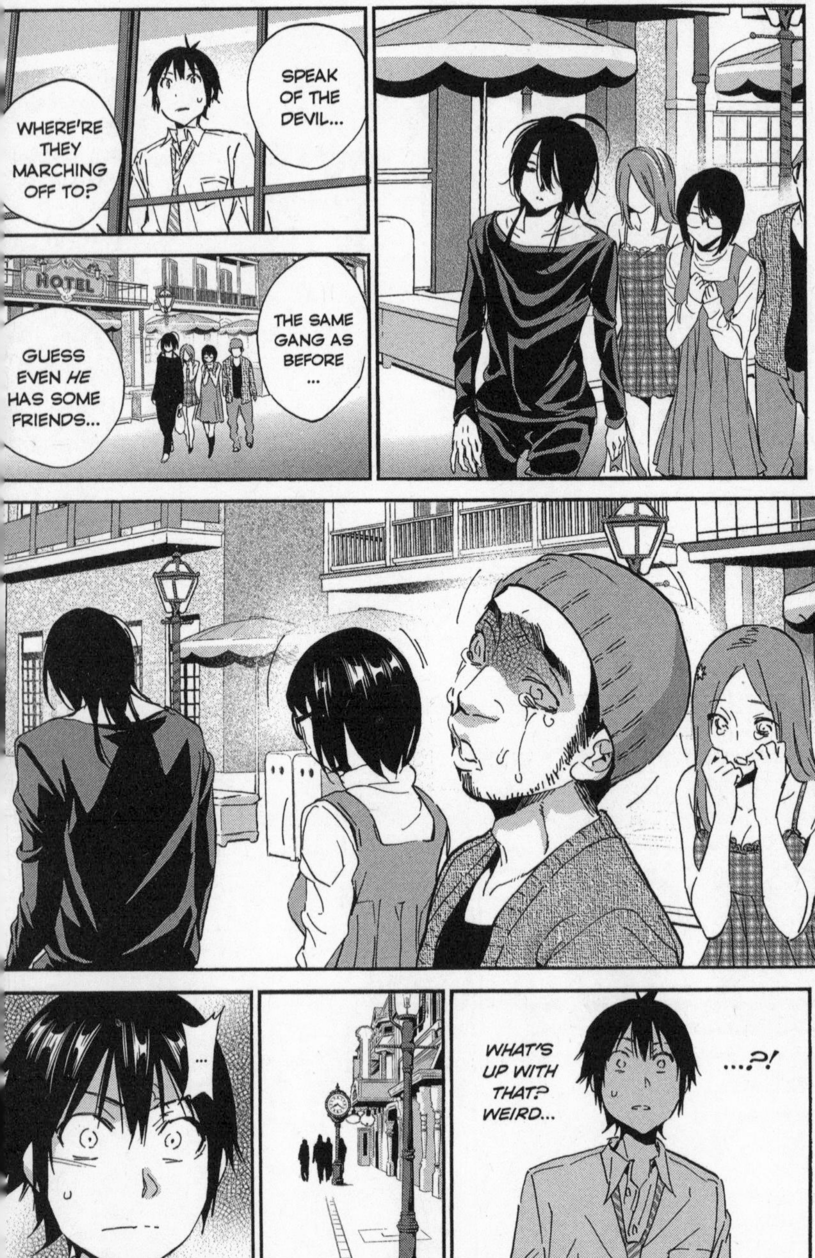
SPEAK OF THE DEVIL...
WHERE'RE THEY MARCHING OFF TO?
THE SAME GANG AS BEFORE ...
GUESS EVEN *HE* HAS SOME FRIENDS...
...?!
WHAT'S UP WITH THAT? WEIRD...
...

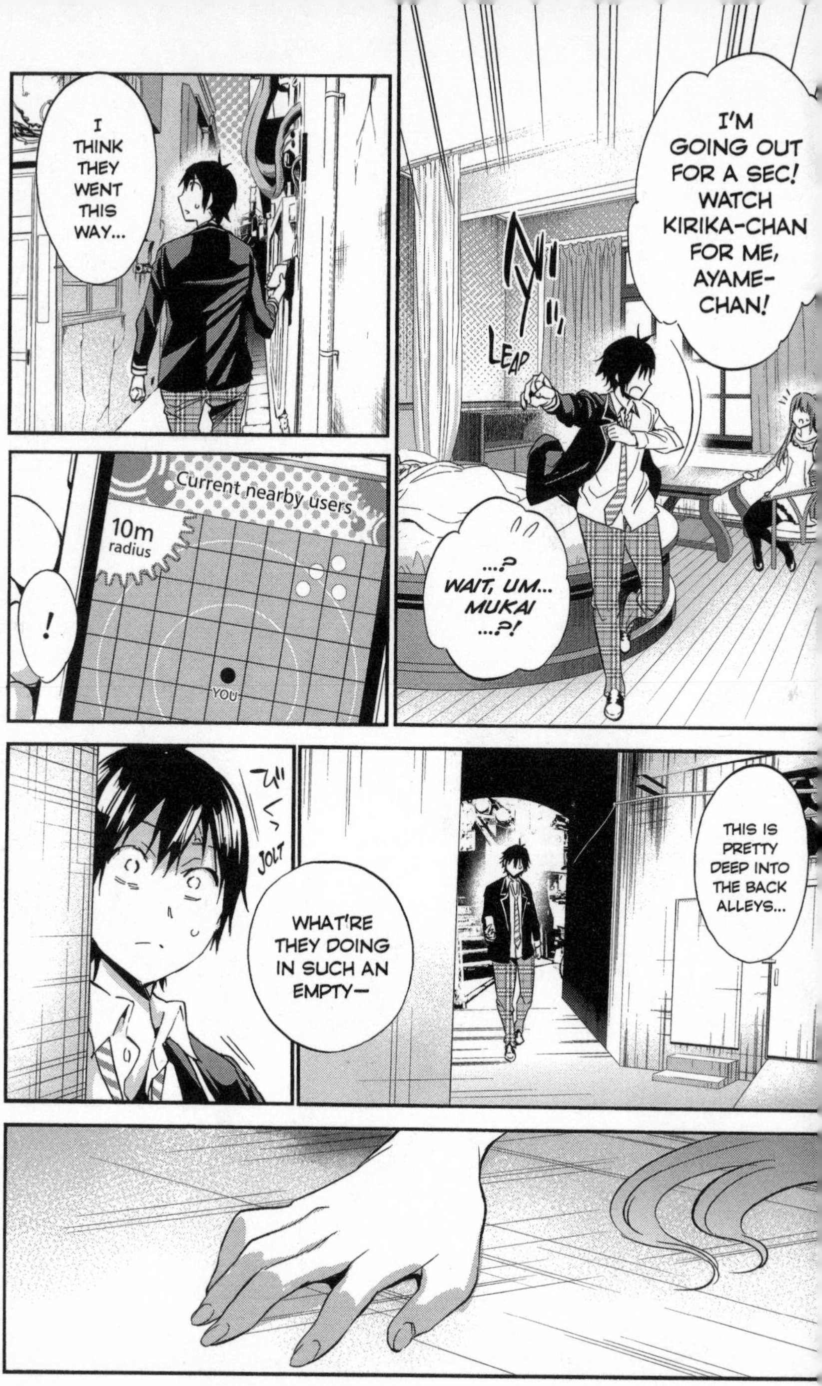
I'M GOING OUT FOR A SEC! WATCH KIRIKA-CHAN FOR ME, AYAME-CHAN!
LEAP
...? WAIT, UM... MUKAI ...?!
I THINK THEY WENT THIS WAY...
Current nearby users
10m radius
YOU
!
THIS IS PRETTY DEEP INTO THE BACK ALLEYS...
JOLT
WHAT'RE THEY DOING IN SUCH AN EMPTY—

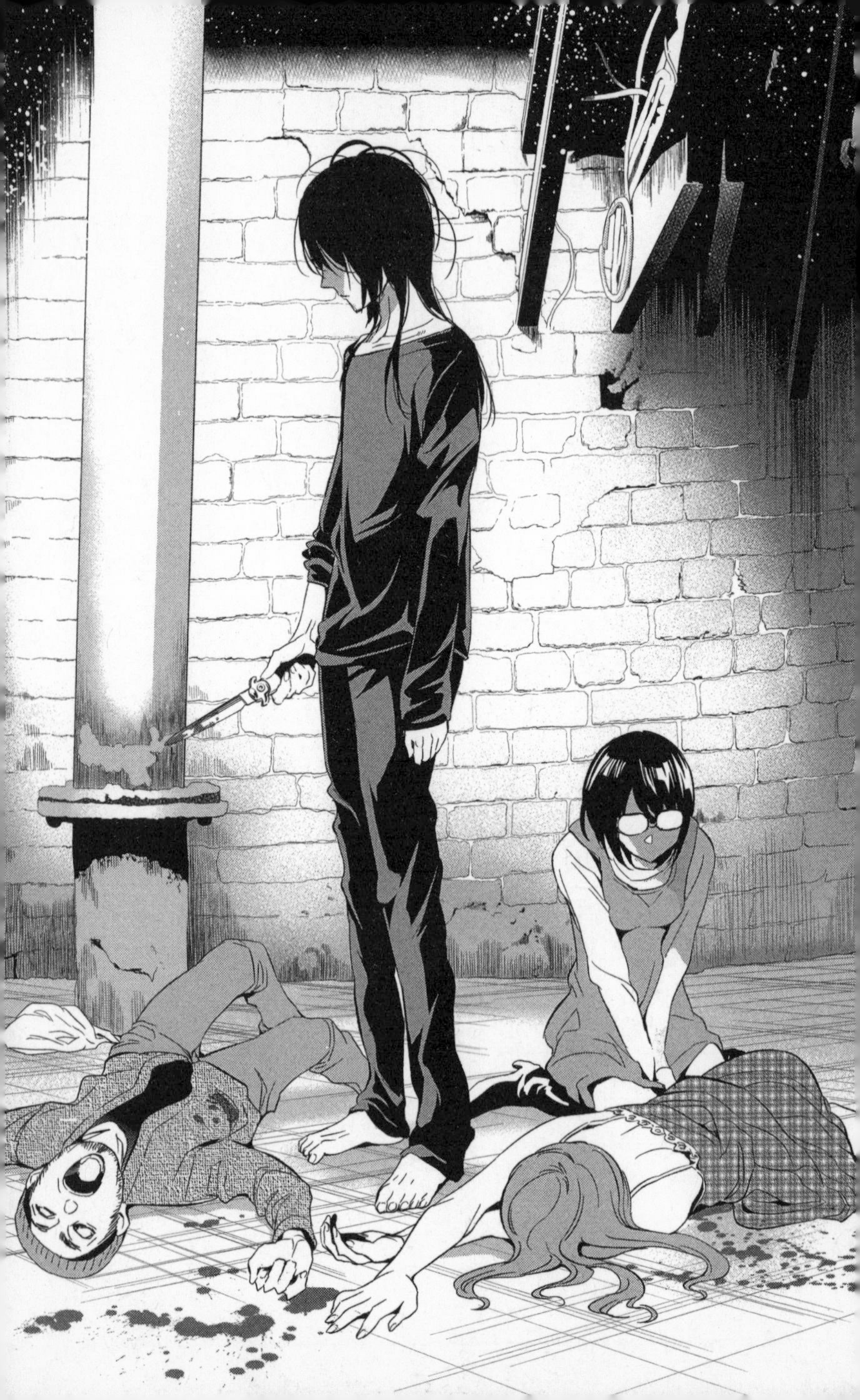

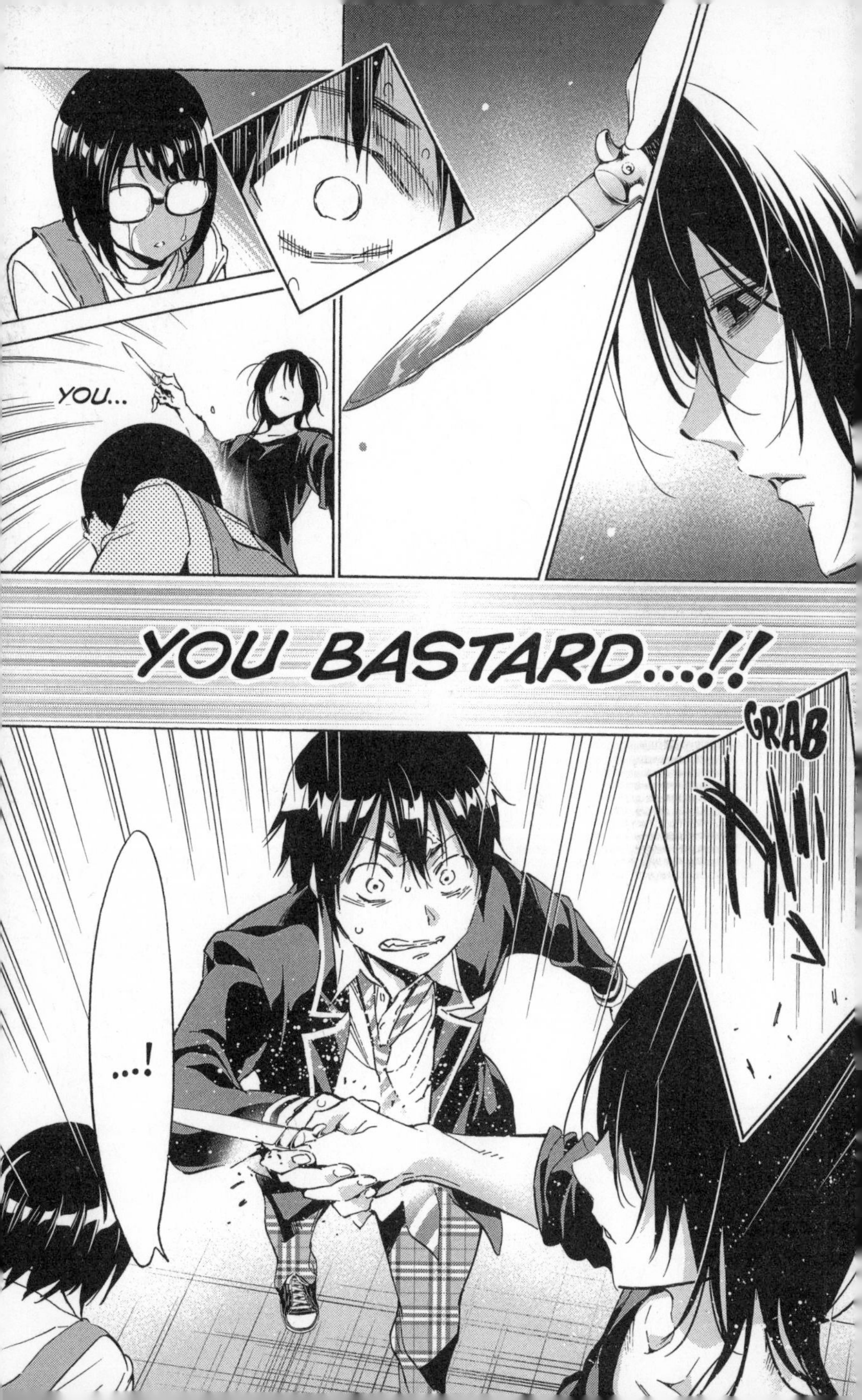
YOU...
YOU BASTARD...!!
GRAB
...!

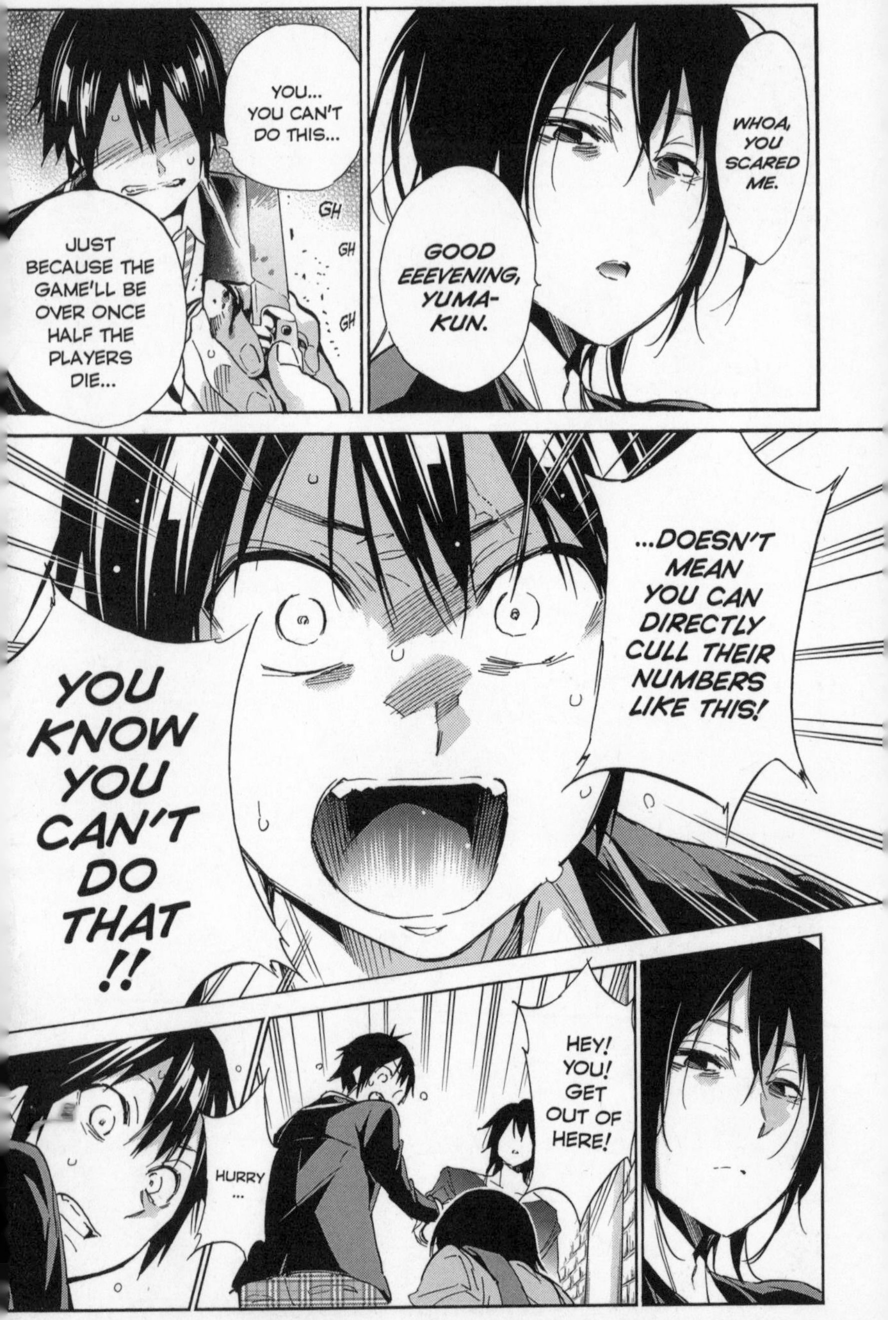
WHOA, YOU SCARED ME.
GOOD EEEVENING, YUMA-KUN.
YOU... YOU CAN'T DO THIS...
GH
GH
GH
JUST BECAUSE THE GAME'LL BE OVER ONCE HALF THE PLAYERS DIE...
...DOESN'T MEAN YOU CAN DIRECTLY CULL THEIR NUMBERS LIKE THIS!
YOU KNOW YOU CAN'T DO THAT!!
HEY! YOU! GET OUT OF HERE!
HURRY ...

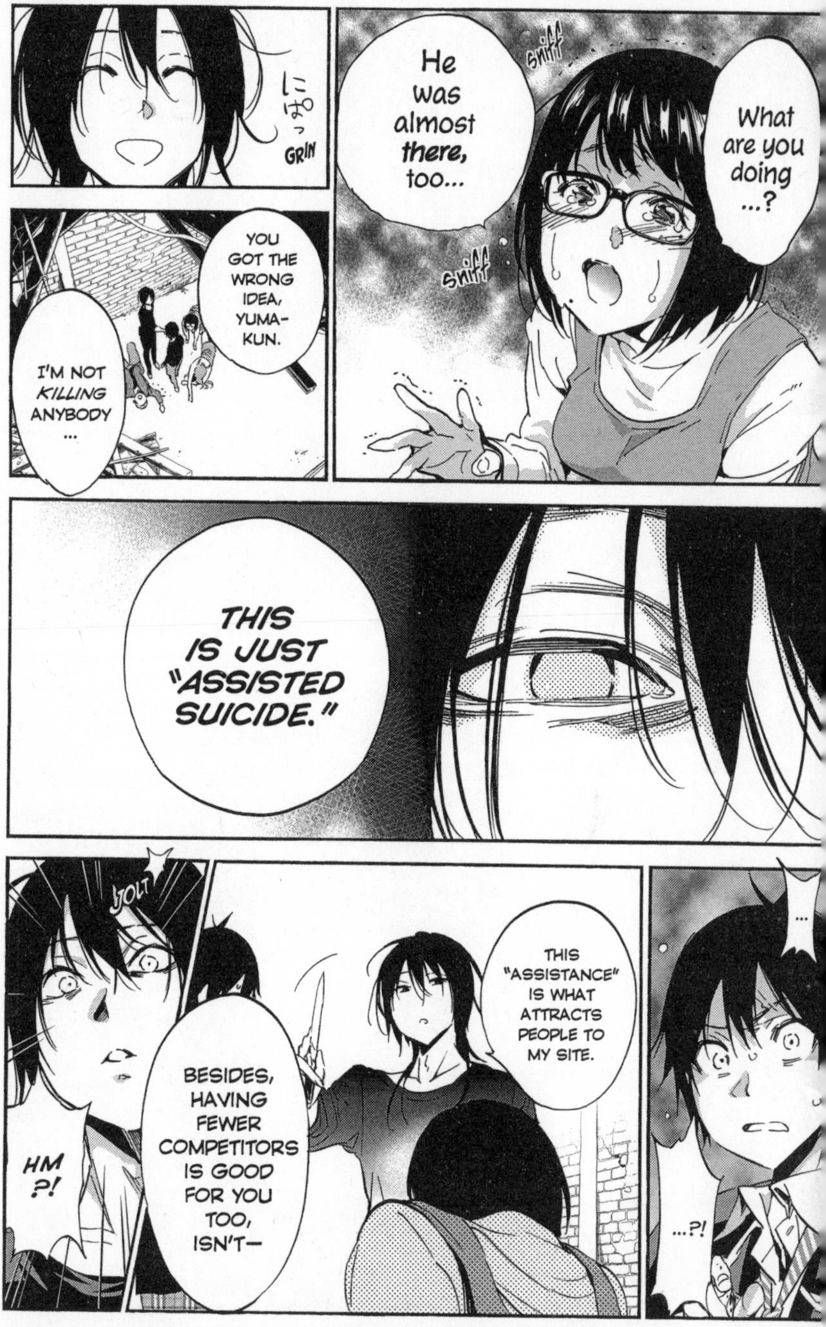
What are you doing ...?
sniff
He was almost *there,* too...
sniff
にぱっ
GRIN
YOU GOT THE WRONG IDEA, YUMA-KUN.
I'M NOT *KILLING* ANYBODY ...
THIS IS JUST "ASSISTED SUICIDE."
...
...?!
THIS "ASSISTANCE" IS WHAT ATTRACTS PEOPLE TO MY SITE.
BESIDES, HAVING FEWER COMPETITORS IS GOOD FOR YOU TOO, ISN'T—
JOLT
HM ?!

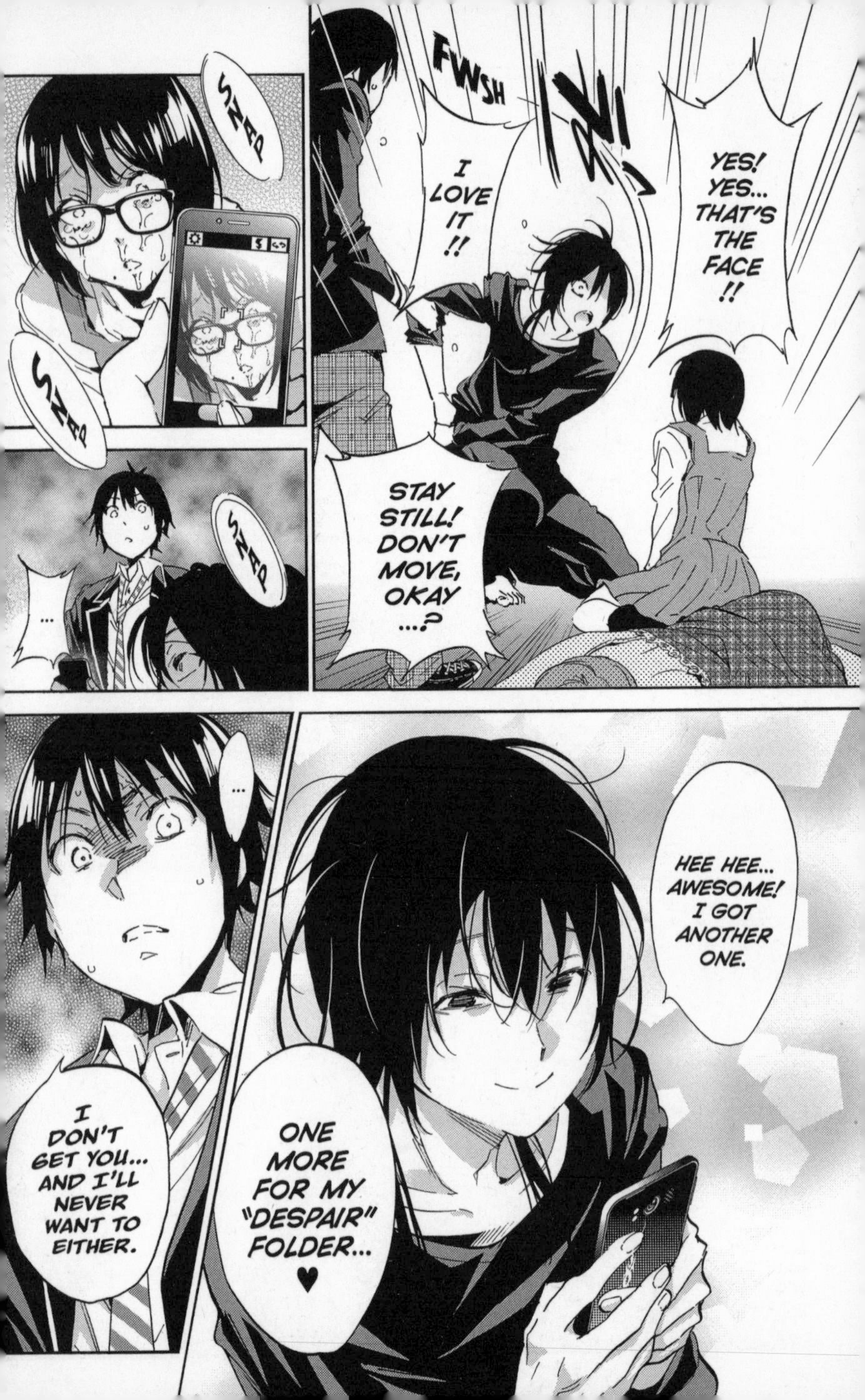
YES! YES... THAT'S THE FACE!!
FWSH
I LOVE IT!!
STAY STILL! DON'T MOVE, OKAY ...?
SZAP
SZAP
SZAP
...
HEE HEE... AWESOME! I GOT ANOTHER ONE.
ONE MORE FOR MY "DESPAIR" FOLDER... ♥
...
I DON'T GET YOU... AND I'LL NEVER WANT TO EITHER.

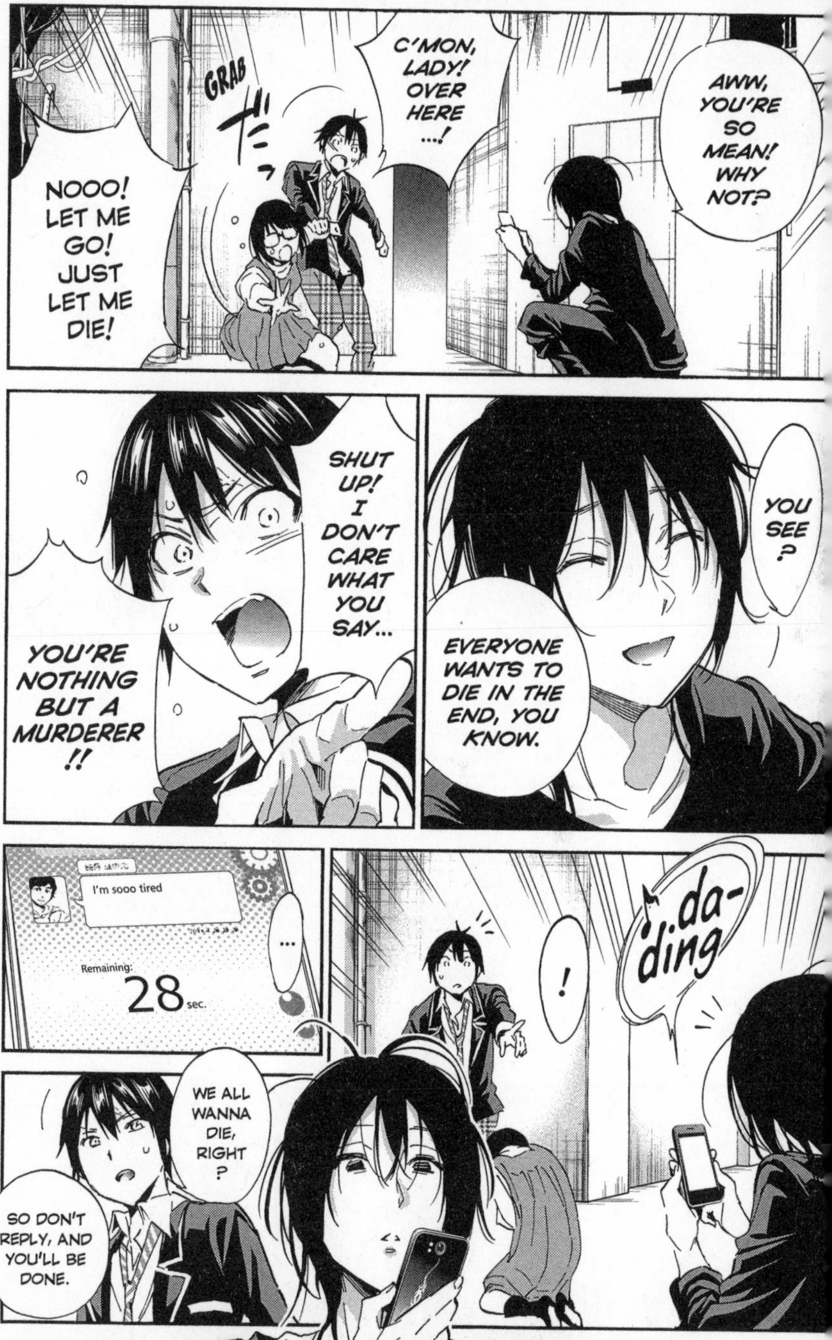
AWW, YOU'RE SO MEAN! WHY NOT?
C'MON, LADY! OVER HERE...!
GRAB
NOOO! LET ME GO! JUST LET ME DIE!
YOU SEE?
EVERYONE WANTS TO DIE IN THE END, YOU KNOW.
SHUT UP! I DON'T CARE WHAT YOU SAY...
YOU'RE NOTHING BUT A MURDERER!!
da-ding
!
I'm sooo tired
Remaining:
28 sec.
...
WE ALL WANNA DIE, RIGHT?
SO DON'T REPLY, AND YOU'LL BE DONE.

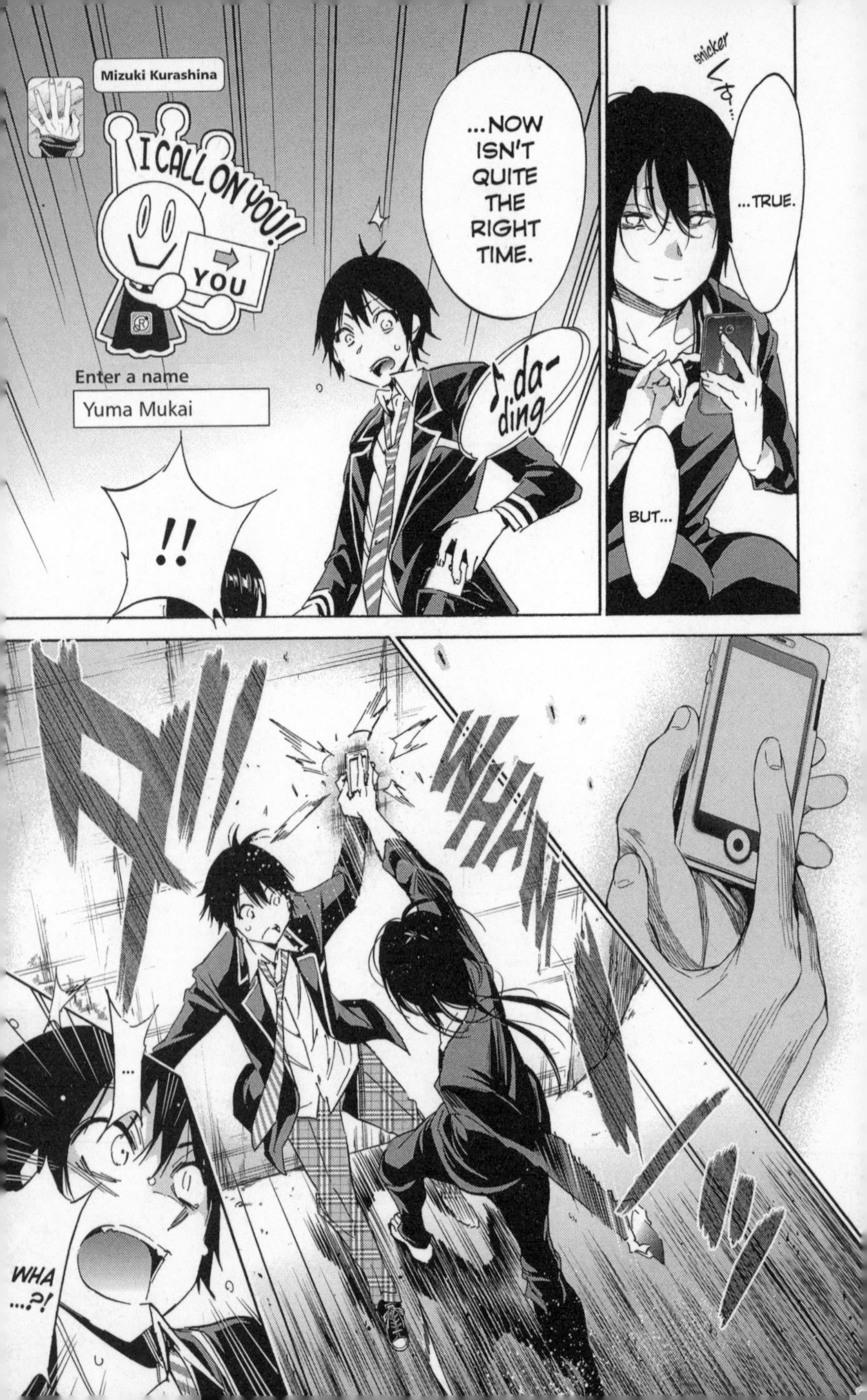
snicker
...TRUE.
BUT...
...NOW ISN'T QUITE THE RIGHT TIME.
♪da-ding
Mizuki Kurashina
I CALL ON YOU!!
YOU
Enter a name
Yuma Mukai
!!
WHAM
...
WHA...?!

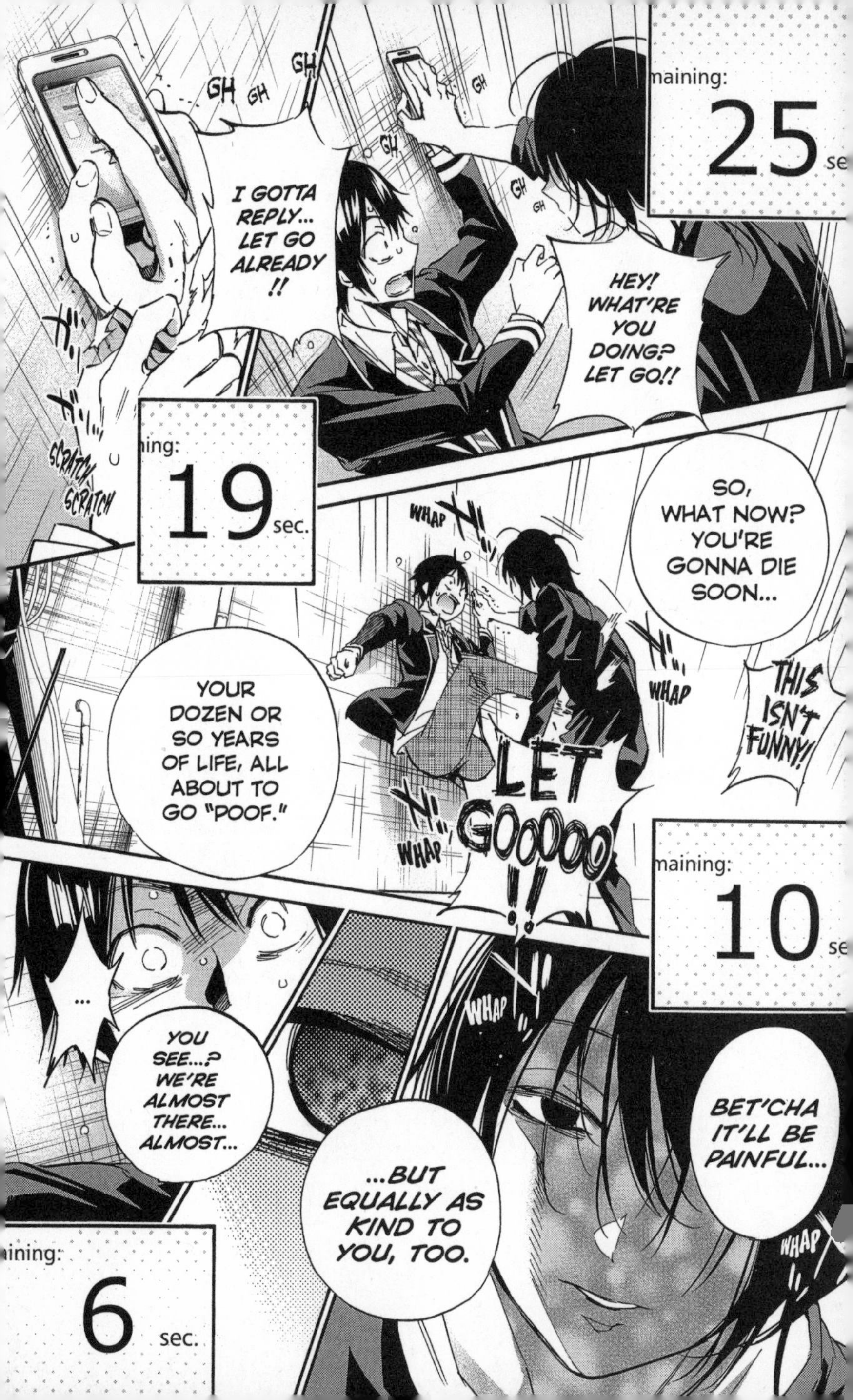maining:
25 se
GH GH GH GH GH GH GH
HEY! WHAT'RE YOU DOING? LET GO!!
I GOTTA REPLY... LET GO ALREADY!!
SCRATCH SCRATCH
ning:
19 sec.
SO, WHAT NOW? YOU'RE GONNA DIE SOON...
WHAP
THIS ISN'T FUNNY!
WHAP
LET GOOOOO!!
YOUR DOZEN OR SO YEARS OF LIFE, ALL ABOUT TO GO "POOF."
WHAP
maining:
10 se
WHAP
BET'CHA IT'LL BE PAINFUL...
WHAP
...BUT EQUALLY AS KIND TO YOU, TOO.
...
YOU SEE...? WE'RE ALMOST THERE... ALMOST...
ining:
6 sec.

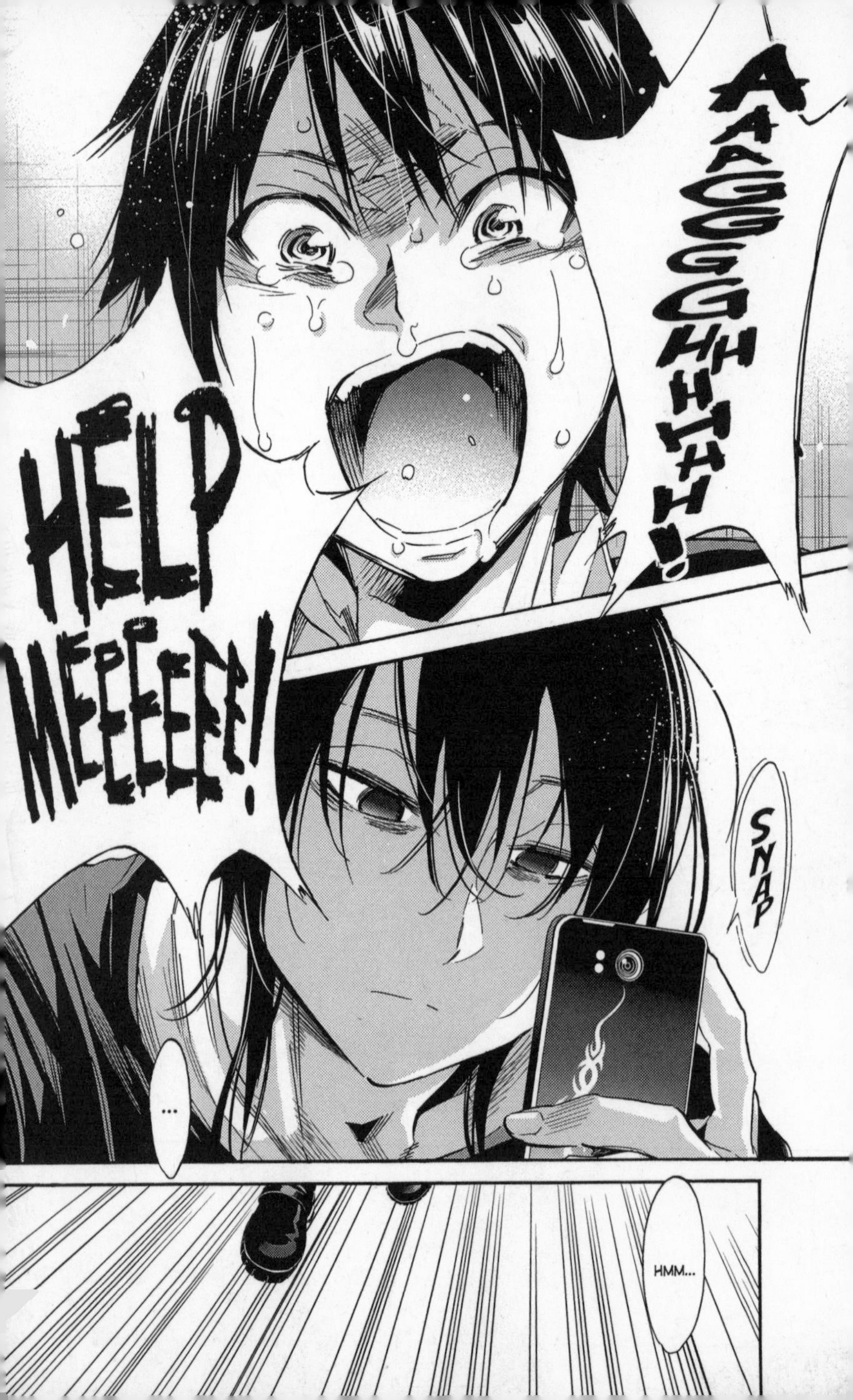
AAAGGGHHHHHH!
HELP MEEEEEE!
SNAP
...
HMM...

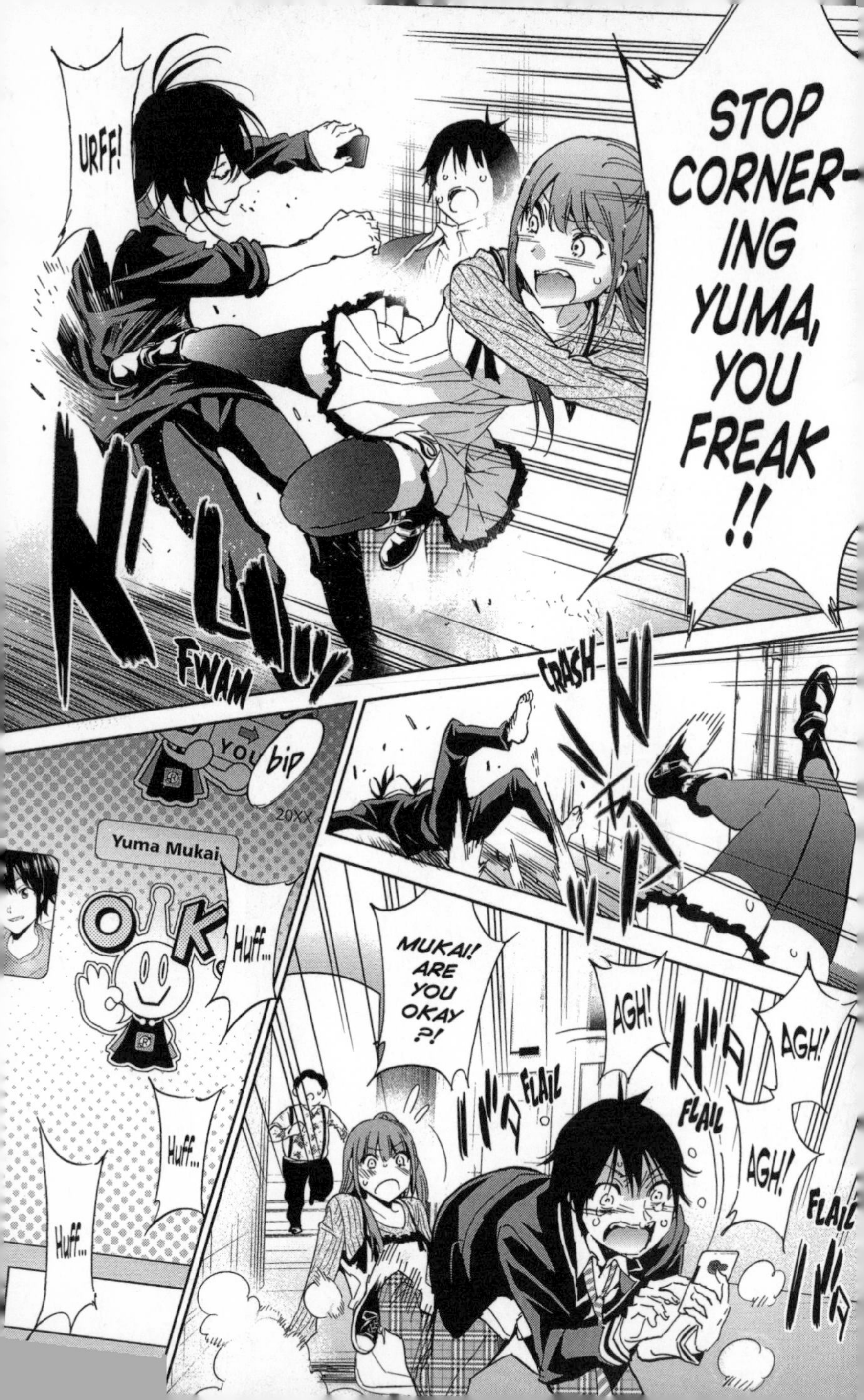

STOP CORNER-ING YUMA, YOU FREAK!!
URFF!
FWAM
CRASH
YOU
bip
20XX
Yuma Mukai
OK
Huff...
Huff...
Huff...
MUKAI! ARE YOU OKAY?!
AGH!
AGH!
AGH!
FLAIL
FLAIL
FLAIL

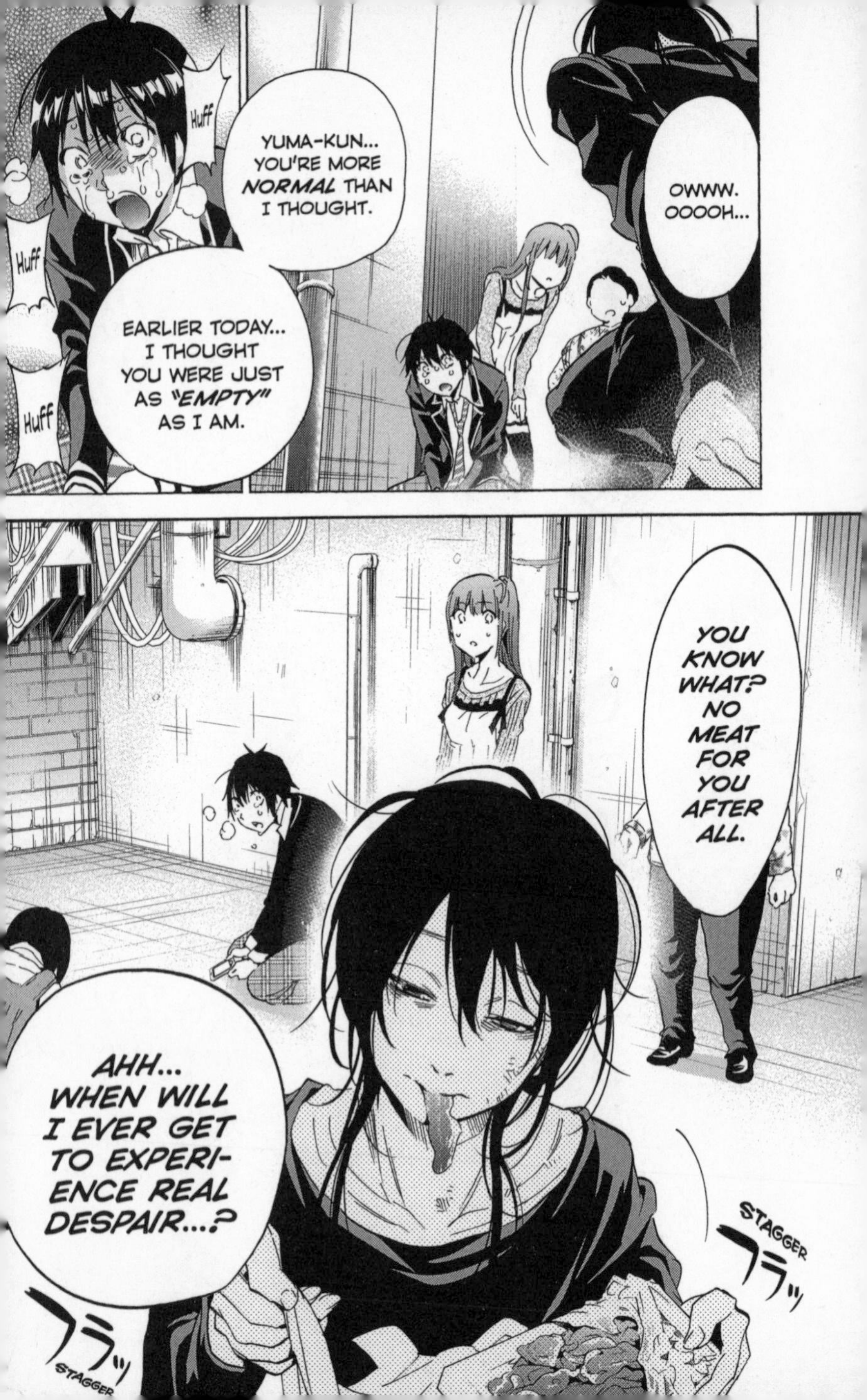
OWWW. OOOOH...
YUMA-KUN... YOU'RE MORE NORMAL THAN I THOUGHT.
EARLIER TODAY... I THOUGHT YOU WERE JUST AS "EMPTY" AS I AM.
Huff
Huff
Huff
YOU KNOW WHAT? NO MEAT FOR YOU AFTER ALL.
AHH... WHEN WILL I EVER GET TO EXPERIENCE REAL DESPAIR...?
フラッ
STAGGER
フラッ
STAGGER

ACCOUNT 17 Digital Tattoos

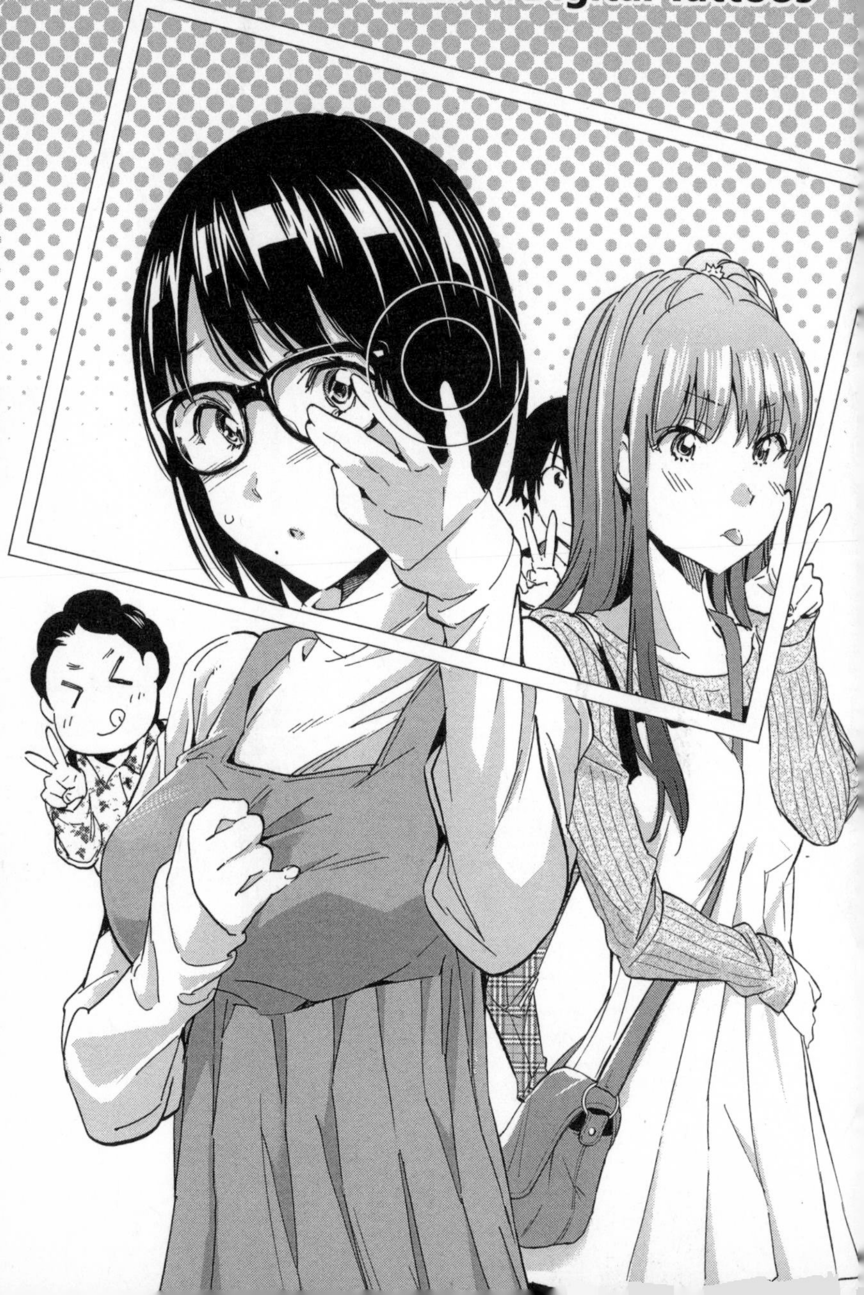

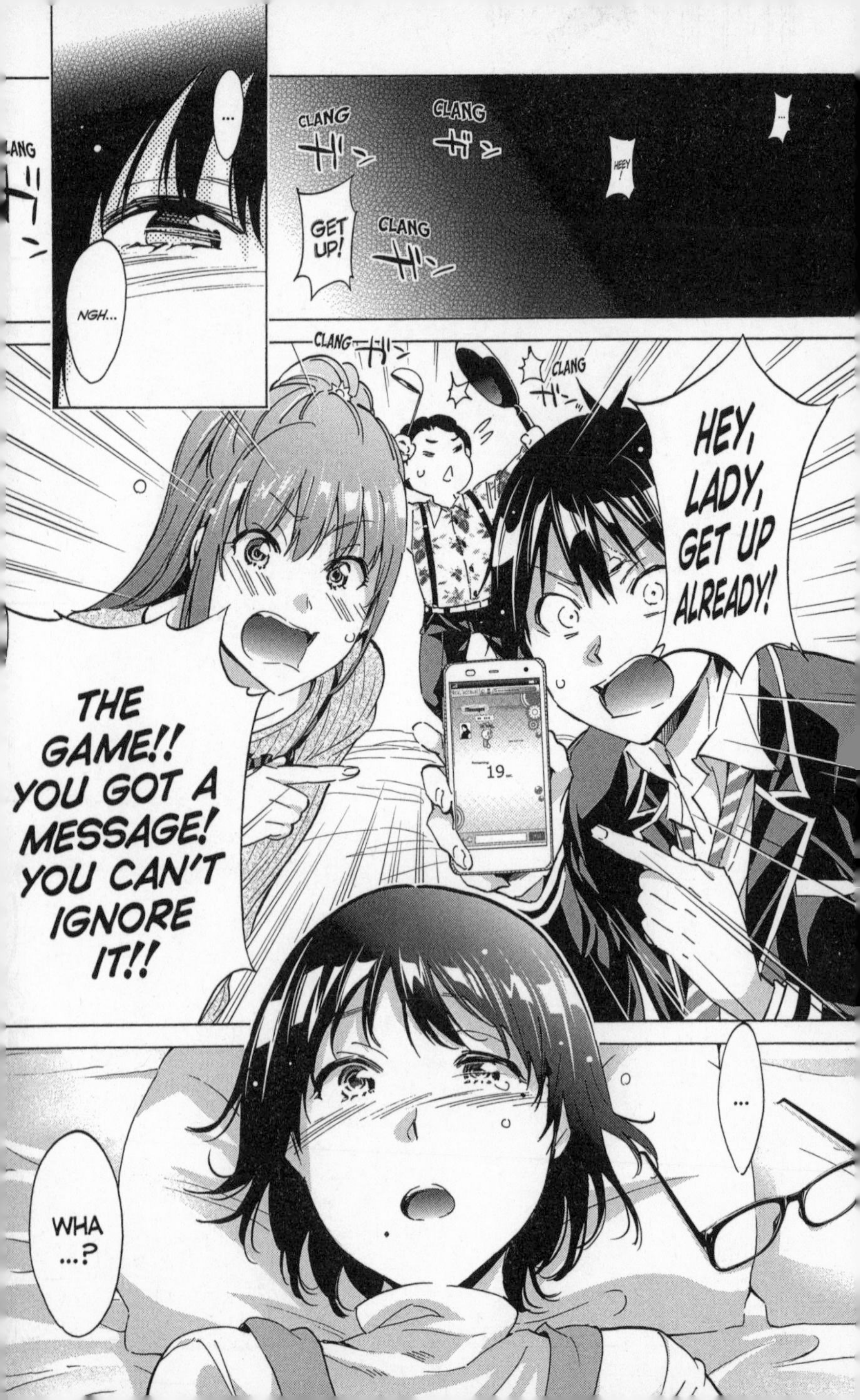
...
HEY!
CLANG
CLANG
GET UP!
CLANG
CLANG
...
NGH...
CLANG
HEY, LADY, GET UP ALREADY!
CLANG
THE GAME!! YOU GOT A MESSAGE! YOU CAN'T IGNORE IT!!
...
WHA ...?

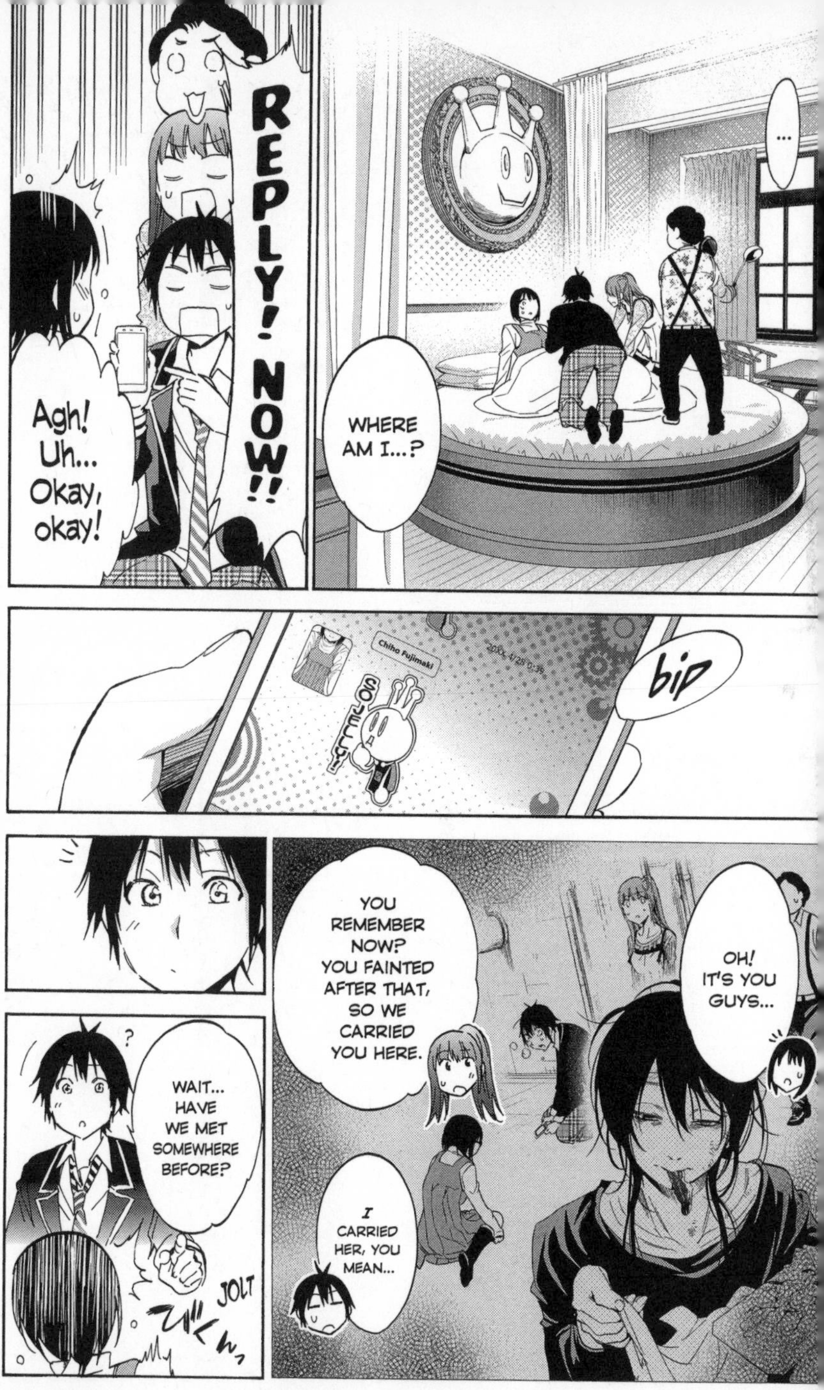
...
WHERE AM I...?
REPLY! NOW!!
Agh! Uh... Okay, okay!
Chiho Fujimaki
SO JELLY!
bip
OH! IT'S YOU GUYS...
YOU REMEMBER NOW? YOU FAINTED AFTER THAT, SO WE CARRIED YOU HERE.
I CARRIED HER, YOU MEAN...
WAIT... HAVE WE MET SOMEWHERE BEFORE?
JOLT
びくんっ

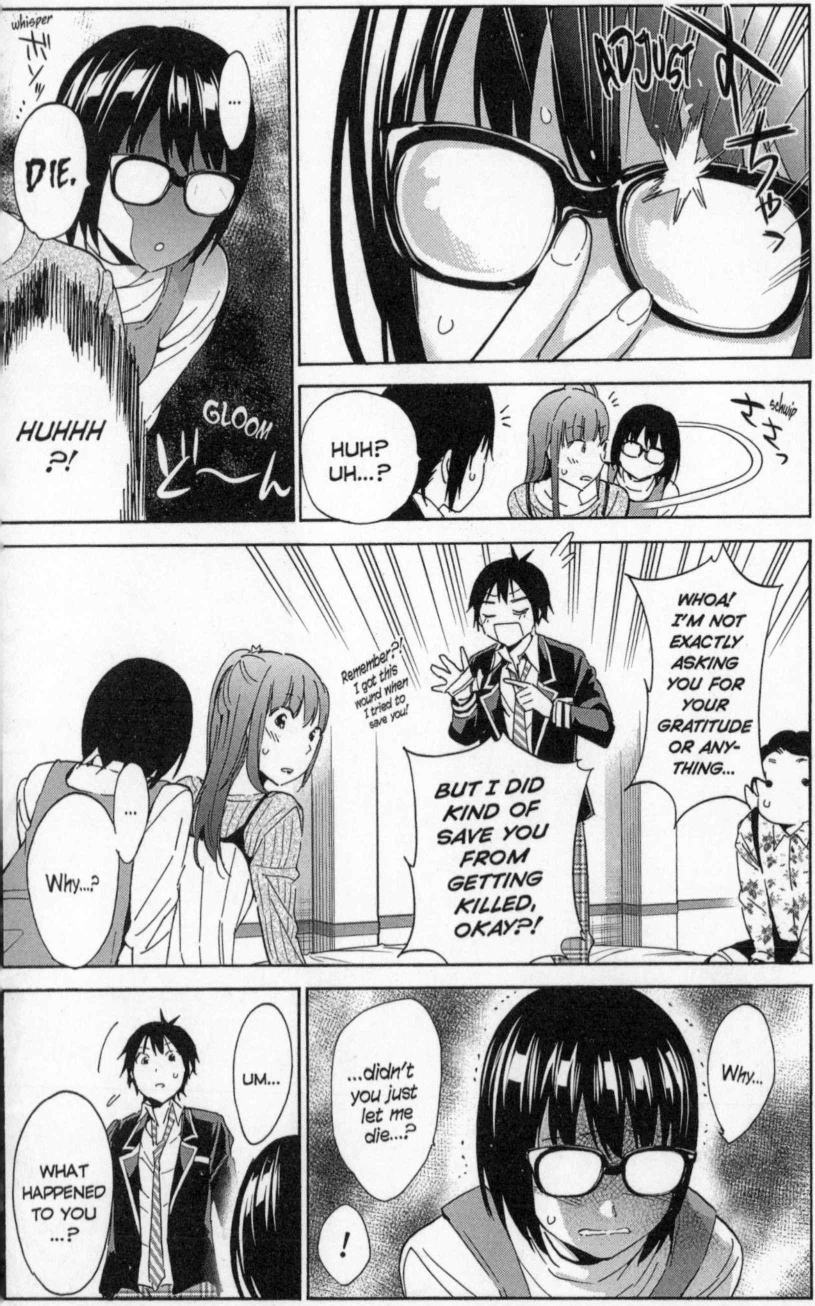

ADJUST
ちゃっ
schwip
さっ
HUH? UH...?
whisper
ボソッ
...
DIE.
HUHHH?!
GLOOM
ど～ん
WHOA! I'M NOT EXACTLY ASKING YOU FOR YOUR GRATITUDE OR ANY-THING...
BUT I DID KIND OF SAVE YOU FROM GETTING KILLED, OKAY?!
Remember?! I got this wound when I tried to save you!
...
Why...?
Why...
...didn't you just let me die...?
!
UM...
WHAT HAPPENED TO YOU ...?

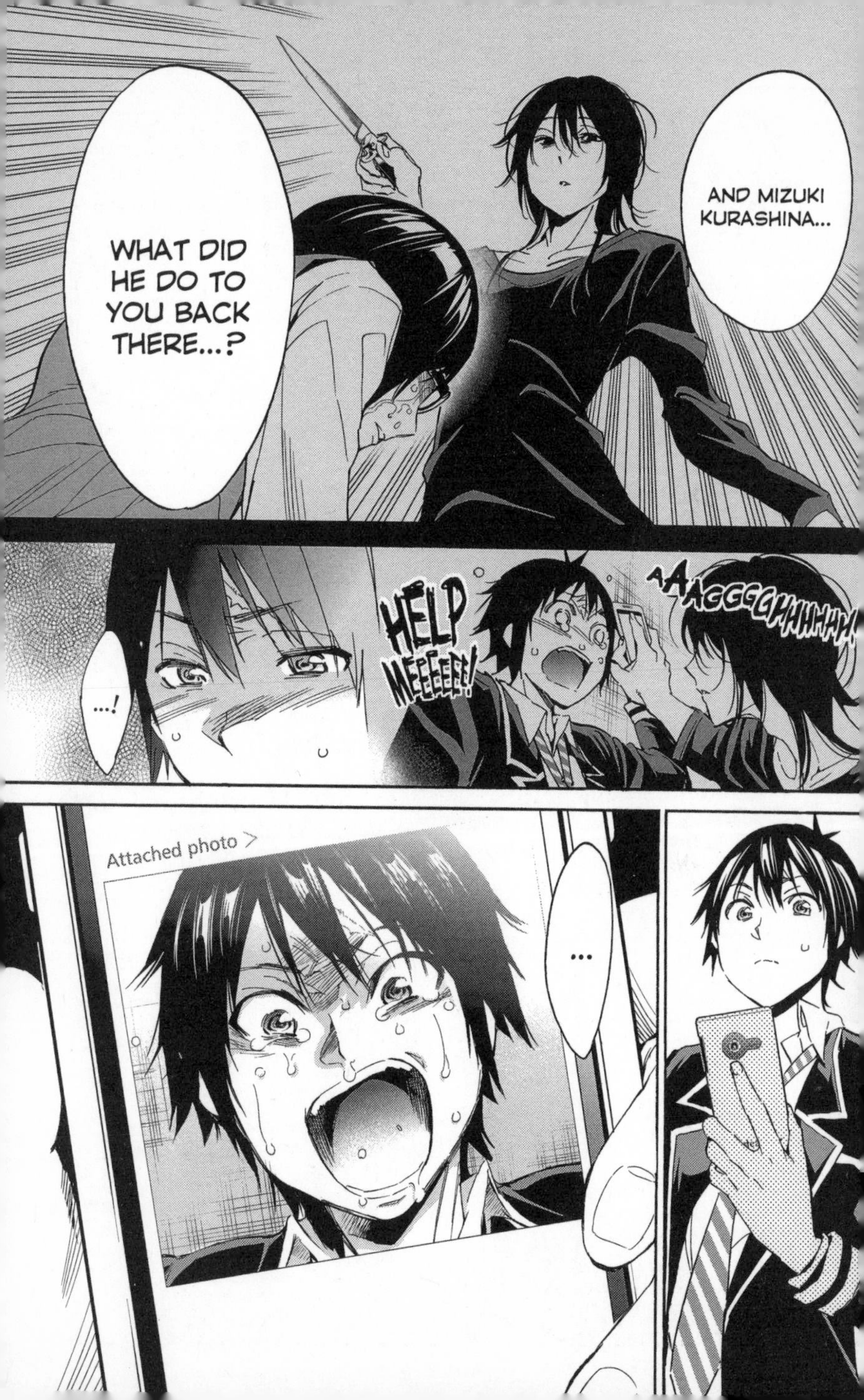
AND MIZUKI KURASHINA...
WHAT DID HE DO TO YOU BACK THERE...?
AAAGGGGHHHHHH!
HELP MEEEEEE!
...!
...
Attached photo >

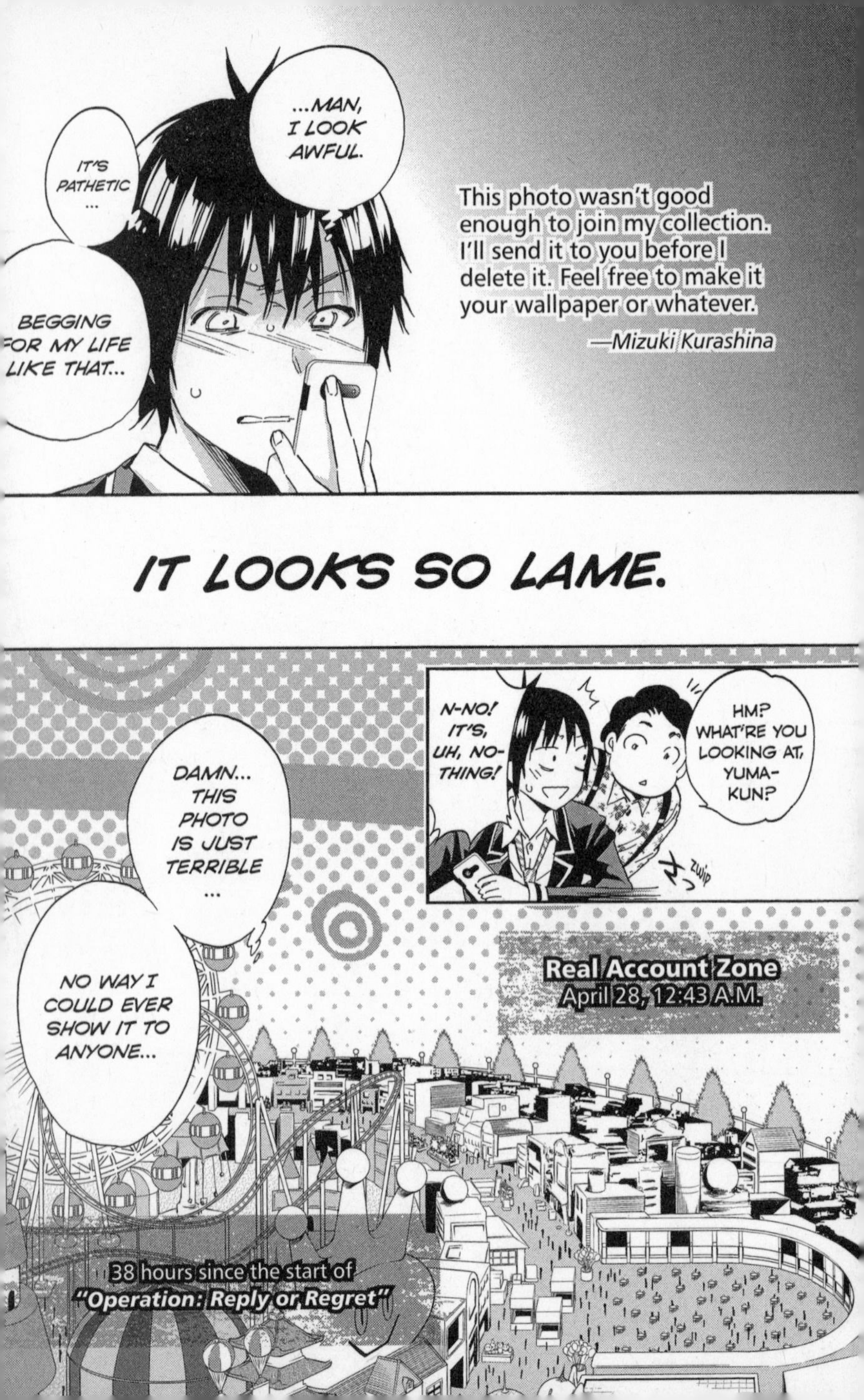
This photo wasn't good enough to join my collection. I'll send it to you before I delete it. Feel free to make it your wallpaper or whatever.
—Mizuki Kurashina
...MAN, I LOOK AWFUL.
IT'S PATHETIC...
BEGGING FOR MY LIFE LIKE THAT...
IT LOOKS SO LAME.
HM? WHAT'RE YOU LOOKING AT, YUMA-KUN?
N-NO! IT'S, UH, NOTHING!
ZWIP
Real Account Zone
April 28, 12:43 A.M.
DAMN... THIS PHOTO IS JUST TERRIBLE...
NO WAY I COULD EVER SHOW IT TO ANYONE...
38 hours since the start of
"Operation: Reply or Regret"

Current players: 2213 Number of deaths left: 678

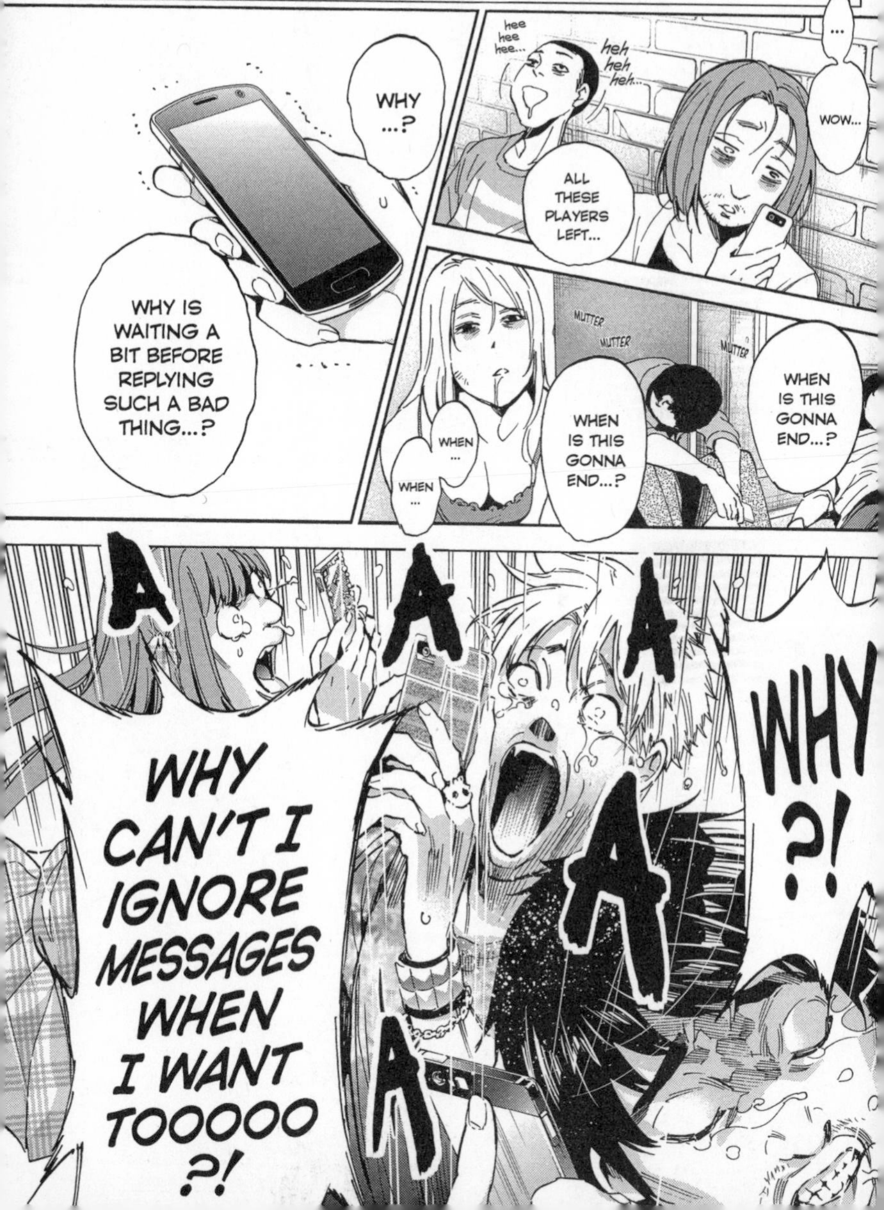
...
WOW...
heh heh heh...
hee hee hee...
ALL THESE PLAYERS LEFT...
MUTTER
MUTTER
MUTTER
WHEN IS THIS GONNA END...?
WHEN IS THIS GONNA END...?
WHEN ...
WHEN ...
WHY ...?
WHY IS WAITING A BIT BEFORE REPLYING SUCH A BAD THING...?
WHY ?!
A
A
A
A
A
A
WHY CAN'T I IGNORE MESSAGES WHEN I WANT TOOOOO ?!

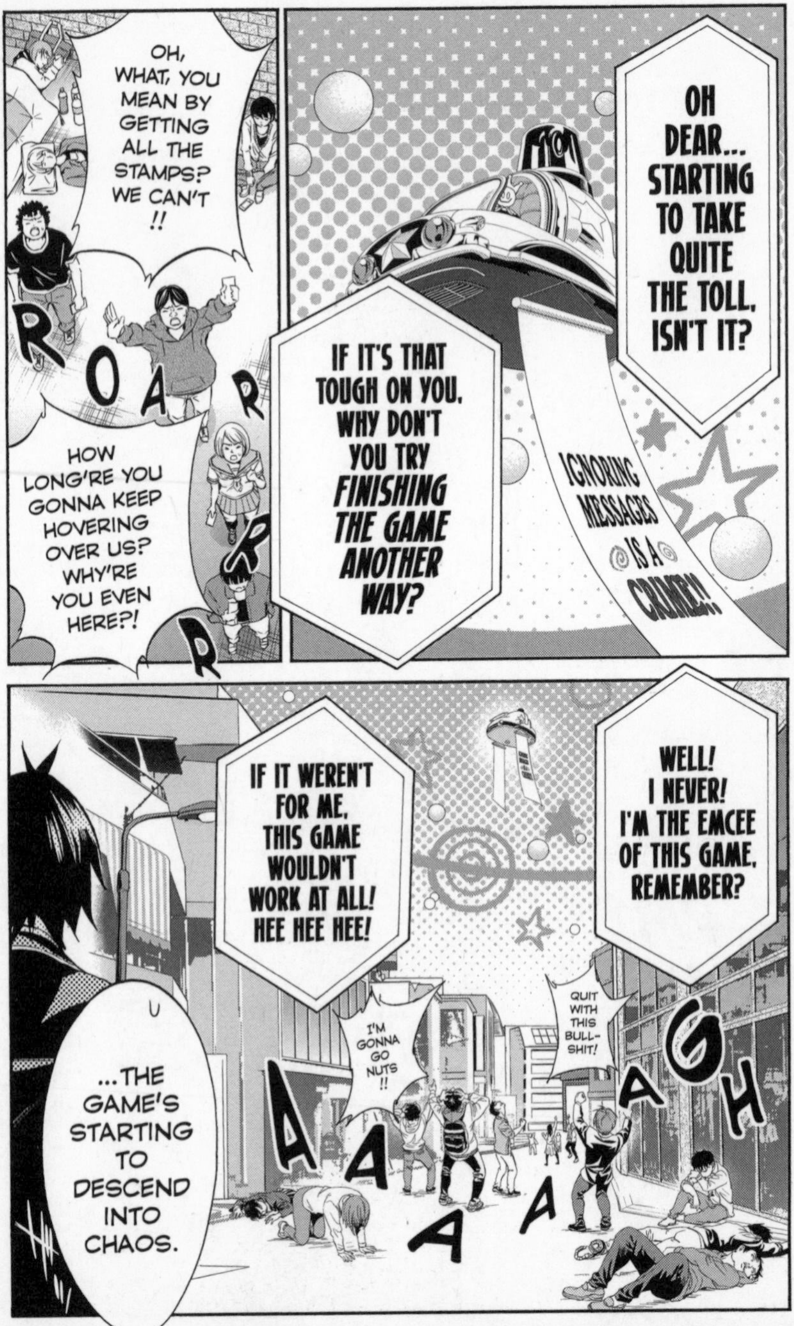
OH DEAR... STARTING TO TAKE QUITE THE TOLL, ISN'T IT?
IGNORING MESSAGES IS A CRIME!!
IF IT'S THAT TOUGH ON YOU, WHY DON'T YOU TRY FINISHING THE GAME ANOTHER WAY?
OH, WHAT, YOU MEAN BY GETTING ALL THE STAMPS? WE CAN'T !!
ROARRR
HOW LONG'RE YOU GONNA KEEP HOVERING OVER US? WHY'RE YOU EVEN HERE?!
WELL! I NEVER! I'M THE EMCEE OF THIS GAME, REMEMBER?
IF IT WEREN'T FOR ME, THIS GAME WOULDN'T WORK AT ALL! HEE HEE HEE!
QUIT WITH THIS BULL-SHIT!
AGH
I'M GONNA GO NUTS !!
AAAAA
U
...THE GAME'S STARTING TO DESCEND INTO CHAOS.

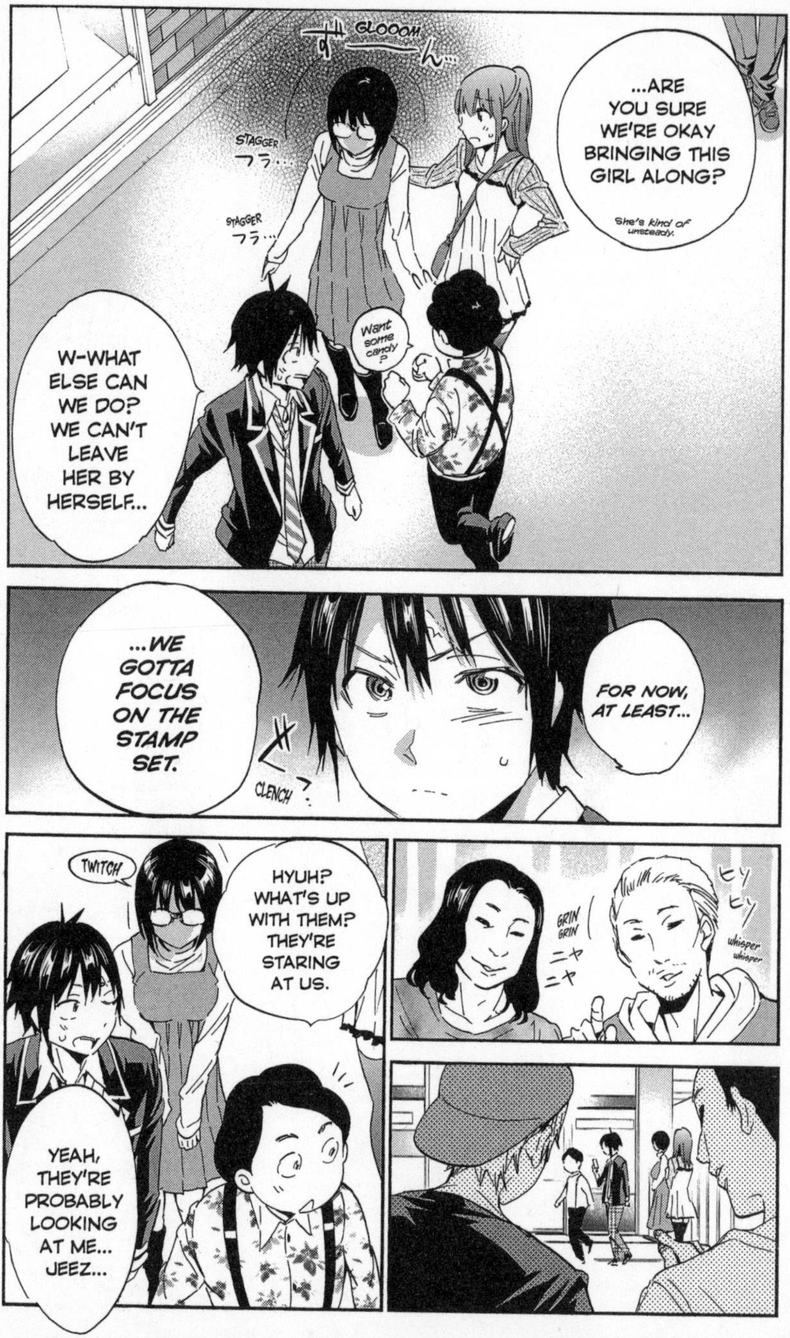
GLOOOM
...ARE YOU SURE WE'RE OKAY BRINGING THIS GIRL ALONG?
She's kind of unsteady.
STAGGER
STAGGER
Want some candy?
W-WHAT ELSE CAN WE DO? WE CAN'T LEAVE HER BY HERSELF...
FOR NOW, AT LEAST...
...WE GOTTA FOCUS ON THE STAMP SET.
CLENCH
whisper whisper
GRIN GRIN
HYUH? WHAT'S UP WITH THEM? THEY'RE STARING AT US.
TWITCH
YEAH, THEY'RE PROBABLY LOOKING AT ME... JEEZ...

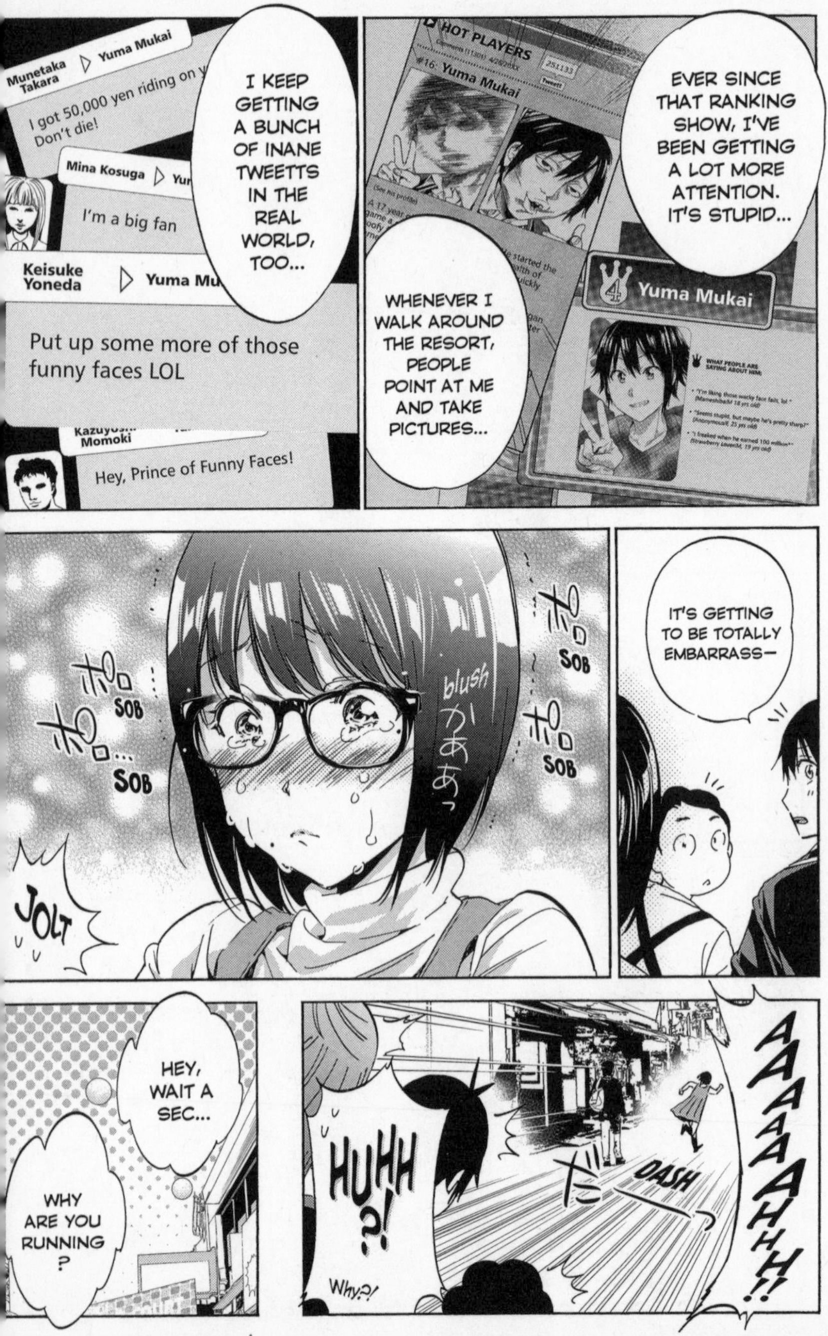
HOT PLAYERS
#16: Yuma Mukai
EVER SINCE THAT RANKING SHOW, I'VE BEEN GETTING A LOT MORE ATTENTION. IT'S STUPID...
WHENEVER I WALK AROUND THE RESORT, PEOPLE POINT AT ME AND TAKE PICTURES...
Yuma Mukai
I KEEP GETTING A BUNCH OF INANE TWEETTS IN THE REAL WORLD, TOO...
Munetaka Takara ▷ Yuma Mukai
I got 50,000 yen riding on y
Don't die!
Mina Kosuga ▷ Yu
I'm a big fan
Keisuke Yoneda ▷ Yuma Mu
Put up some more of those funny faces LOL
Momoki
Hey, Prince of Funny Faces!
IT'S GETTING TO BE TOTALLY EMBARRASS—
SOB
SOB
blush
かあっ
SOB
SOB
JOLT
AAAAAAAHHH!!
DASH
HUHH?!
Why?!
HEY, WAIT A SEC...
WHY ARE YOU RUNNING?

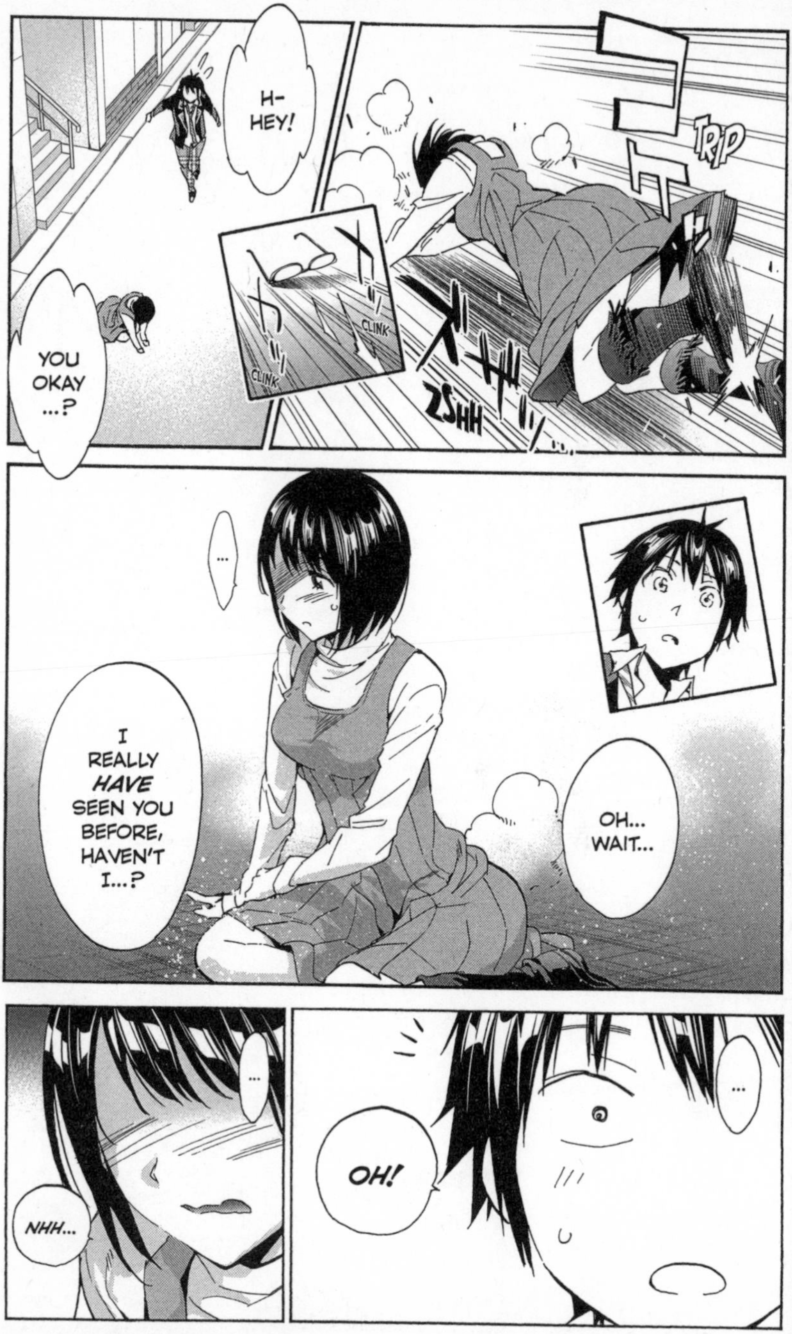
TRIP
ZSHH
CLINK
CLINK
H-HEY!
YOU OKAY ...?
...
OH... WAIT...
I REALLY *HAVE* SEEN YOU BEFORE, HAVEN'T I...?
...
OH!
...
NHH...

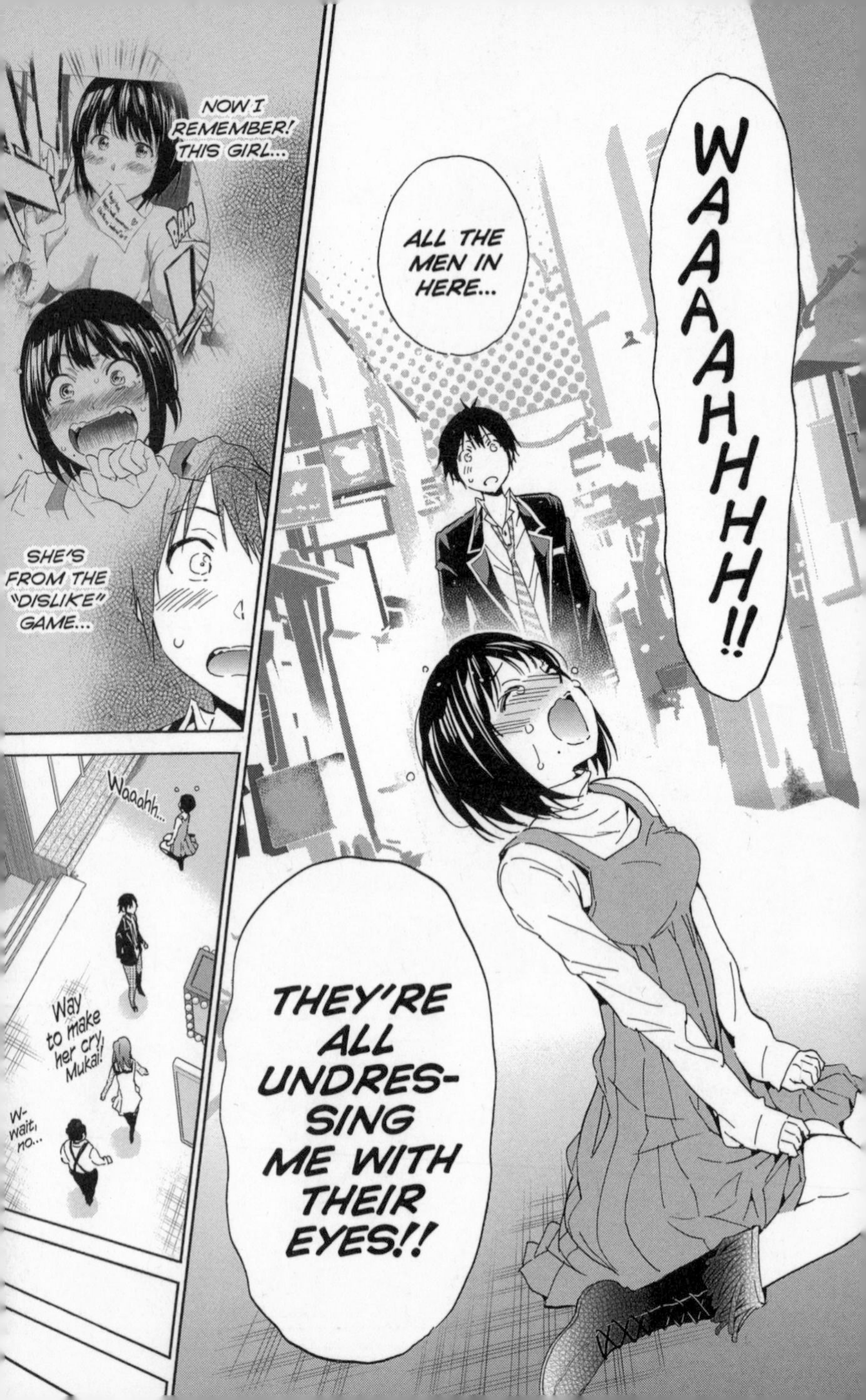
WAAAAHHHHH!!
ALL THE MEN IN HERE...
THEY'RE ALL UNDRES-SING ME WITH THEIR EYES!!
NOW I REMEMBER! THIS GIRL...
BAM
SHE'S FROM THE "DISLIKE" GAME...
Waaahh...
Way to make her cry, Mukai!
W-wait, no...

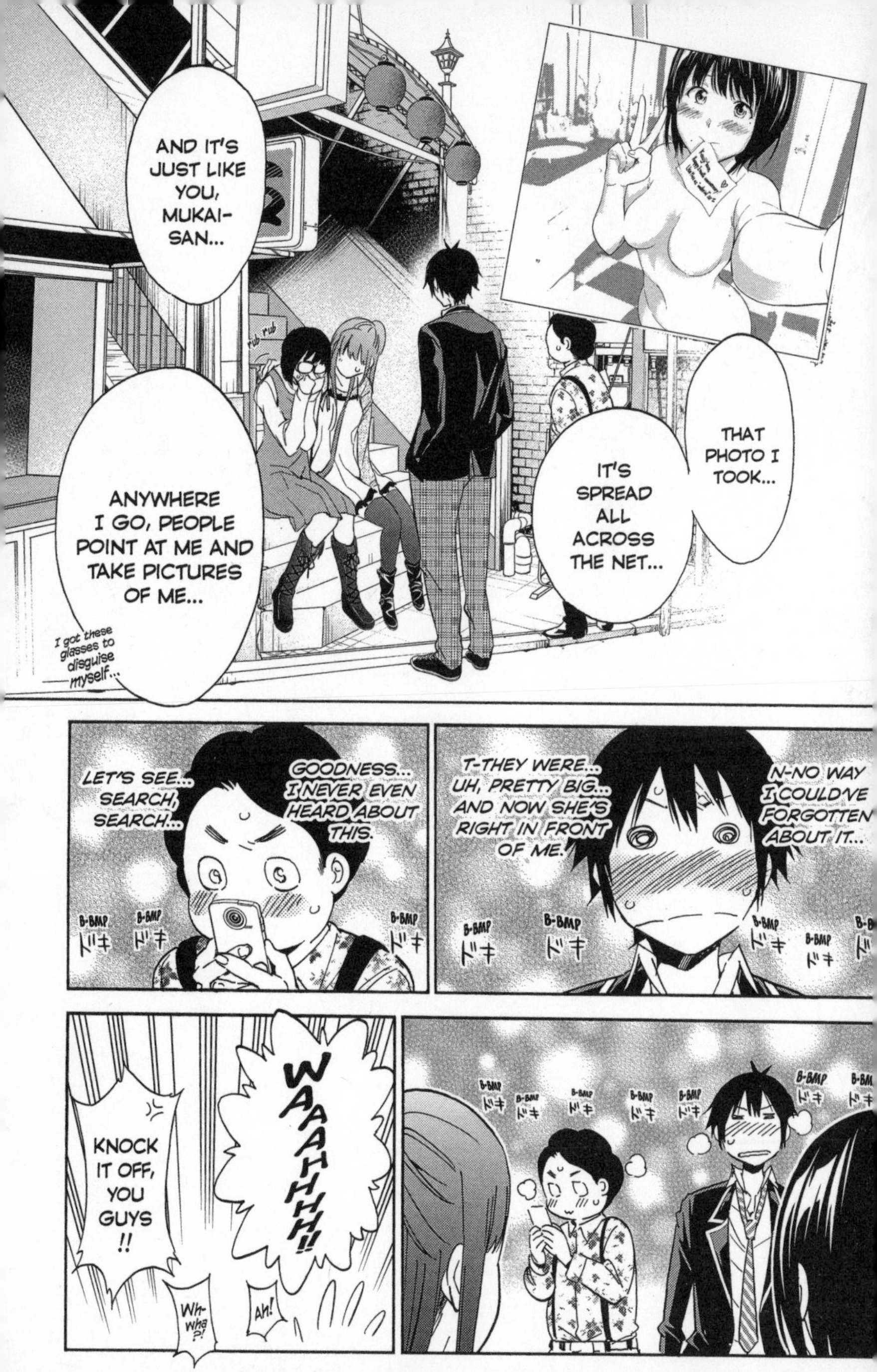
THAT PHOTO I TOOK...
IT'S SPREAD ALL ACROSS THE NET...
AND IT'S JUST LIKE YOU, MUKAI-SAN...
rub rub
ANYWHERE I GO, PEOPLE POINT AT ME AND TAKE PICTURES OF ME...
I got these glasses to disguise myself...
N-NO WAY I COULD'VE FORGOTTEN ABOUT IT...
T-THEY WERE... UH, PRETTY BIG... AND NOW SHE'S RIGHT IN FRONT OF ME.
B-BMP ドキ
B-BMP ドキ
B-BMP ドキ
B-BMP ドキ
GOODNESS... I NEVER EVEN HEARD ABOUT THIS.
LET'S SEE... SEARCH, SEARCH...
B-BMP ドキ
B-BMP ドキ
B-BMP ドキ
B-BMP ドキ
B-BMP ドキ
B-BMP ドキ
B-BMP ドキ
B-BMP ドキ
B-BMP ドキ
WAAAHHHH!!
KNOCK IT OFF, YOU GUYS !!
Ah!
Wh-wha?!

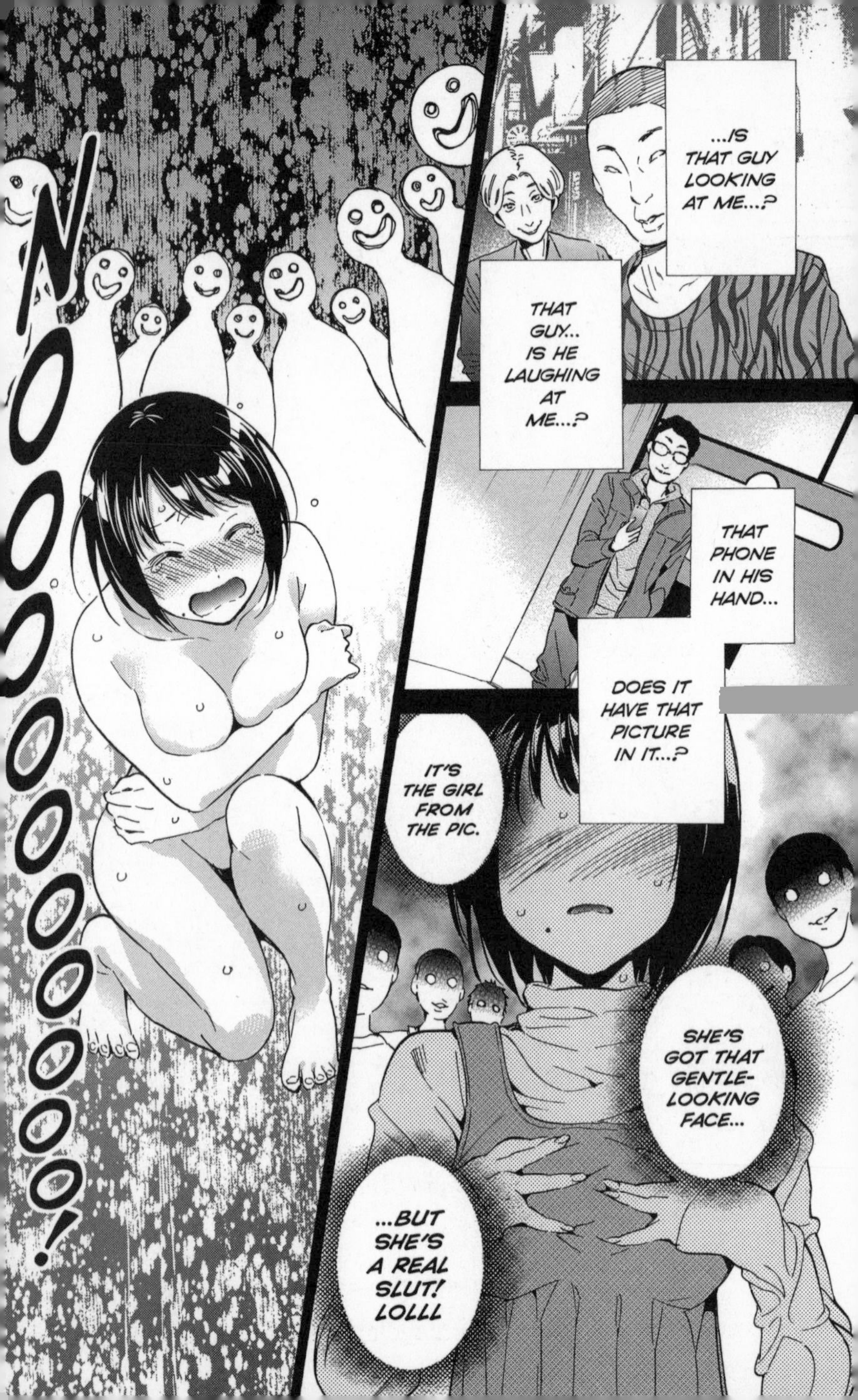
...IS THAT GUY LOOKING AT ME...?
THAT GUY... IS HE LAUGHING AT ME...?
THAT PHONE IN HIS HAND...
DOES IT HAVE THAT PICTURE IN IT...?
IT'S THE GIRL FROM THE PIC.
SHE'S GOT THAT GENTLE-LOOKING FACE...
...BUT SHE'S A REAL SLUT! LOLLL
NOOOOOOOOOOO!

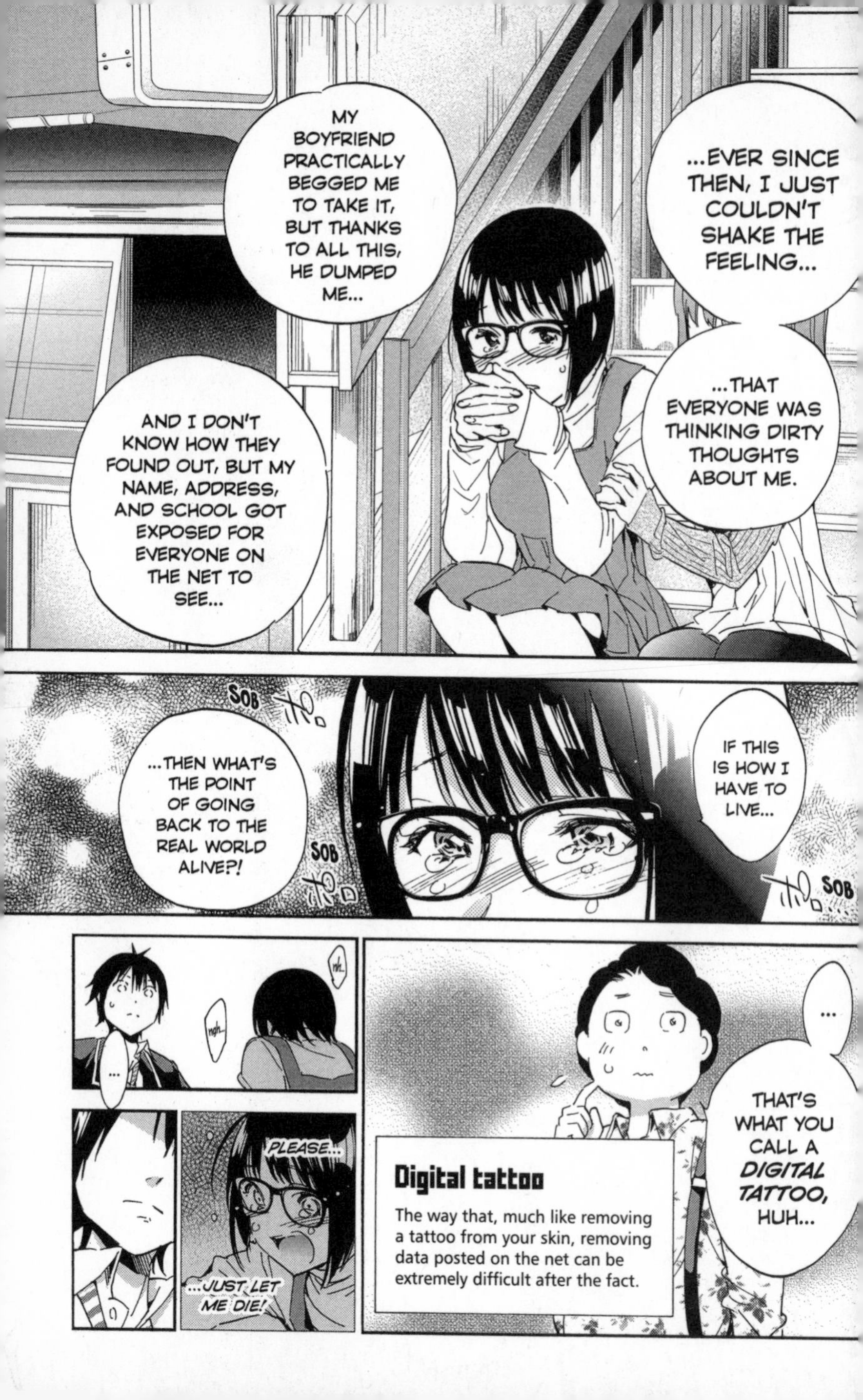
...EVER SINCE THEN, I JUST COULDN'T SHAKE THE FEELING...
...THAT EVERYONE WAS THINKING DIRTY THOUGHTS ABOUT ME.
MY BOYFRIEND PRACTICALLY BEGGED ME TO TAKE IT, BUT THANKS TO ALL THIS, HE DUMPED ME...
AND I DON'T KNOW HOW THEY FOUND OUT, BUT MY NAME, ADDRESS, AND SCHOOL GOT EXPOSED FOR EVERYONE ON THE NET TO SEE...
SOB
IF THIS IS HOW I HAVE TO LIVE...
SOB
...THEN WHAT'S THE POINT OF GOING BACK TO THE REAL WORLD ALIVE?!
SOB
...
THAT'S WHAT YOU CALL A *DIGITAL TATTOO,* HUH...
Digital tattoo
The way that, much like removing a tattoo from your skin, removing data posted on the net can be extremely difficult after the fact.
nk
ngh...
...
PLEASE...
...JUST LET ME DIE!

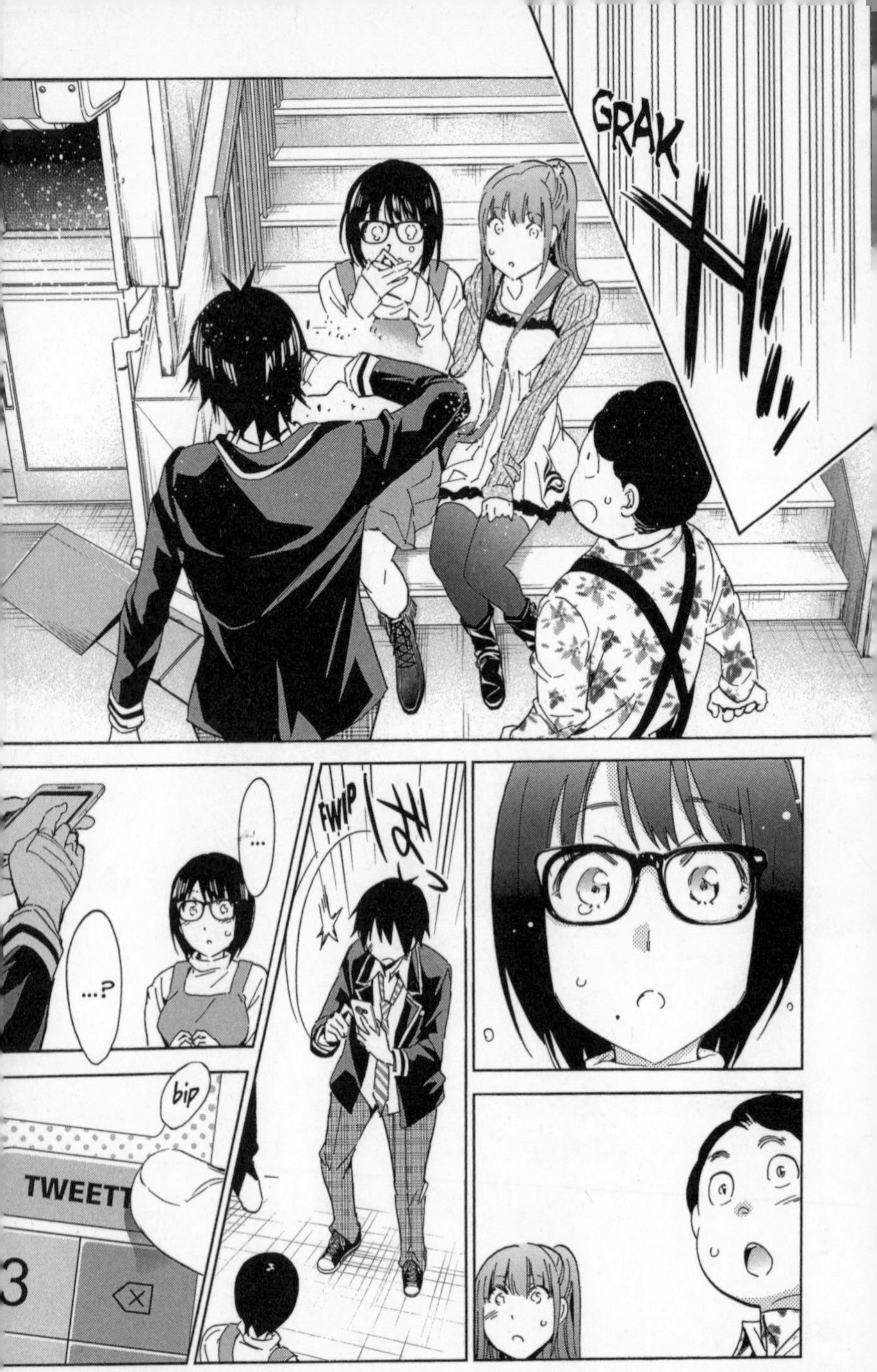
GRAK
FWIP
...
...?
bip
TWEET
3

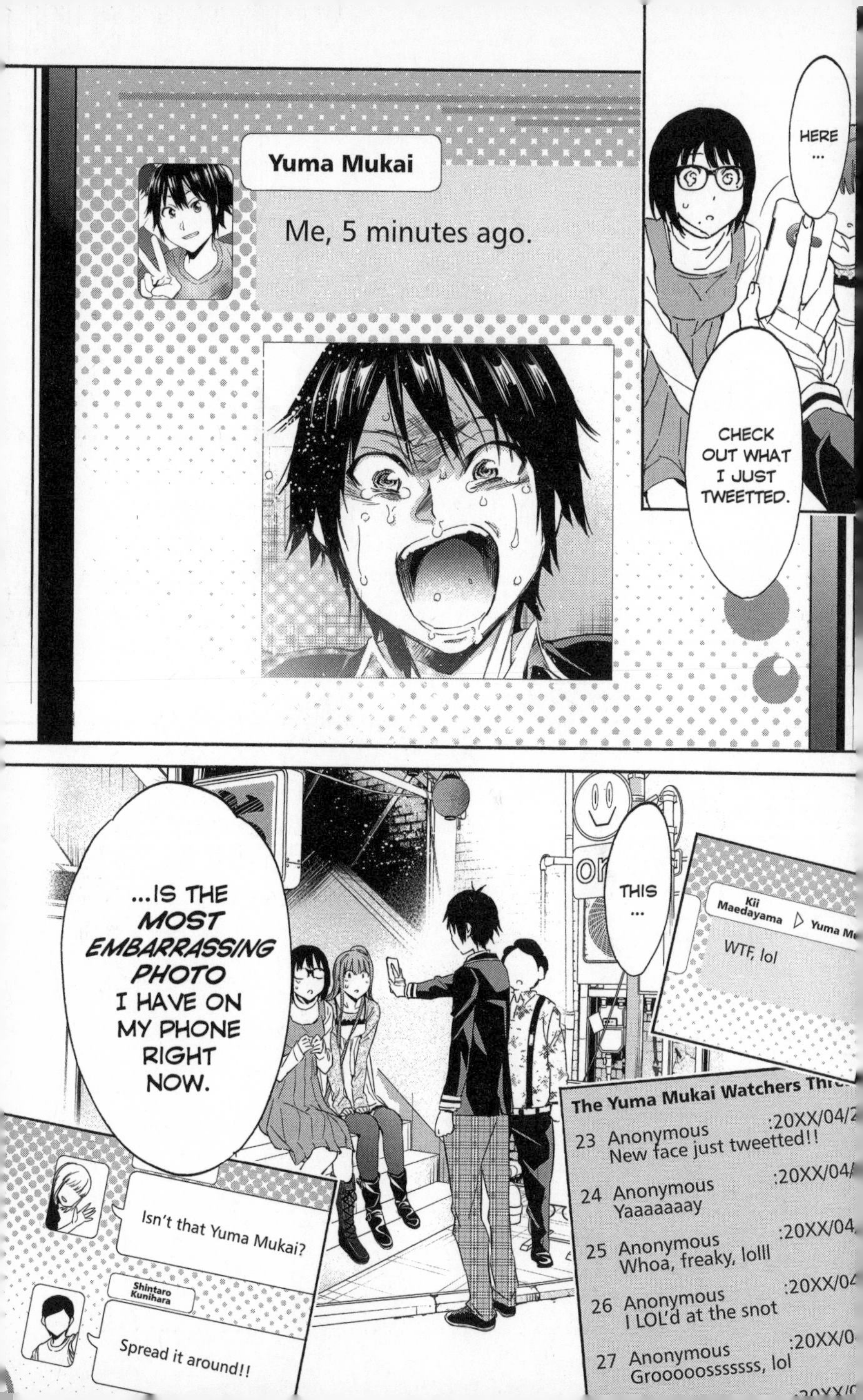
HERE...
CHECK OUT WHAT I JUST TWEETTED.
Yuma Mukai
Me, 5 minutes ago.
THIS...
Kii Maedayama ▷ Yuma M
WTF, lol
...IS THE MOST EMBARRASSING PHOTO I HAVE ON MY PHONE RIGHT NOW.
The Yuma Mukai Watchers Thre
23 Anonymous :20XX/04/2
New face just tweetted!!
24 Anonymous :20XX/04/
Yaaaaaay
25 Anonymous :20XX/04,
Whoa, freaky, lolll
26 Anonymous :20XX/04
I LOL'd at the snot
27 Anonymous :20XX/0
Groooosssssss, lol
Isn't that Yuma Mukai?
Shintaro Kunihara
Spread it around!!

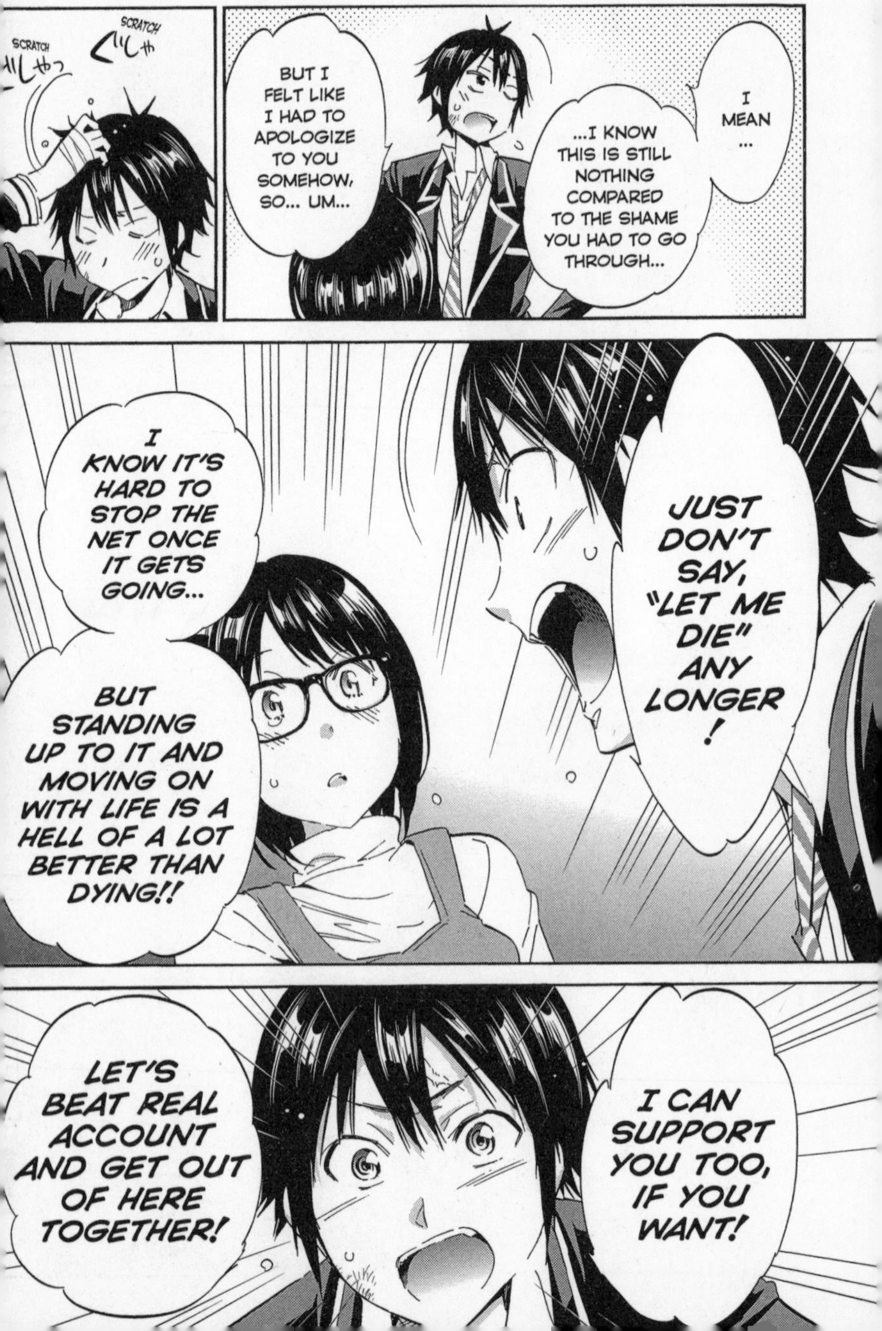
I MEAN...
...I KNOW THIS IS STILL NOTHING COMPARED TO THE SHAME YOU HAD TO GO THROUGH...
BUT I FELT LIKE I HAD TO APOLOGIZE TO YOU SOMEHOW, SO... UM...
SCRATCH
ぐしゃ
SCRATCH
JUST DON'T SAY, "LET ME DIE" ANY LONGER!
I KNOW IT'S HARD TO STOP THE NET ONCE IT GETS GOING...
BUT STANDING UP TO IT AND MOVING ON WITH LIFE IS A HELL OF A LOT BETTER THAN DYING!!
I CAN SUPPORT YOU TOO, IF YOU WANT!
LET'S BEAT REAL ACCOUNT AND GET OUT OF HERE TOGETHER!

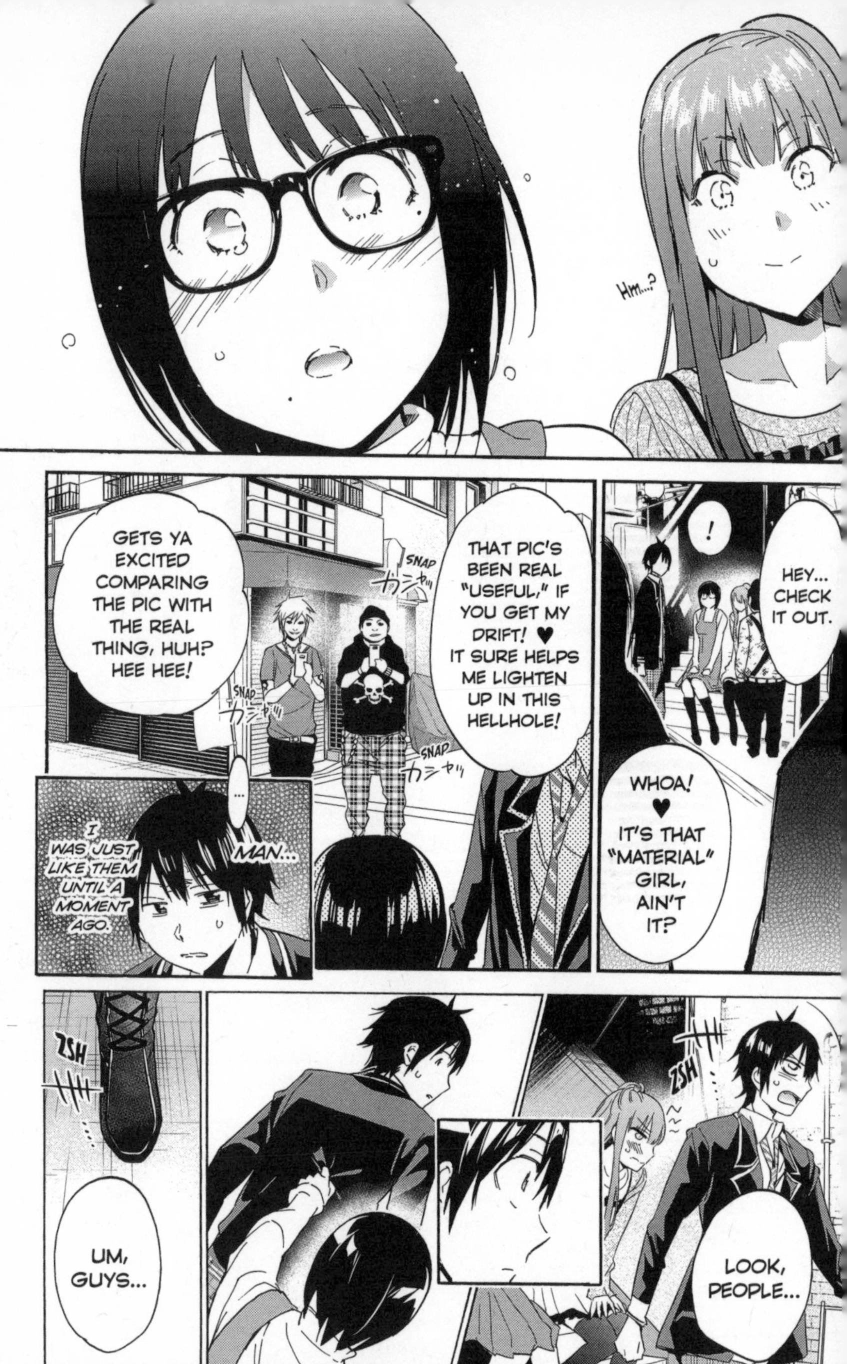

Hm...?
!
HEY... CHECK IT OUT.
WHOA! ♥ IT'S THAT "MATERIAL" GIRL, AIN'T IT?
THAT PIC'S BEEN REAL "USEFUL," IF YOU GET MY DRIFT! ♥ IT SURE HELPS ME LIGHTEN UP IN THIS HELLHOLE!
SNAP
GETS YA EXCITED COMPARING THE PIC WITH THE REAL THING, HUH? HEE HEE!
SNAP
SNAP
...
MAN...
I WAS JUST LIKE THEM UNTIL A MOMENT AGO.
ZSH
LOOK, PEOPLE...
ZSH
UM, GUYS...

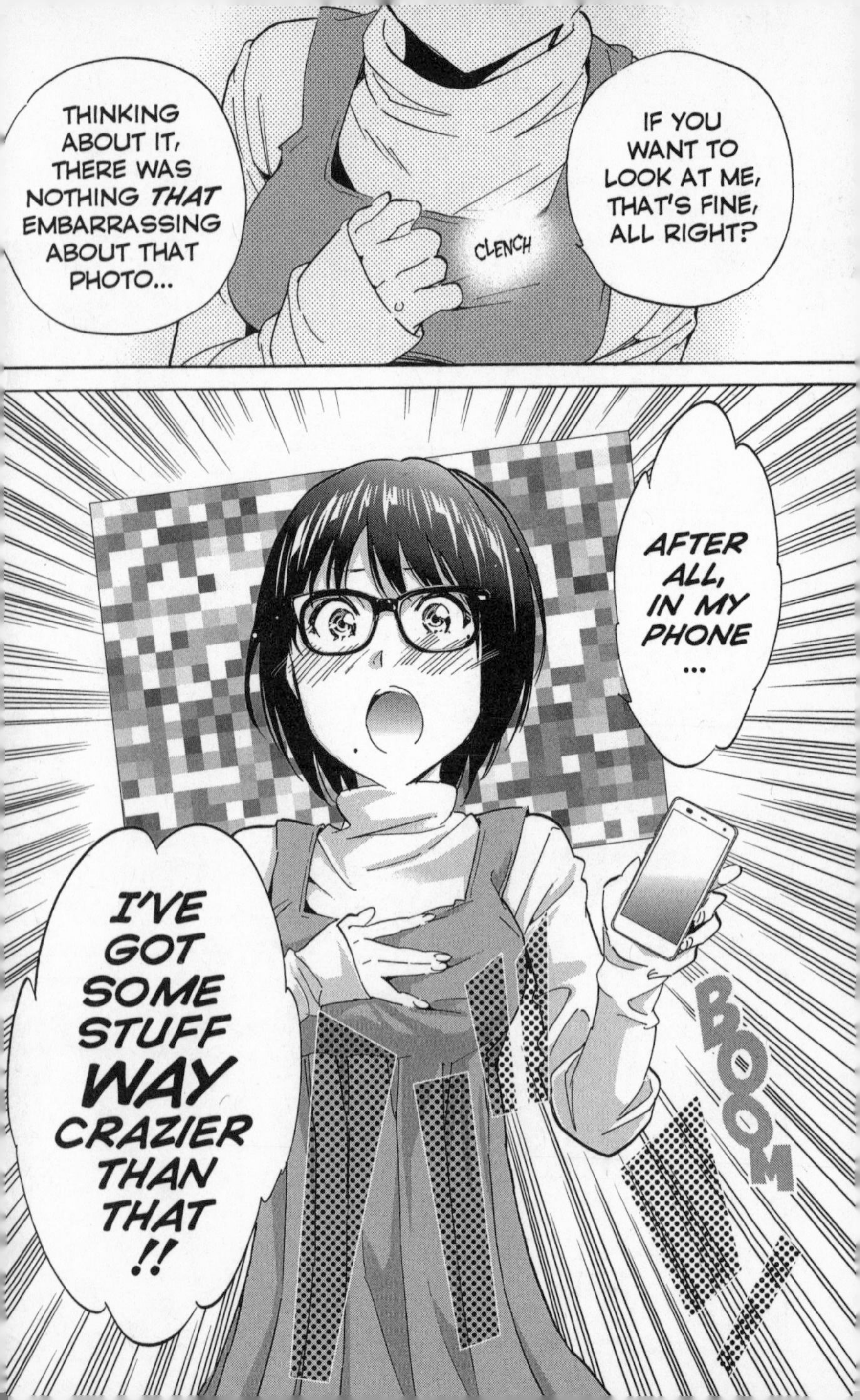
IF YOU WANT TO LOOK AT ME, THAT'S FINE, ALL RIGHT?
CLENCH
THINKING ABOUT IT, THERE WAS NOTHING *THAT* EMBARRASSING ABOUT THAT PHOTO...
AFTER ALL, IN MY PHONE ...
BOOM
*I'VE GOT SOME STUFF **WAY** CRAZIER THAN THAT !!*

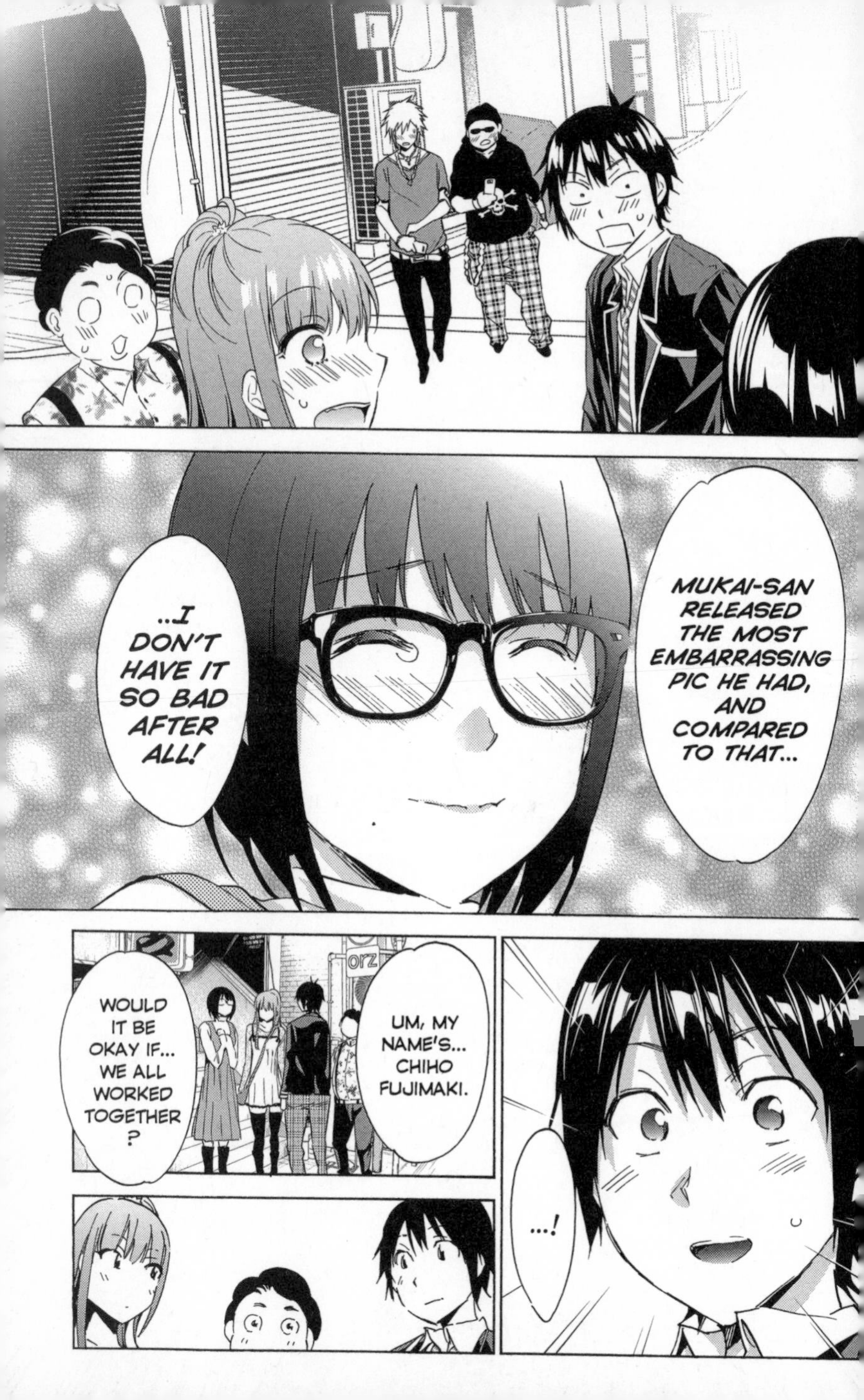
MUKAI-SAN RELEASED THE MOST EMBARRASSING PIC HE HAD, AND COMPARED TO THAT...
..I DON'T HAVE IT SO BAD AFTER ALL!
...!
UM, MY NAME'S... CHIHO FUJIMAKI.
WOULD IT BE OKAY IF... WE ALL WORKED TOGETHER?
orz

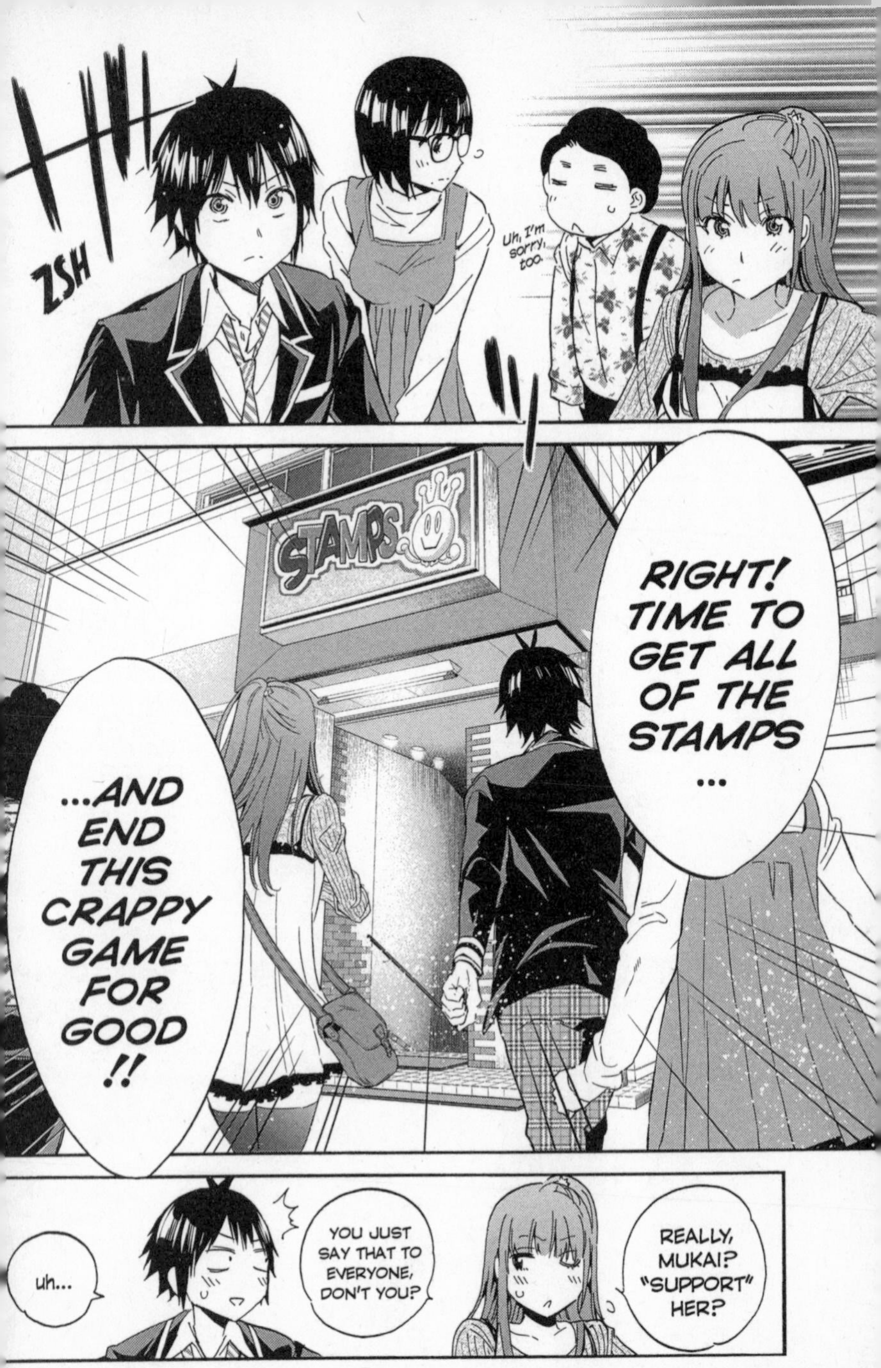
Uh, I'm sorry, too.
ZSH
STAMPS
RIGHT! TIME TO GET ALL OF THE STAMPS ...
...AND END THIS CRAPPY GAME FOR GOOD!!
REALLY, MUKAI? "SUPPORT" HER?
YOU JUST SAY THAT TO EVERYONE, DON'T YOU?
uh...

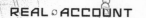

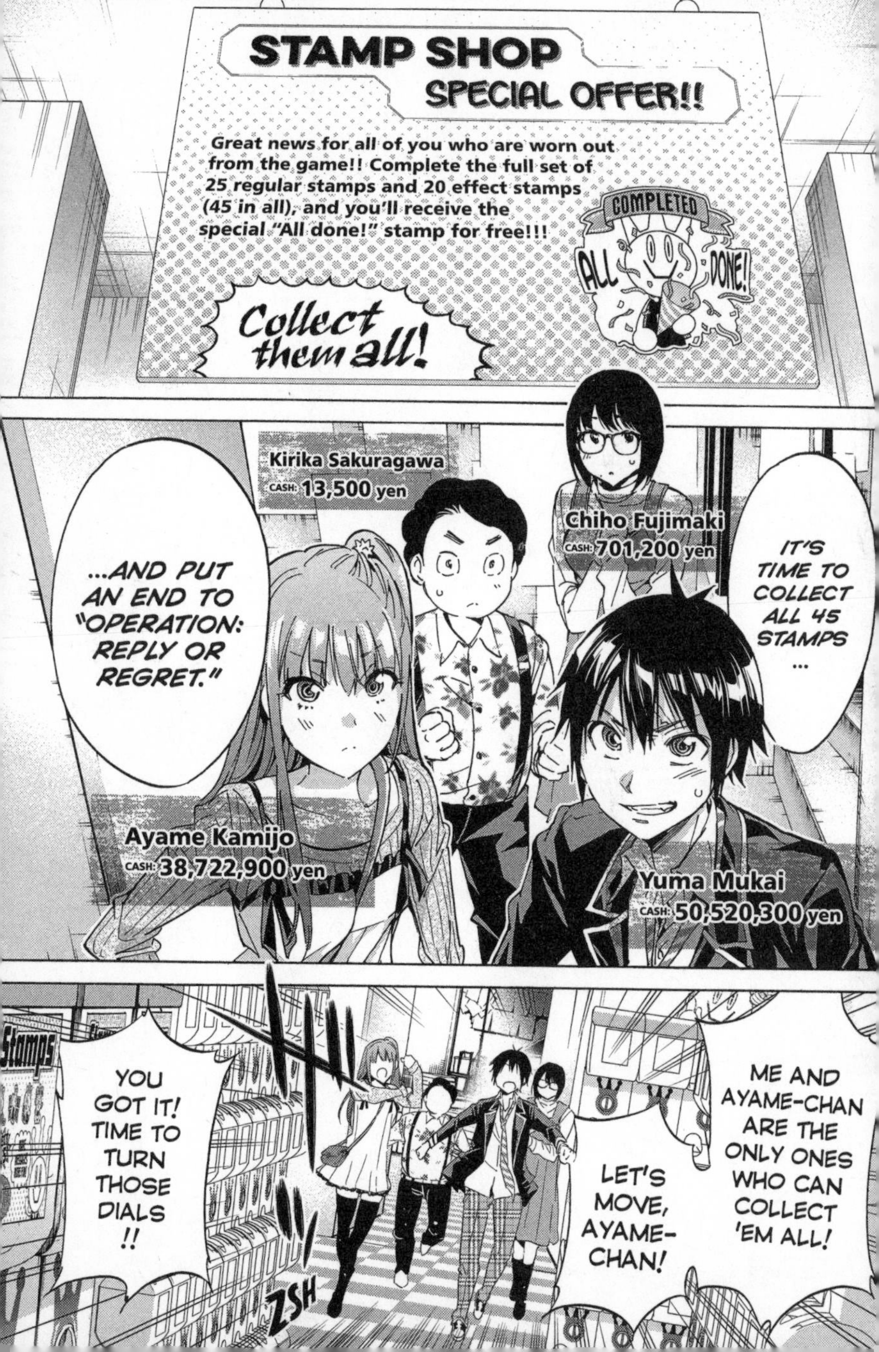
STAMP SHOP
SPECIAL OFFER!!
Great news for all of you who are worn out from the game!! Complete the full set of 25 regular stamps and 20 effect stamps (45 in all), and you'll receive the special "All done!" stamp for free!!!
COMPLETED
ALL DONE!
Collect them all!
IT'S TIME TO COLLECT ALL 45 STAMPS ...
...AND PUT AN END TO "OPERATION: REPLY OR REGRET."
Chiho Fujimaki
CASH: 701,200 yen
Kirika Sakuragawa
CASH: 13,500 yen
Yuma Mukai
CASH: 50,520,300 yen
Ayame Kamijo
CASH: 38,722,900 yen
ME AND AYAME-CHAN ARE THE ONLY ONES WHO CAN COLLECT 'EM ALL!
LET'S MOVE, AYAME-CHAN!
YOU GOT IT! TIME TO TURN THOSE DIALS !!
Stamps
ZSH

ACCOUNT 18 The Collector's Nightmare!

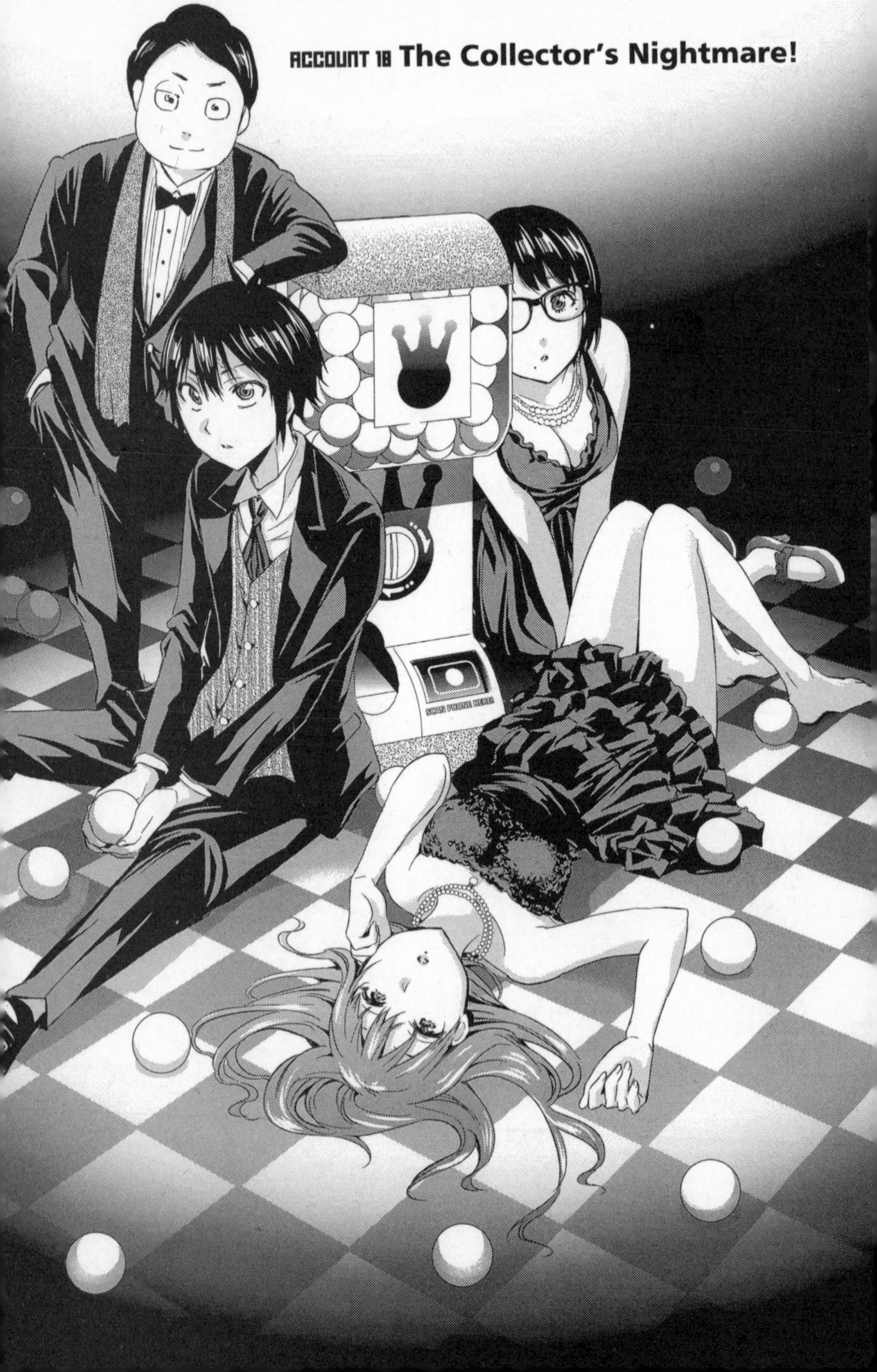
SCAN PHONE HERE!

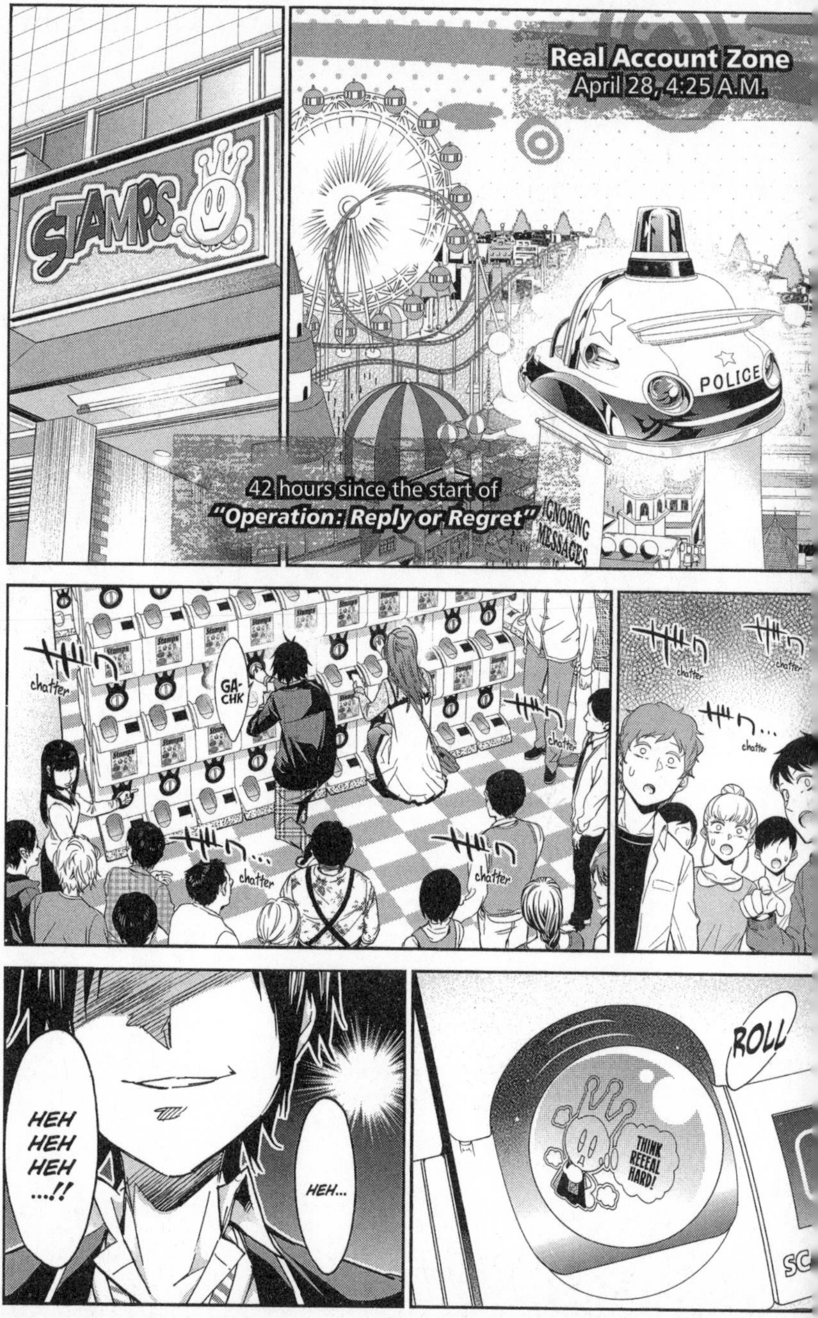
Real Account Zone
April 28, 4:25 A.M.
POLICE
IGNORING MESSAGES
42 hours since the start of
"Operation: Reply or Regret"
STAMPS
chatter
chatter
chatter...
chatter
GA-CHK
chatter
chatter...
chatter
ROLL
THINK REEEAL HARD!
HEH...
HEH HEH HEH ...!!

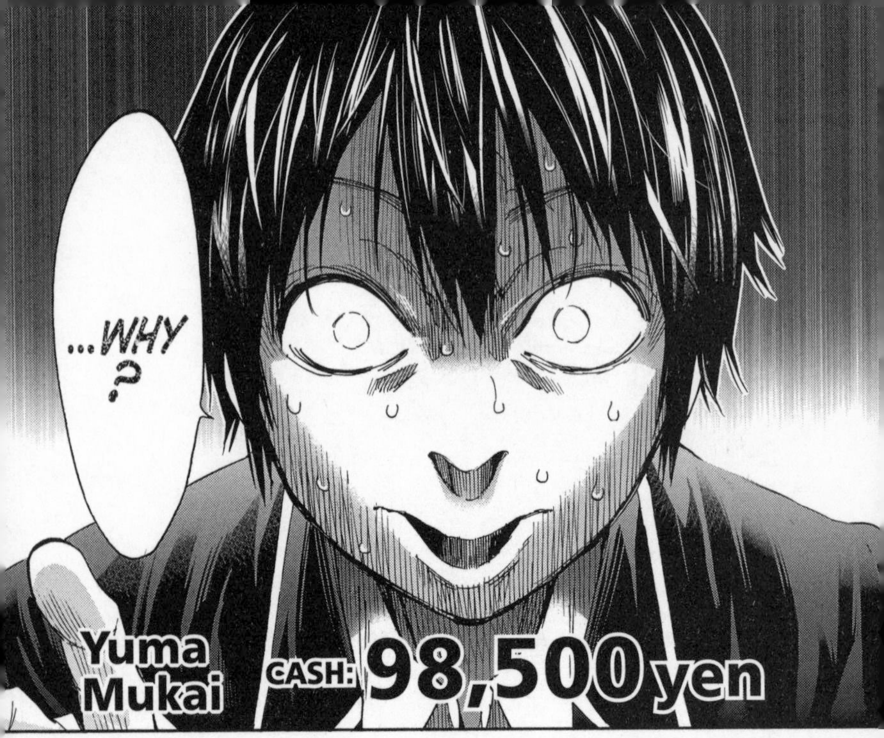
...WHY?
Yuma Mukai
CASH: 98,500 yen

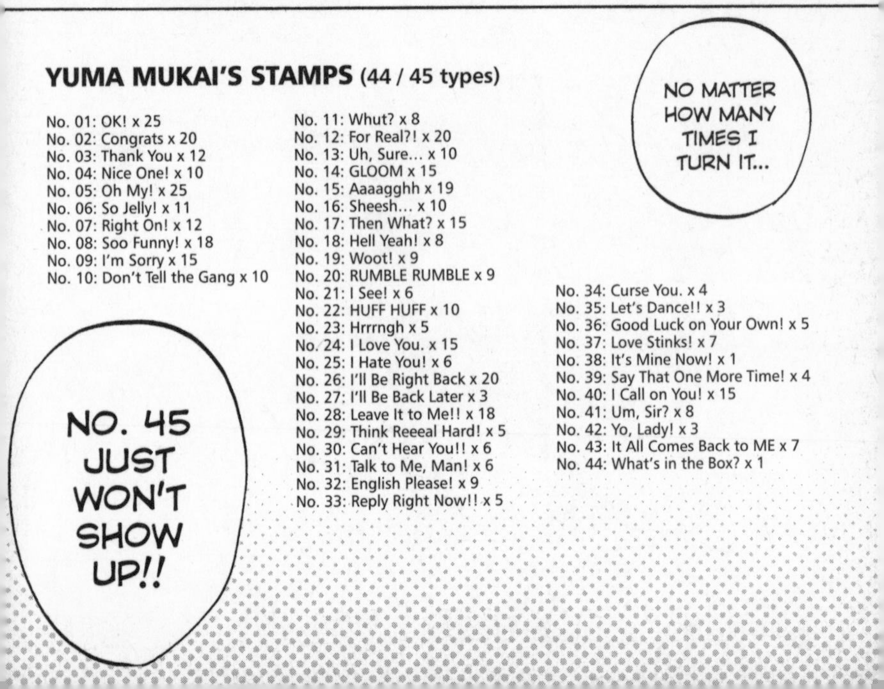
NO MATTER HOW MANY TIMES I TURN IT...
YUMA MUKAI'S STAMPS (44 / 45 types)
No. 01: OK! x 25
No. 02: Congrats x 20
No. 03: Thank You x 12
No. 04: Nice One! x 10
No. 05: Oh My! x 25
No. 06: So Jelly! x 11
No. 07: Right On! x 12
No. 08: Soo Funny! x 18
No. 09: I'm Sorry x 15
No. 10: Don't Tell the Gang x 10
No. 11: Whut? x 8
No. 12: For Real?! x 20
No. 13: Uh, Sure... x 10
No. 14: GLOOM x 15
No. 15: Aaaagghh x 19
No. 16: Sheesh... x 10
No. 17: Then What? x 15
No. 18: Hell Yeah! x 8
No. 19: Woot! x 9
No. 20: RUMBLE RUMBLE x 9
No. 21: I See! x 6
No. 22: HUFF HUFF x 10
No. 23: Hrrrngh x 5
No. 24: I Love You. x 15
No. 25: I Hate You! x 6
No. 26: I'll Be Right Back x 20
No. 27: I'll Be Back Later x 3
No. 28: Leave It to Me!! x 18
No. 29: Think Reeeal Hard! x 5
No. 30: Can't Hear You!! x 6
No. 31: Talk to Me, Man! x 6
No. 32: English Please! x 9
No. 33: Reply Right Now!! x 5
No. 34: Curse You. x 4
No. 35: Let's Dance!! x 3
No. 36: Good Luck on Your Own! x 5
No. 37: Love Stinks! x 7
No. 38: It's Mine Now! x 1
No. 39: Say That One More Time! x 4
No. 40: I Call on You! x 15
No. 41: Um, Sir? x 8
No. 42: Yo, Lady! x 3
No. 43: It All Comes Back to ME x 7
No. 44: What's in the Box? x 1
NO. 45 JUST WON'T SHOW UP!!

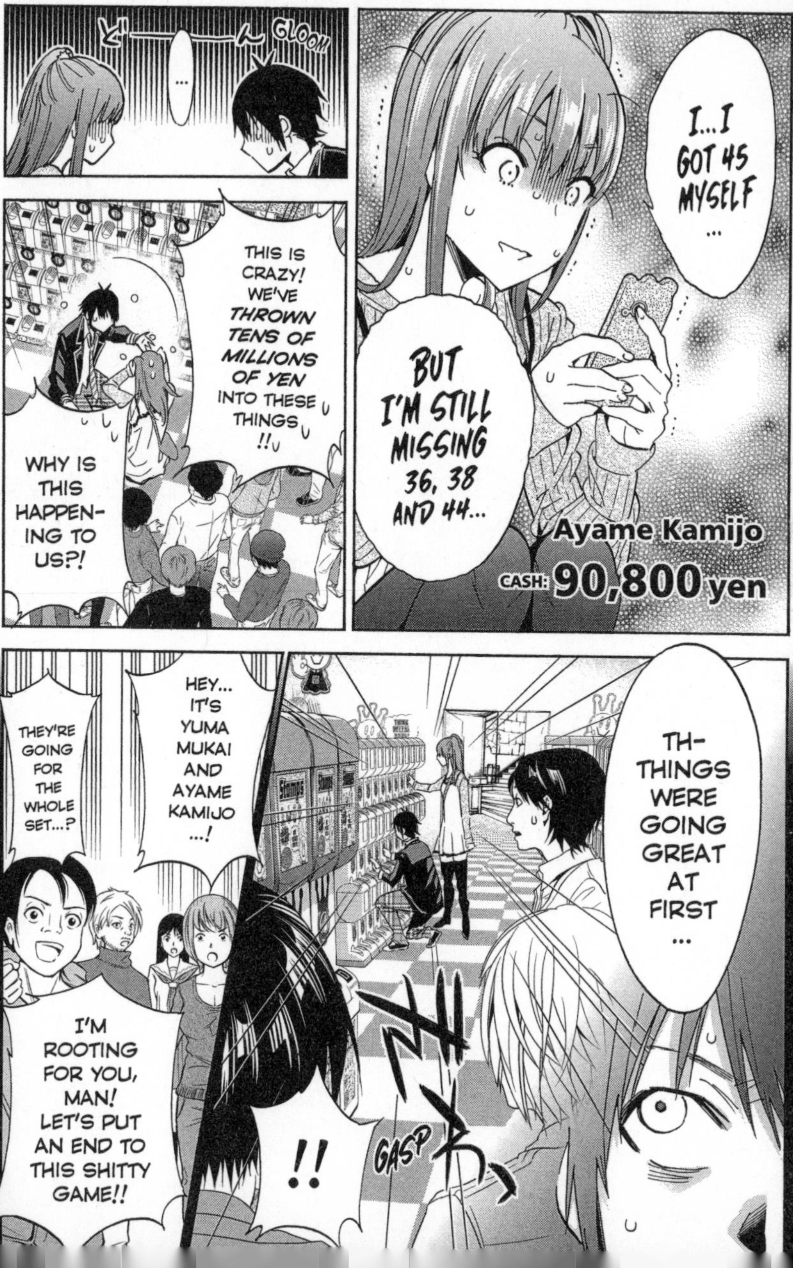
I...I GOT 45 MYSELF ...
BUT I'M STILL MISSING 36, 38 AND 44...
Ayame Kamijo
CASH: 90,800 yen
どーーーん GLOOM
...
THIS IS CRAZY! WE'VE THROWN TENS OF MILLIONS OF YEN INTO THESE THINGS!!
WHY IS THIS HAPPENING TO US?!
TH-THINGS WERE GOING GREAT AT FIRST...
GASP
!!
HEY... IT'S YUMA MUKAI AND AYAME KAMIJO...!
THEY'RE GOING FOR THE WHOLE SET...?
I'M ROOTING FOR YOU, MAN! LET'S PUT AN END TO THIS SHITTY GAME!!

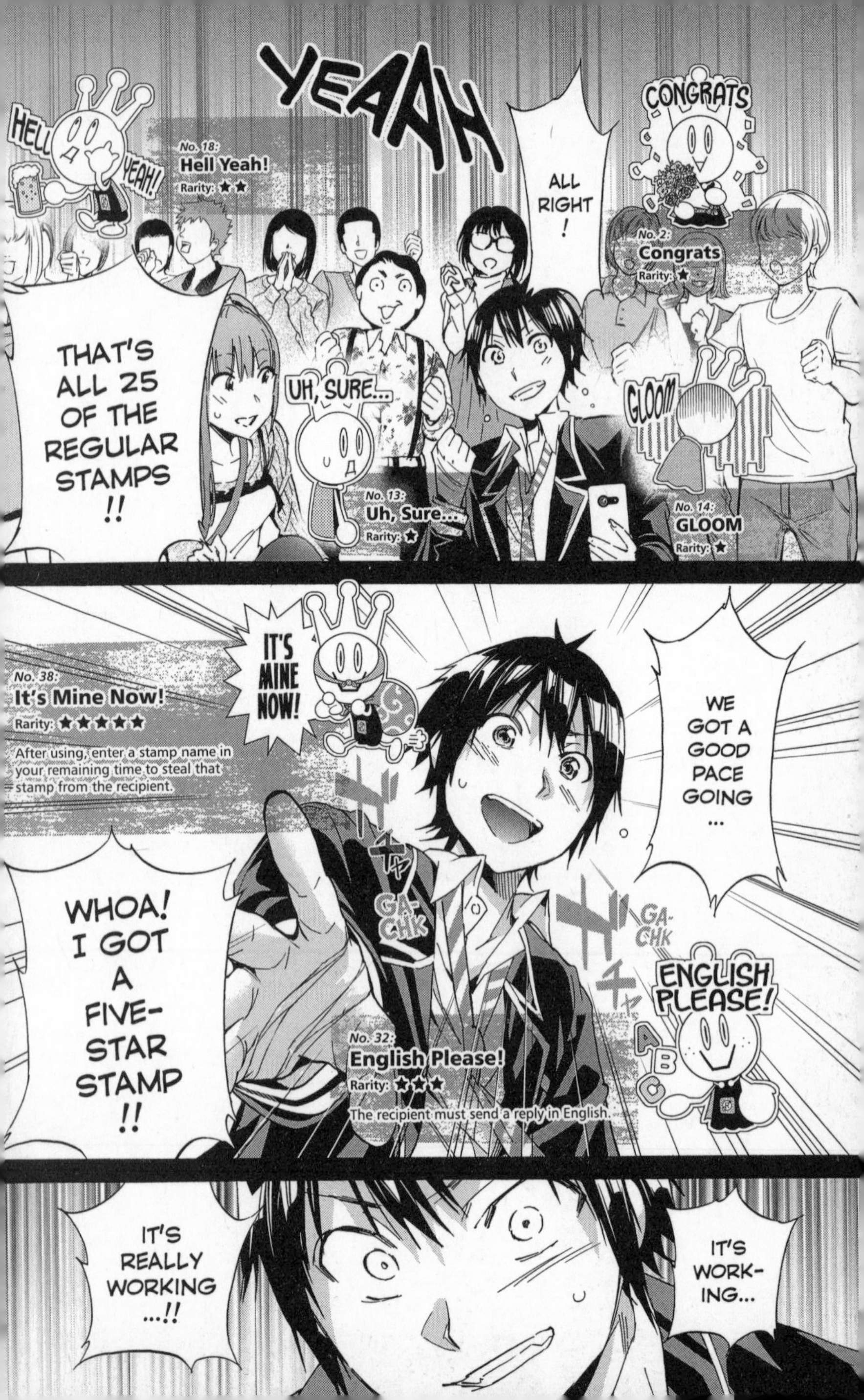
CONGRATS
No. 2: Congrats
Rarity: ★
ALL RIGHT!
YEAAAH
HELL YEAH!
No. 18: Hell Yeah!
Rarity: ★★
GLOOM
No. 14: GLOOM
Rarity: ★
UH, SURE...
No. 13: Uh, Sure...
Rarity: ★
THAT'S ALL 25 OF THE REGULAR STAMPS!!
WE GOT A GOOD PACE GOING...
IT'S MINE NOW!
No. 38: It's Mine Now!
Rarity: ★★★★★
After using, enter a stamp name in your remaining time to steal that stamp from the recipient.
GA-CHK
GA-CHK
ENGLISH PLEASE!
ABC
No. 32: English Please!
Rarity: ★★★
The recipient must send a reply in English.
WHOA! I GOT A FIVE-STAR STAMP!!
IT'S WORKING...
IT'S REALLY WORKING...!!

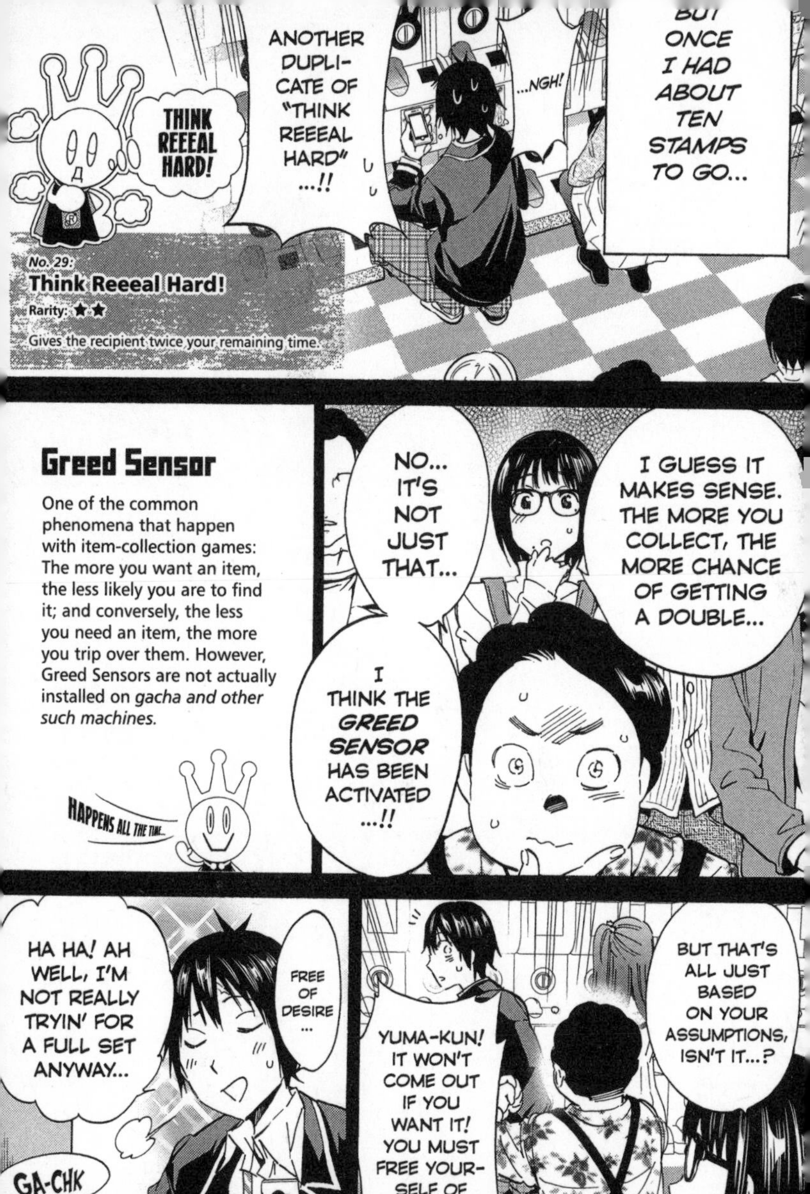
BUT ONCE I HAD ABOUT TEN STAMPS TO GO...
...NGH!
ANOTHER DUPLICATE OF "THINK REEEAL HARD" ...!!
THINK REEEAL HARD!
No. 29:
Think Reeeal Hard!
Rarity: ★★
Gives the recipient twice your remaining time.
I GUESS IT MAKES SENSE. THE MORE YOU COLLECT, THE MORE CHANCE OF GETTING A DOUBLE...
NO... IT'S NOT JUST THAT...
I THINK THE GREED SENSOR HAS BEEN ACTIVATED ...!!
Greed Sensor
One of the common phenomena that happen with item-collection games: The more you want an item, the less likely you are to find it; and conversely, the less you need an item, the more you trip over them. However, Greed Sensors are not actually installed on gacha and other such machines.
HAPPENS ALL THE TIME...
BUT THAT'S ALL JUST BASED ON YOUR ASSUMPTIONS, ISN'T IT...?
YUMA-KUN! IT WON'T COME OUT IF YOU WANT IT! YOU MUST FREE YOURSELF OF DESIRE!!
FREE OF DESIRE ...
HA HA! AH WELL, I'M NOT REALLY TRYIN' FOR A FULL SET ANYWAY...
GA-CHK

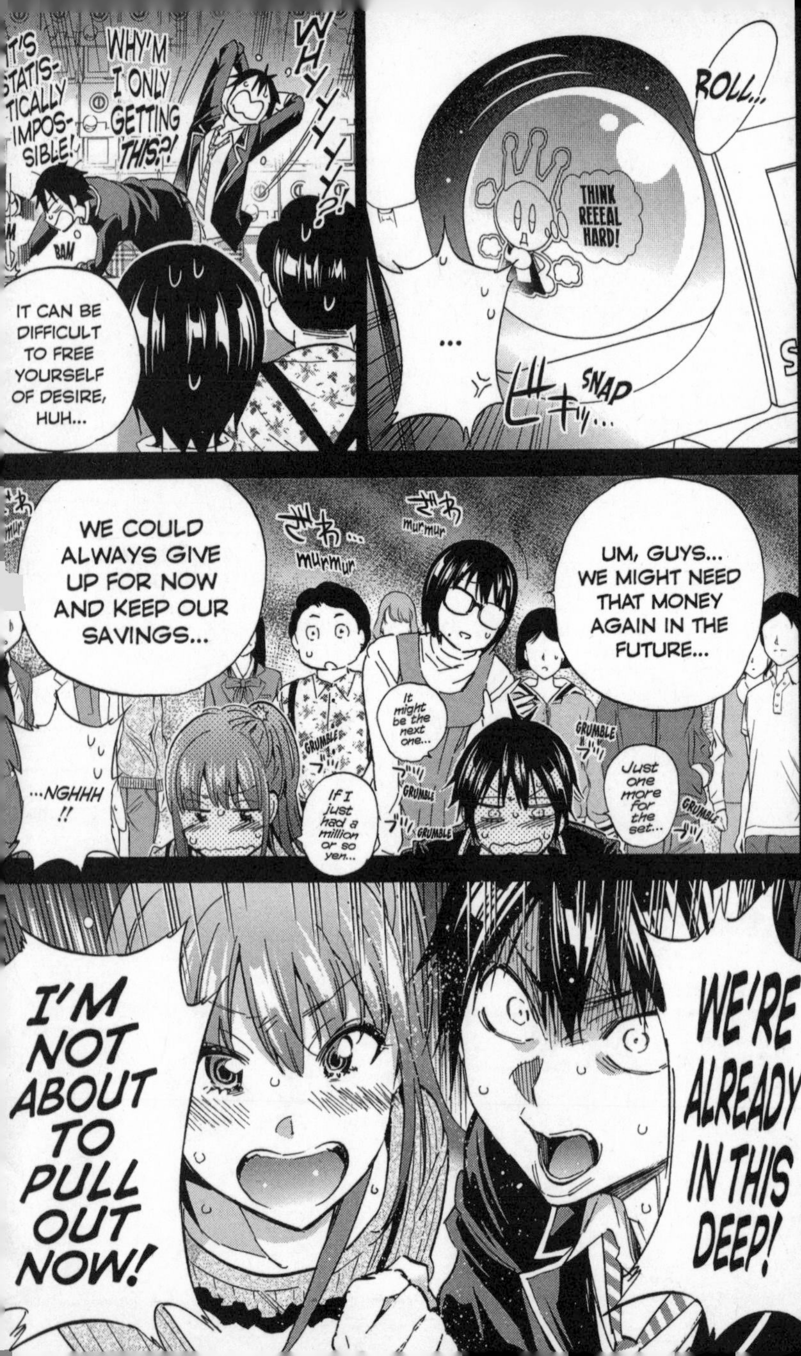
ROLL...
THINK REEEAL HARD!
...
SNAP
WHYYYYYY?!
WHY'M I ONLY GETTING THIS?!
IT'S STATISTICALLY IMPOSSIBLE!
BAM
IT CAN BE DIFFICULT TO FREE YOURSELF OF DESIRE, HUH...
UM, GUYS... WE MIGHT NEED THAT MONEY AGAIN IN THE FUTURE...
murmur
murmur
GRUMBLE
Just one more for the set...
GRUMBLE
It might be the next one...
GRUMBLE
If I just had a million or so yen...
GRUMBLE
GRUMBLE
WE COULD ALWAYS GIVE UP FOR NOW AND KEEP OUR SAVINGS...
murmur
...NGHHH!!
WE'RE ALREADY IN THIS DEEP!
I'M NOT ABOUT TO PULL OUT NOW!

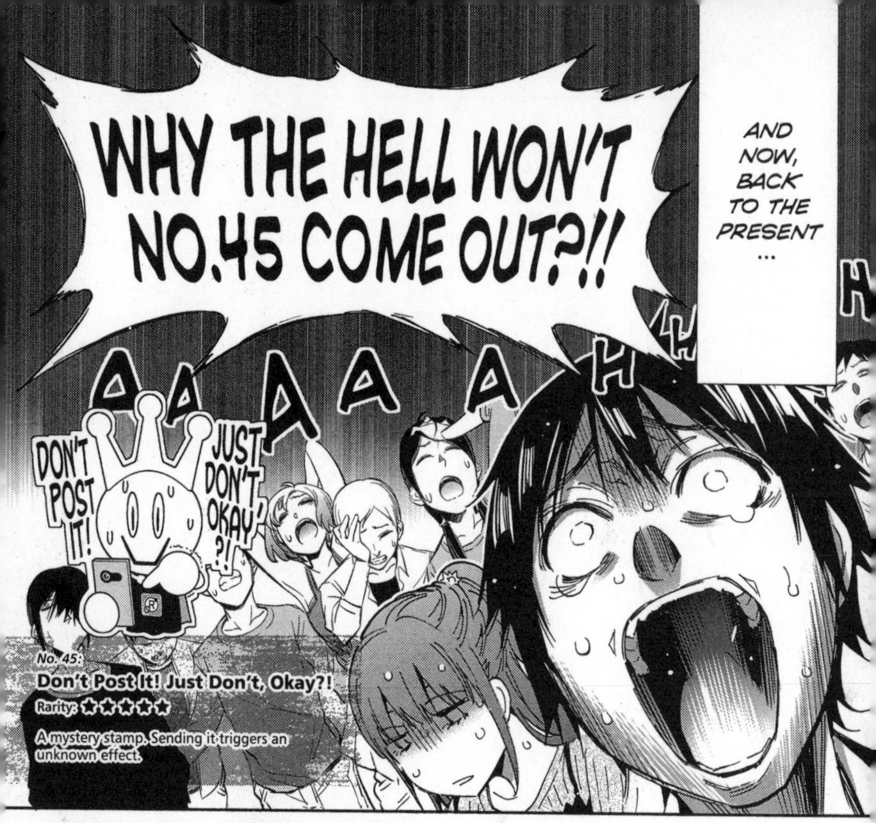
AND NOW, BACK TO THE PRESENT...
WHY THE HELL WON'T NO.45 COME OUT?!!
AAAAAAHHH
JUST DON'T OKAY?!
DON'T POST IT!
No. 45:
Don't Post It! Just Don't, Okay?!
Rarity: ★★★★★
A mystery stamp. Sending it triggers an unknown effect.

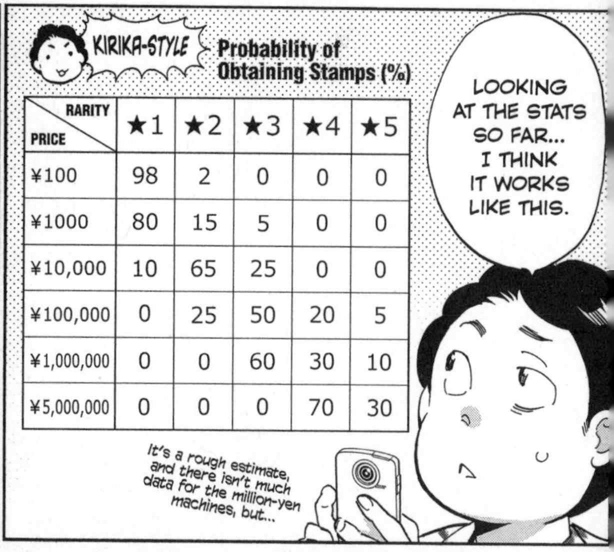
LOOKING AT THE STATS SO FAR... I THINK IT WORKS LIKE THIS.
KIRIKA-STYLE
Probability of Obtaining Stamps (%)
It's a rough estimate, and there isn't much data for the million-yen machines, but...

PRICE \ RARITY	★1	★2	★3	★4	★5
¥100	98	2	0	0	0
¥1000	80	15	5	0	0
¥10,000	10	65	25	0	0
¥100,000	0	25	50	20	5
¥1,000,000	0	0	60	30	10
¥5,000,000	0	0	0	70	30

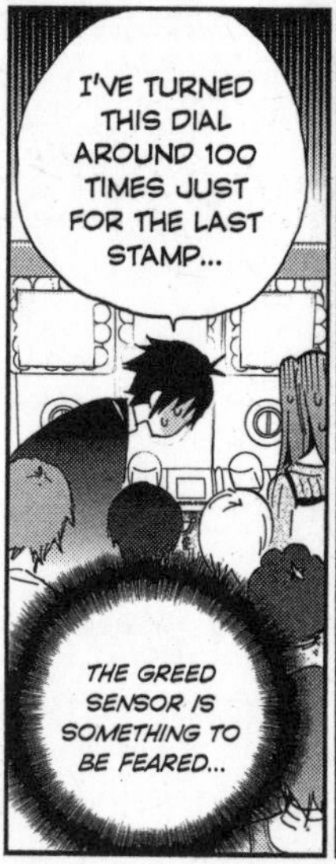
I'VE TURNED THIS DIAL AROUND 100 TIMES JUST FOR THE LAST STAMP...
THE GREED SENSOR IS SOMETHING TO BE FEARED...

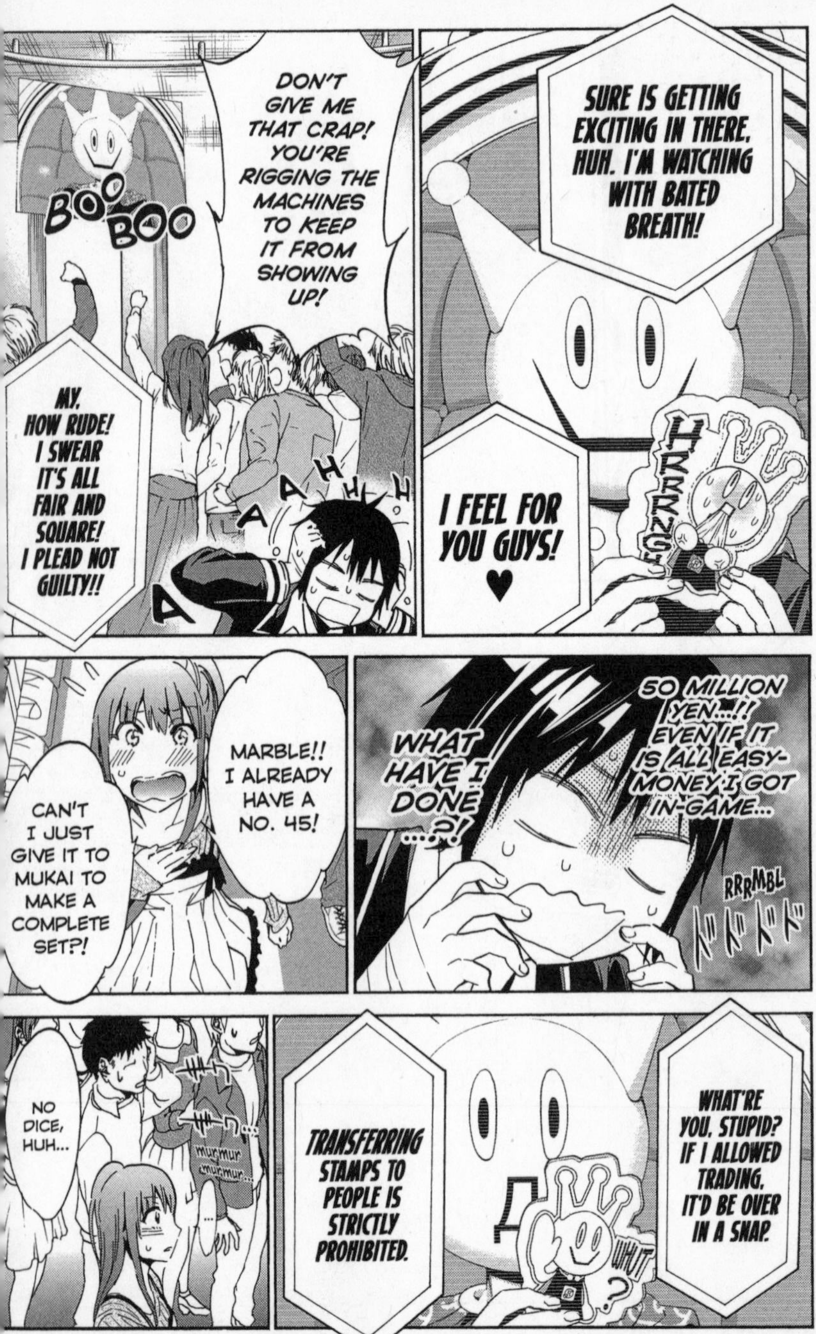
SURE IS GETTING EXCITING IN THERE, HUH. I'M WATCHING WITH BATED BREATH!
HRRRNGH
I FEEL FOR YOU GUYS! ♥
DON'T GIVE ME THAT CRAP! YOU'RE RIGGING THE MACHINES TO KEEP IT FROM SHOWING UP!
BOO BOO
MY, HOW RUDE! I SWEAR IT'S ALL FAIR AND SQUARE! I PLEAD NOT GUILTY!!
AAAHHH
50 MILLION YEN...!! EVEN IF IT IS ALL EASY-MONEY I GOT IN-GAME...
WHAT HAVE I DONE...?!
RRRMBL
ドドドド
MARBLE!! I ALREADY HAVE A NO. 45!
CAN'T I JUST GIVE IT TO MUKAI TO MAKE A COMPLETE SET?!
WHAT'RE YOU, STUPID? IF I ALLOWED TRADING, IT'D BE OVER IN A SNAP.
TRANSFERRING STAMPS TO PEOPLE IS STRICTLY PROHIBITED.
WHUT ?
NO DICE, HUH...
murmur murmur...
...

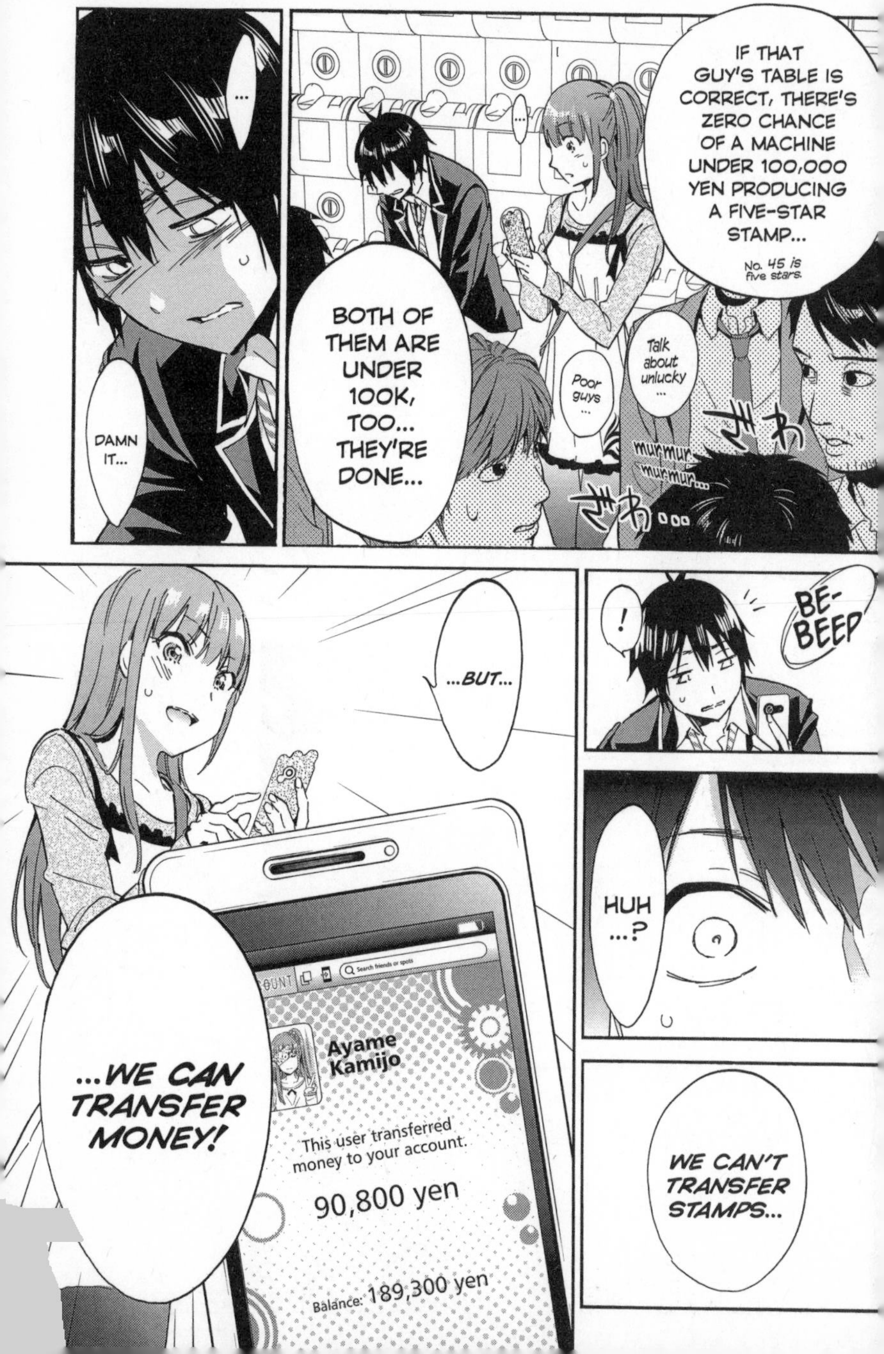
IF THAT GUY'S TABLE IS CORRECT, THERE'S ZERO CHANCE OF A MACHINE UNDER 100,000 YEN PRODUCING A FIVE-STAR STAMP...
No. 45 is five stars.
...
Talk about unlucky ...
Poor guys ...
murmur murmur...
BOTH OF THEM ARE UNDER 100K, TOO... THEY'RE DONE...
...
DAMN IT...
BE-BEEP
!
HUH ...?
WE CAN'T TRANSFER STAMPS...
...BUT...
...WE CAN TRANSFER MONEY!
Search friends or spots
Ayame Kamijo
This user transferred money to your account.
90,800 yen
Balance: 189,300 yen

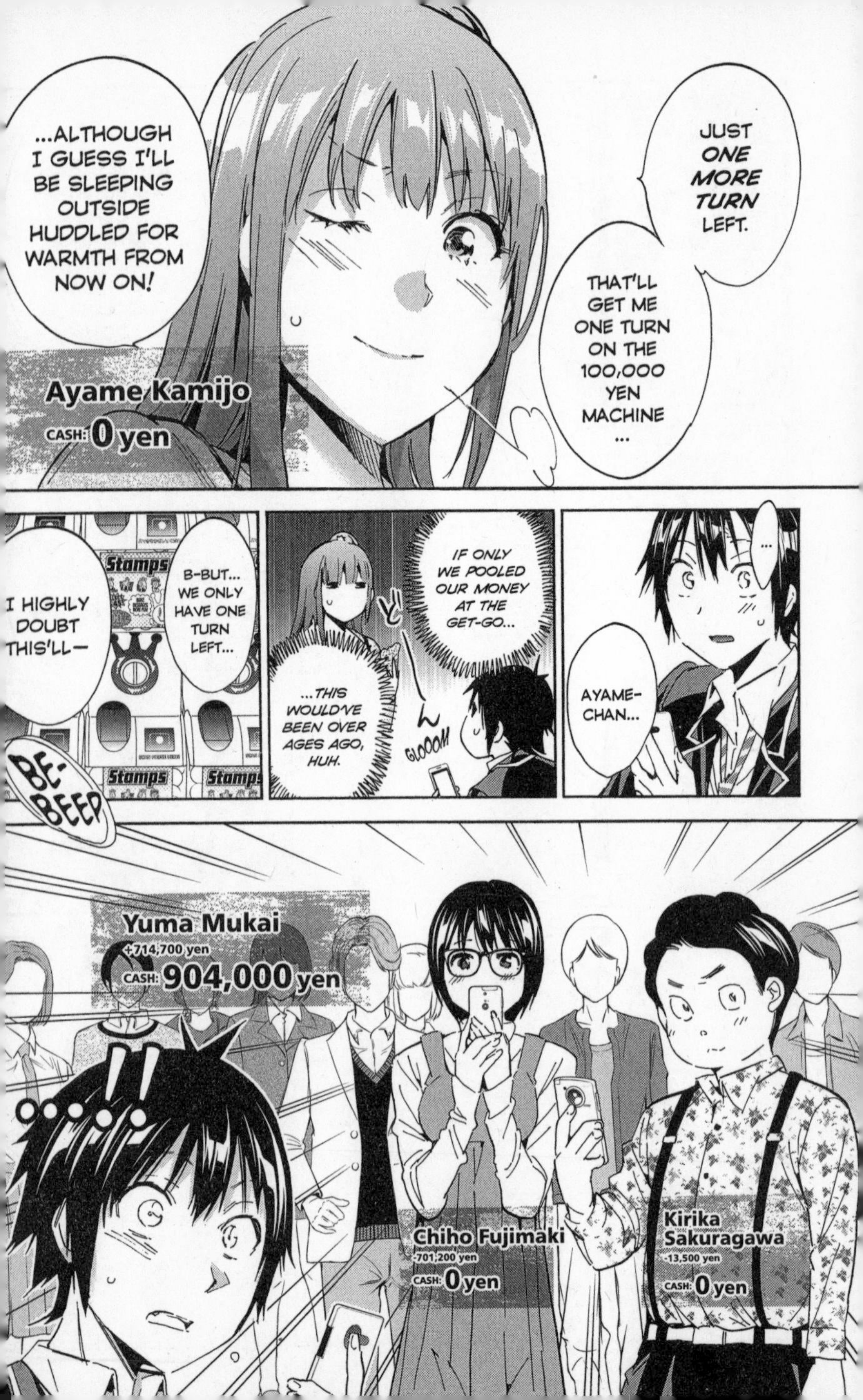
JUST *ONE MORE TURN* LEFT.
THAT'LL GET ME ONE TURN ON THE 100,000 YEN MACHINE ...
...ALTHOUGH I GUESS I'LL BE SLEEPING OUTSIDE HUDDLED FOR WARMTH FROM NOW ON!
Ayame Kamijo
CASH: 0 yen
...
AYAME-CHAN...
IF ONLY WE POOLED OUR MONEY AT THE GET-GO...
...THIS WOULD'VE BEEN OVER AGES AGO, HUH.
GLOOOM
Stamps
B-BUT... WE ONLY HAVE ONE TURN LEFT...
I HIGHLY DOUBT THIS'LL—
BE-BEEP
Kirika Sakuragawa
-13,500 yen
CASH: 0 yen
Chiho Fujimaki
-701,200 yen
CASH: 0 yen
Yuma Mukai
+714,700 yen
CASH: 904,000 yen
......!!

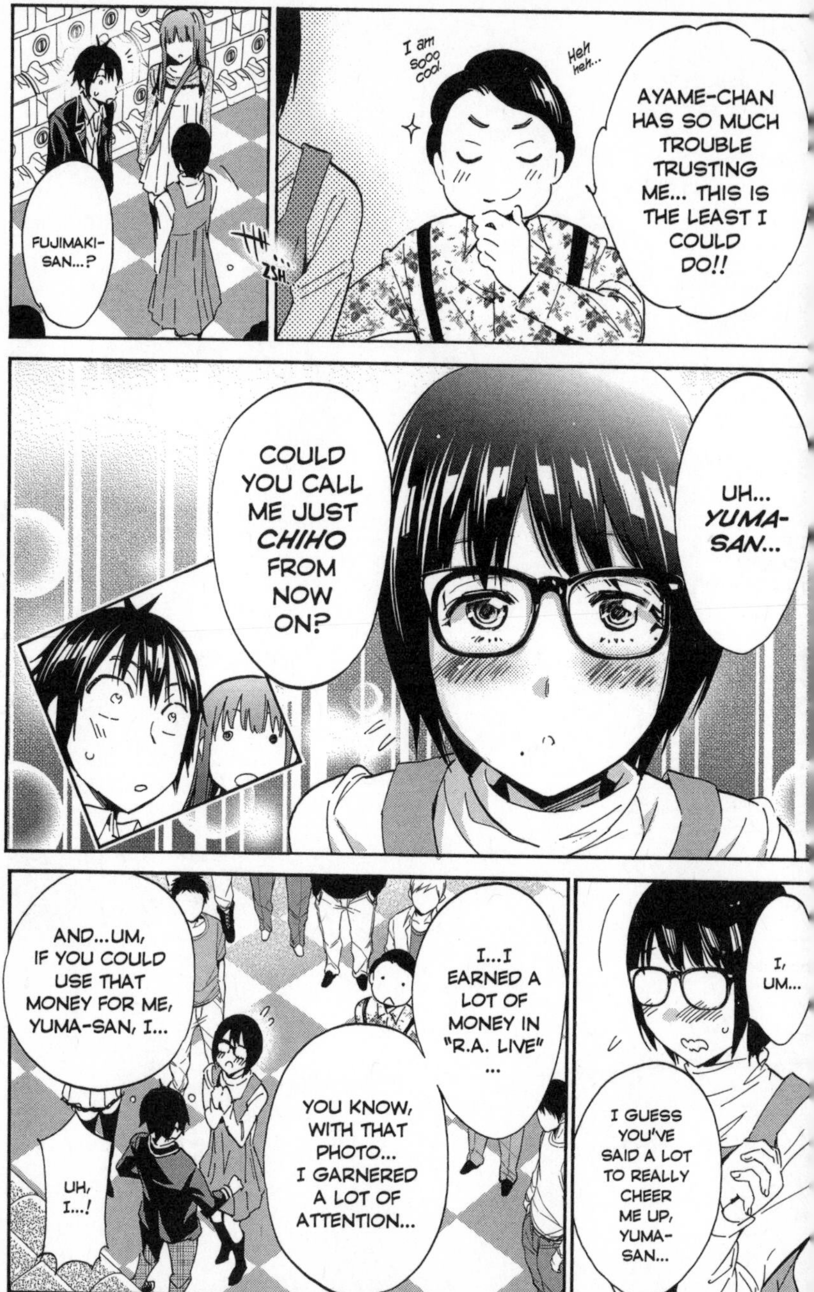
AYAME-CHAN HAS SO MUCH TROUBLE TRUSTING ME... THIS IS THE LEAST I COULD DO!!
Heh heh...
I am sooo cool.
ZSH
FUJIMAKI-SAN...?
UH... *YUMA-SAN*...
COULD YOU CALL ME JUST *CHIHO* FROM NOW ON?
I, UM...
I GUESS YOU'VE SAID A LOT TO REALLY CHEER ME UP, YUMA-SAN...
I...I EARNED A LOT OF MONEY IN "R.A. LIVE" ...
YOU KNOW, WITH THAT PHOTO... I GARNERED A LOT OF ATTENTION...
AND...UM, IF YOU COULD USE THAT MONEY FOR ME, YUMA-SAN, I...
UH, I...!

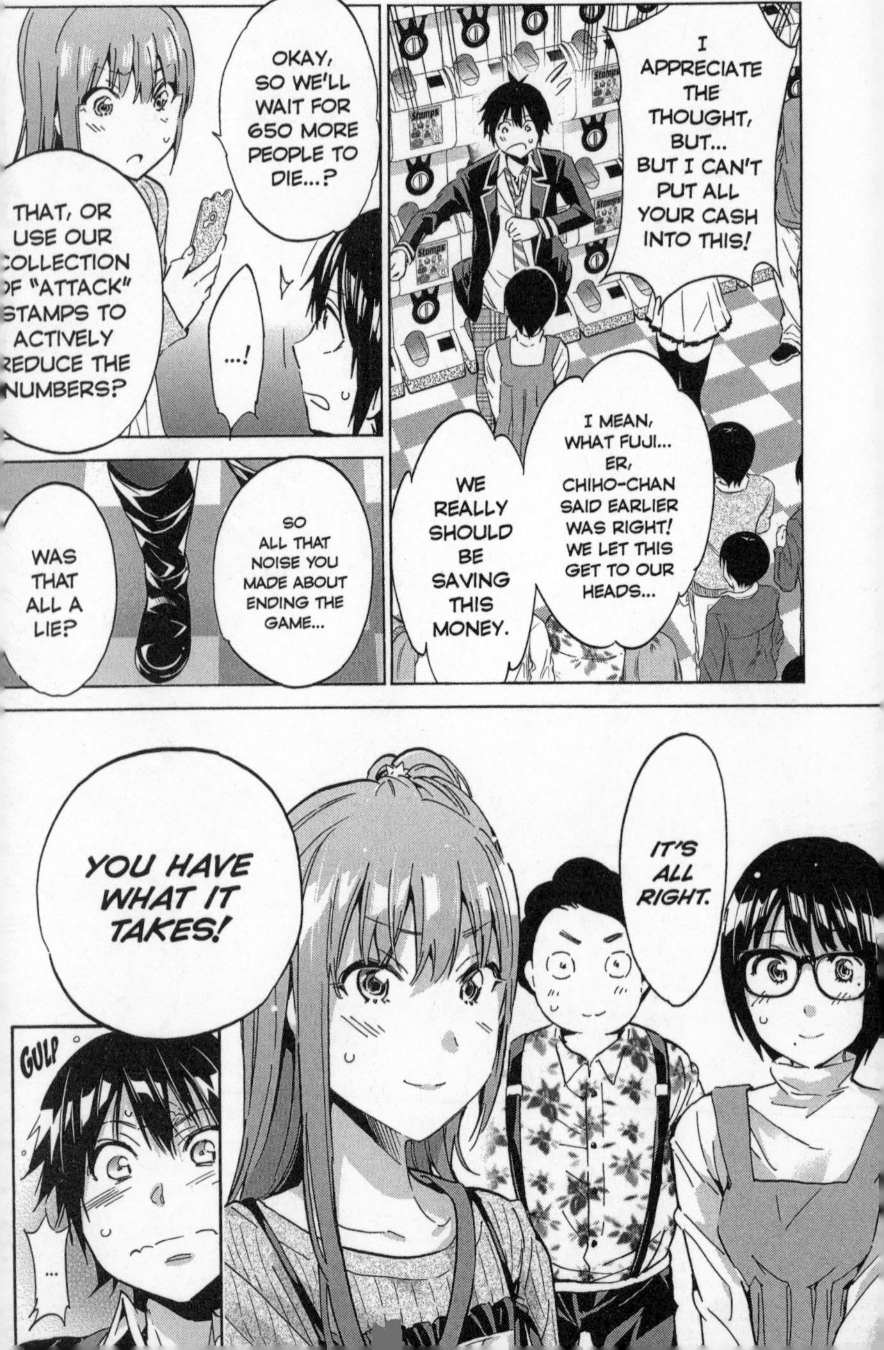
I APPRECIATE THE THOUGHT, BUT... BUT I CAN'T PUT ALL YOUR CASH INTO THIS!
I MEAN, WHAT FUJI... ER, CHIHO-CHAN SAID EARLIER WAS RIGHT! WE LET THIS GET TO OUR HEADS...
WE REALLY SHOULD BE SAVING THIS MONEY.
OKAY, SO WE'LL WAIT FOR 650 MORE PEOPLE TO DIE...?
...!
THAT, OR USE OUR COLLECTION OF "ATTACK" STAMPS TO ACTIVELY REDUCE THE NUMBERS?
SO ALL THAT NOISE YOU MADE ABOUT ENDING THE GAME...
WAS THAT ALL A LIE?
IT'S ALL RIGHT.
YOU HAVE WHAT IT TAKES!
GULP
...

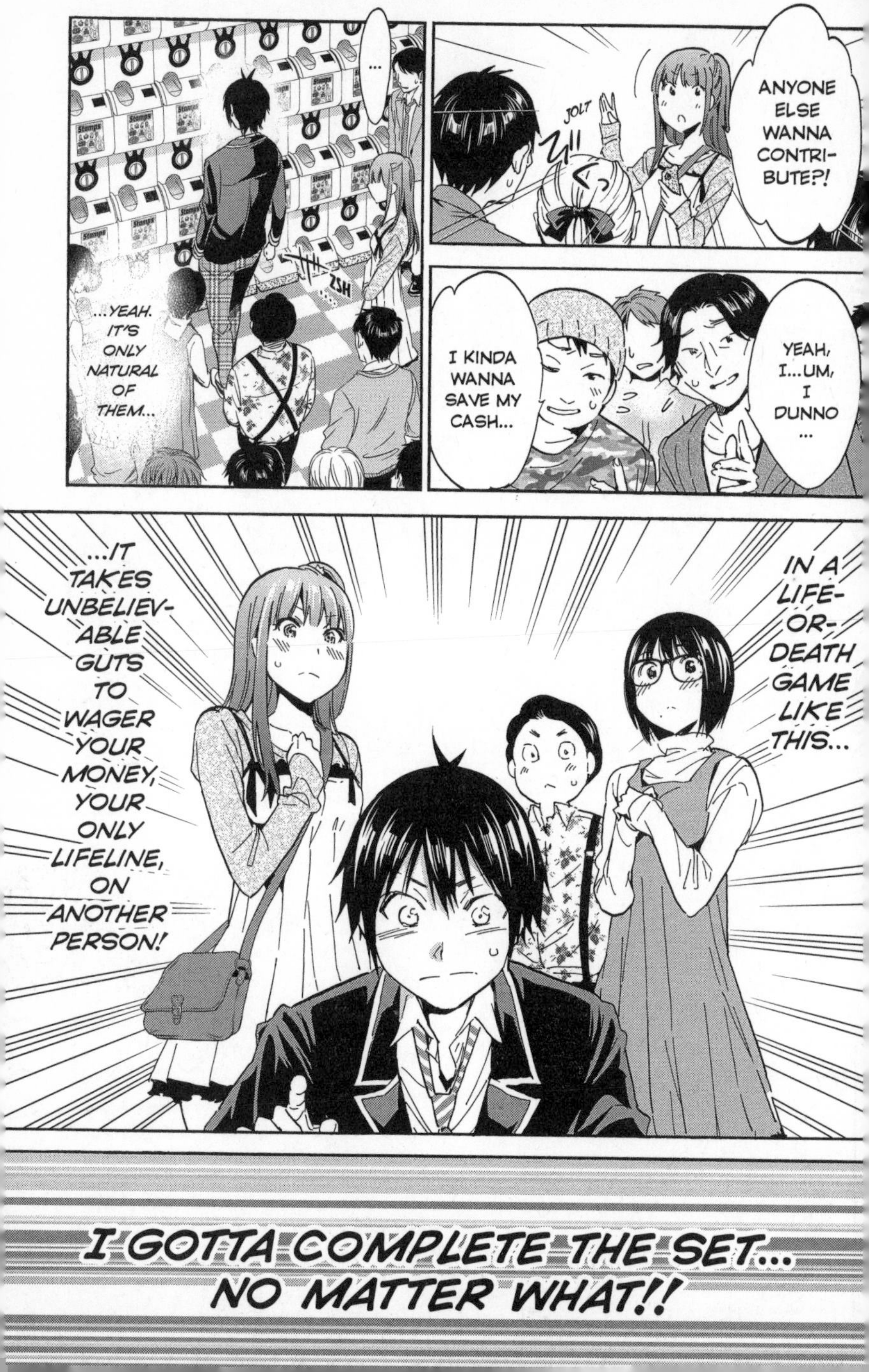
ANYONE ELSE WANNA CONTRIBUTE?!
JOLT
YEAH, I...UM, I DUNNO...
I KINDA WANNA SAVE MY CASH...
...
ZSH
...YEAH. IT'S ONLY NATURAL OF THEM...
IN A LIFE-OR-DEATH GAME LIKE THIS...
...IT TAKES UNBELIEVABLE GUTS TO WAGER YOUR MONEY, YOUR ONLY LIFELINE, ON ANOTHER PERSON!
I GOTTA COMPLETE THE SET... NO MATTER WHAT!!

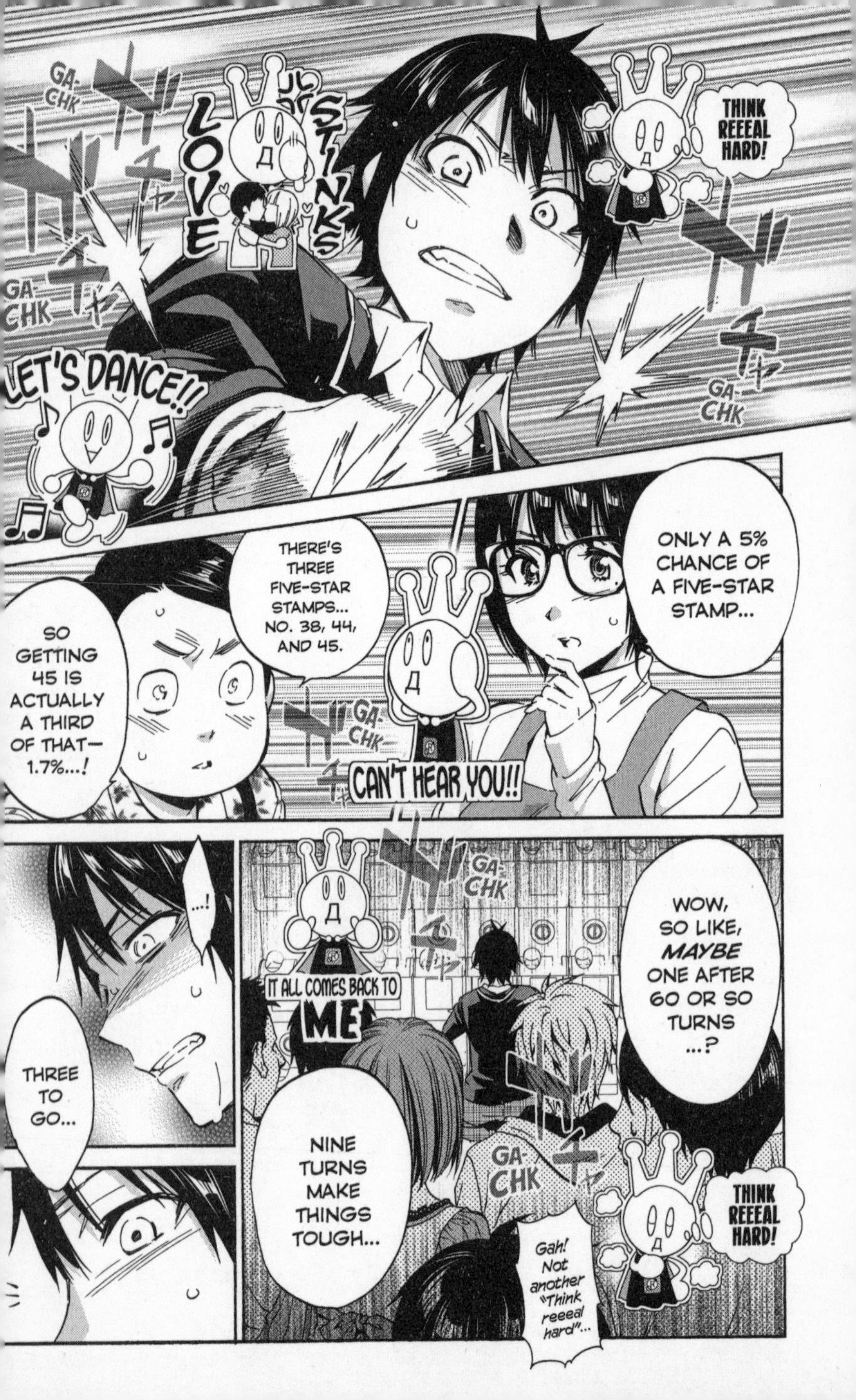

THINK REEEAL HARD!
GA-CHK
LOVE STINKS
GA-CHK
GA-CHK
LET'S DANCE!!
ONLY A 5% CHANCE OF A FIVE-STAR STAMP...
GA-CHK
CAN'T HEAR YOU!!
THERE'S THREE FIVE-STAR STAMPS... NO. 38, 44, AND 45.
SO GETTING 45 IS ACTUALLY A THIRD OF THAT—1.7%...!
WOW, SO LIKE, *MAYBE* ONE AFTER 60 OR SO TURNS ...?
GA-CHK
IT ALL COMES BACK TO ME
THINK REEEAL HARD!
GA-CHK
NINE TURNS MAKE THINGS TOUGH...
Gah! Not another "Think reeeal hard"...
...!
THREE TO GO...

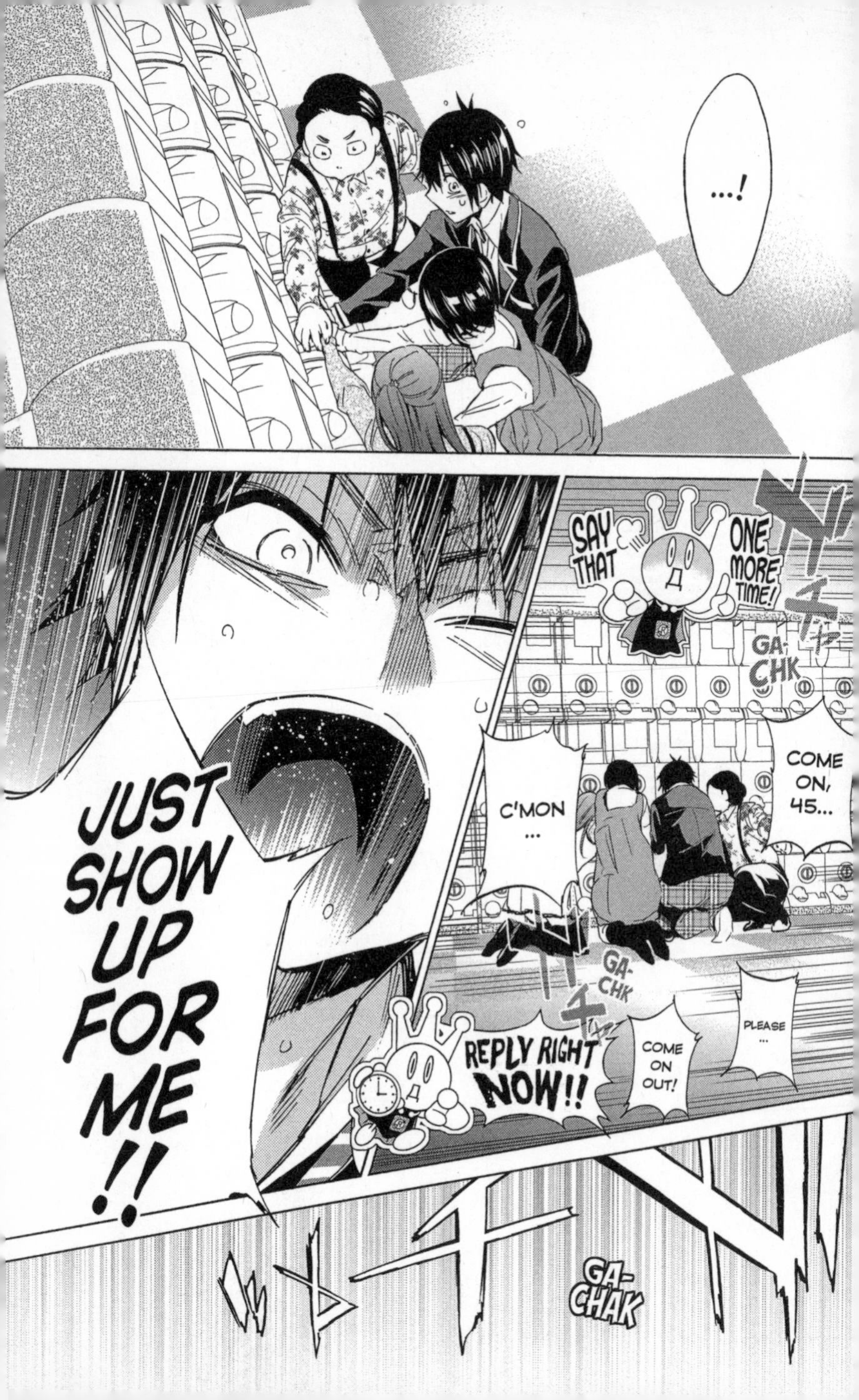
...!
SAY THAT ONE MORE TIME!
GA-CHK
COME ON, 45...
C'MON ...
PLEASE ...
COME ON OUT!
GA-CHK
REPLY RIGHT NOW!!
JUST SHOW UP FOR ME!!
GA-CHAK

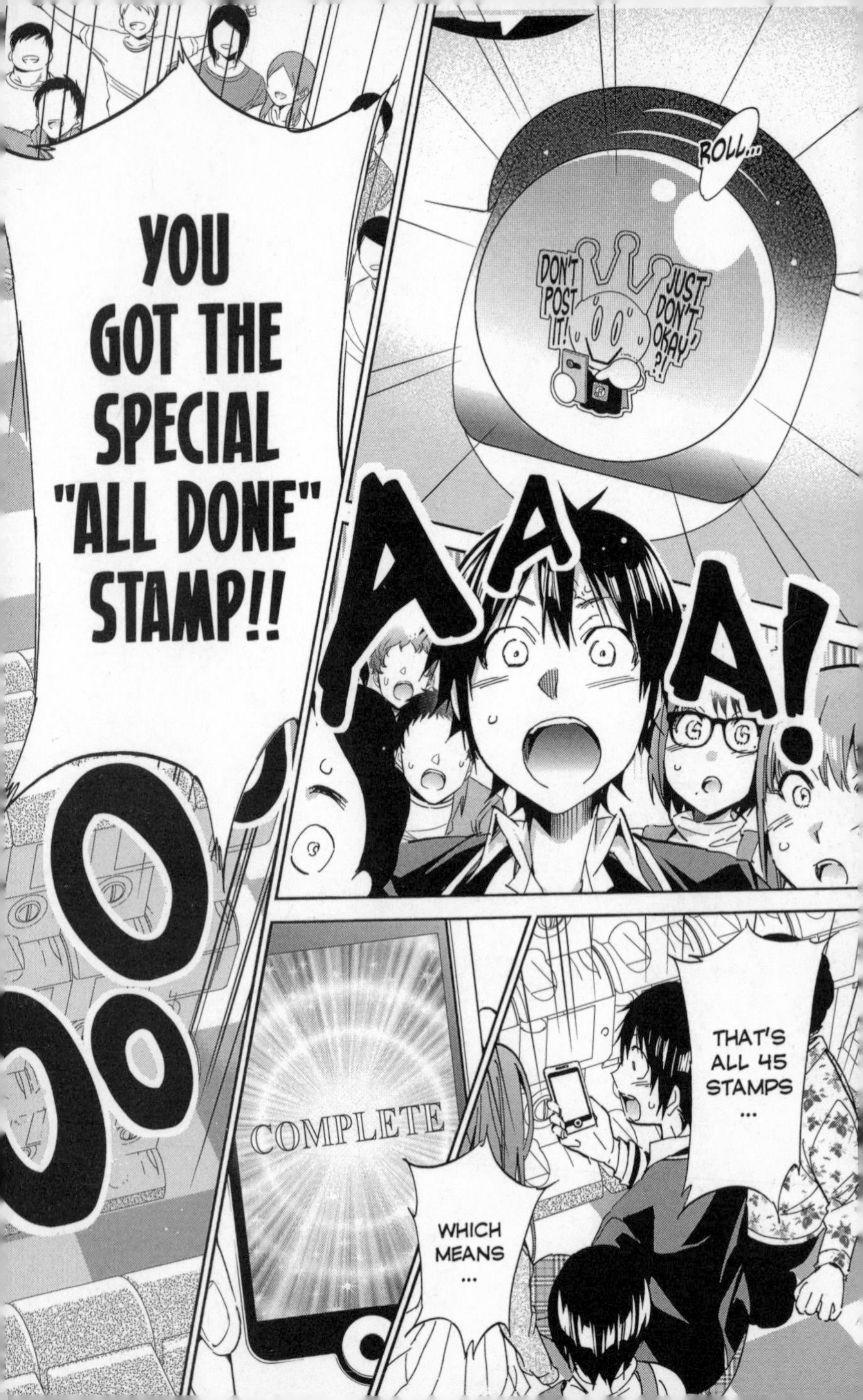
ROLL...
DON'T POST IT!
JUST DON'T, OKAY?!
AAA!
THAT'S ALL 45 STAMPS ...
WHICH MEANS ...
COMPLETE
YOU GOT THE SPECIAL "ALL DONE" STAMP!!
OOO

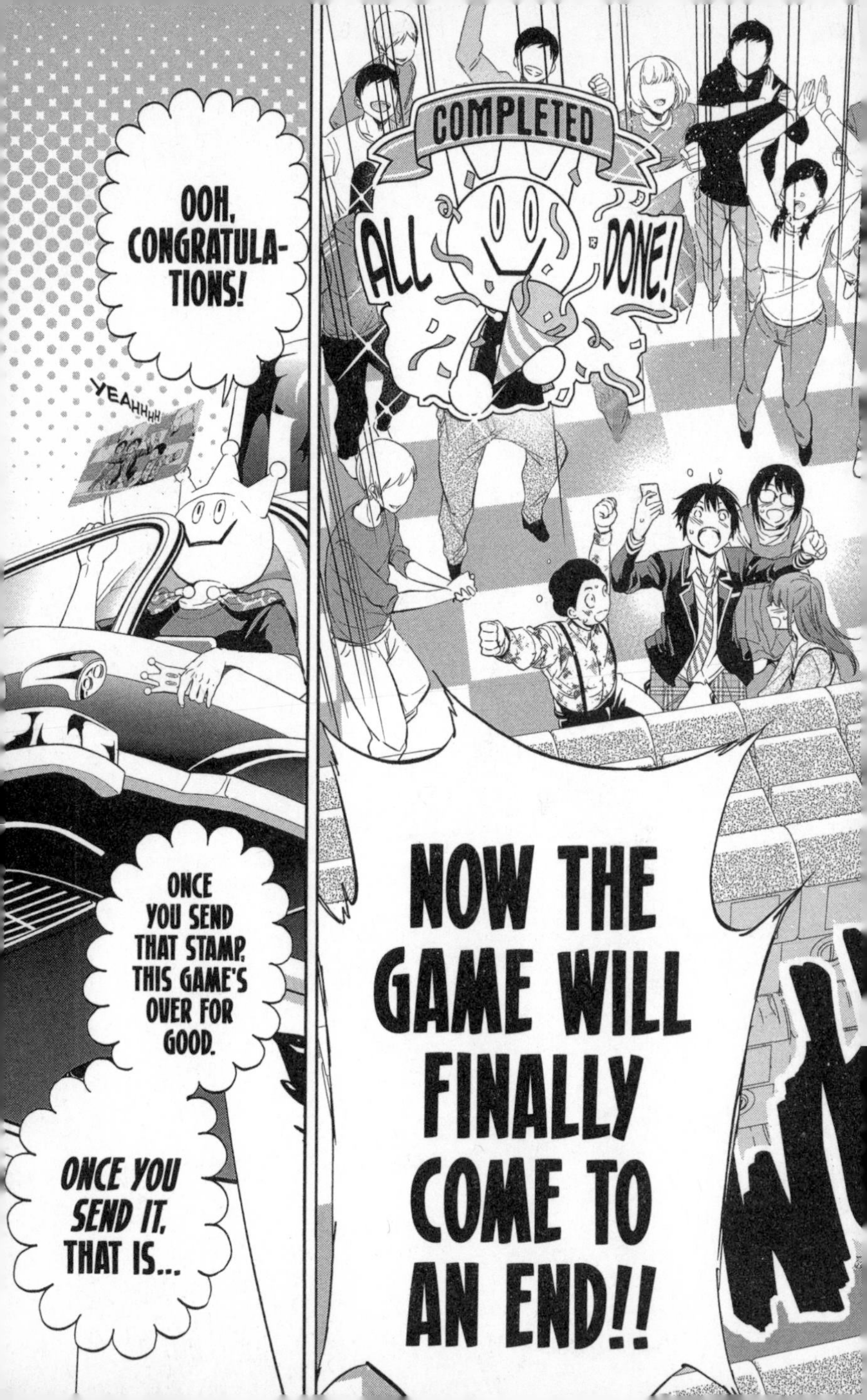
COMPLETED
ALL DONE!
NOW THE GAME WILL FINALLY COME TO AN END!!
OOH, CONGRATULATIONS!
YEAHHHH
ONCE YOU SEND THAT STAMP, THIS GAME'S OVER FOR GOOD.
ONCE YOU SEND IT, THAT IS...

REAL ACCOUNT

OPERATION: REPLY or REGRET
STAMP LIST
1 OK!
2 CONGRATS
3 THANK YOU
4 NICE ONE!
5 OH MY!
6 SO JELLY!
7 RIGHT ON!
8 SOO FUNNY!
9 I'M SORRY
10 DON'T TELL THE GANG
11 WHUT?
12 FOR REAL?!
13 UH, SURE...
14 GLOOM
15 AAAAAGGGH
16 SHEESH!
17 THEN WHAT?
18 HELL YEAH!
19 WOOT!
20 RUMBLE RUMBLE
21 I SEE!
22 HUFF HUFF
23 HRRRNGH
24 I LOVE YOU.
25 I HATE YOU!
26 I'LL BE RIGHT BACK
27 I'LL BE BACK LATER
28 LEAVE IT TO ME!!
29 THINK REEEAL HARD!
30 CAN'T HEAR YOU!!
31 TALK TO ME, MAN!
32 ENGLISH PLEASE!
33 REPLY RIGHT NOW!!
34 CURSE YOU.
35 LET'S DANCE!!
36 GOOD LUCK ON YOUR OWN!
37 LOVE STINKS
38 IT'S MINE NOW!
39 SAY THAT ONE MORE TIME!
40 I CALL ON YOU!! YOU
41 UM, SIR?
42 YO, LADY!
43 IT ALL COMES BACK TO ME
44 WHAT'S IN THE BOX?
45 DON'T POST IT! JUST DON'T, OKAY?!

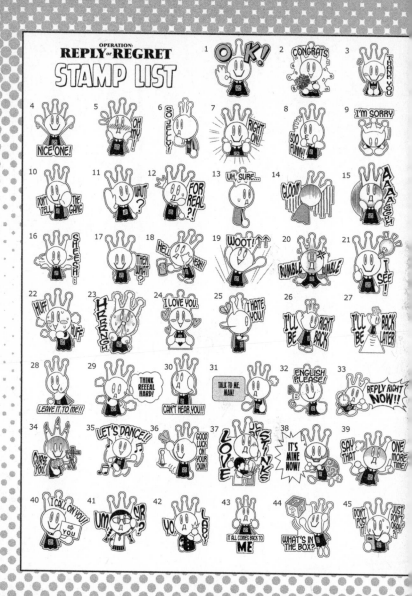

ACCOUNT 19 All is Lost!!

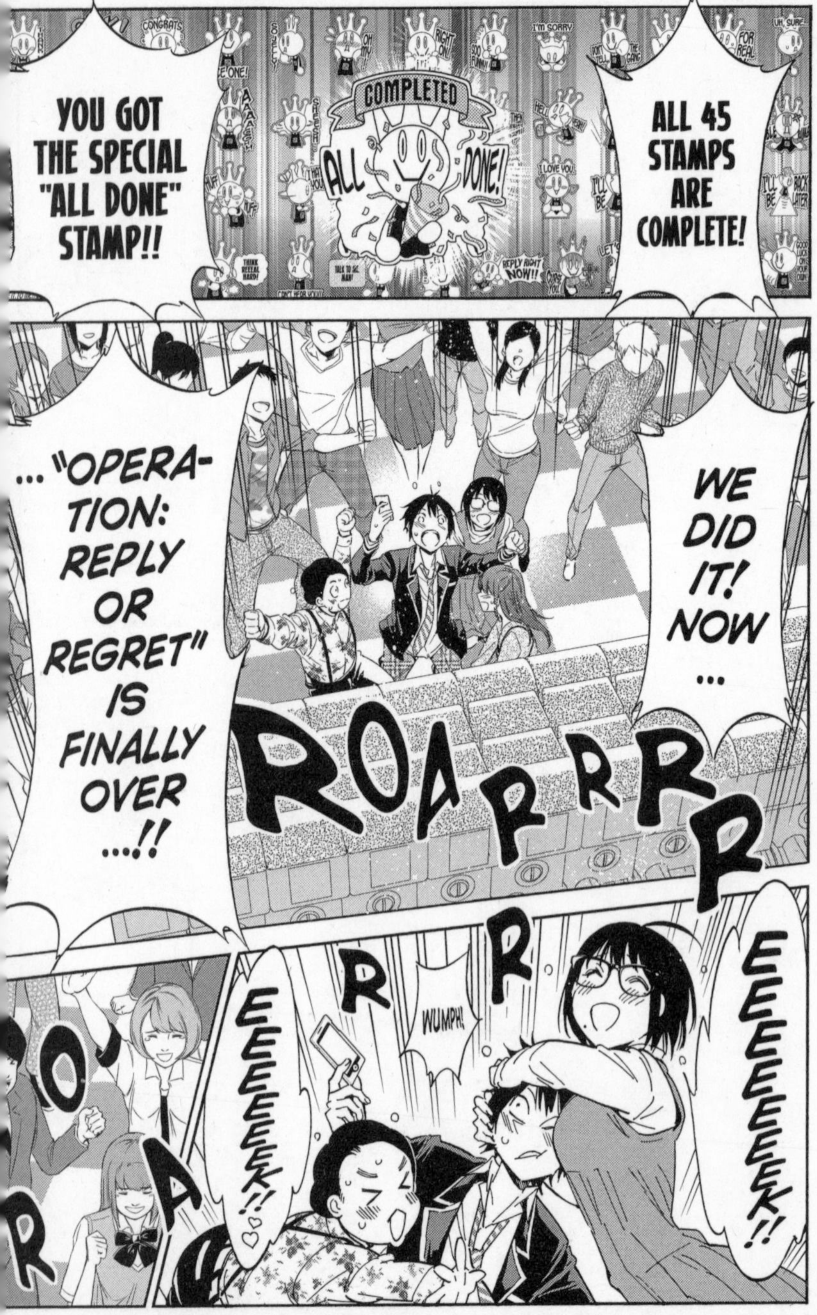
ALL 45 STAMPS ARE COMPLETE!
COMPLETED
ALL DONE!
YOU GOT THE SPECIAL "ALL DONE" STAMP!!
WE DID IT! NOW ...
... "OPERATION: REPLY OR REGRET" IS FINALLY OVER ...!!
ROARRRR
EEEEEEEEK!!
R R
WUMPH!
EEEEEEEK!! ♡
ROAR

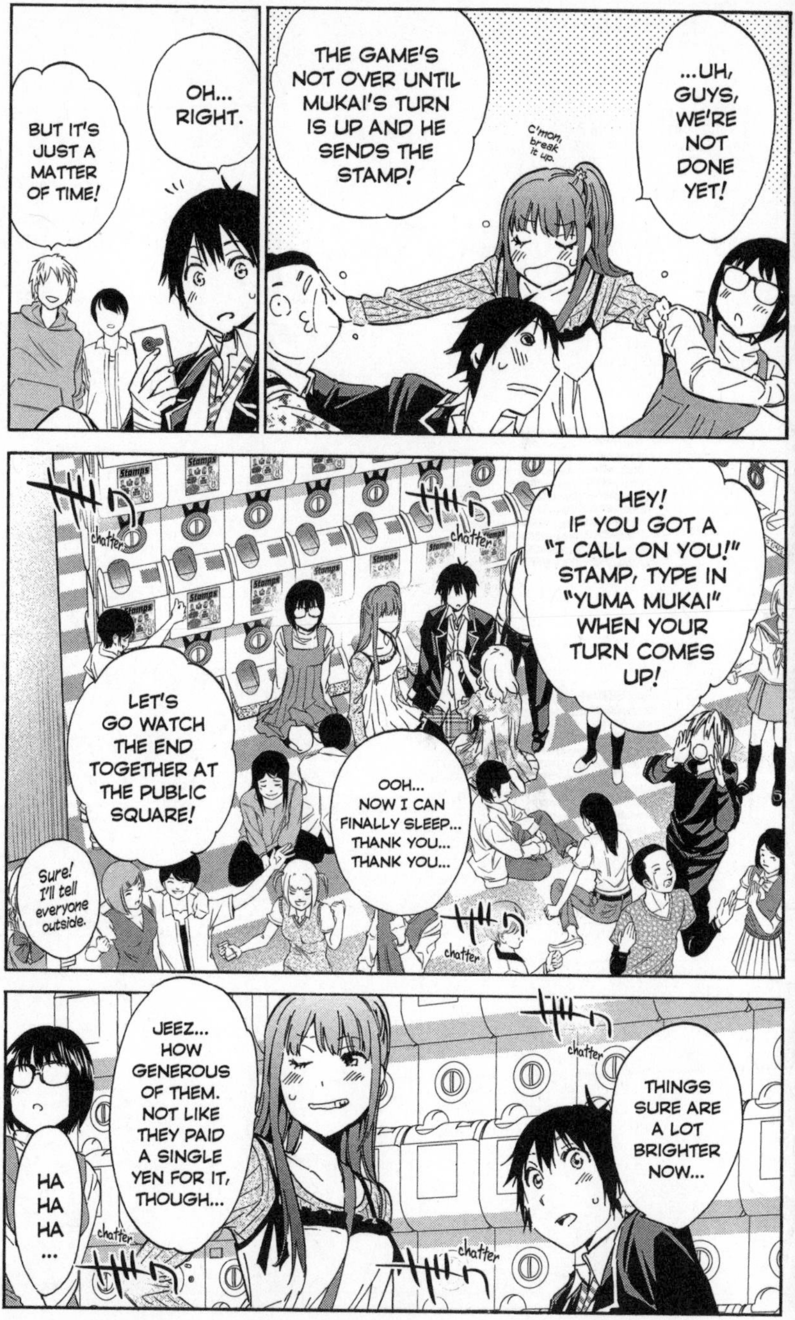
...UH, GUYS, WE'RE NOT DONE YET!
THE GAME'S NOT OVER UNTIL MUKAI'S TURN IS UP AND HE SENDS THE STAMP!
C'mon, break it up.
OH... RIGHT.
BUT IT'S JUST A MATTER OF TIME!
HEY! IF YOU GOT A "I CALL ON YOU!" STAMP, TYPE IN "YUMA MUKAI" WHEN YOUR TURN COMES UP!
chatter
chatter
LET'S GO WATCH THE END TOGETHER AT THE PUBLIC SQUARE!
OOH... NOW I CAN FINALLY SLEEP... THANK YOU... THANK YOU...
Sure! I'll tell everyone outside.
chatter
THINGS SURE ARE A LOT BRIGHTER NOW...
chatter
JEEZ... HOW GENEROUS OF THEM. NOT LIKE THEY PAID A SINGLE YEN FOR IT, THOUGH...
HA HA HA ...
chatter
chatter

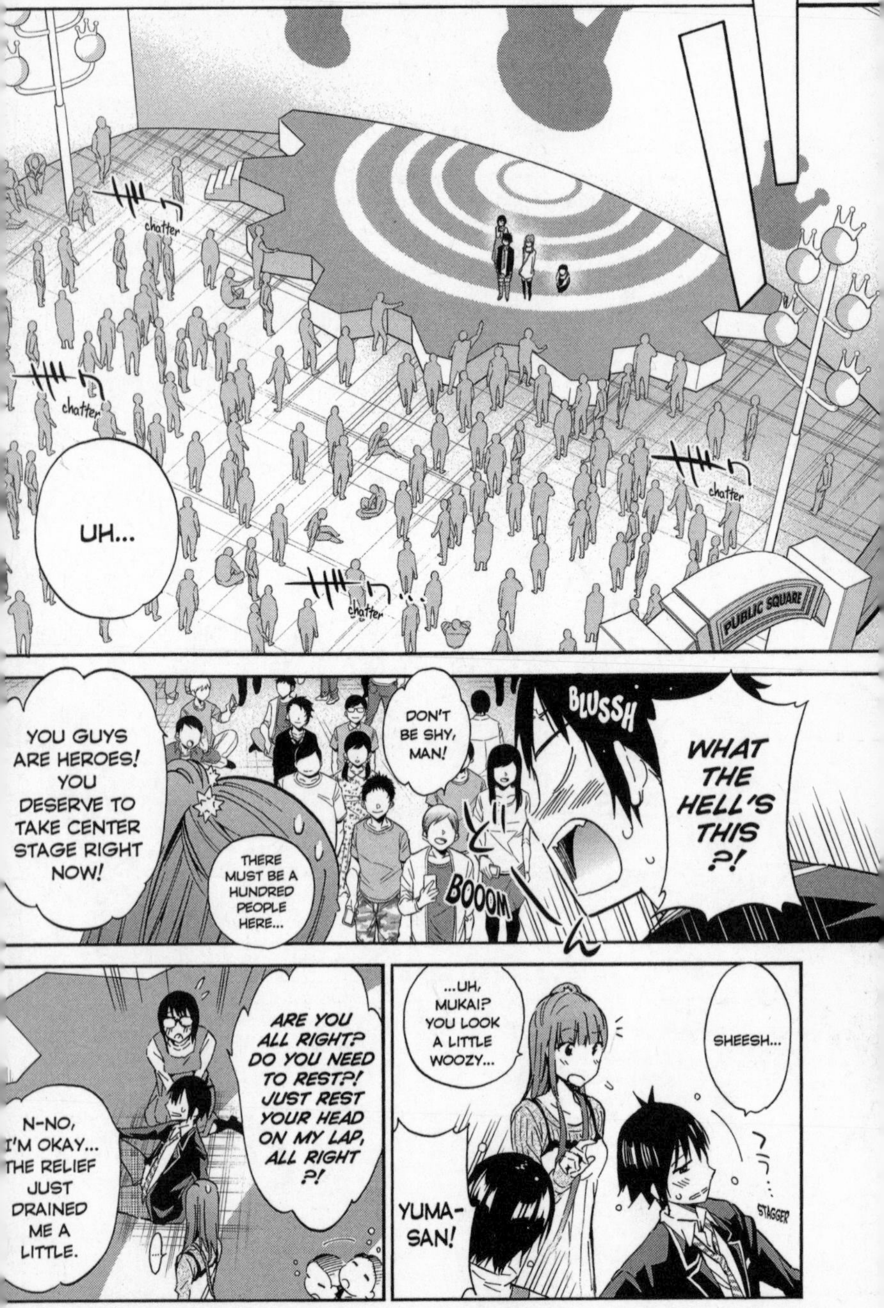
chatter
chatter
chatter
UH...
chatter
PUBLIC SQUARE
BLUSSH
WHAT THE HELL'S THIS?!
DON'T BE SHY, MAN!
BOOOM
THERE MUST BE A HUNDRED PEOPLE HERE...
YOU GUYS ARE HEROES! YOU DESERVE TO TAKE CENTER STAGE RIGHT NOW!
SHEESH...
STAGGER
...UH, MUKAI? YOU LOOK A LITTLE WOOZY...
YUMA-SAN!
ARE YOU ALL RIGHT? DO YOU NEED TO REST?! JUST REST YOUR HEAD ON MY LAP, ALL RIGHT?!
N-NO, I'M OKAY... THE RELIEF JUST DRAINED ME A LITTLE.
...

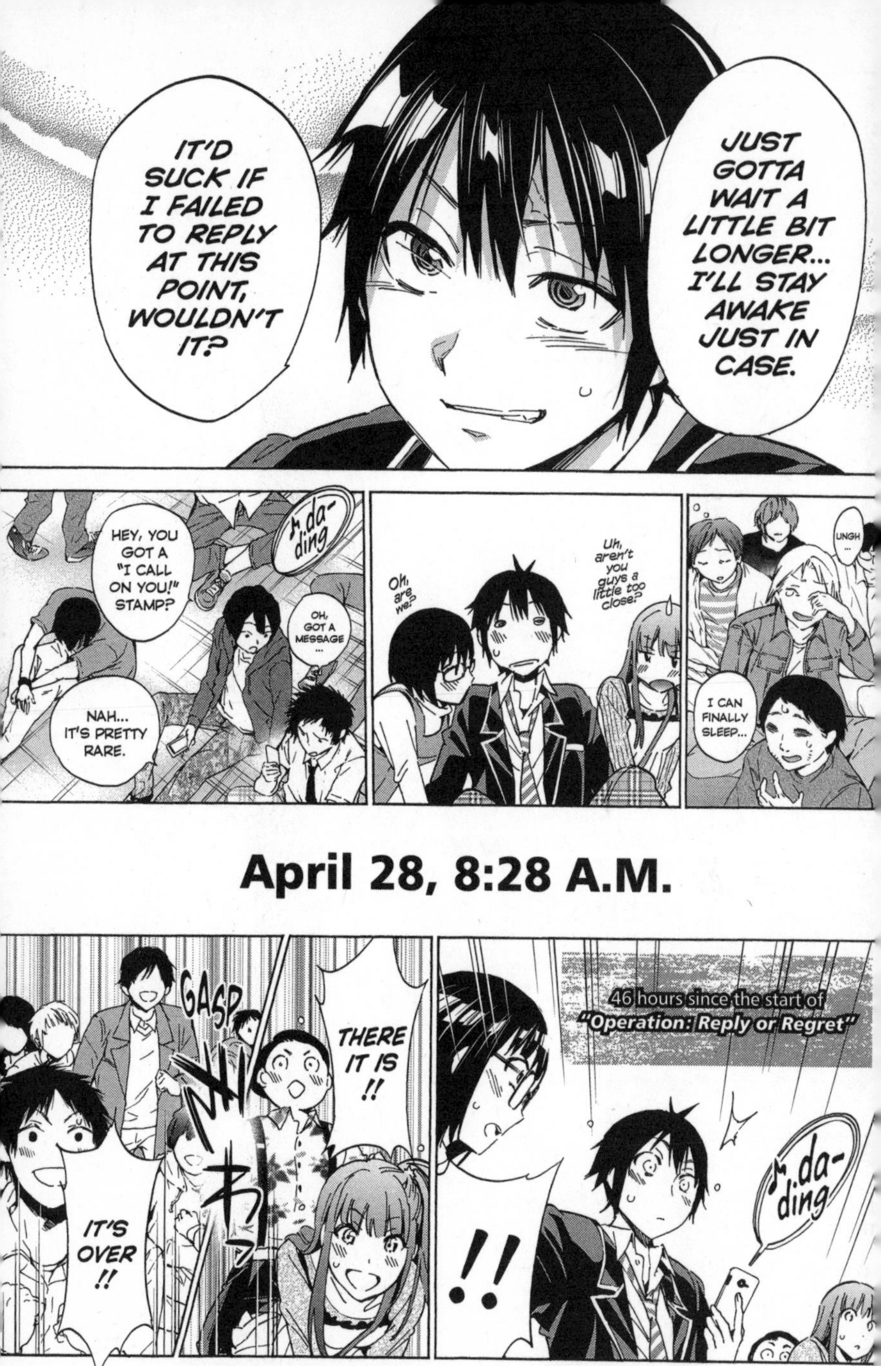
JUST GOTTA WAIT A LITTLE BIT LONGER... I'LL STAY AWAKE JUST IN CASE.
IT'D SUCK IF I FAILED TO REPLY AT THIS POINT, WOULDN'T IT?
UNGH ...
I CAN FINALLY SLEEP...
Uh, aren't you guys a little too close?
Oh, are we?
♪da-ding
OH, GOT A MESSAGE ...
HEY, YOU GOT A "I CALL ON YOU!" STAMP?
NAH... IT'S PRETTY RARE.
April 28, 8:28 A.M.
46 hours since the start of "Operation: Reply or Regret"
♪da-ding
!!
THERE IT IS !!
GASP
IT'S OVER !!

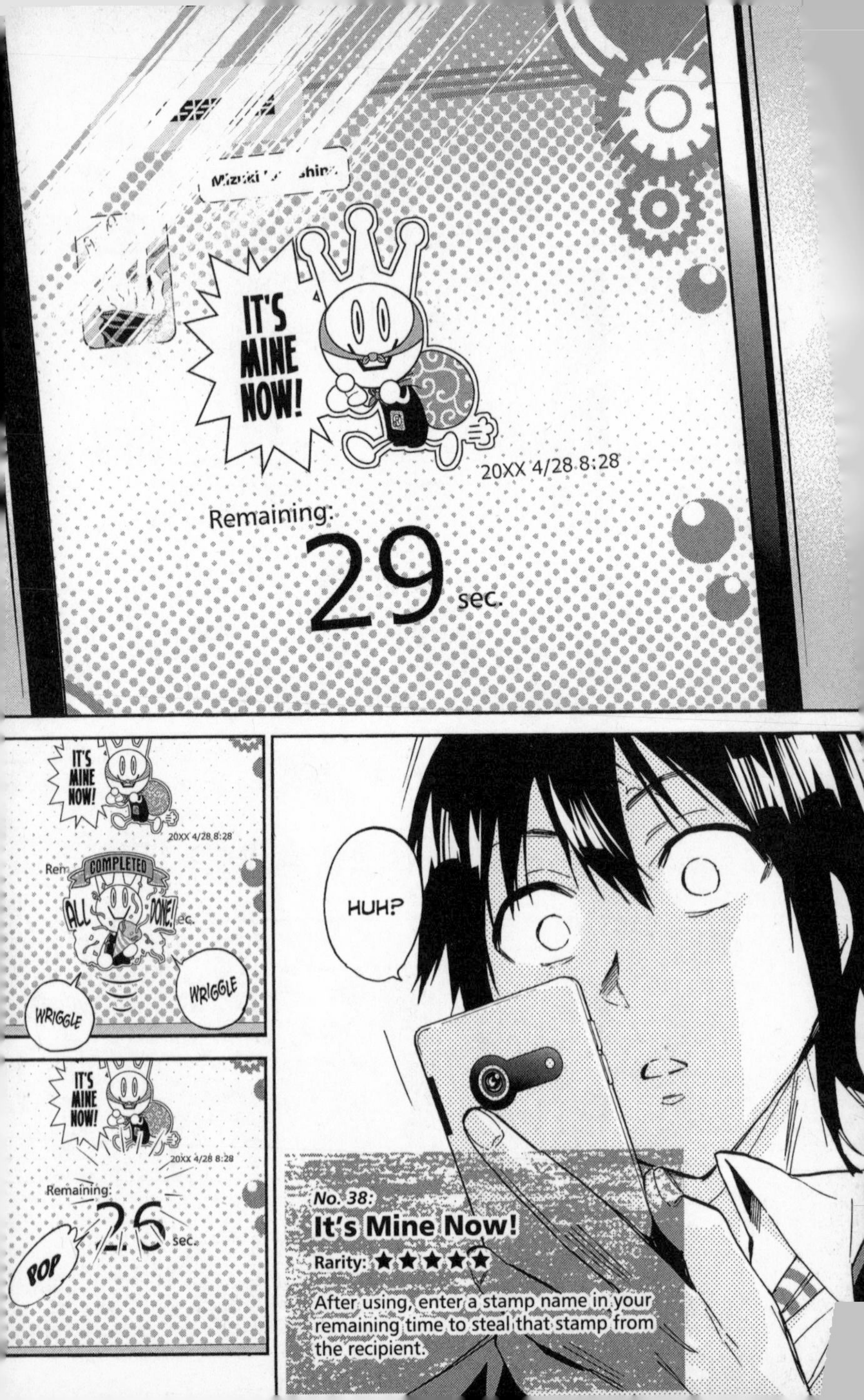
IT'S MINE NOW!
20XX 4/28 8:28
Remaining:
29 sec.
HUH?
No. 38:
It's Mine Now!
Rarity: ★★★★★
After using, enter a stamp name in your remaining time to steal that stamp from the recipient.
IT'S MINE NOW!
20XX 4/28 8:28
COMPLETED
ALL DONE!
WRIGGLE
WRIGGLE
IT'S MINE NOW!
20XX 4/28 8:28
Remaining:
26 sec.
POP

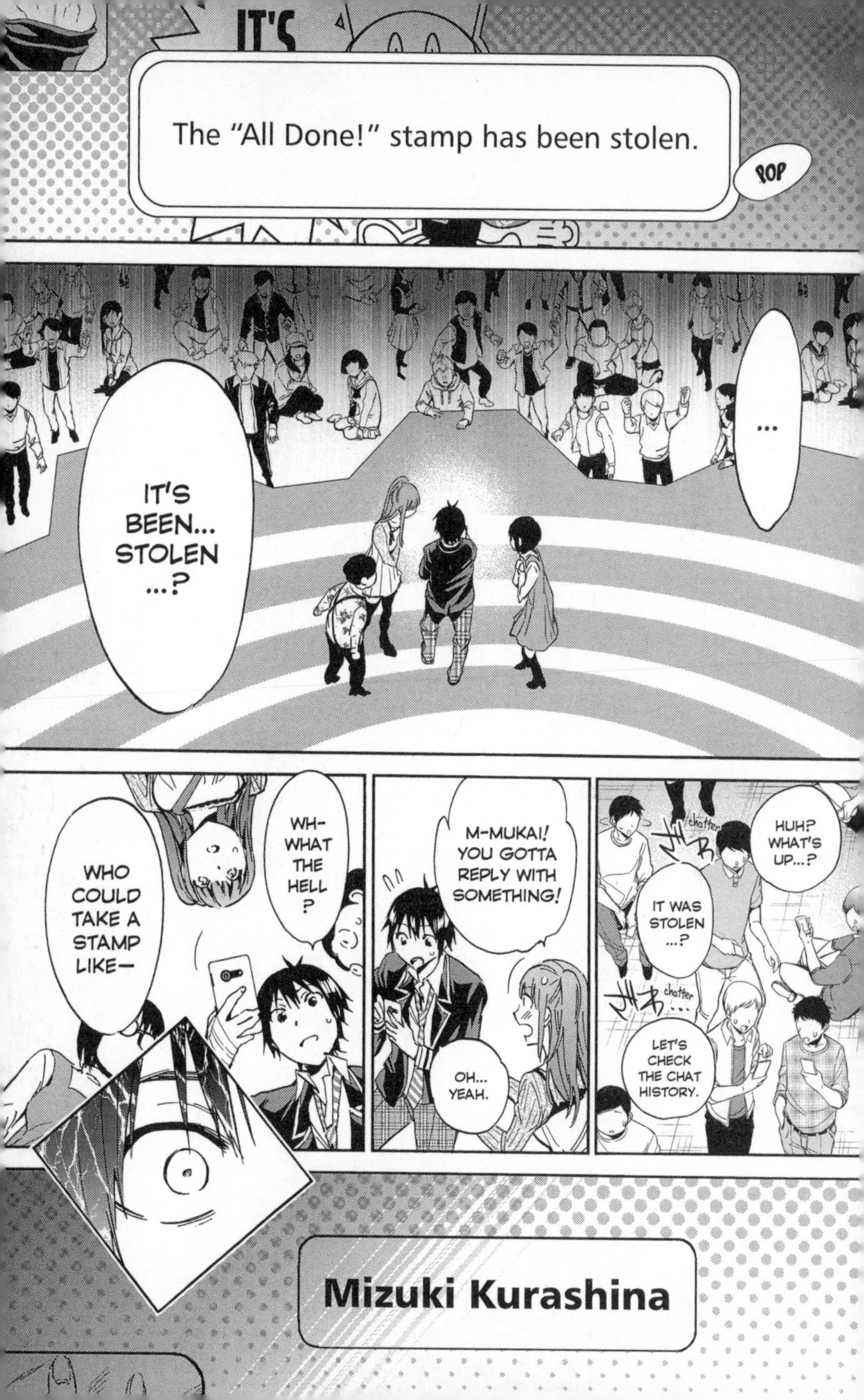
IT'S
The "All Done!" stamp has been stolen.
POP
...
IT'S BEEN... STOLEN...?
HUH? WHAT'S UP...?
chatter
IT WAS STOLEN...?
chatter...
LET'S CHECK THE CHAT HISTORY.
M-MUKAI! YOU GOTTA REPLY WITH SOMETHING!
OH... YEAH.
WH-WHAT THE HELL?
WHO COULD TAKE A STAMP LIKE—
Mizuki Kurashina

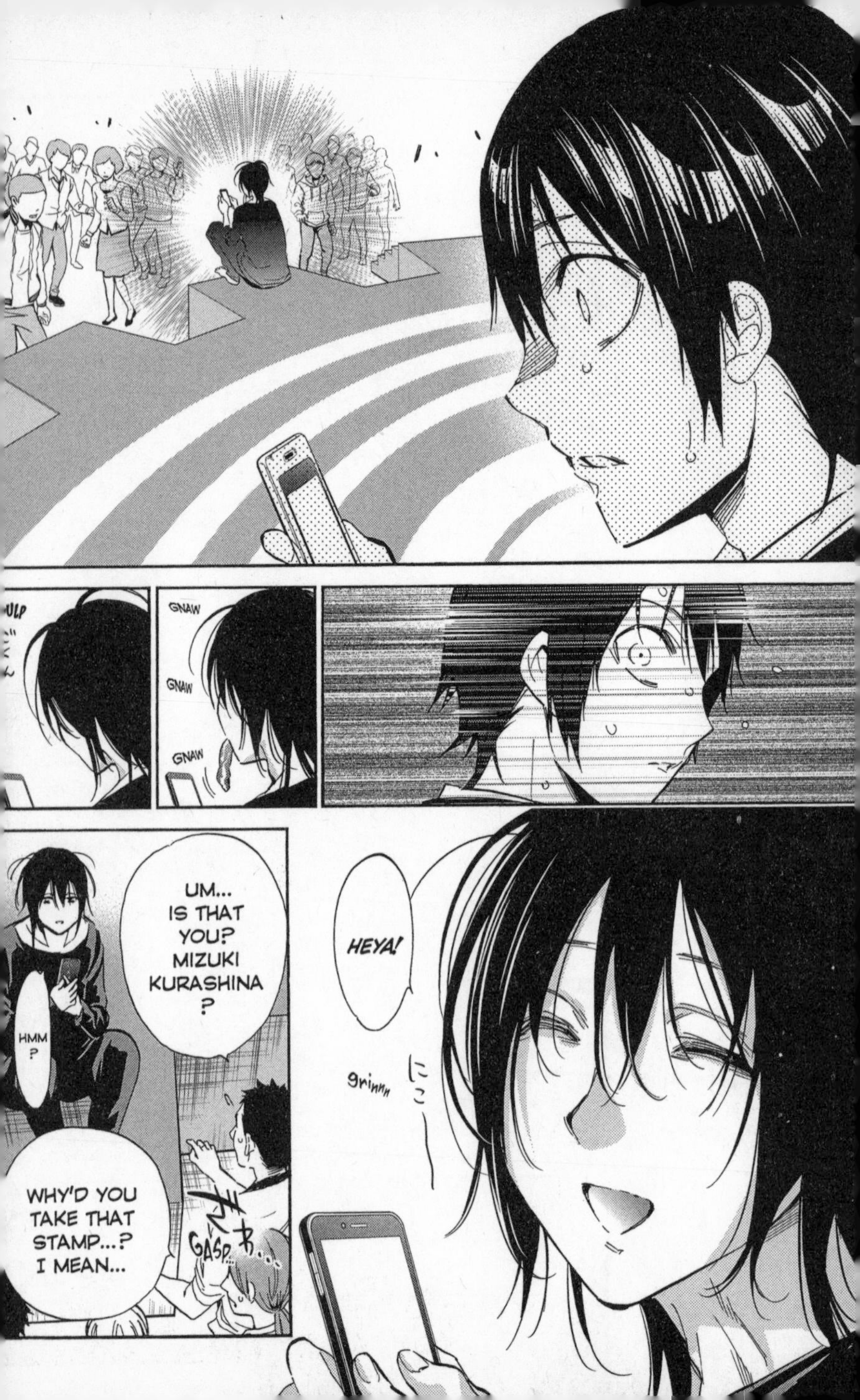
GNAW
GNAW
GNAW
HEYA!
grinnn
にこー
UM... IS THAT YOU? MIZUKI KURASHINA?
HMM?
WHY'D YOU TAKE THAT STAMP...? I MEAN...
GASP...

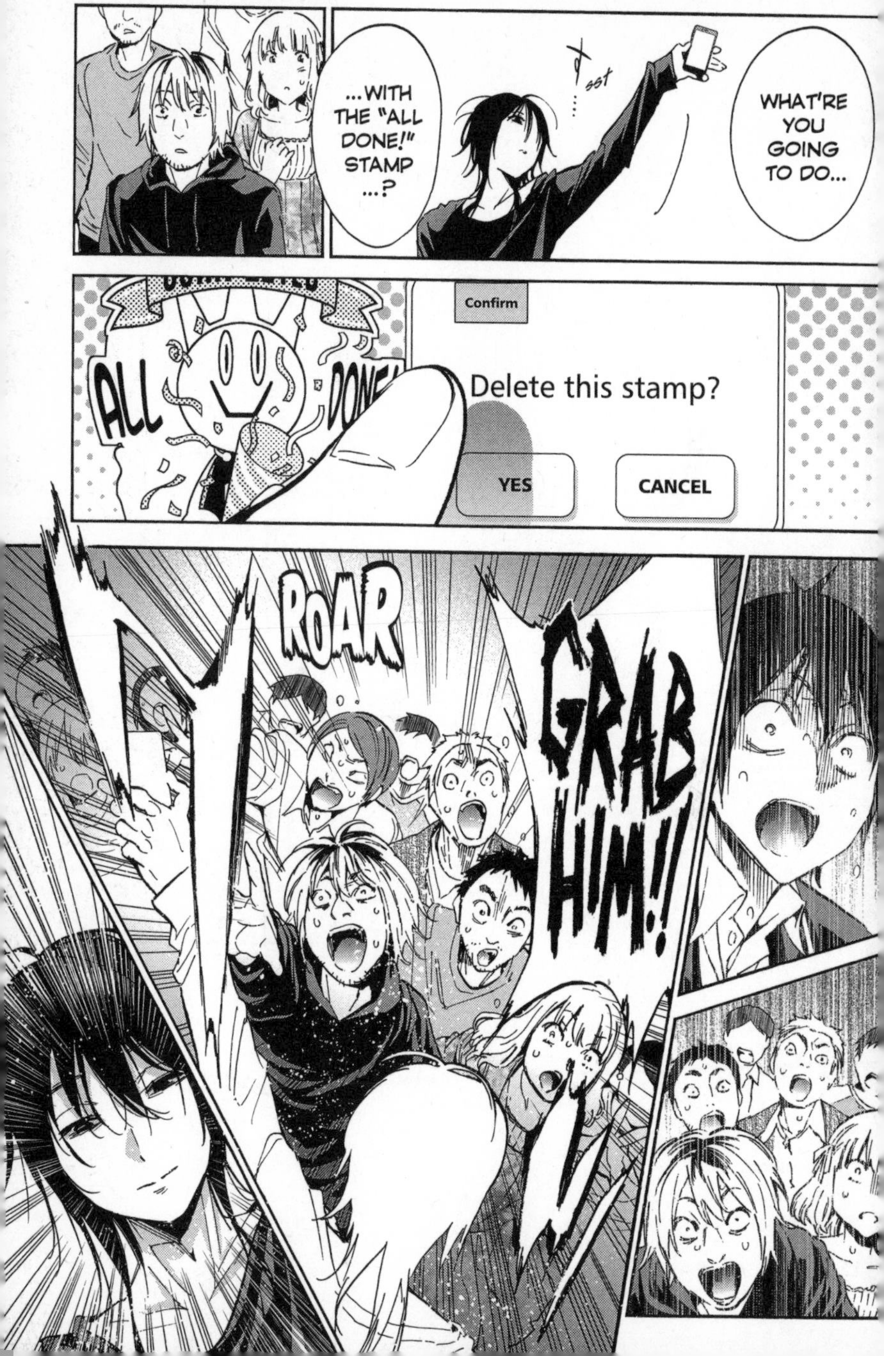
WHAT'RE YOU GOING TO DO...
tsst
...WITH THE "ALL DONE!" STAMP ...?
Confirm
Delete this stamp?
YES
CANCEL
ALL DONE!
ROAR
GRAB HIM!!

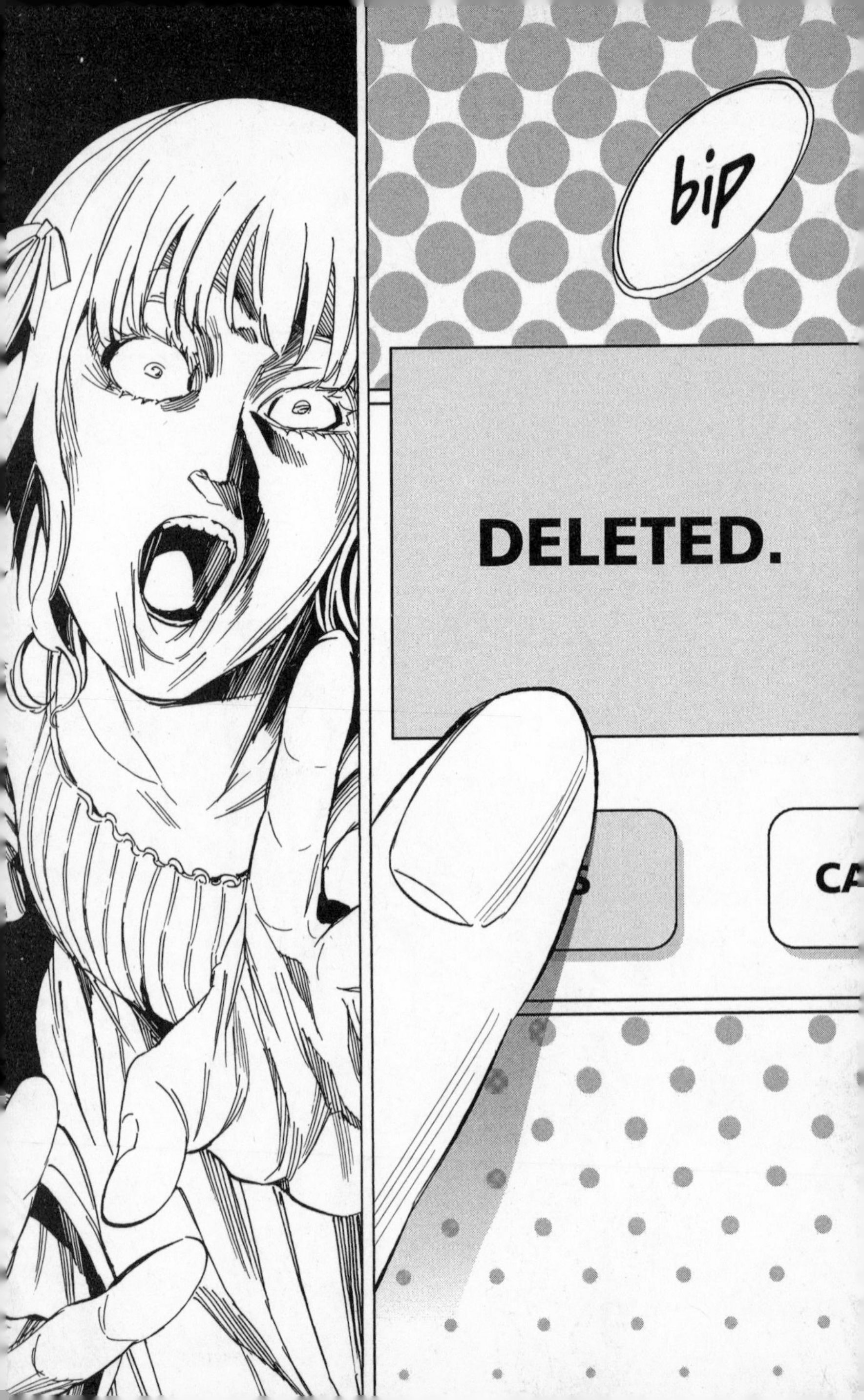
bip
DELETED.

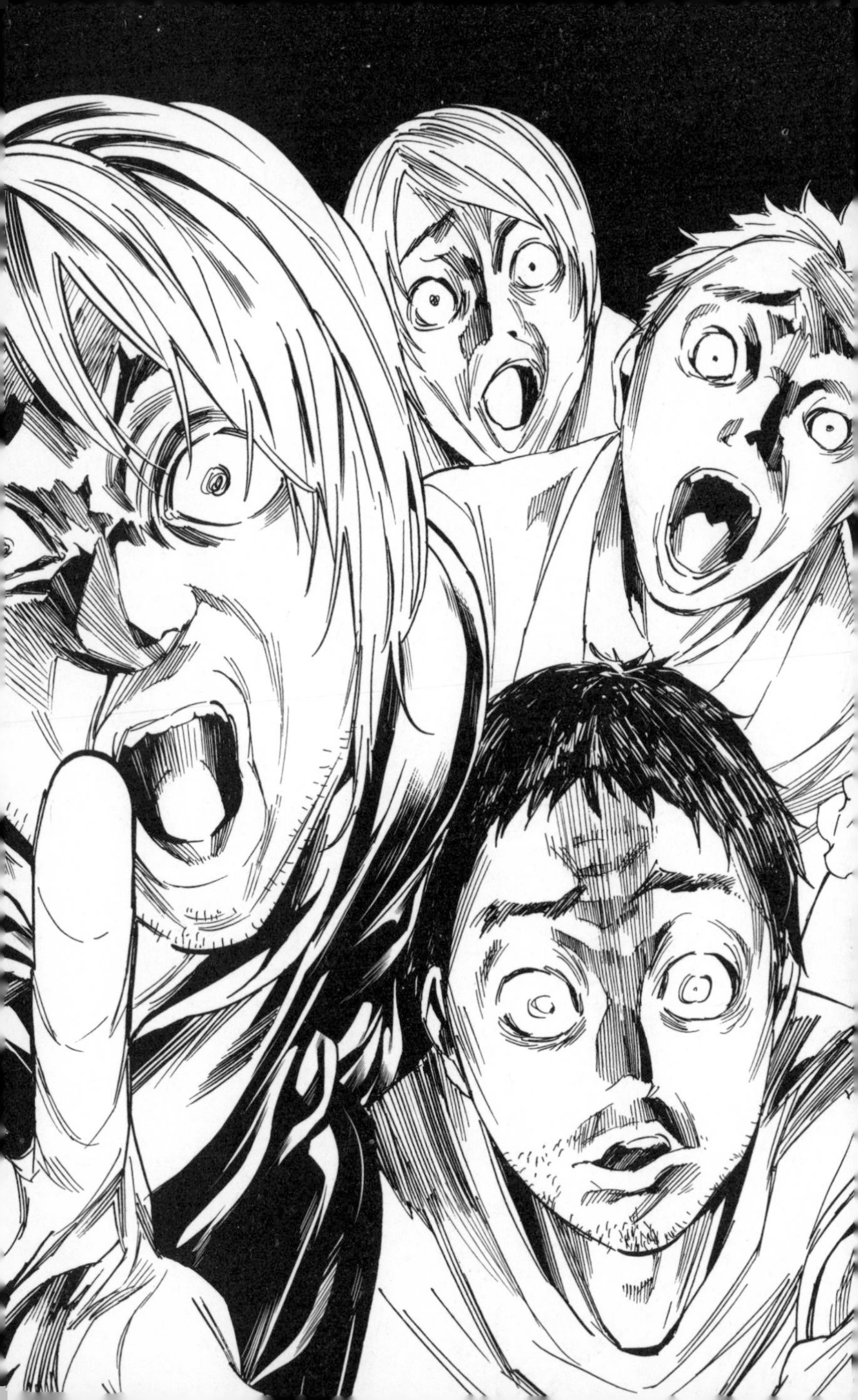

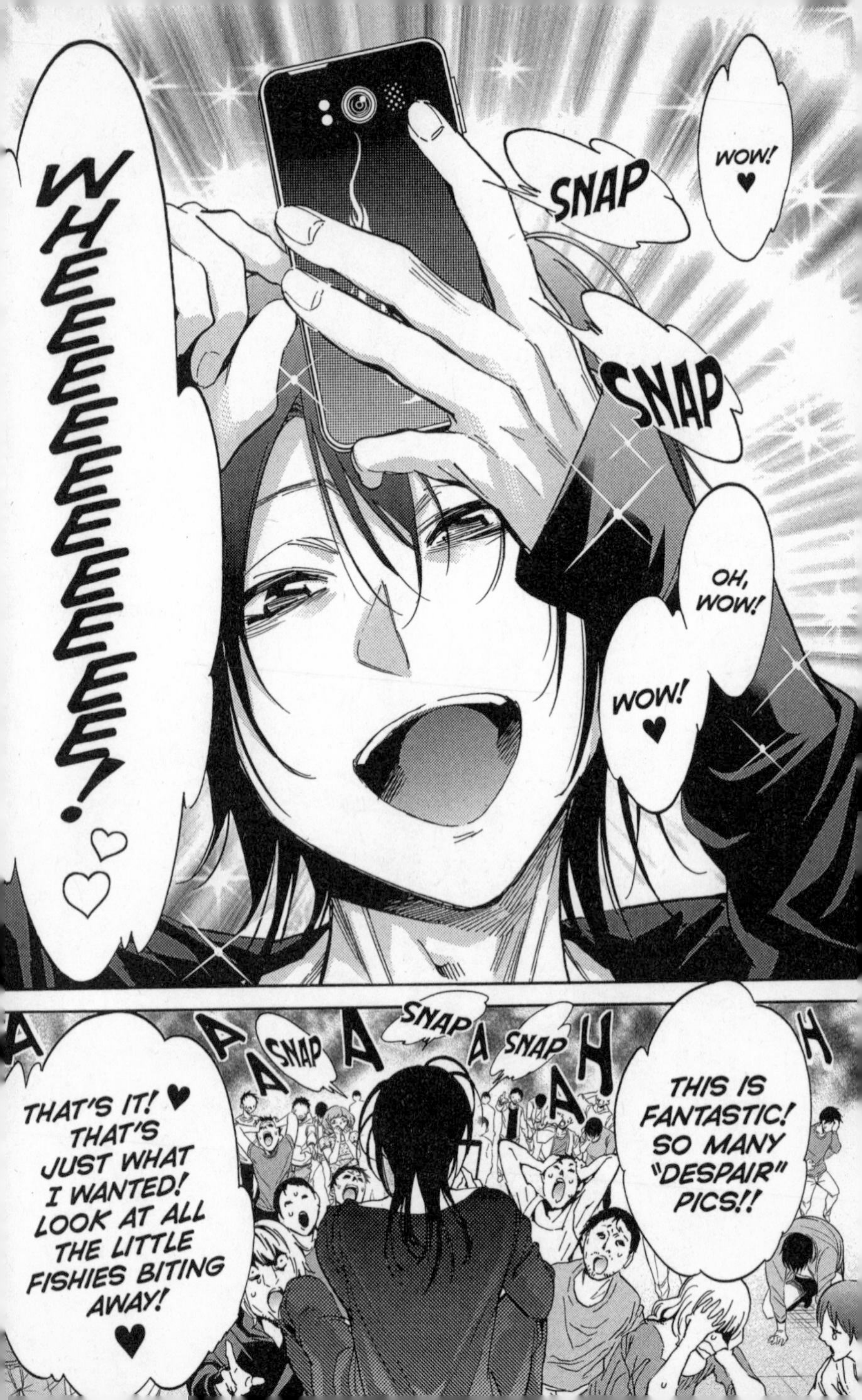
WOW! ♥
SNAP
SNAP
OH, WOW!
WOW! ♥
WHEEEEEEEEEES! ♡ ♡
AAAAAAHH
SNAP
SNAP
SNAP
THIS IS FANTASTIC! SO MANY "DESPAIR" PICS!!
THAT'S IT! ♥ THAT'S JUST WHAT I WANTED! LOOK AT ALL THE LITTLE FISHIES BITING AWAY! ♥

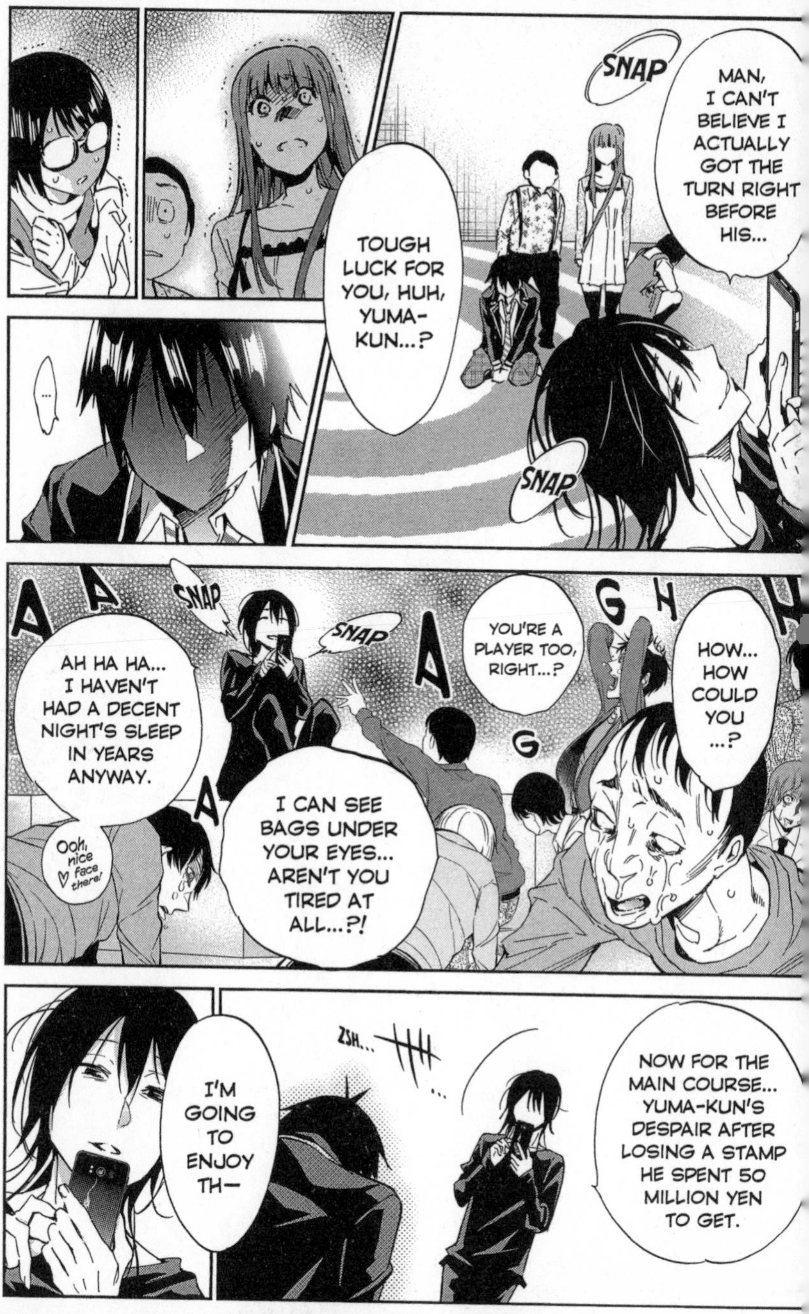
SNAP
MAN, I CAN'T BELIEVE I ACTUALLY GOT THE TURN RIGHT BEFORE HIS...
TOUGH LUCK FOR YOU, HUH, YUMA-KUN...?
SNAP
...
HOW... HOW COULD YOU ...?
AAAAGGHH
YOU'RE A PLAYER TOO, RIGHT...?
SNAP
I CAN SEE BAGS UNDER YOUR EYES... AREN'T YOU TIRED AT ALL...?!
SNAP
AH HA HA... I HAVEN'T HAD A DECENT NIGHT'S SLEEP IN YEARS ANYWAY.
Ooh, nice ♡ face there!
NOW FOR THE MAIN COURSE... YUMA-KUN'S DESPAIR AFTER LOSING A STAMP HE SPENT 50 MILLION YEN TO GET.
ZSH...
...
I'M GOING TO ENJOY TH—

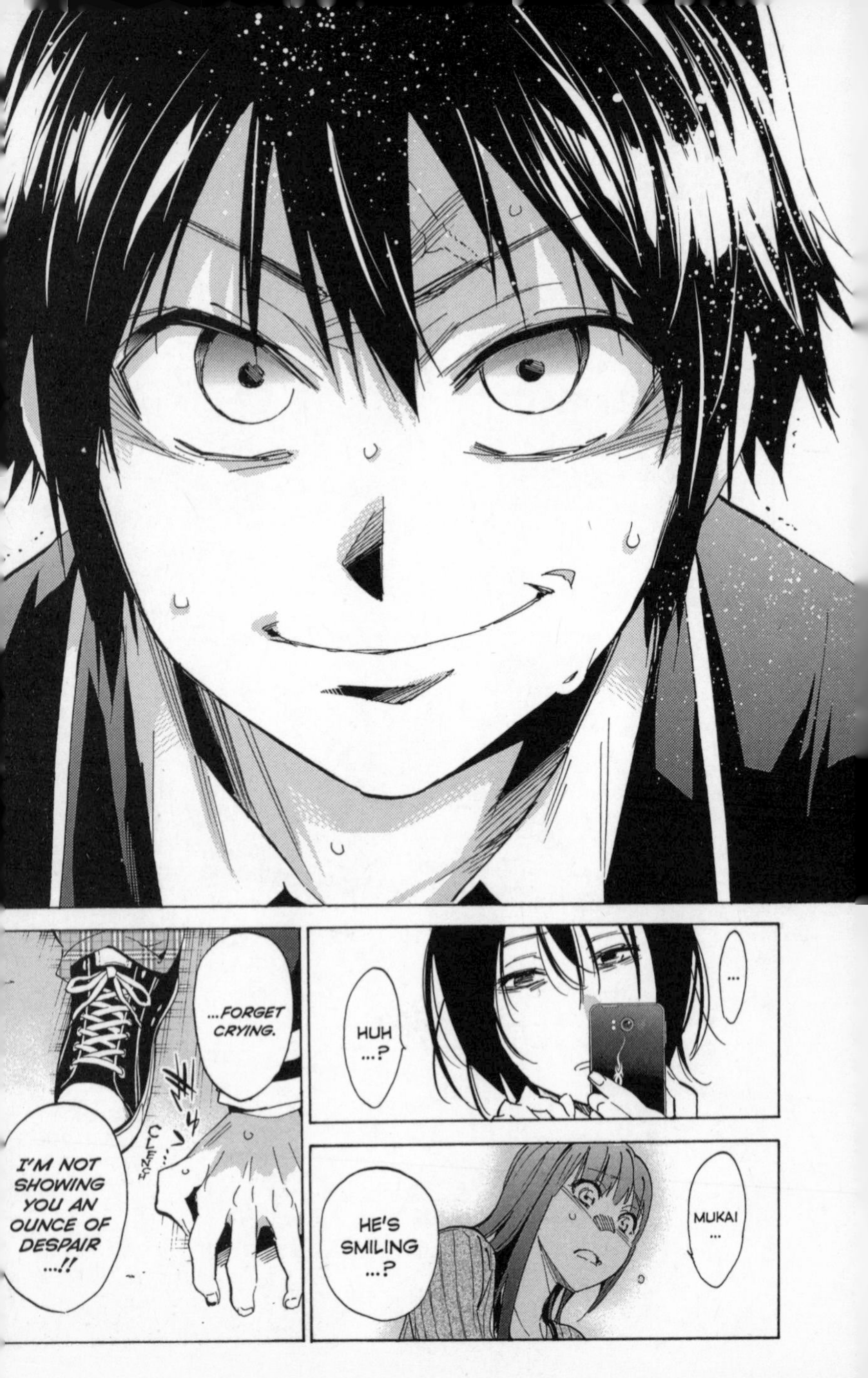
...
HUH ...?
MUKAI ...
HE'S SMILING ...?
...FORGET CRYING.
CLENCH
I'M NOT SHOWING YOU AN OUNCE OF DESPAIR ...!!

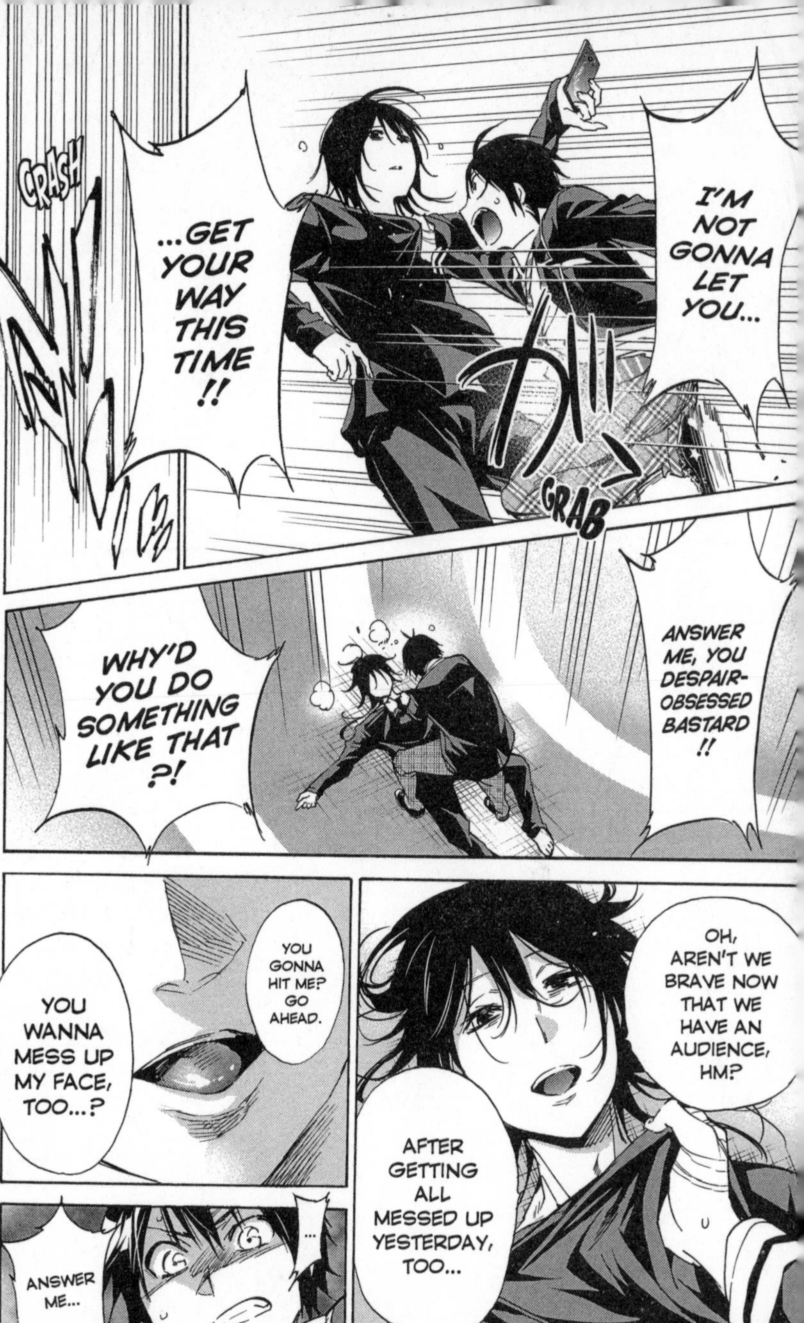
I'M NOT GONNA LET YOU...
GRAB
...GET YOUR WAY THIS TIME!!
CRASH
ANSWER ME, YOU DESPAIR-OBSESSED BASTARD!!
WHY'D YOU DO SOMETHING LIKE THAT?!
OH, AREN'T WE BRAVE NOW THAT WE HAVE AN AUDIENCE, HM?
AFTER GETTING ALL MESSED UP YESTERDAY, TOO...
YOU GONNA HIT ME? GO AHEAD.
YOU WANNA MESS UP MY FACE, TOO...?
...
ANSWER ME...

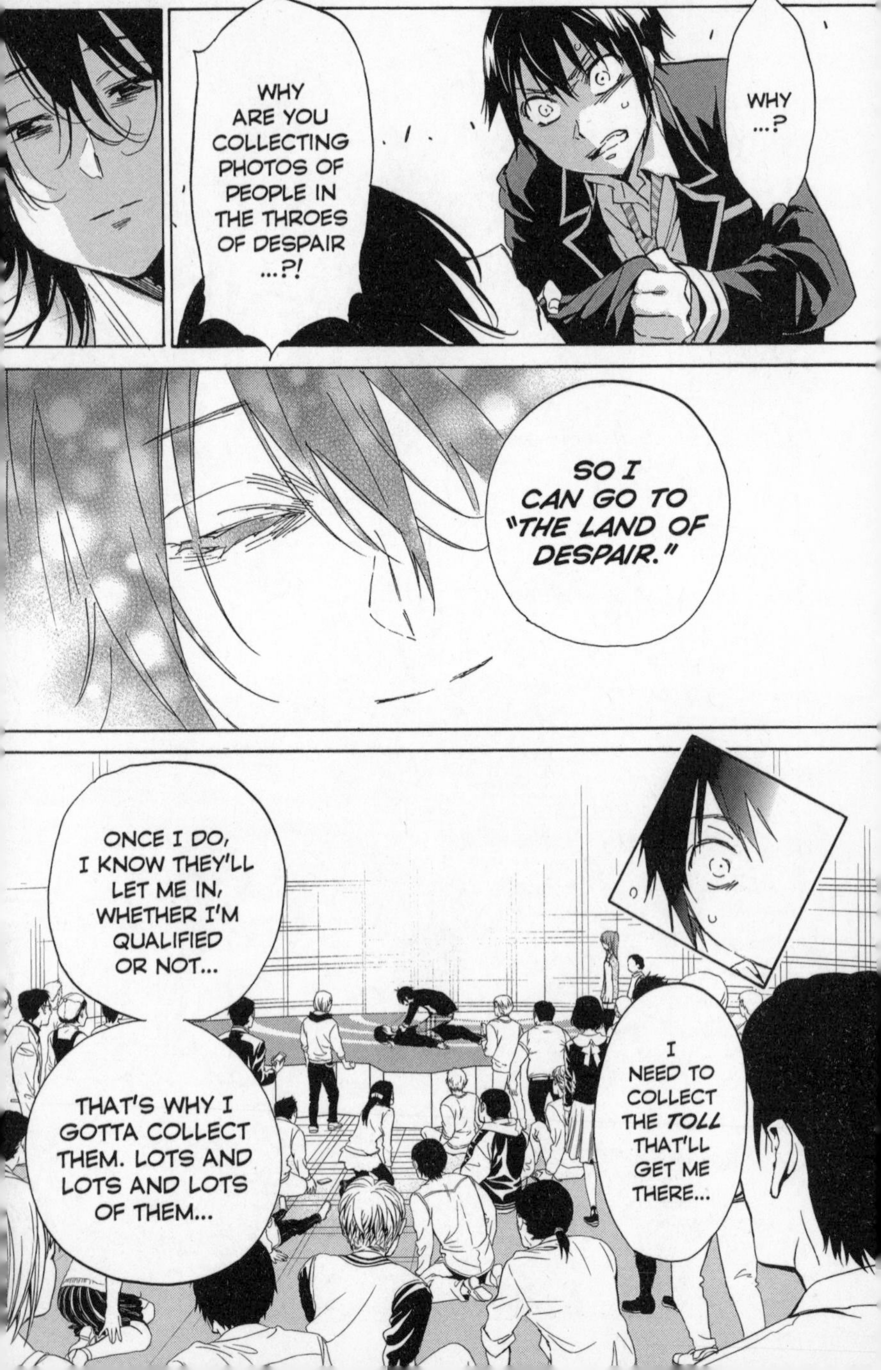
WHY ...?
WHY ARE YOU COLLECTING PHOTOS OF PEOPLE IN THE THROES OF DESPAIR ...?!
SO I CAN GO TO *"THE LAND OF DESPAIR."*
I NEED TO COLLECT THE *TOLL* THAT'LL GET ME THERE...
ONCE I DO, I KNOW THEY'LL LET ME IN, WHETHER I'M QUALIFIED OR NOT...
THAT'S WHY I GOTTA COLLECT THEM. LOTS AND LOTS AND LOTS OF THEM...

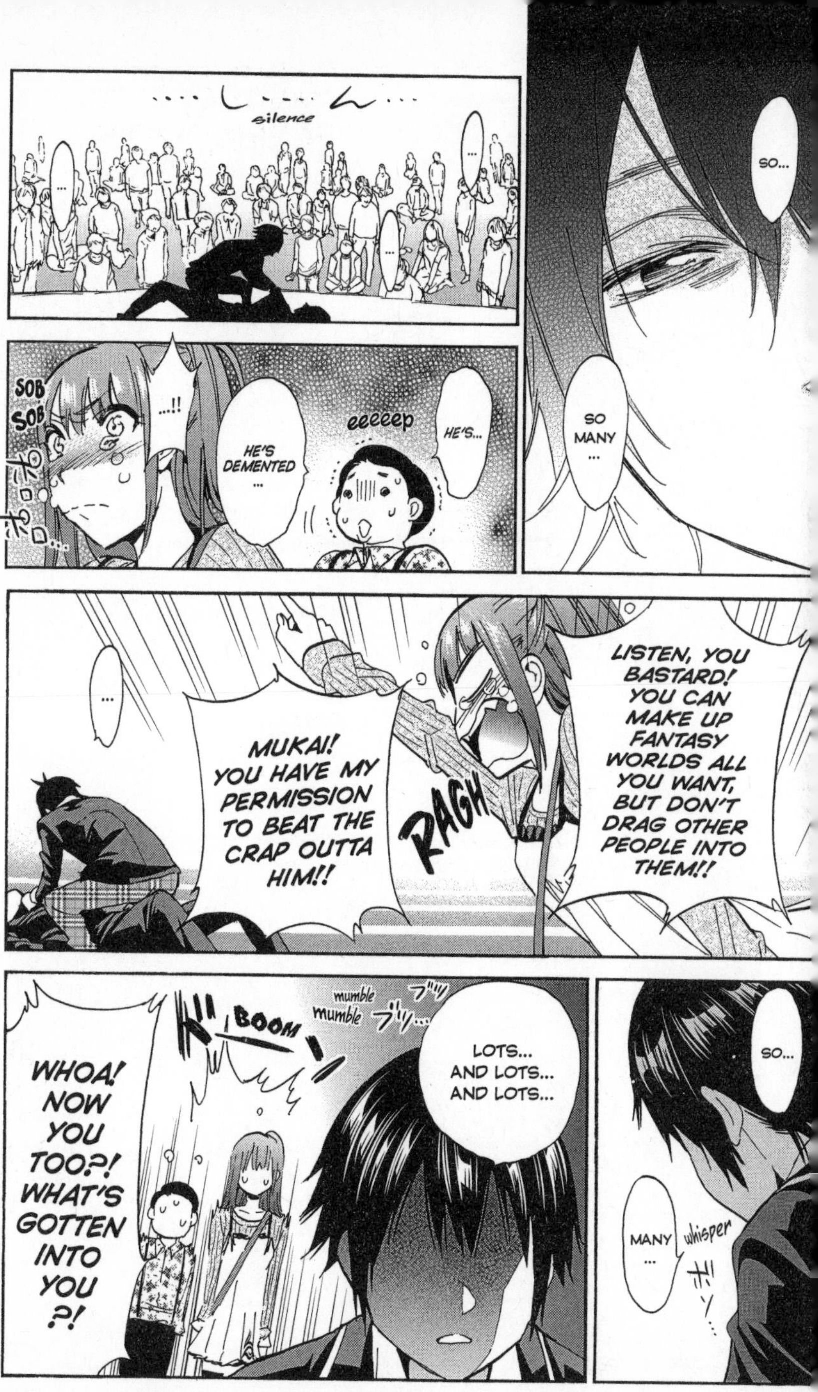
SO...
SO MANY ...
silence
...
...
...
HE'S...
eeeeep
HE'S DEMENTED ...
...!!
SOB SOB
LISTEN, YOU BASTARD! YOU CAN MAKE UP FANTASY WORLDS ALL YOU WANT, BUT DON'T DRAG OTHER PEOPLE INTO THEM!!
RAGH
MUKAI! YOU HAVE MY PERMISSION TO BEAT THE CRAP OUTTA HIM!!
...
SO...
MANY ...
whisper
LOTS... AND LOTS... AND LOTS...
mumble mumble
BOOM
WHOA! NOW YOU TOO?! WHAT'S GOTTEN INTO YOU ?!

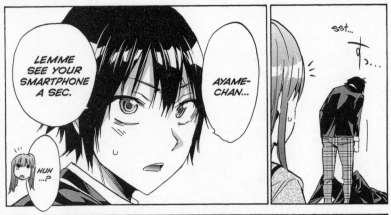

sst...
すっ...
AYAME-CHAN...
LEMME SEE YOUR SMARTPHONE A SEC.
HUH ...?
MY, MY, MY! NOW THAT'S A SURPRISE !!
I WAS ALL READY TO DECLARE THIS FINISHED, BUT NOW THINGS HAVE FLIPPED AND WE GOTTA KEEP GOING!!
IGNORING MESSAGES
ALL RIGHT, EVERYONE! NOW'S NO TIME TO WALLOW IN DESPAIR!
FOR REAL ...?
TRY TO KEEP UP WITH ALL OF YOUR MESSAGES. OKAAAAAY? ♥
I CAN'T ...
DAMN IT...

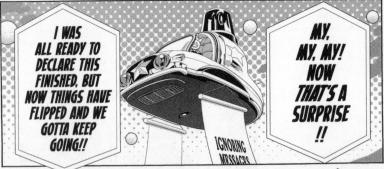

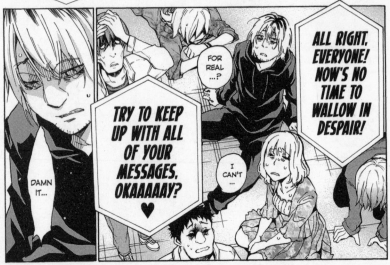

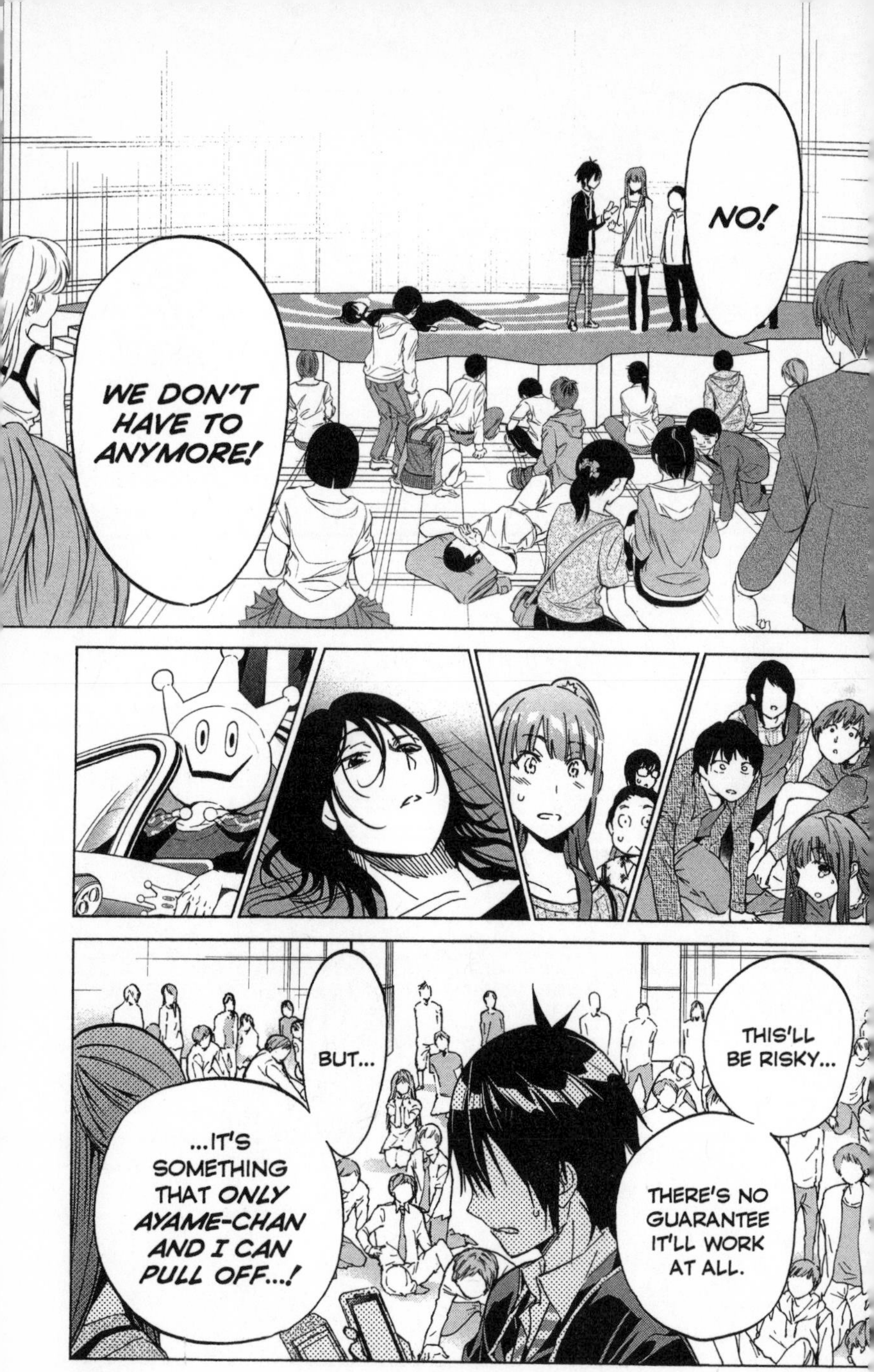
NO!
WE DON'T HAVE TO ANYMORE!
THIS'LL BE RISKY...
THERE'S NO GUARANTEE IT'LL WORK AT ALL.
BUT...
...IT'S SOMETHING THAT ONLY AYAME-CHAN AND I CAN PULL OFF...!

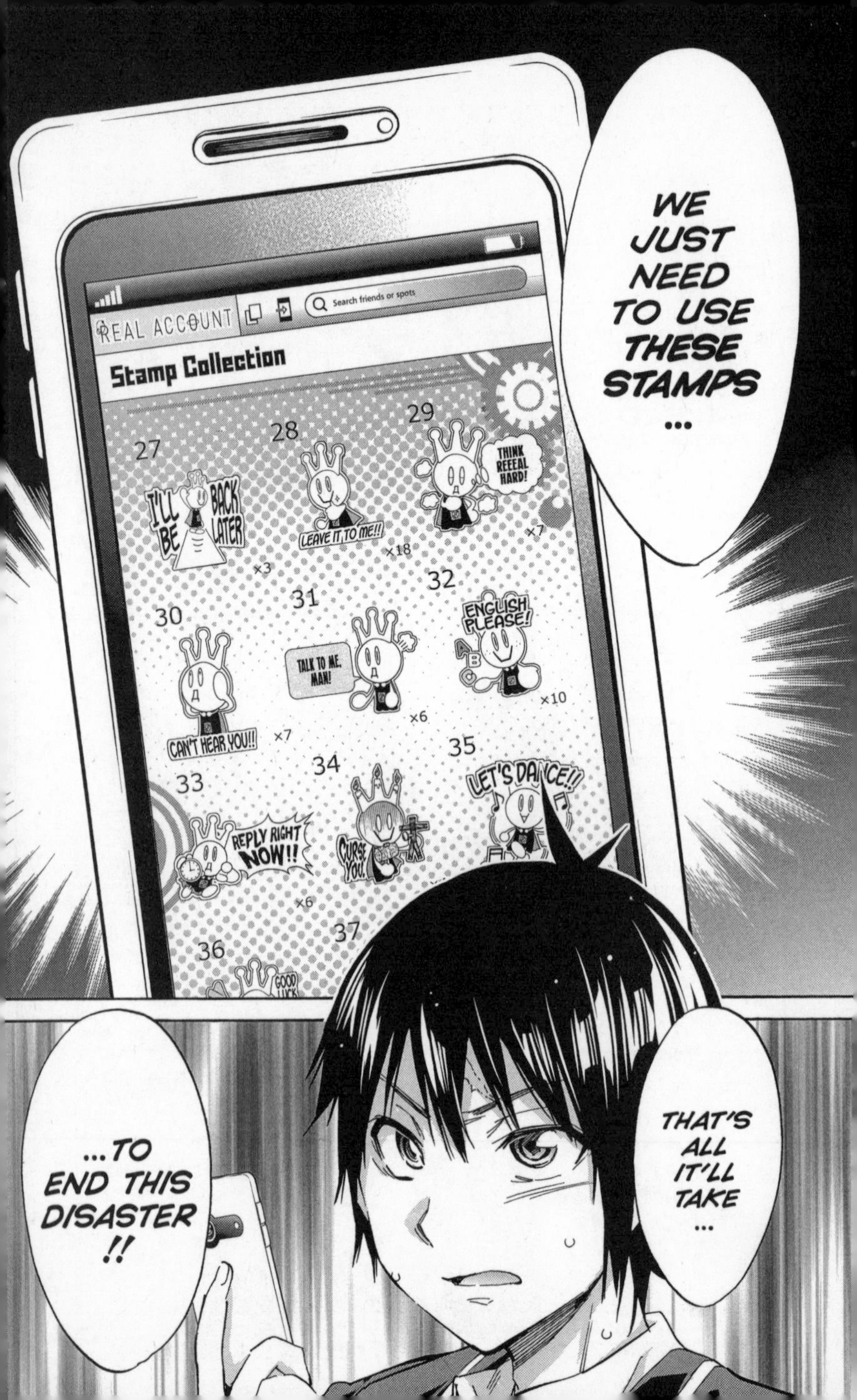
WE JUST NEED TO USE THESE STAMPS...
REAL ACCOUNT
Search friends or spots
Stamp Collection
27
I'LL BE BACK LATER
×3
28
LEAVE IT TO ME!!
×18
29
THINK REEEAL HARD!
×7
30
CAN'T HEAR YOU!!
×7
31
TALK TO ME, MAN!
×6
32
ENGLISH PLEASE!
×10
33
REPLY RIGHT NOW!!
×6
34
CURSE YOU!
35
LET'S DANCE!!
36
37
GOOD
THAT'S ALL IT'LL TAKE...
...TO END THIS DISASTER!!

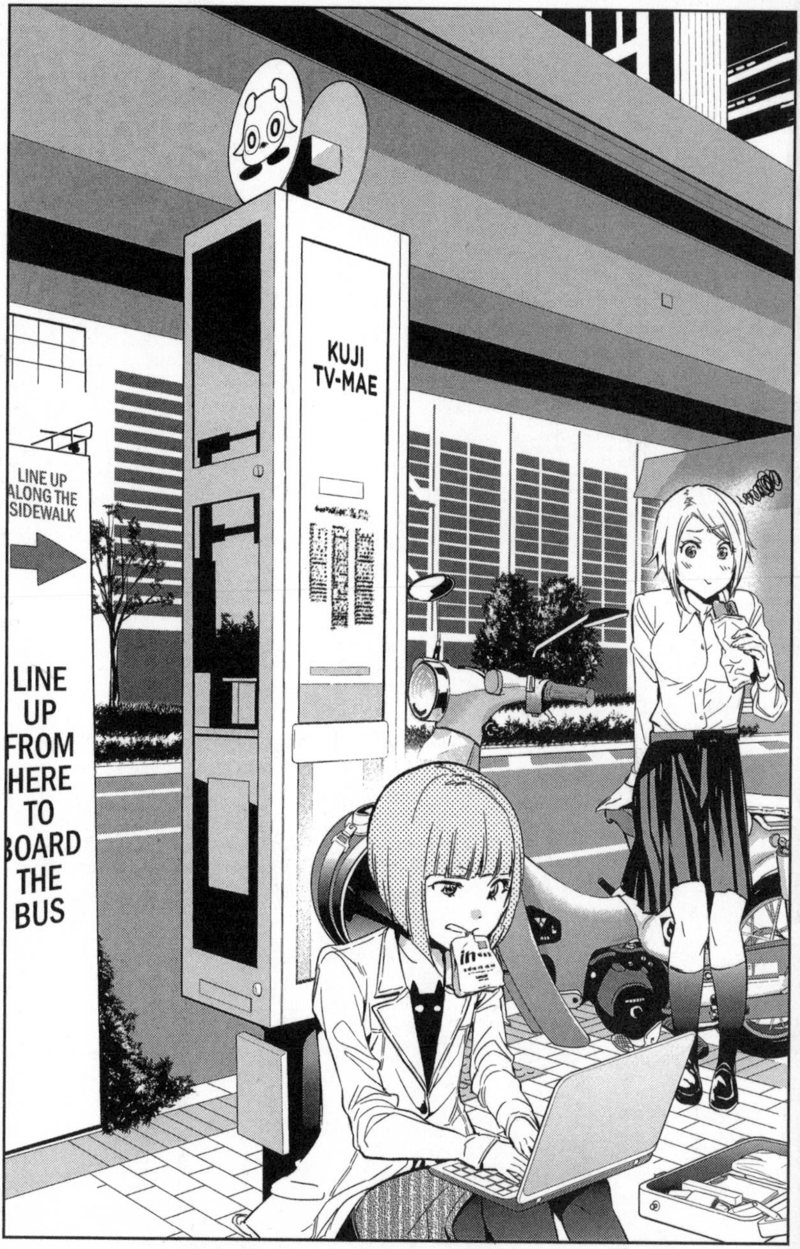
KUJI
TV-MAE
LINE UP
ALONG THE
SIDEWALK
LINE
UP
FROM
HERE
TO
BOARD
THE
BUS

ACCOUNT 20 Long Live the Freedom to Ignore

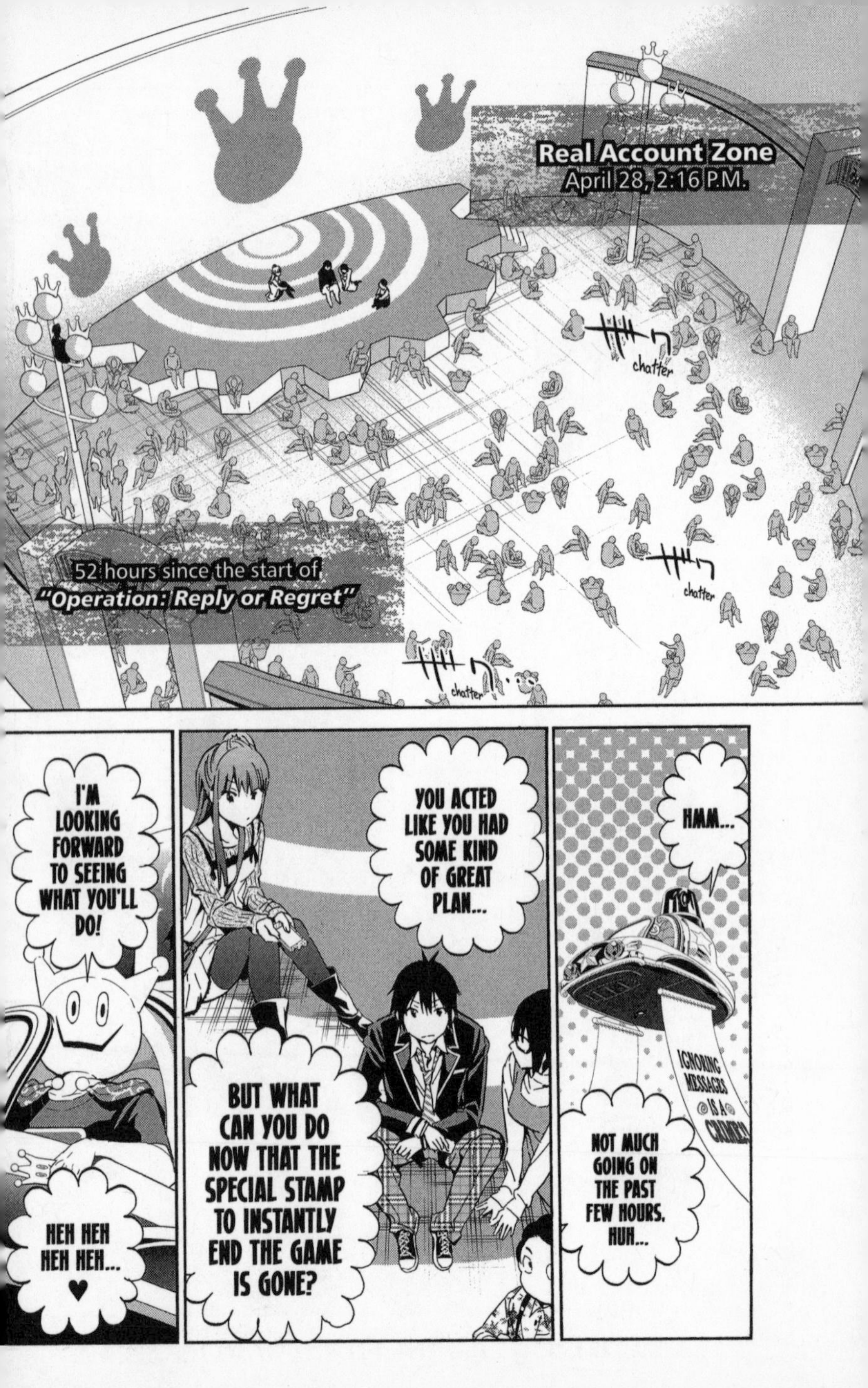
Real Account Zone
April 28, 2:16 P.M.
chatter
chatter
52 hours since the start of "Operation: Reply or Regret"
chatter
HMM...
IGNORING MESSAGES IS A CRIME!!
NOT MUCH GOING ON THE PAST FEW HOURS, HUH...
YOU ACTED LIKE YOU HAD SOME KIND OF GREAT PLAN...
BUT WHAT CAN YOU DO NOW THAT THE SPECIAL STAMP TO INSTANTLY END THE GAME IS GONE?
I'M LOOKING FORWARD TO SEEING WHAT YOU'LL DO!
HEH HEH HEH HEH... ♥

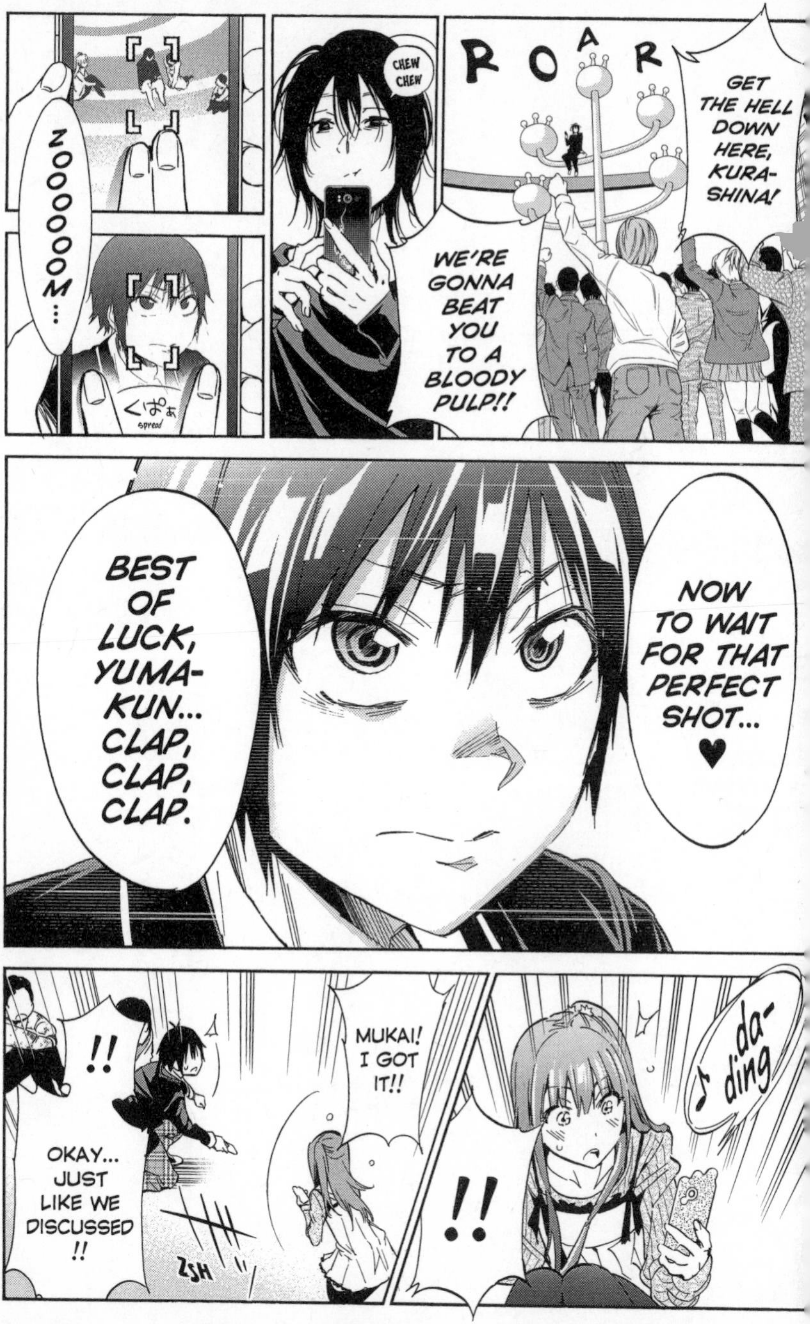
GET THE HELL DOWN HERE, KURA-SHINA!
ROAR
WE'RE GONNA BEAT YOU TO A BLOODY PULP!!
CHEW CHEW
ZOOOOOOOM...
くぱぁ
spread
NOW TO WAIT FOR THAT PERFECT SHOT... ♥
BEST OF LUCK, YUMA-KUN... CLAP, CLAP, CLAP.
♪ da-ding
!!
MUKAI! I GOT IT!!
!!
OKAY... JUST LIKE WE DISCUSSED!!
ZSH

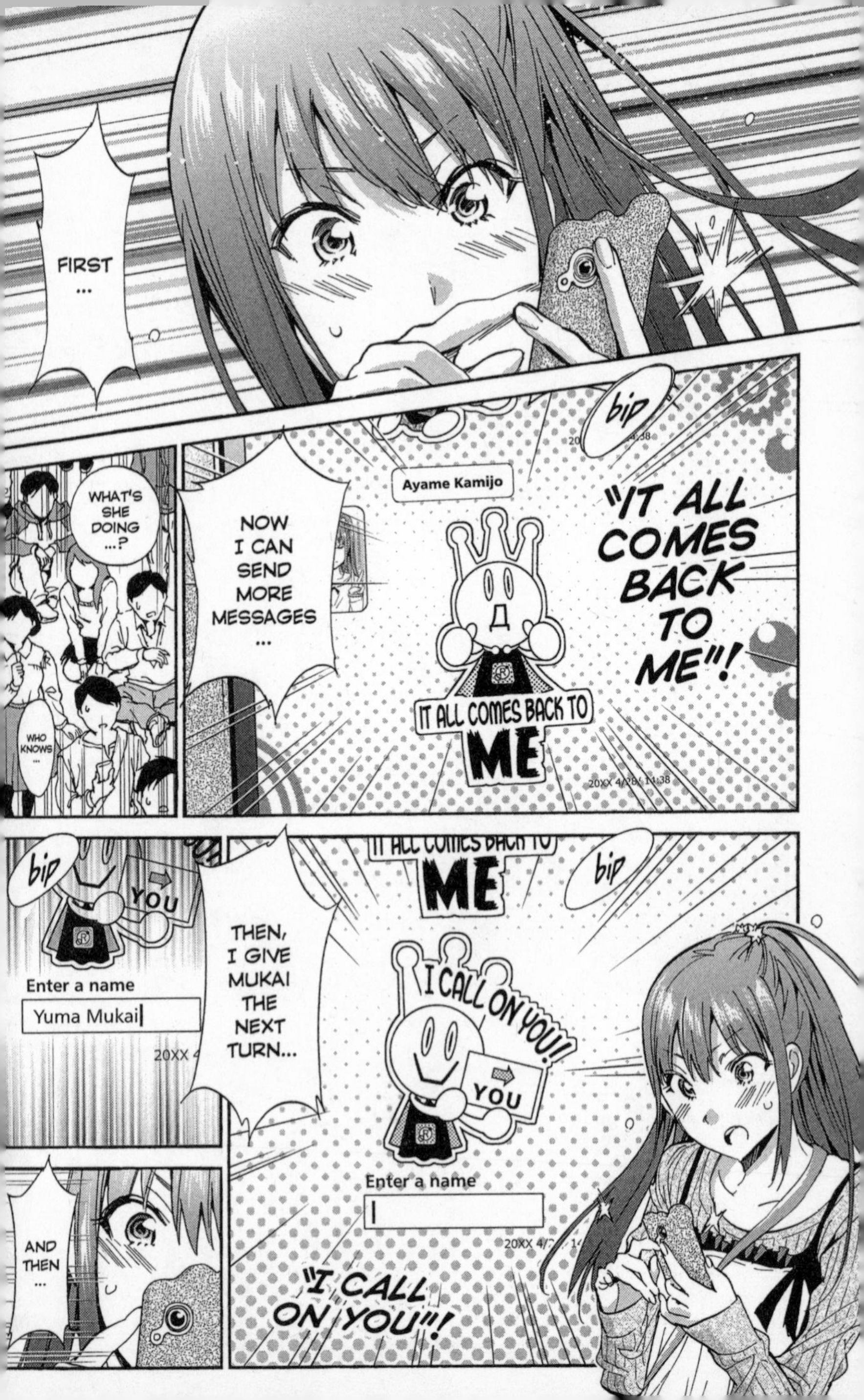
FIRST ...
bip
"IT ALL COMES BACK TO ME"!
Ayame Kamijo
NOW I CAN SEND MORE MESSAGES ...
IT ALL COMES BACK TO ME
20XX 4/28 14:38
WHAT'S SHE DOING ...?
WHO KNOWS ...
bip
ME
I CALL ON YOU!!
YOU
Enter a name
"I CALL ON YOU"!
THEN, I GIVE MUKAI THE NEXT TURN...
bip
YOU
Enter a name
Yuma Mukai
AND THEN ...

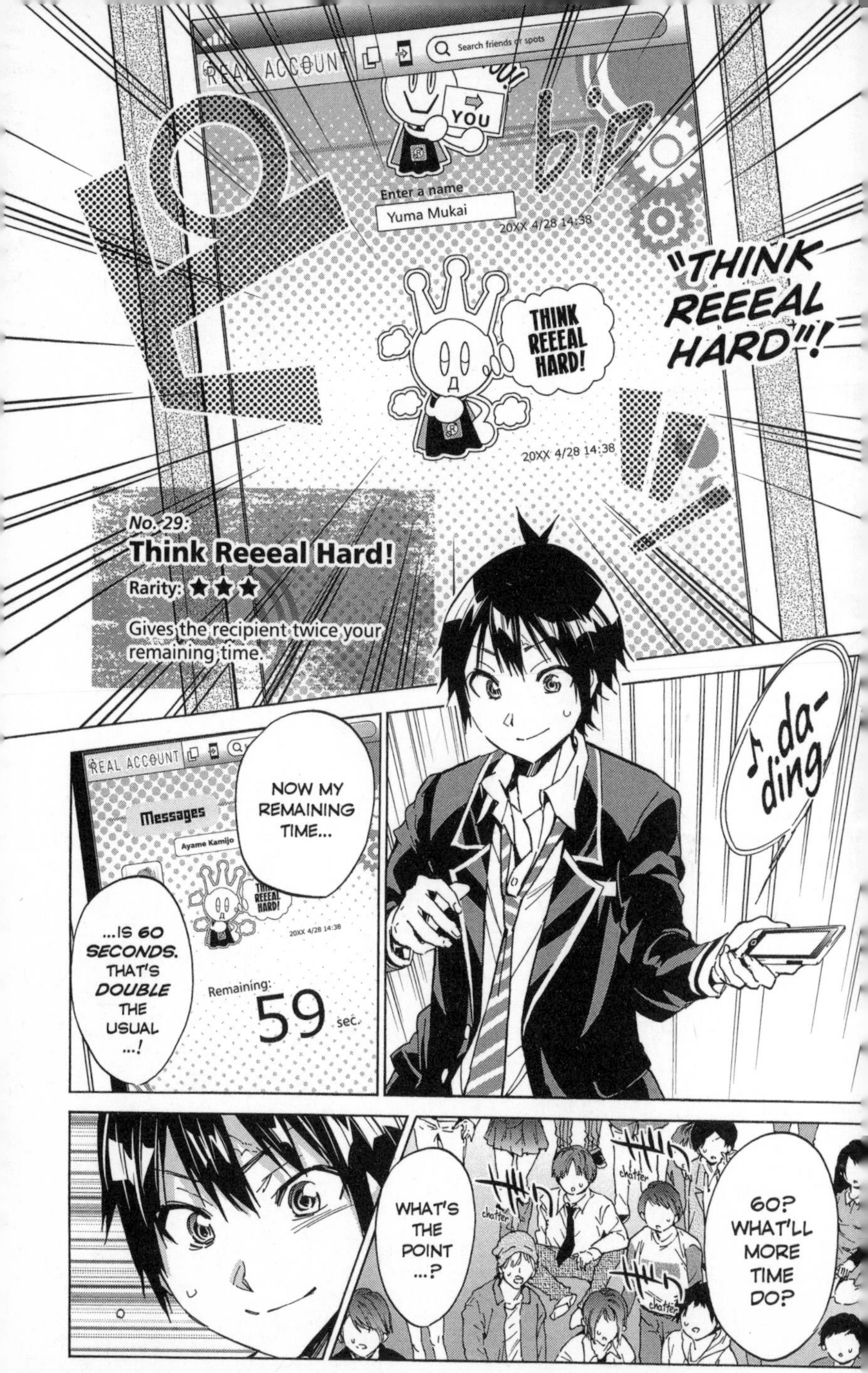
REAL ACCOUNT
Search friends or spots
YOU
Enter a name
Yuma Mukai
20XX 4/28 14:38
"THINK REEEAL HARD"!
THINK REEEAL HARD!
20XX 4/28 14:38
No. 29:
Think Reeeal Hard!
Rarity: ★★★
Gives the recipient twice your remaining time.
♪ da-ding
NOW MY REMAINING TIME...
REAL ACCOUNT
Messages
Ayame Kamijo
THINK REEEAL HARD!
20XX 4/28 14:38
Remaining:
59 sec.
...IS 60 SECONDS. THAT'S DOUBLE THE USUAL ...!
60? WHAT'LL MORE TIME DO?
chatter
chatter
chatter
WHAT'S THE POINT ...?

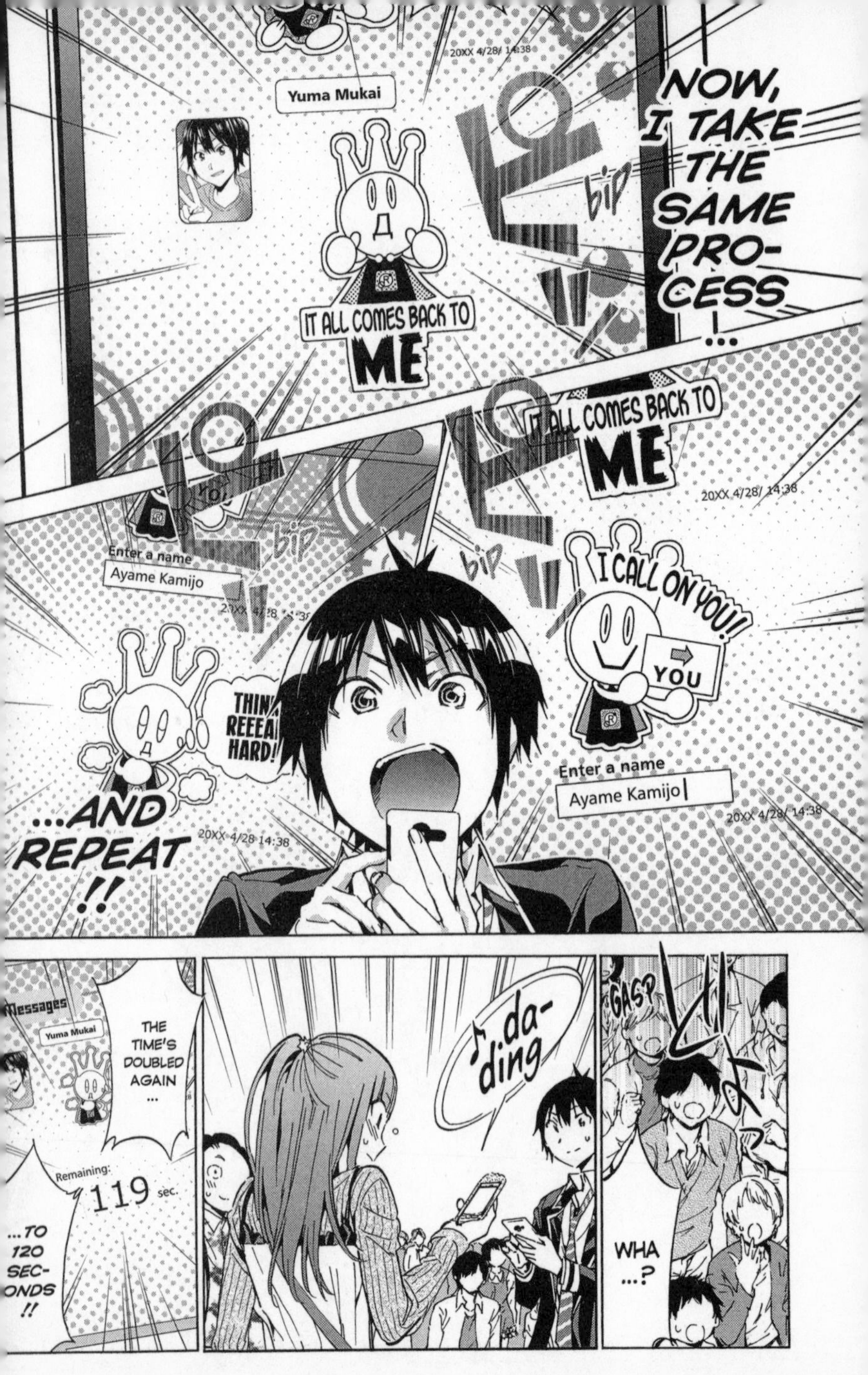
NOW, I TAKE THE SAME PROCESS...
20XX 4/28/ 14:38
Yuma Mukai
IT ALL COMES BACK TO ME
bip
IT ALL COMES BACK TO ME
20XX 4/28/ 14:38
bip
I CALL ON YOU!!
YOU
Enter a name
Ayame Kamijo
20XX 4/28/ 14:38
Enter a name
Ayame Kamijo
THIN REEEA HARD!
...AND REPEAT!!
20XX 4/28 14:38
GASP
WHA...?
da-ding
Messages
Yuma Mukai
THE TIME'S DOUBLED AGAIN...
Remaining:
119 sec.
...TO 120 SECONDS!!

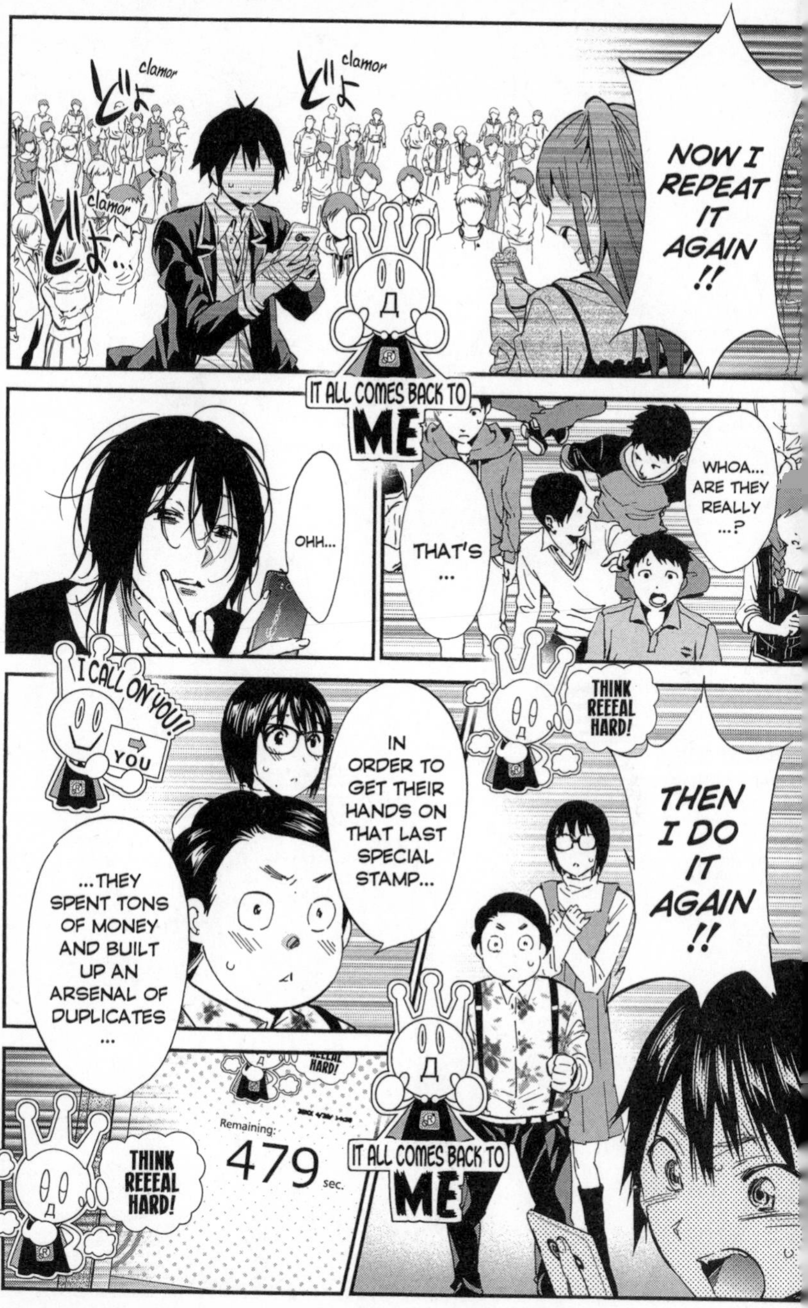
NOW I REPEAT IT AGAIN!!
どよ clamor
どよ clamor
どよ… clamor
IT ALL COMES BACK TO ME
WHOA... ARE THEY REALLY ...?
THAT'S ...
OHH...
THINK REEEAL HARD!
THEN I DO IT AGAIN!!
IN ORDER TO GET THEIR HANDS ON THAT LAST SPECIAL STAMP...
...THEY SPENT TONS OF MONEY AND BUILT UP AN ARSENAL OF DUPLICATES ...
I CALL ON YOU!!
YOU
IT ALL COMES BACK TO ME
Remaining: 479 sec.
THINK REEEAL HARD!

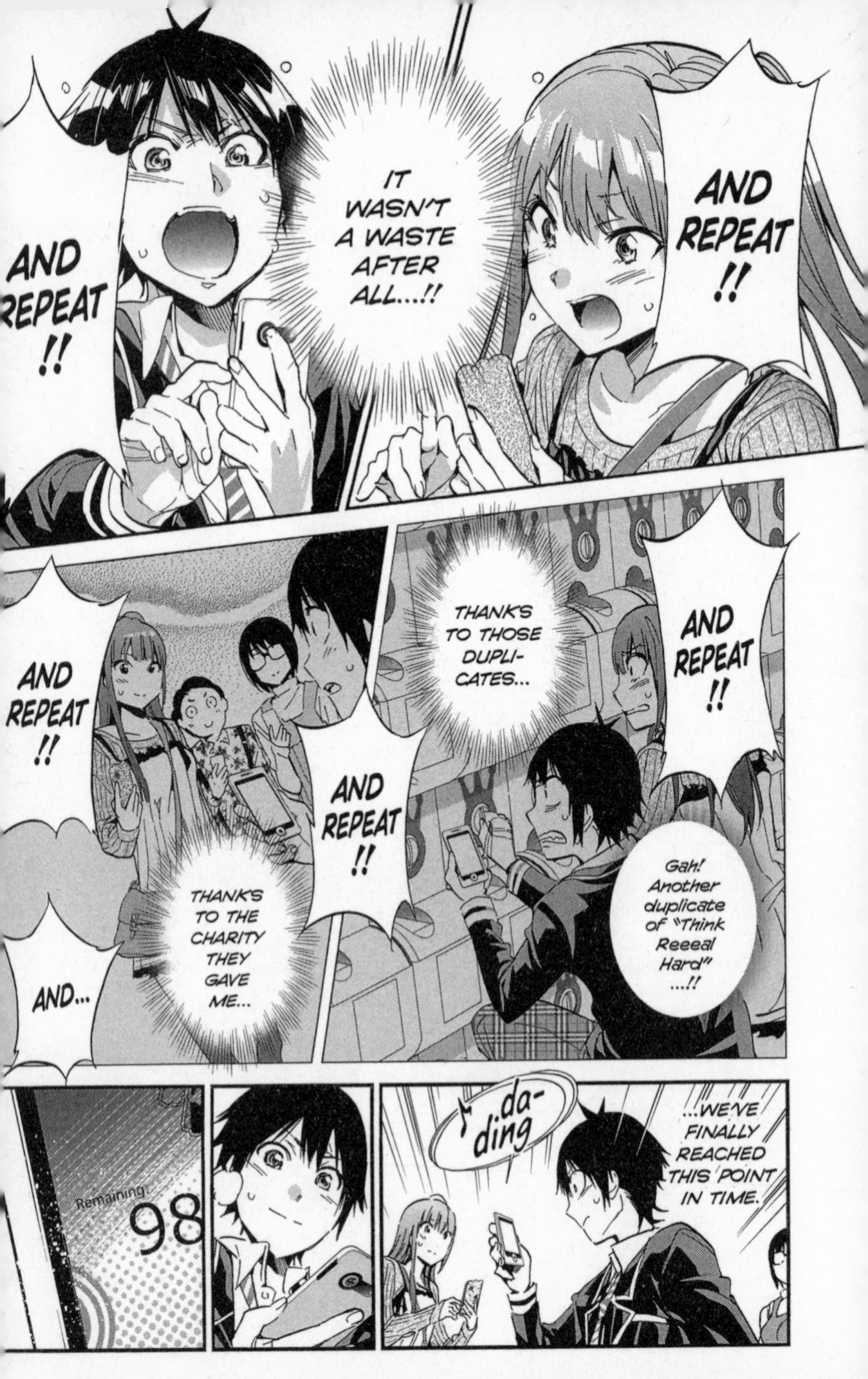
AND REPEAT!!
IT WASN'T A WASTE AFTER ALL...!!
AND REPEAT!!
AND REPEAT!!
THANKS TO THOSE DUPLICATES...
Gah! Another duplicate of "Think Reeeal Hard"...!!
AND REPEAT!!
AND REPEAT!!
THANKS TO THE CHARITY THEY GAVE ME...
AND...
da-ding
...WE'VE FINALLY REACHED THIS POINT IN TIME.
Remaining: 98

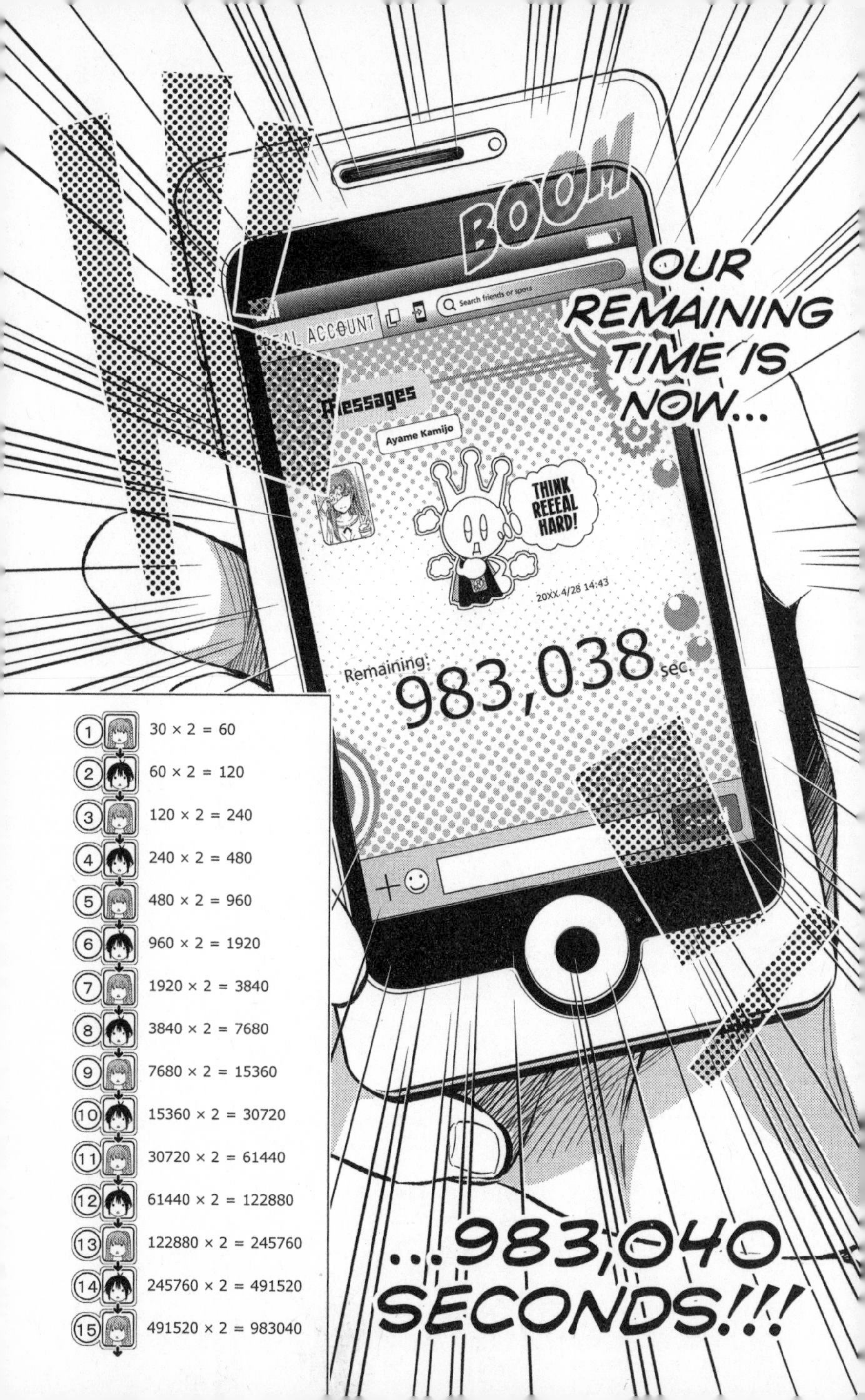
OUR REMAINING TIME IS NOW...
BOOM
EAL ACCOUNT
Search friends or spots
Messages
Ayame Kamijo
THINK REEEAL HARD!
20XX 4/28 14:43
Remaining: 983,038 sec.
...983,040 SECONDS!!!
1 30 × 2 = 60
2 60 × 2 = 120
3 120 × 2 = 240
4 240 × 2 = 480
5 480 × 2 = 960
6 960 × 2 = 1920
7 1920 × 2 = 3840
8 3840 × 2 = 7680
9 7680 × 2 = 15360
10 15360 × 2 = 30720
11 30720 × 2 = 61440
12 61440 × 2 = 122880
13 122880 × 2 = 245760
14 245760 × 2 = 491520
15 491520 × 2 = 983040

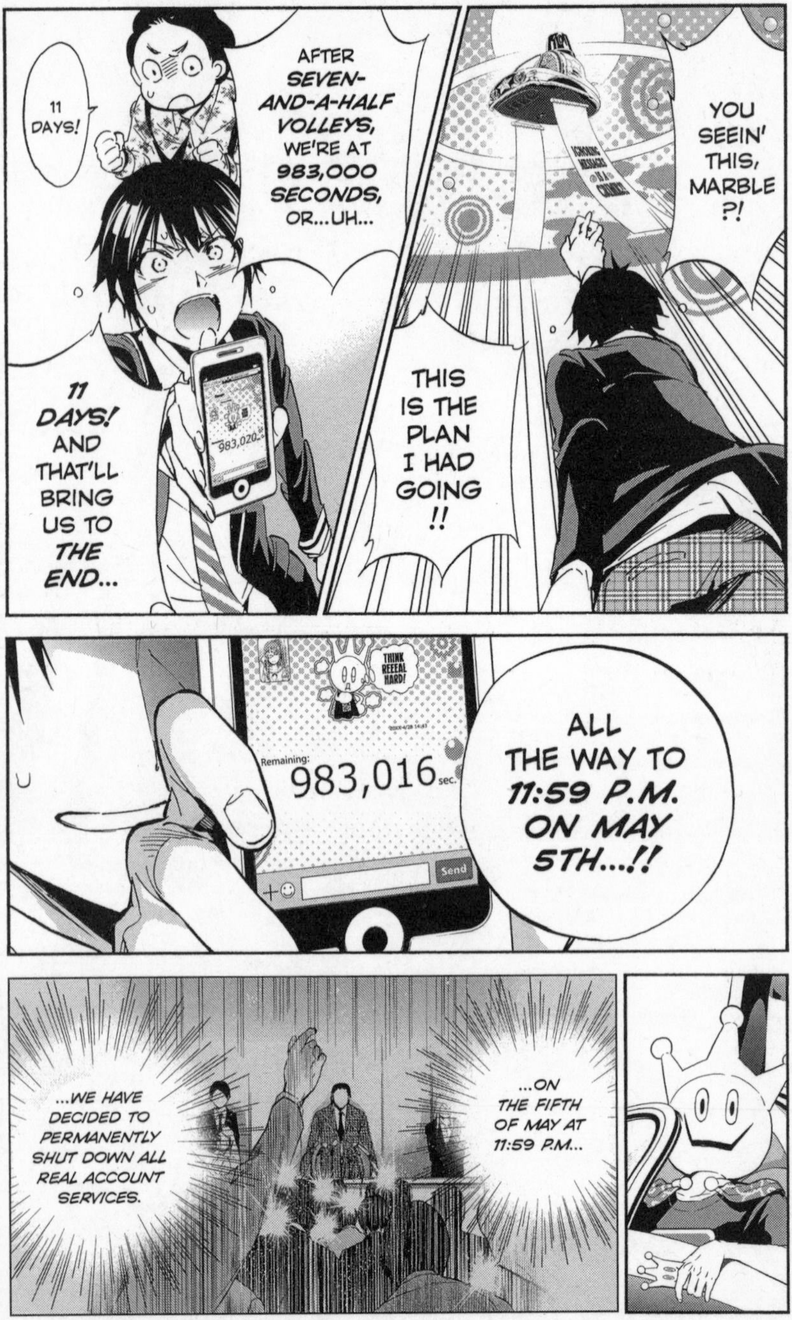
YOU SEEIN' THIS, MARBLE?!
THIS IS THE PLAN I HAD GOING!!
AFTER SEVEN-AND-A-HALF VOLLEYS, WE'RE AT 983,000 SECONDS, OR...UH...
11 DAYS!
11 DAYS! AND THAT'LL BRING US TO THE END...
983,020
THINK REEEAL HARD!
Remaining: 983,016 sec.
Send
ALL THE WAY TO 11:59 P.M. ON MAY 5TH...!!
...ON THE FIFTH OF MAY AT 11:59 P.M...
...WE HAVE DECIDED TO PERMANENTLY SHUT DOWN ALL REAL ACCOUNT SERVICES.

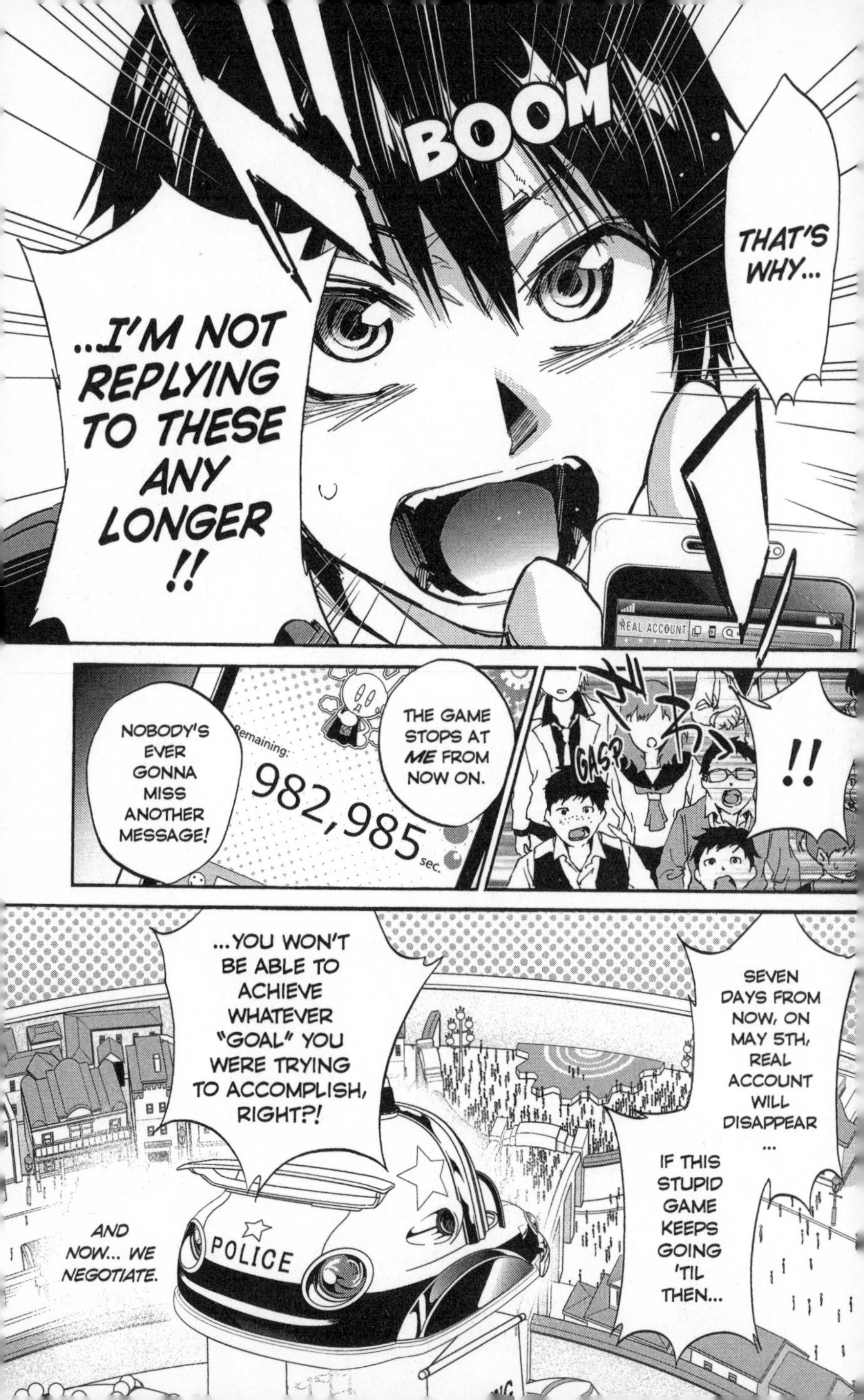
THAT'S WHY...
BOOM
...I'M NOT REPLYING TO THESE ANY LONGER !!
REAL ACCOUNT
!!
GASP
THE GAME STOPS AT *ME* FROM NOW ON.
NOBODY'S EVER GONNA MISS ANOTHER MESSAGE!
Remaining:
982,985 sec.
SEVEN DAYS FROM NOW, ON MAY 5TH, REAL ACCOUNT WILL DISAPPEAR ...
IF THIS STUPID GAME KEEPS GOING 'TIL THEN...
...YOU WON'T BE ABLE TO ACHIEVE WHATEVER "GOAL" YOU WERE TRYING TO ACCOMPLISH, RIGHT?!
POLICE
AND NOW... WE NEGOTIATE.

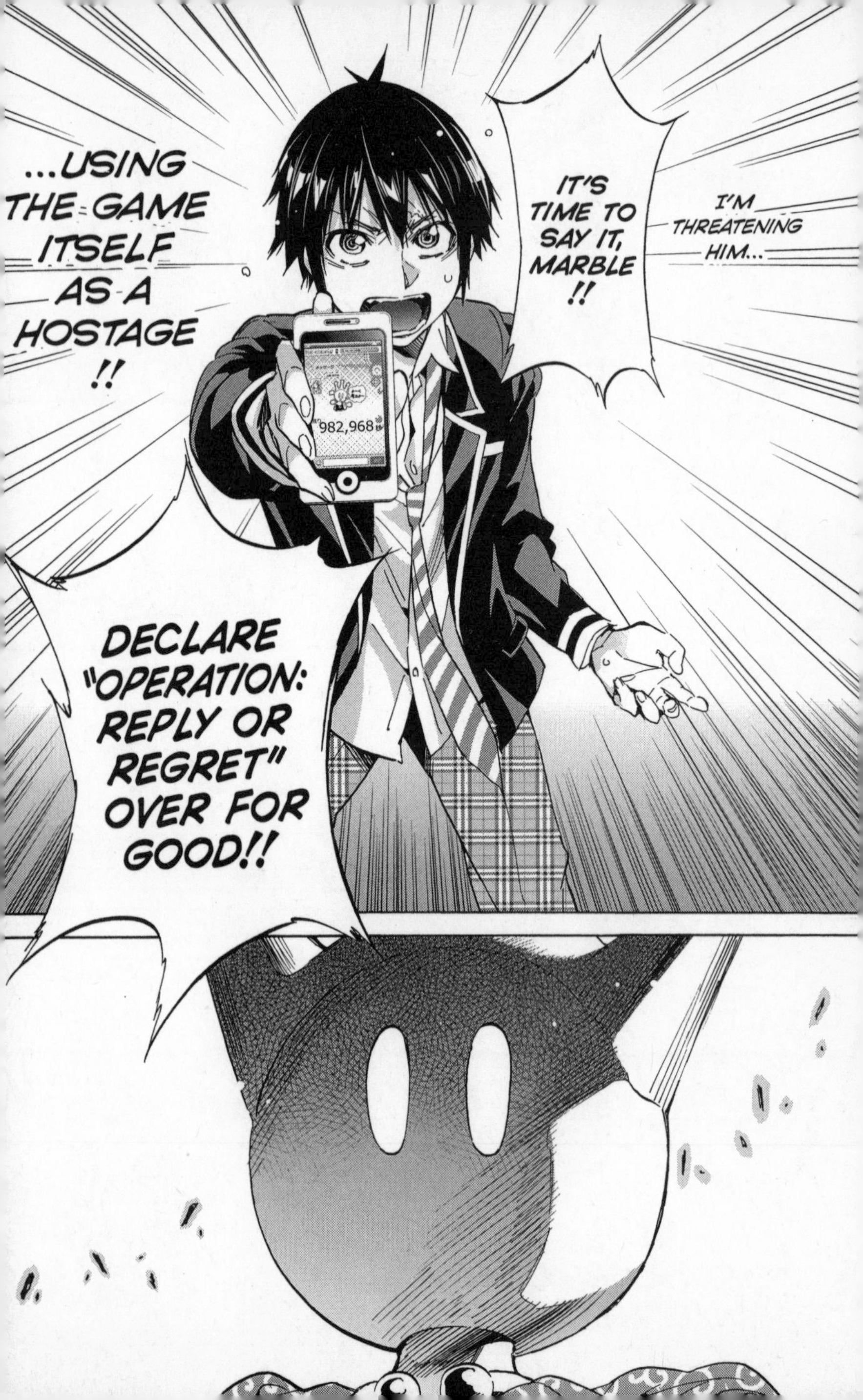
I'M THREATENING HIM...
IT'S TIME TO SAY IT, MARBLE!!
...USING THE GAME ITSELF AS A HOSTAGE!!
982,968
DECLARE "OPERATION: REPLY OR REGRET" OVER FOR GOOD!!

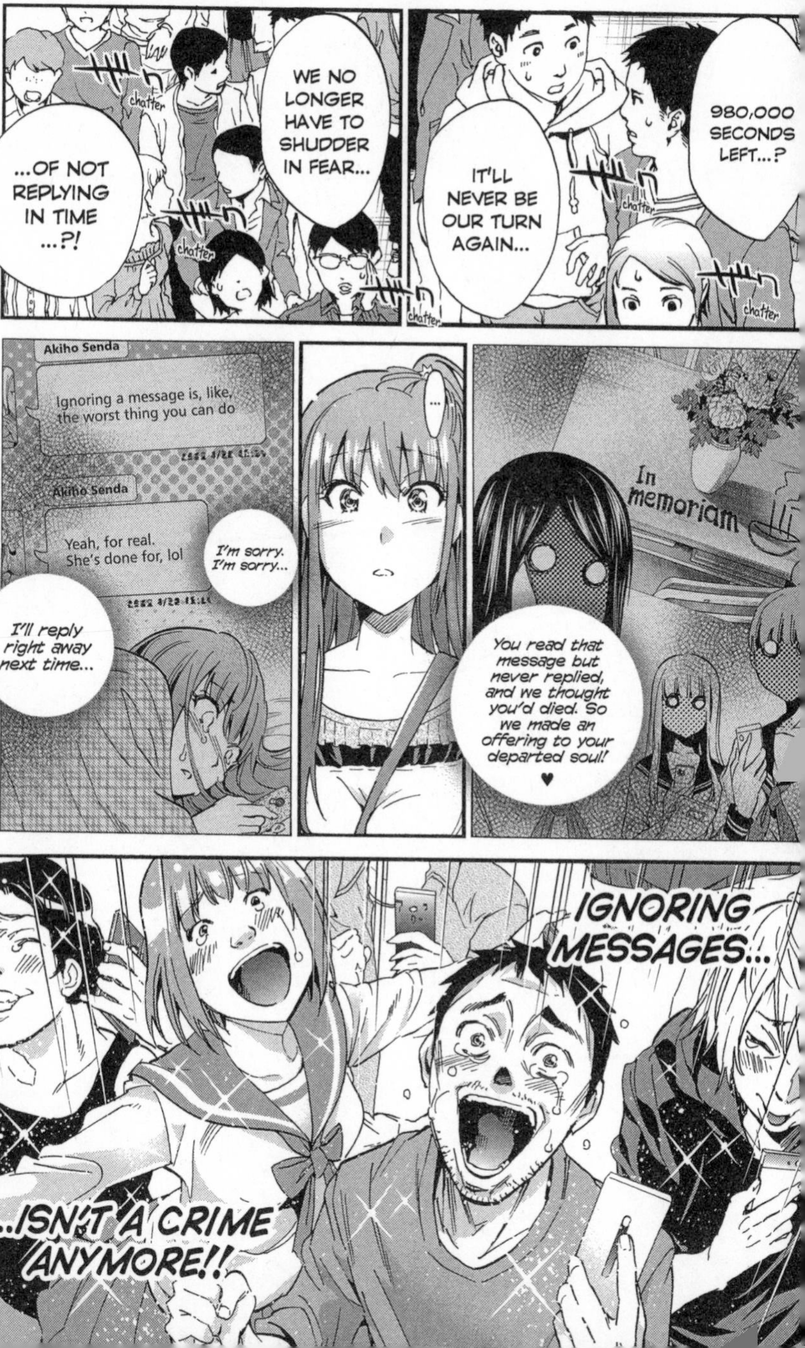
980,000 SECONDS LEFT...?
IT'LL NEVER BE OUR TURN AGAIN...
chatter
chatter
chatter
WE NO LONGER HAVE TO SHUDDER IN FEAR...
...OF NOT REPLYING IN TIME ...?!
chatter
chatter
chatter
In memoriam
You read that message but never replied, and we thought you'd died. So we made an offering to your departed soul! ♥
...
Akiho Senda
Ignoring a message is, like, the worst thing you can do
Akiho Senda
Yeah, for real. She's done for, lol
I'm sorry. I'm sorry...
I'll reply right away next time...
IGNORING MESSAGES...
...ISN'T A CRIME ANYMORE!!

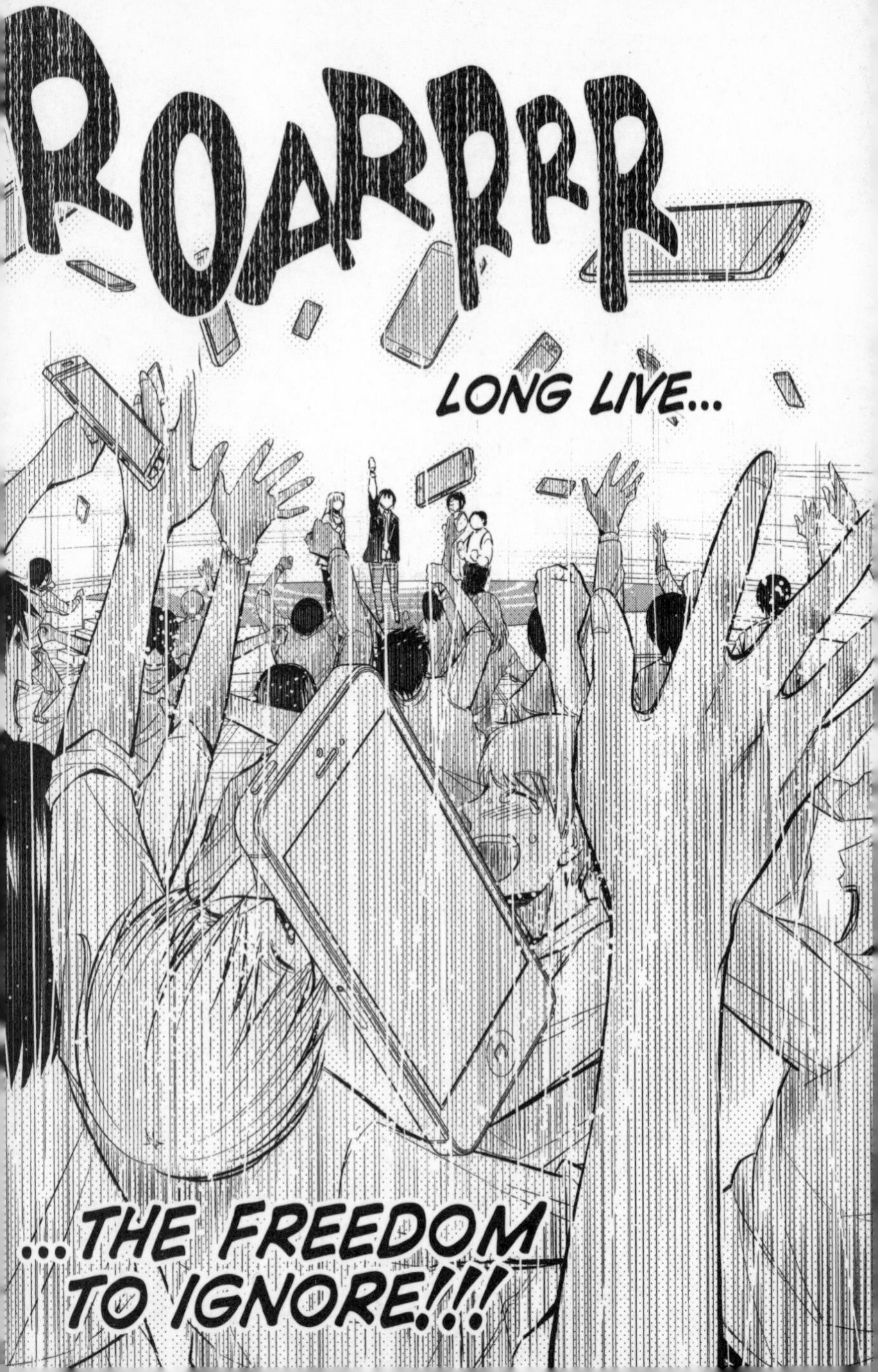
ROARRRR
LONG LIVE...
...THE FREEDOM TO IGNORE!!!

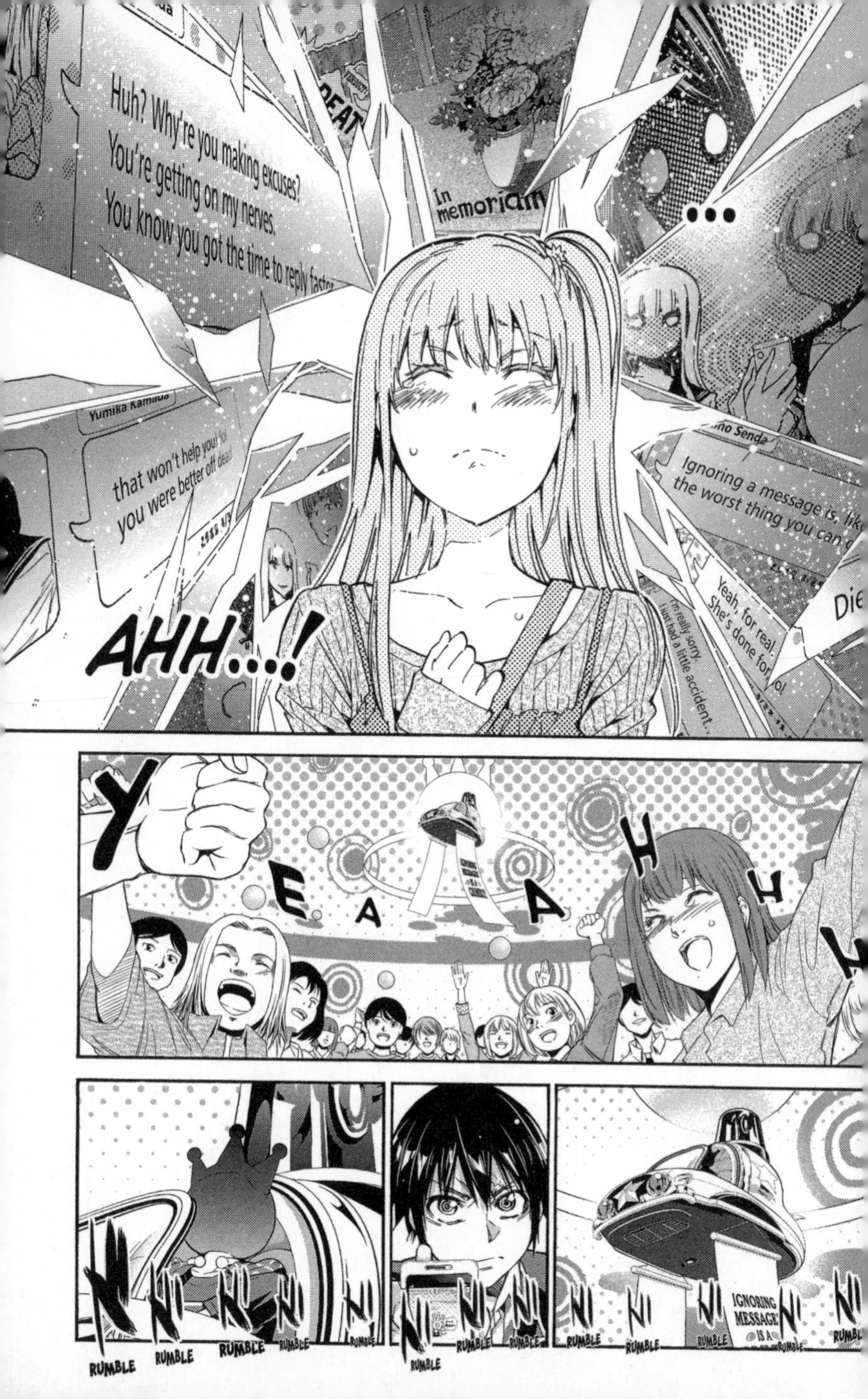
...
In memoriam
Huh? Why're you making excuses? You're getting on my nerves. You know you got the time to reply
Ignoring a message is, like, the worst thing you can
Die
Yeah, for real. She's done for lol
I'm really sorry. I just had a little accident.
Yumika Kamada
that won't help your
you were better off dead
AHH...!
YEAAHHH
RUMBLE RUMBLE RUMBLE RUMBLE
IGNORING MESSAGES IS A
RUMBLE RUMBLE RUMBLE RUMBLE
RUMBLE RUMBLE RUMBLE
RUMBLE RUMBLE RUMBLE RUMBLE RUMBLE

HE'S PLAYING CAT'S CRADLE...

...?

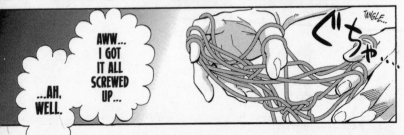

AWW... I GOT IT ALL SCREWED UP...

...AH, WELL.

TANGLE...

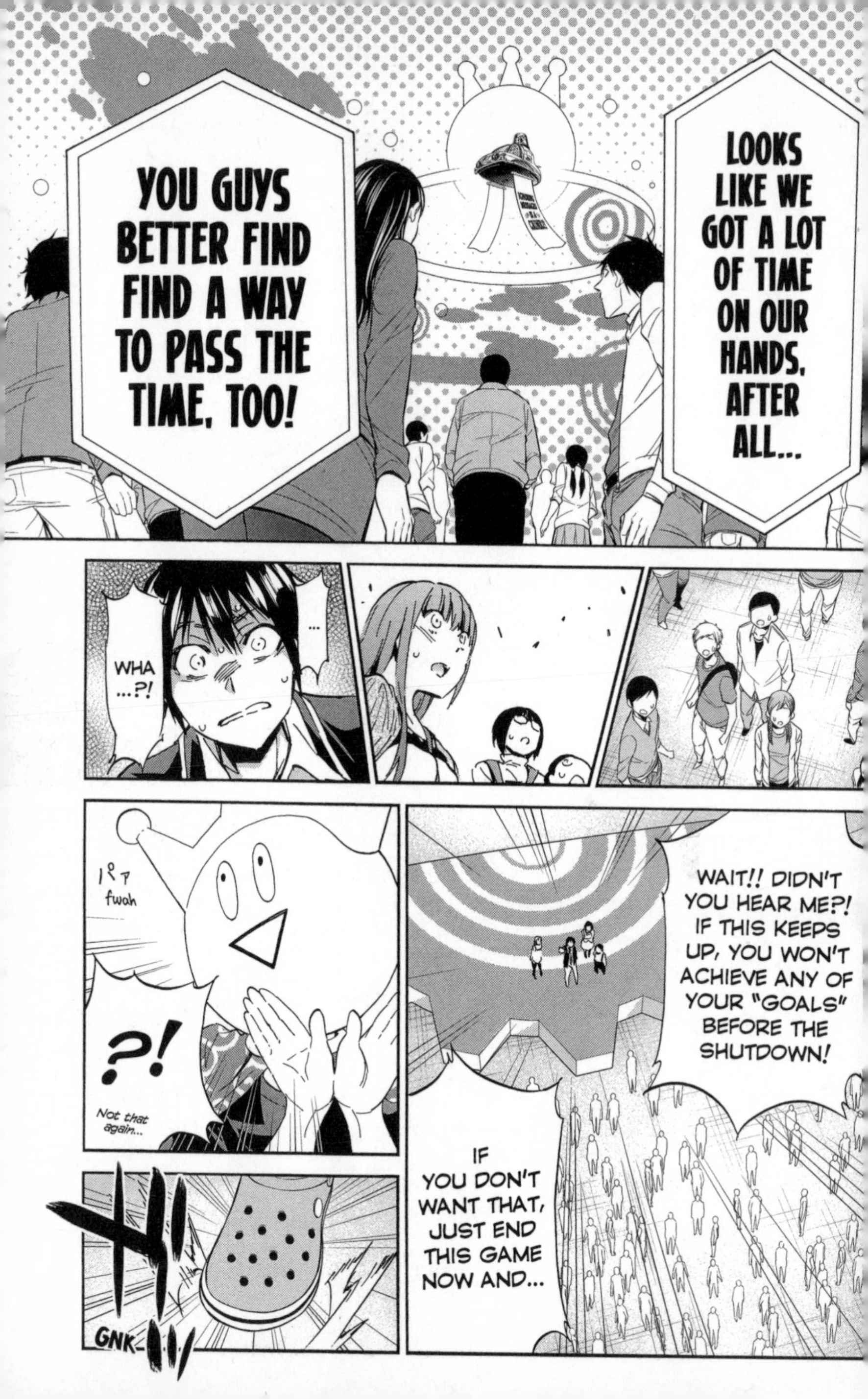
LOOKS LIKE WE GOT A LOT OF TIME ON OUR HANDS, AFTER ALL...
YOU GUYS BETTER FIND FIND A WAY TO PASS THE TIME, TOO!
...
WHA ...?!
WAIT!! DIDN'T YOU HEAR ME?! IF THIS KEEPS UP, YOU WON'T ACHIEVE ANY OF YOUR "GOALS" BEFORE THE SHUTDOWN!
IF YOU DON'T WANT THAT, JUST END THIS GAME NOW AND...
パァ
fwah
?!
Not that again...
GNK

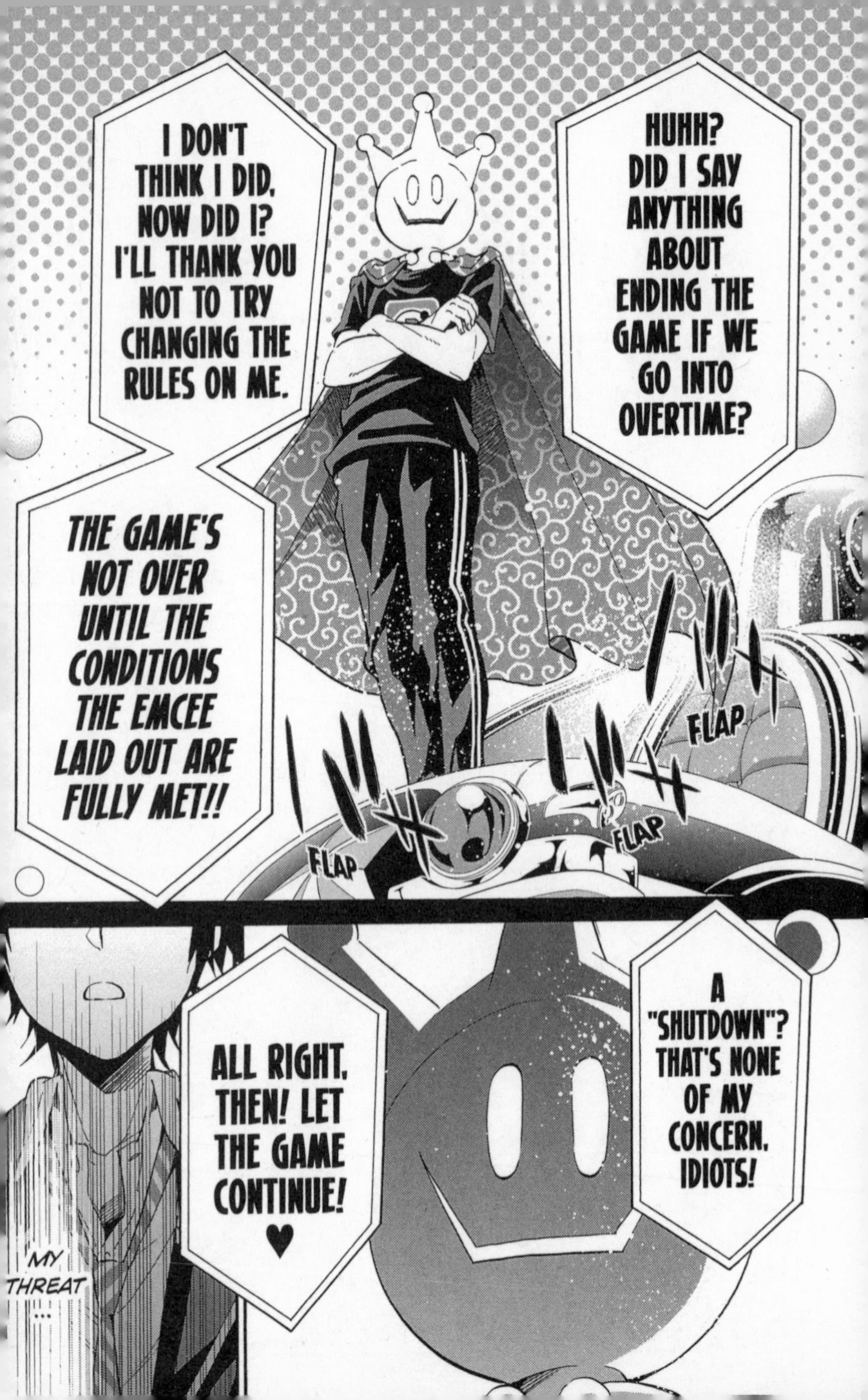
HUHH? DID I SAY ANYTHING ABOUT ENDING THE GAME IF WE GO INTO OVERTIME?
I DON'T THINK I DID, NOW DID I? I'LL THANK YOU NOT TO TRY CHANGING THE RULES ON ME.
THE GAME'S NOT OVER UNTIL THE CONDITIONS THE EMCEE LAID OUT ARE FULLY MET!!
FLAP
FLAP
FLAP
A "SHUTDOWN"? THAT'S NONE OF MY CONCERN, IDIOTS!
ALL RIGHT, THEN! LET THE GAME CONTINUE! ♥
MY THREAT...

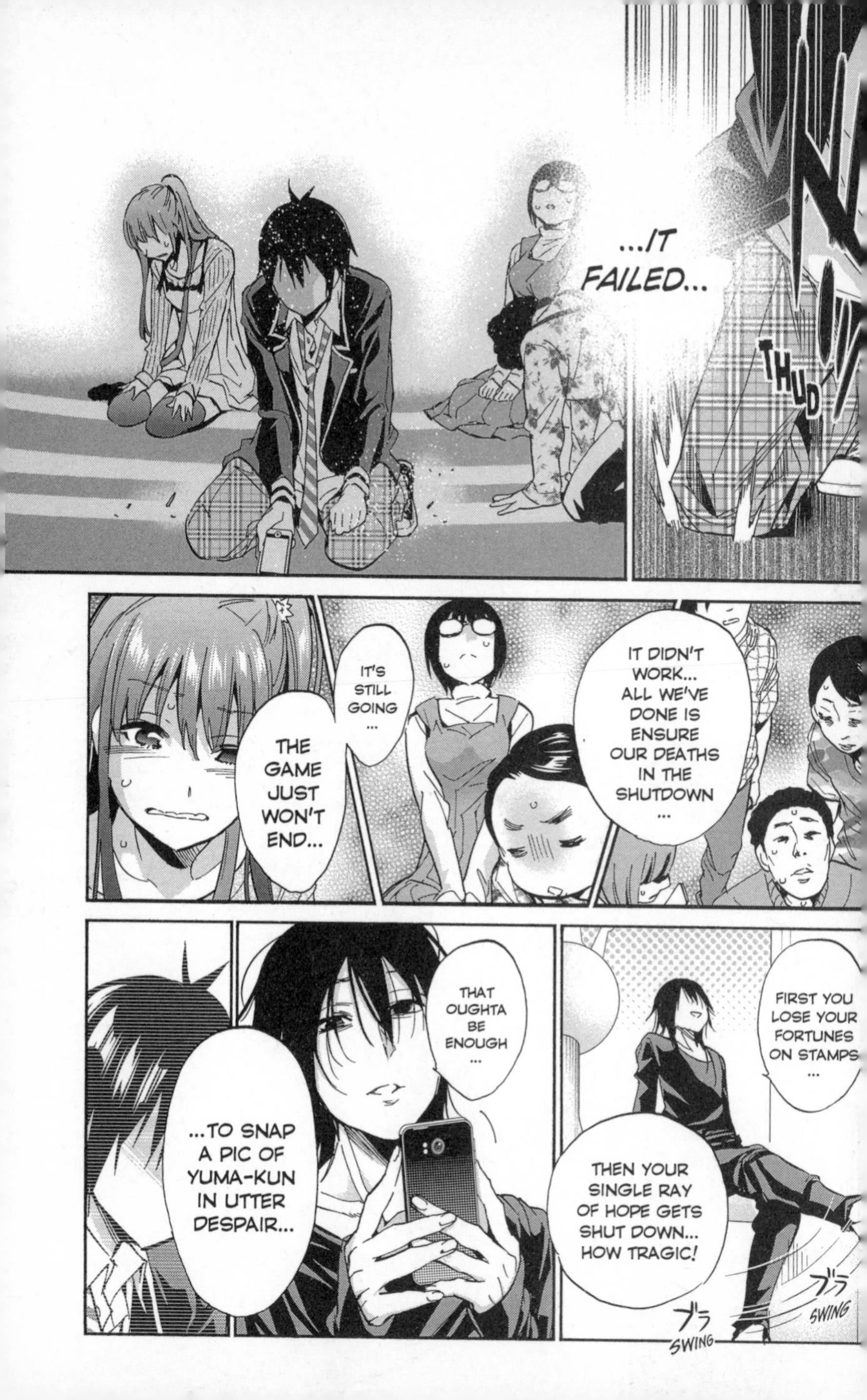
THUD
...IT FAILED...
IT DIDN'T WORK... ALL WE'VE DONE IS ENSURE OUR DEATHS IN THE SHUTDOWN ...
IT'S STILL GOING ...
THE GAME JUST WON'T END...
FIRST YOU LOSE YOUR FORTUNES ON STAMPS ...
THEN YOUR SINGLE RAY OF HOPE GETS SHUT DOWN... HOW TRAGIC!
SWING
SWING
THAT OUGHTA BE ENOUGH ...
...TO SNAP A PIC OF YUMA-KUN IN UTTER DESPAIR...

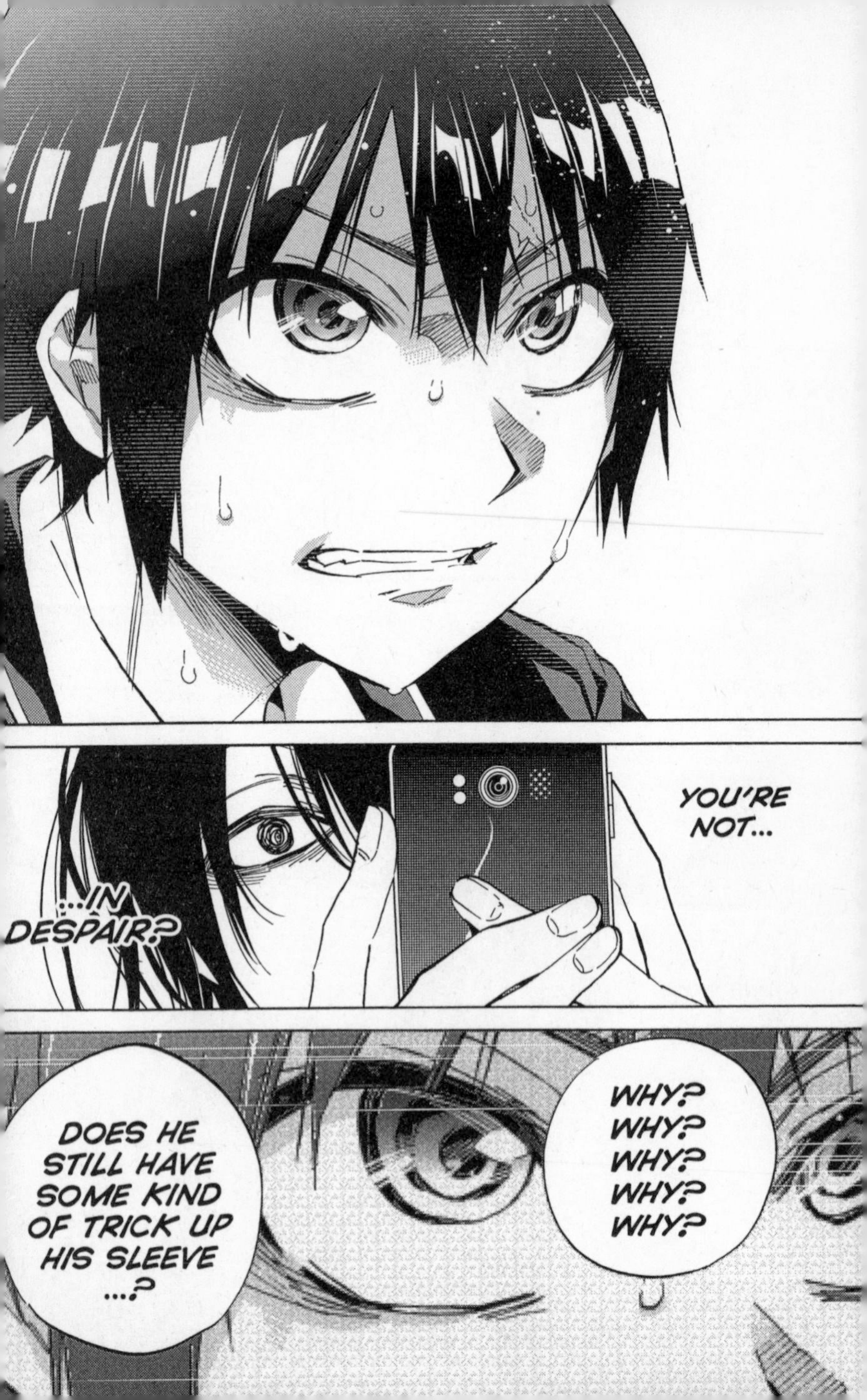
YOU'RE NOT...
...IN DESPAIR?
WHY? WHY? WHY? WHY? WHY?
DOES HE STILL HAVE SOME KIND OF TRICK UP HIS SLEEVE ...?

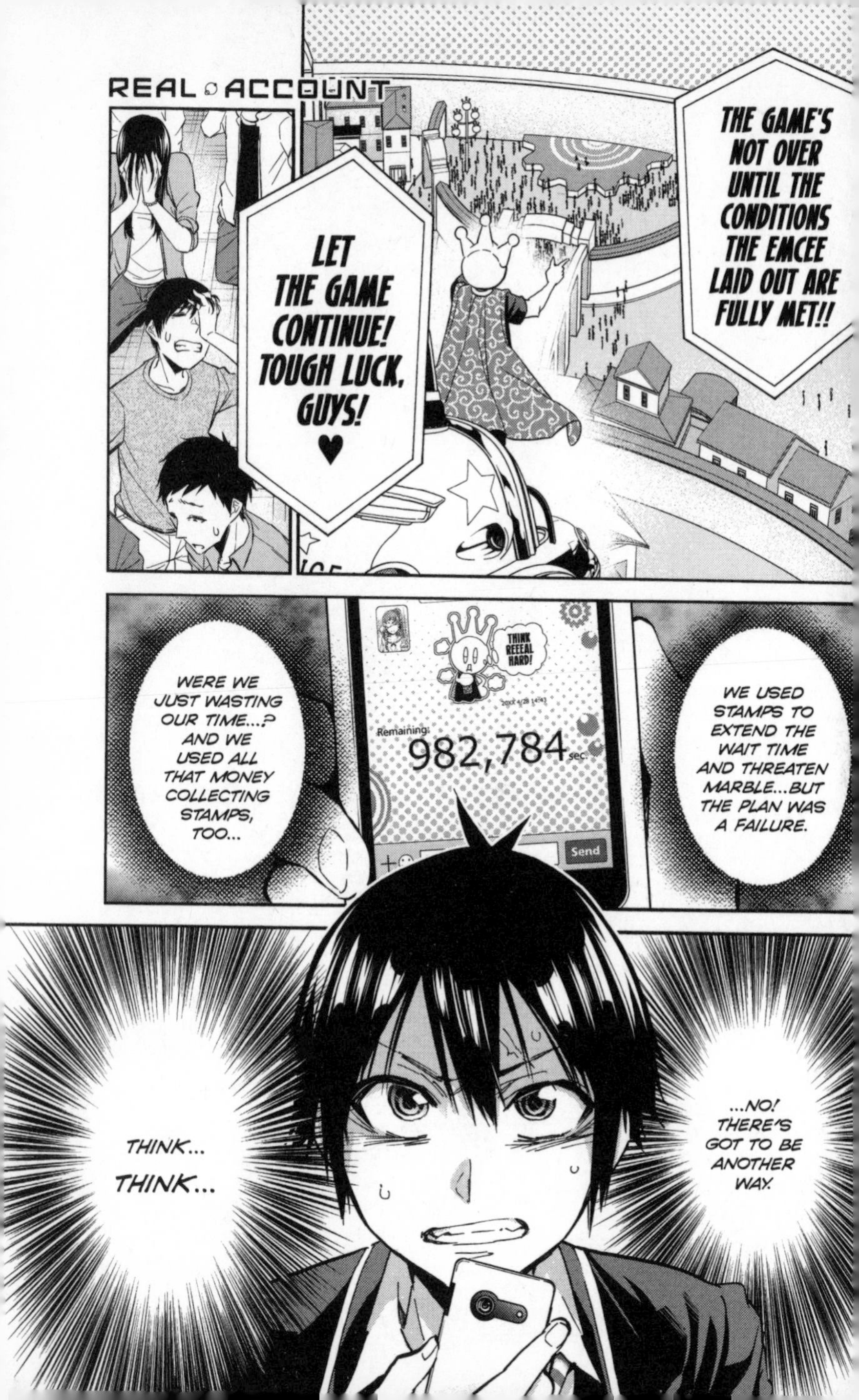
THE GAME'S NOT OVER UNTIL THE CONDITIONS THE EMCEE LAID OUT ARE FULLY MET!!
LET THE GAME CONTINUE! TOUGH LUCK, GUYS! ♥
THINK REEEAL HARD!
Remaining: 982,784 sec.
Send
WE USED STAMPS TO EXTEND THE WAIT TIME AND THREATEN MARBLE...BUT THE PLAN WAS A FAILURE.
WERE WE JUST WASTING OUR TIME...? AND WE USED ALL THAT MONEY COLLECTING STAMPS, TOO...
...NO! THERE'S GOT TO BE ANOTHER WAY.
THINK... THINK...

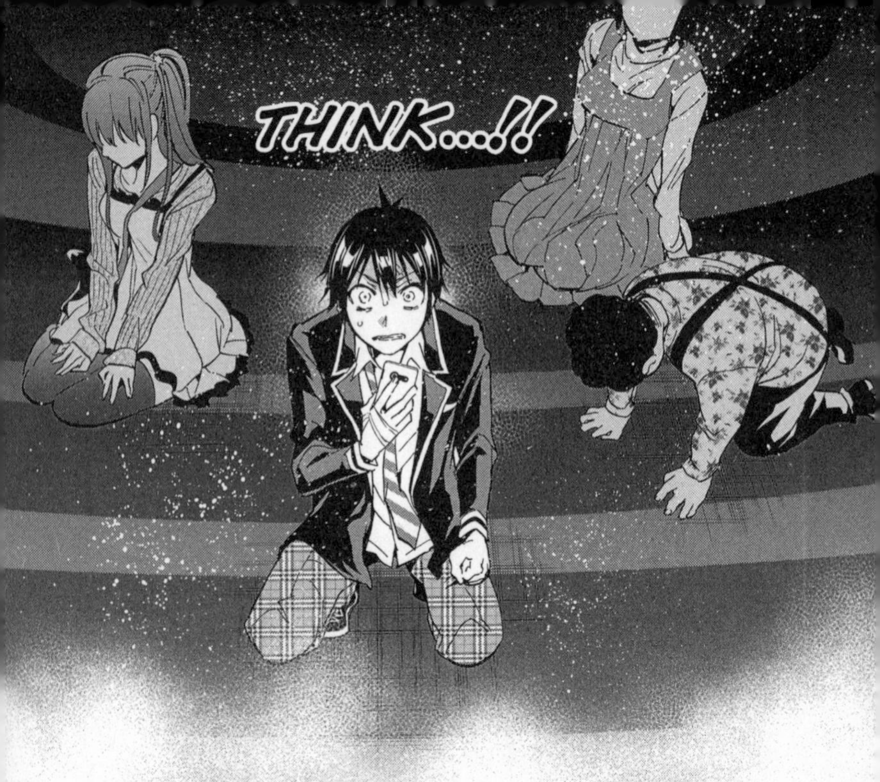
THINK...!!

ACCOUNT 21 Back to the Beginning

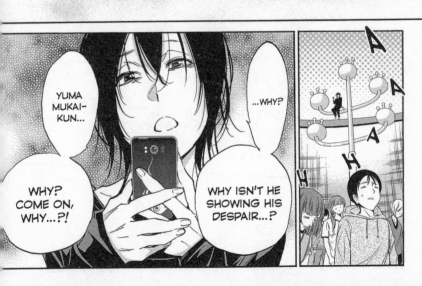

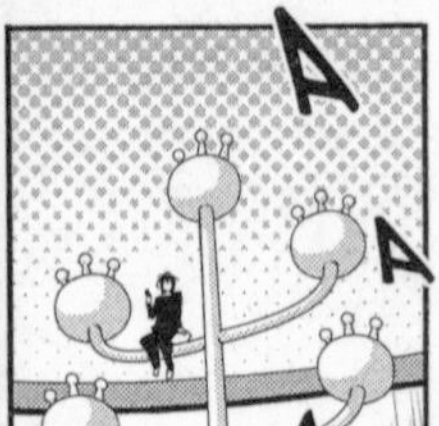
AAAHH

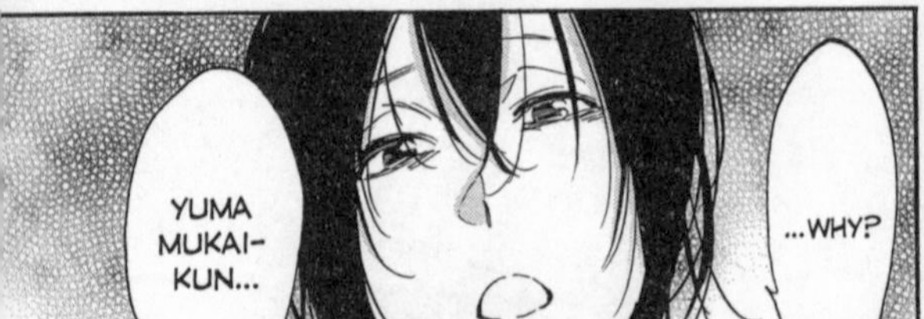
...WHY?
YUMA MUKAI-KUN...
WHY ISN'T HE SHOWING HIS DESPAIR...?
WHY? COME ON, WHY...?!

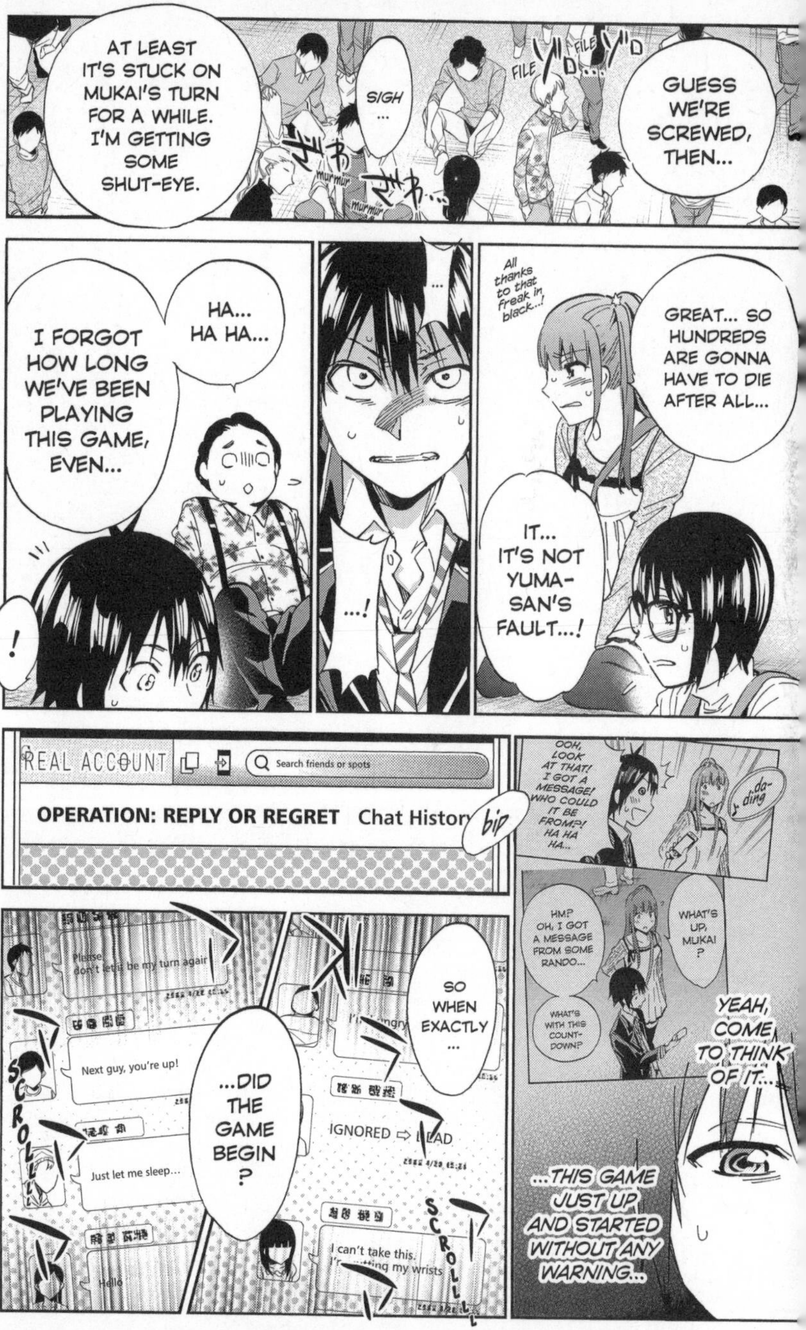
GUESS WE'RE SCREWED, THEN...
FILE
D
FILE
D
SIGH ...
murmur
murmur
AT LEAST IT'S STUCK ON MUKAI'S TURN FOR A WHILE. I'M GETTING SOME SHUT-EYE.
All thanks to that freak in black...!
GREAT... SO HUNDREDS ARE GONNA HAVE TO DIE AFTER ALL...
IT... IT'S NOT YUMA-SAN'S FAULT...!
...
...!
HA... HA HA...
I FORGOT HOW LONG WE'VE BEEN PLAYING THIS GAME, EVEN...
!
OOH, LOOK AT THAT! I GOT A MESSAGE! WHO COULD IT BE FROM?! HA HA HA...
da-ding
WHAT'S UP, MUKAI?
HM? OH, I GOT A MESSAGE FROM SOME RANDO...
WHAT'S WITH THIS COUNT-DOWN?
YEAH, COME TO THINK OF IT...
...THIS GAME JUST UP AND STARTED WITHOUT ANY WARNING...
REAL ACCOUNT
Search friends or spots
OPERATION: REPLY OR REGRET Chat History
bip
SO WHEN EXACTLY ...
IGNORED ⇨
I can't take this.
SCROLL
...DID THE GAME BEGIN ?
Next guy, you're up!
Just let me sleep...
Hello
SCROLL

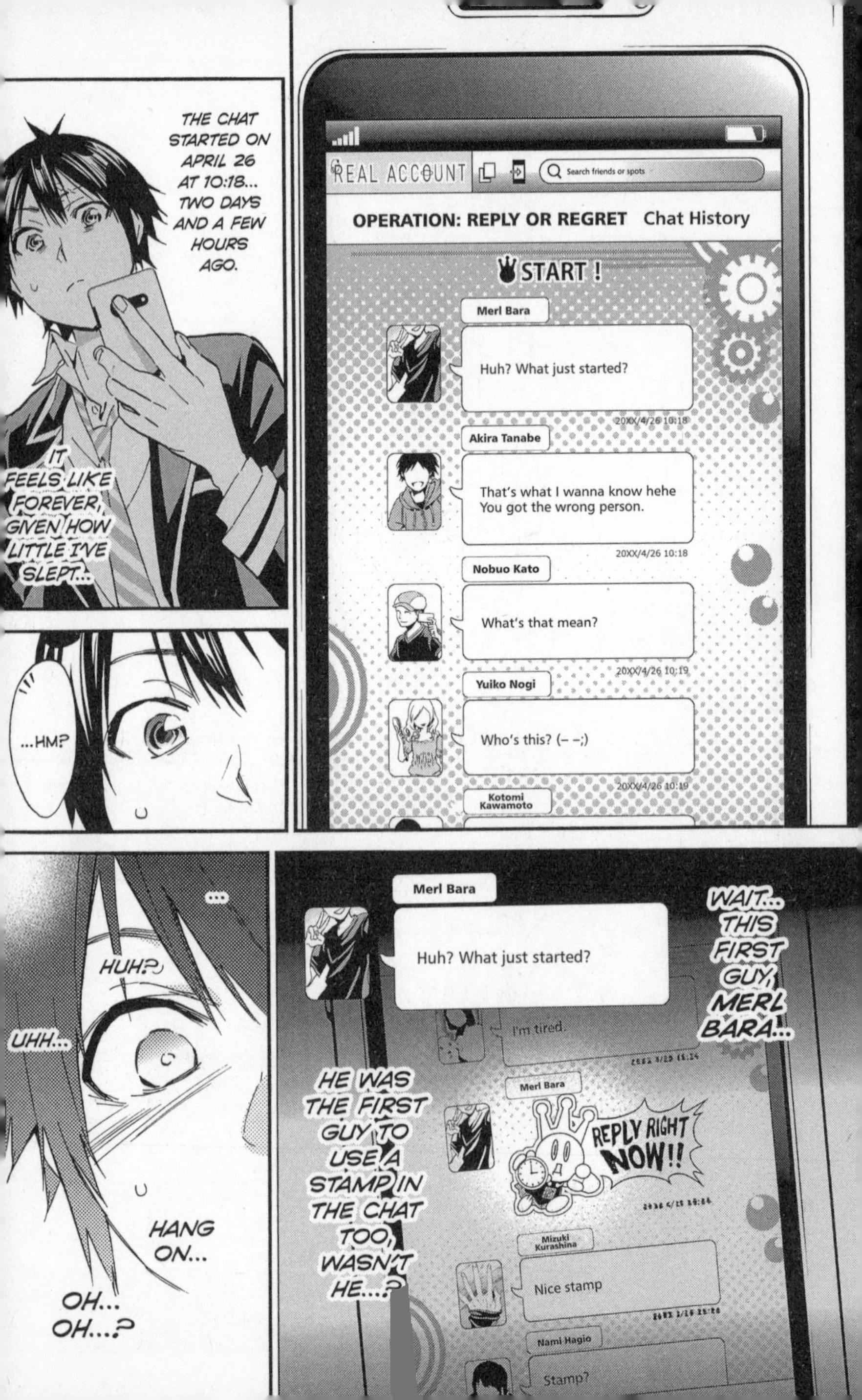
REAL ACCOUNT
Search friends or spots
OPERATION: REPLY OR REGRET Chat History
START !
Merl Bara
Huh? What just started?
20XX/4/26 10:18
Akira Tanabe
That's what I wanna know hehe
You got the wrong person.
20XX/4/26 10:18
Nobuo Kato
What's that mean?
20XX/4/26 10:19
Yuiko Nogi
Who's this? (– –;)
20XX/4/26 10:19
Kotomi Kawamoto
THE CHAT STARTED ON APRIL 26 AT 10:18... TWO DAYS AND A FEW HOURS AGO.
IT FEELS LIKE FOREVER, GIVEN HOW LITTLE I'VE SLEPT...
...HM?
WAIT... THIS FIRST GUY, MERL BARA...
Merl Bara
Huh? What just started?
I'm tired.
Merl Bara
REPLY RIGHT NOW!!
Mizuki Kurashina
Nice stamp
Nami Hagio
Stamp?
HE WAS THE FIRST GUY TO USE A STAMP IN THE CHAT TOO, WASN'T HE...?
...
HUH?
UHH...
HANG ON...
OH... OH...?

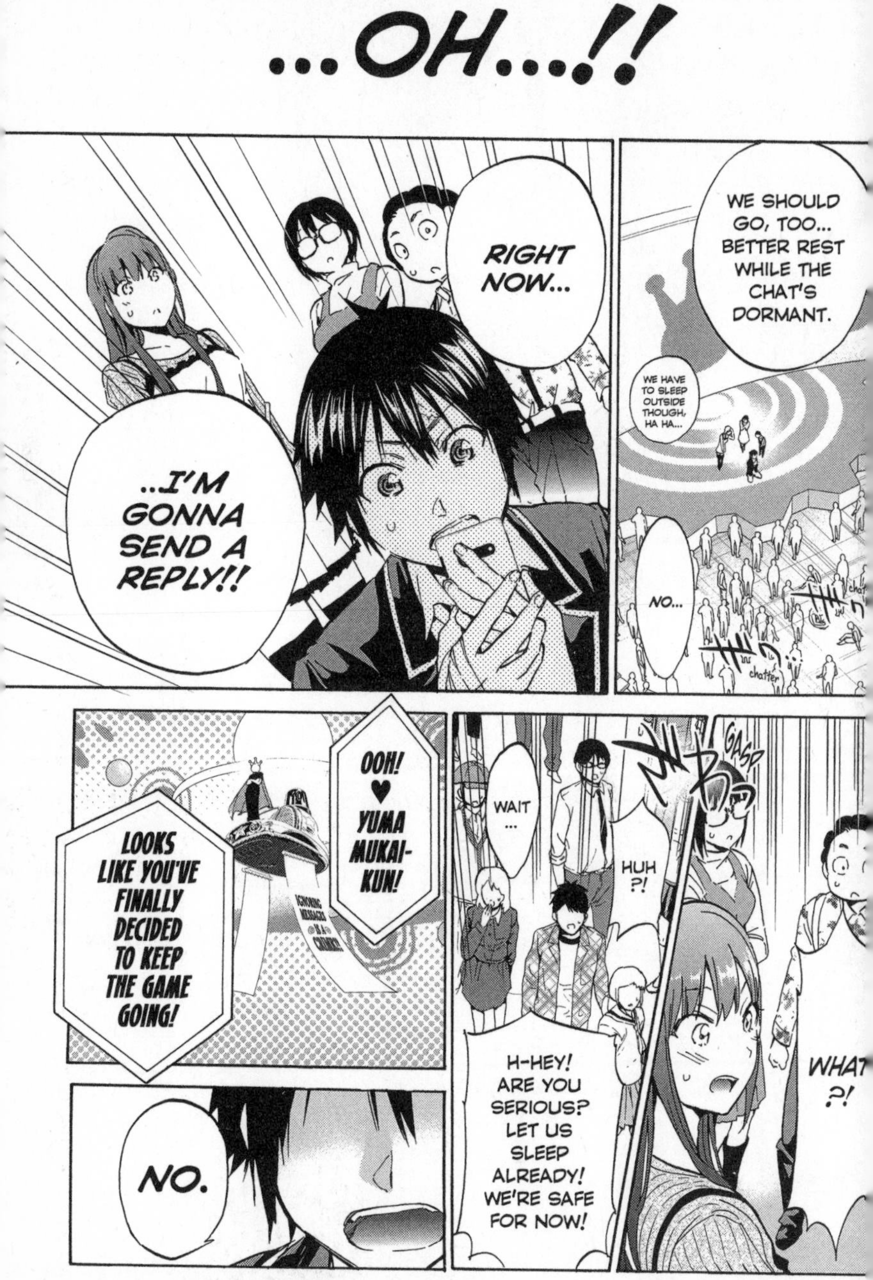
...OH...!!
WE SHOULD GO, TOO... BETTER REST WHILE THE CHAT'S DORMANT.
WE HAVE TO SLEEP OUTSIDE THOUGH, HA HA...
NO...
chatter
chatter
RIGHT NOW...
...I'M GONNA SEND A REPLY!!
GASP
WHAT?!
HUH?!
WAIT...
H-HEY! ARE YOU SERIOUS? LET US SLEEP ALREADY! WE'RE SAFE FOR NOW!
OOH! ♥ YUMA MUKAI-KUN!
LOOKS LIKE YOU'VE FINALLY DECIDED TO KEEP THE GAME GOING!
IGNORING MESSAGES IS A CRIME!!
NO.

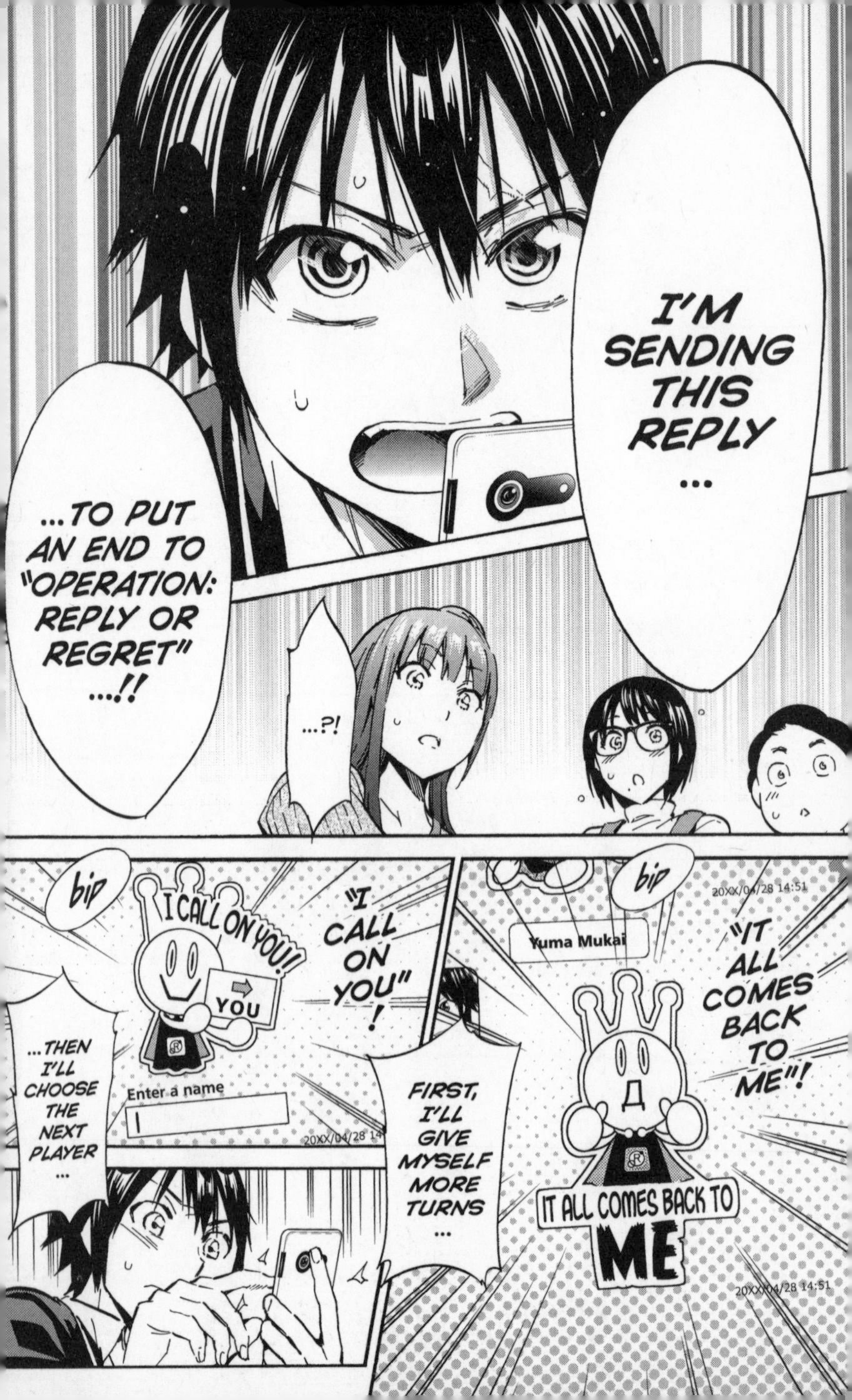
I'M SENDING THIS REPLY...
...TO PUT AN END TO "OPERATION: REPLY OR REGRET"...!!
...?!
bip
20XX/04/28 14:51
Yuma Mukai
FIRST, I'LL GIVE MYSELF MORE TURNS...
"IT ALL COMES BACK TO ME"!
IT ALL COMES BACK TO ME
20XX/04/28 14:51
bip
...THEN I'LL CHOOSE THE NEXT PLAYER...
"I CALL ON YOU"!
I CALL ON YOU!!
YOU
Enter a name
20XX/04/28 14

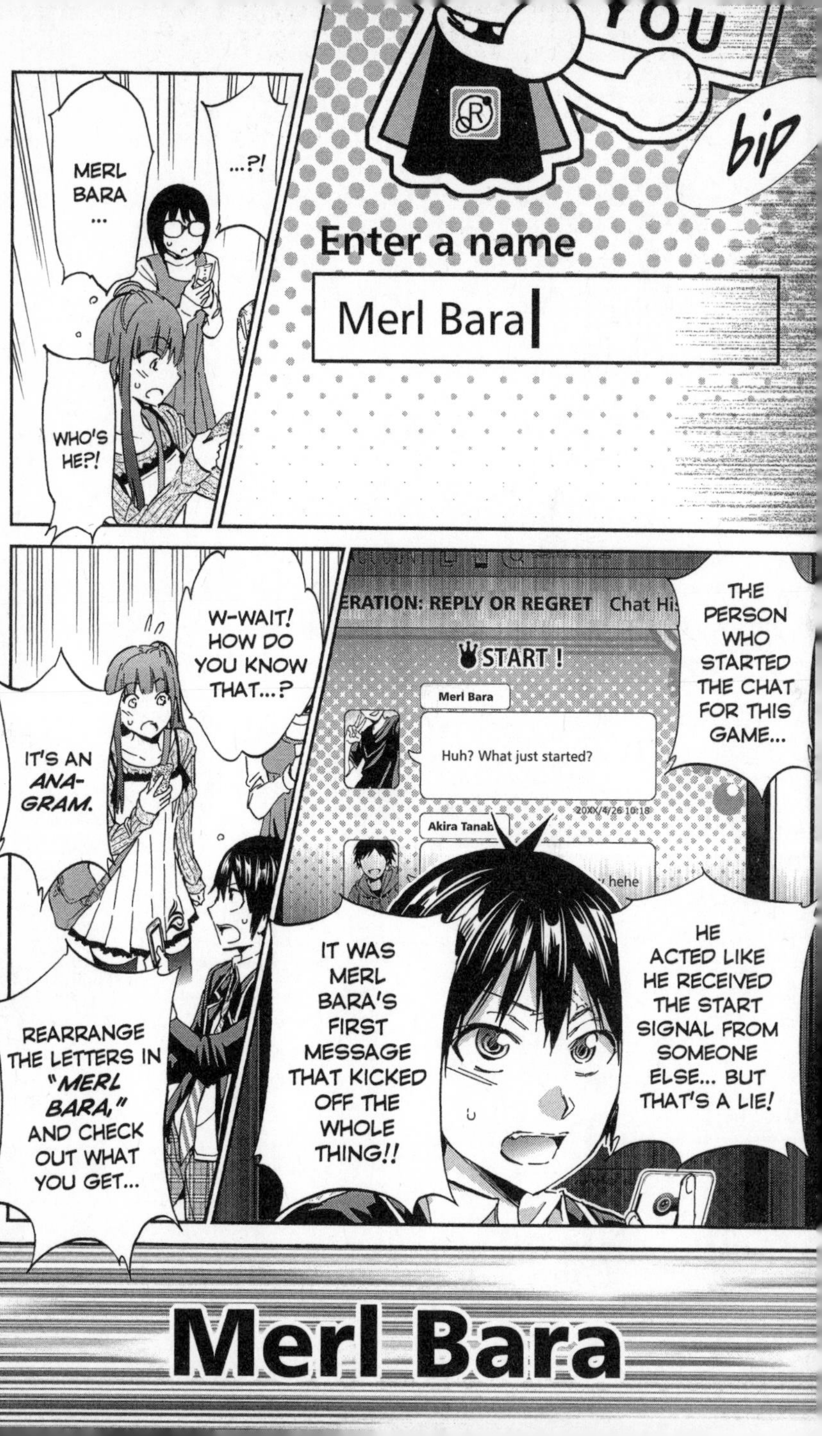
YOU
bip
Enter a name
Merl Bara
...?!
MERL BARA ...
WHO'S HE?!
ERATION: REPLY OR REGRET Chat His
START !
Merl Bara
Huh? What just started?
20XX/4/26 10:18
Akira Tanab
hehe
THE PERSON WHO STARTED THE CHAT FOR THIS GAME...
HE ACTED LIKE HE RECEIVED THE START SIGNAL FROM SOMEONE ELSE... BUT THAT'S A LIE!
IT WAS MERL BARA'S FIRST MESSAGE THAT KICKED OFF THE WHOLE THING!!
W-WAIT! HOW DO YOU KNOW THAT...?
IT'S AN ANAGRAM.
REARRANGE THE LETTERS IN "MERL BARA," AND CHECK OUT WHAT YOU GET...
Merl Bara

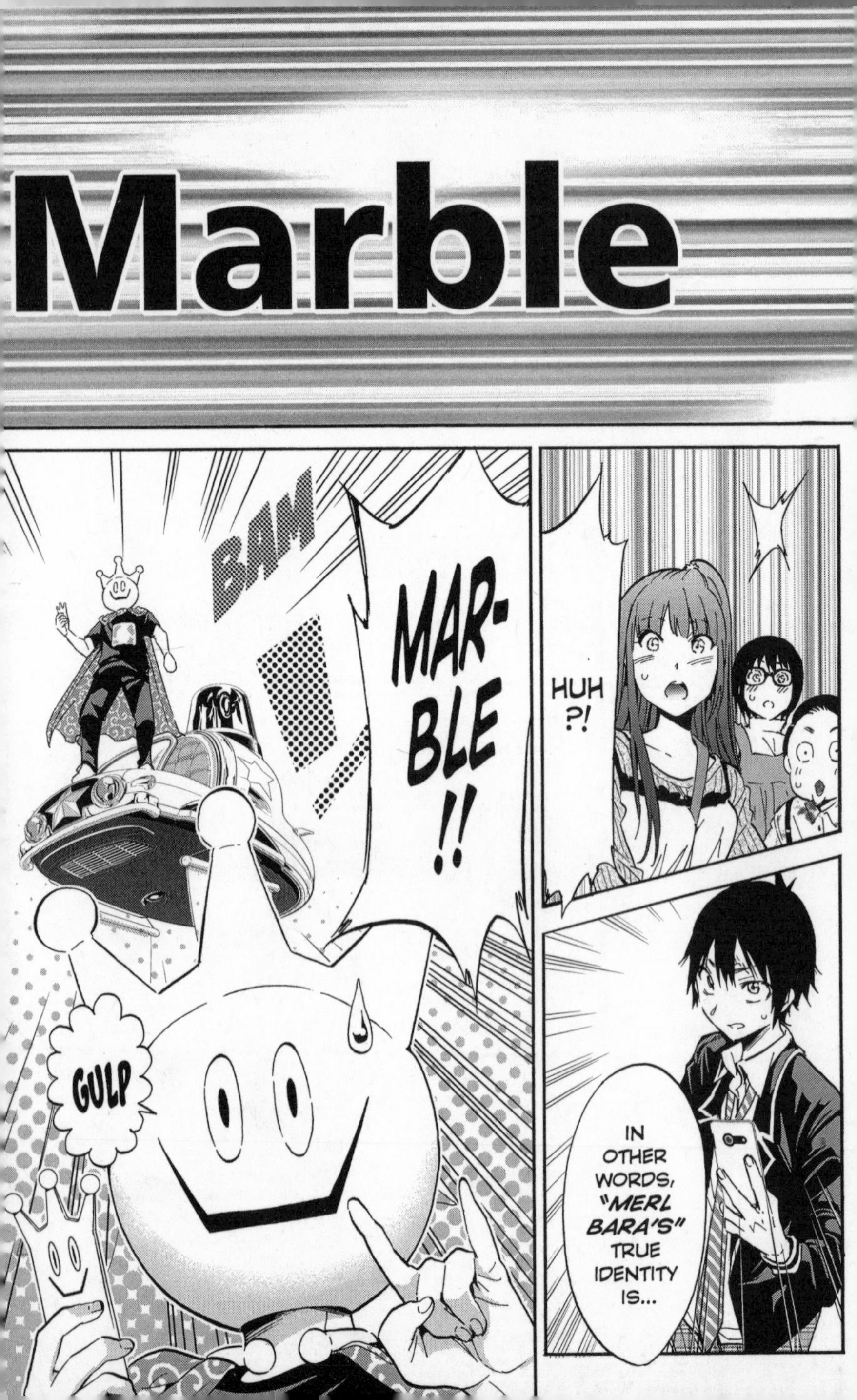
Marble
HUH ?!
IN OTHER WORDS, "MERL BARA'S" TRUE IDENTITY IS...
BAM
MAR-BLE!!
GULP

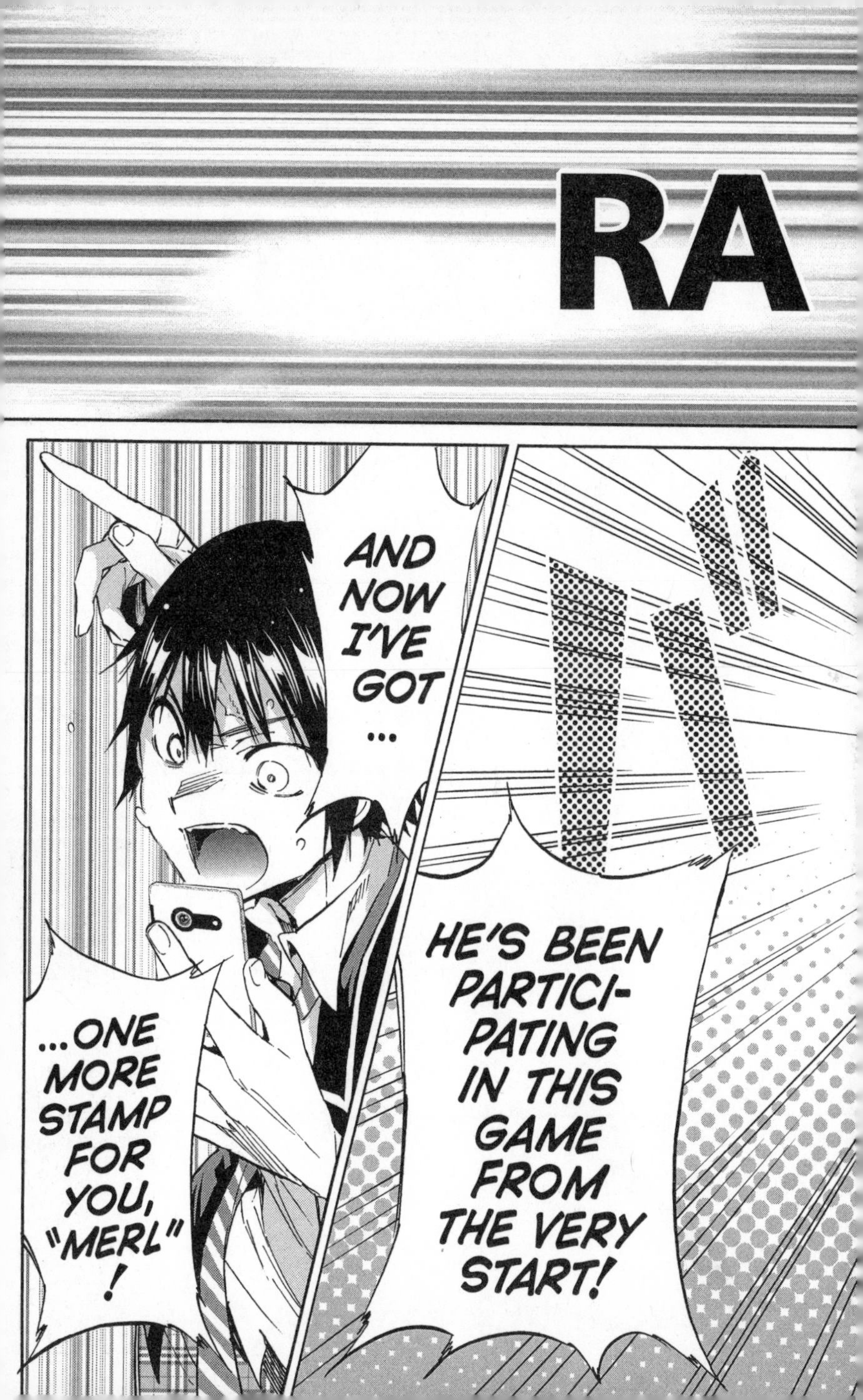
RA
HE'S BEEN PARTICI-PATING IN THIS GAME FROM THE VERY START!
AND NOW I'VE GOT ...
...ONE MORE STAMP FOR YOU, "MERL" !

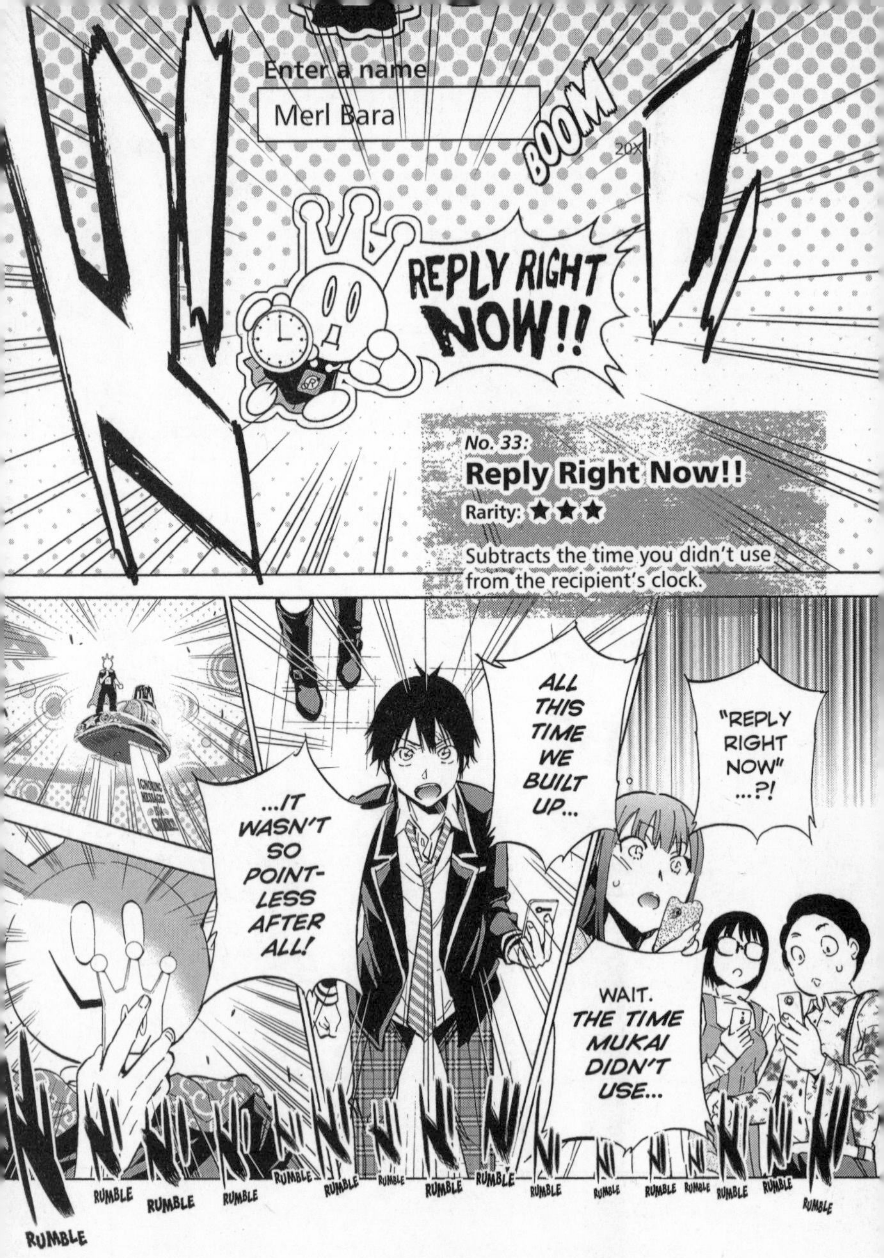
Enter a name
Merl Bara
BOOM
REPLY RIGHT NOW!!
No. 33:
Reply Right Now!!
Rarity: ★★★
Subtracts the time you didn't use from the recipient's clock.
"REPLY RIGHT NOW" ...?!
ALL THIS TIME WE BUILT UP...
...IT WASN'T SO POINTLESS AFTER ALL!
WAIT. THE TIME MUKAI DIDN'T USE...
RUMBLE RUMBLE RUMBLE RUMBLE RUMBLE RUMBLE RUMBLE RUMBLE RUMBLE RUMBLE RUMBLE RUMBLE RUMBLE RUMBLE RUMBLE

[Merl Bara (Marble)'s unused time] [Yuma Mukai's unused time]

30 sec. – 982,535 sec. = ...

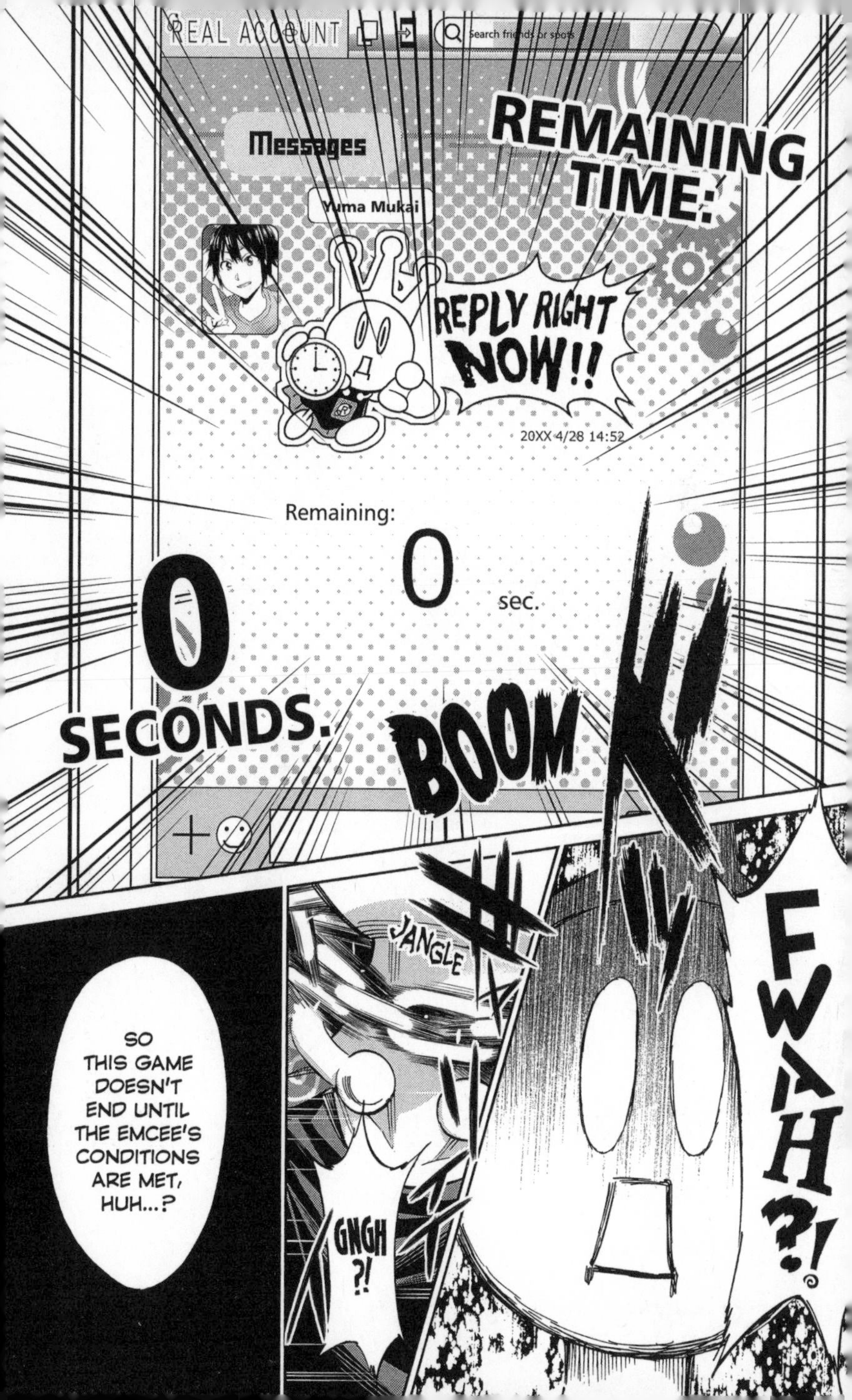
REAL ACCOUNT
Search friends or spots
Messages
Yuma Mukai
REMAINING TIME:
REPLY RIGHT NOW!!
20XX 4/28 14:52
Remaining:
0
sec.
0 SECONDS.
BOOM
FWAH?!
JANGLE
GNGH ?!
SO THIS GAME DOESN'T END UNTIL THE EMCEE'S CONDITIONS ARE MET, HUH...?

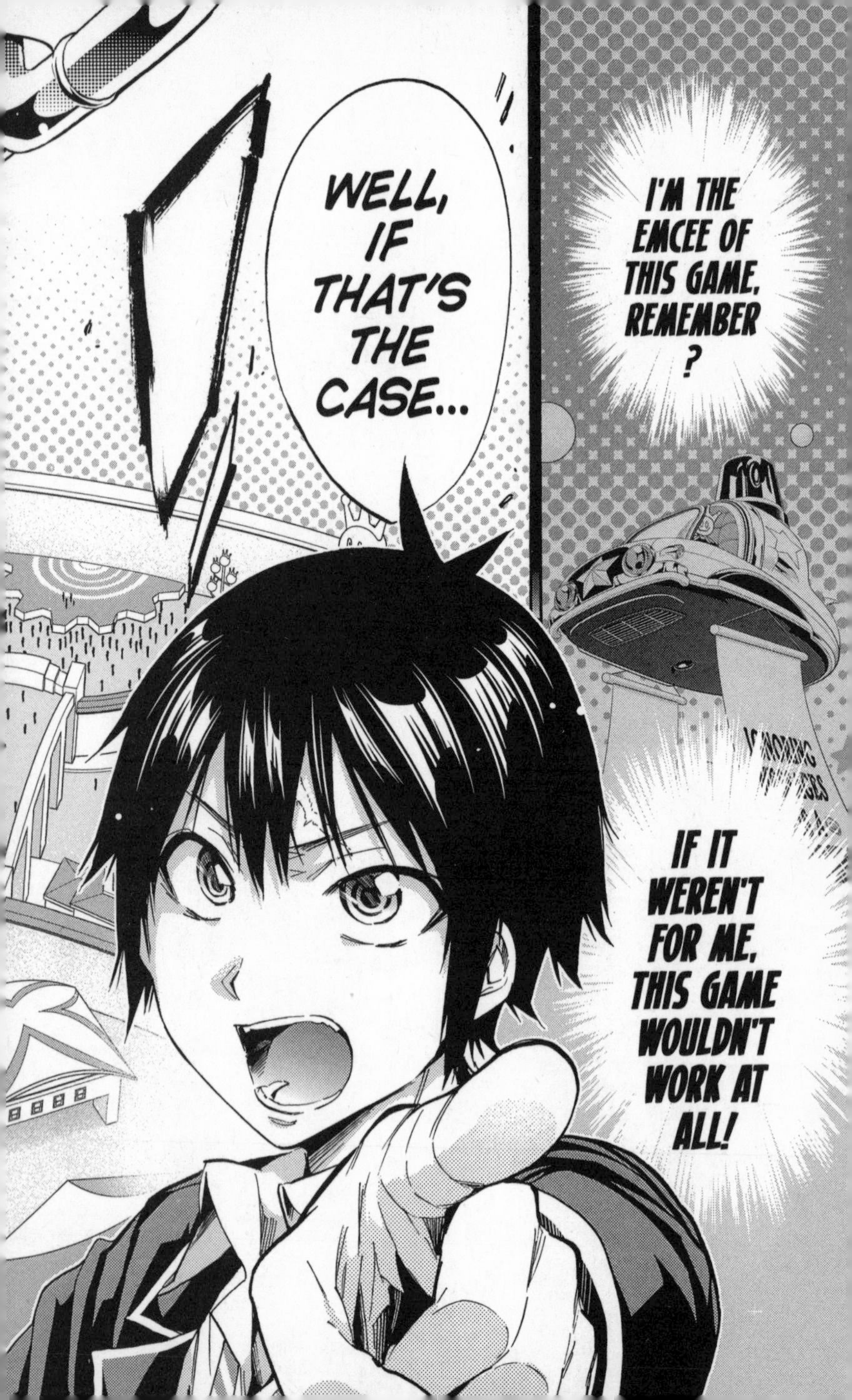
I'M THE EMCEE OF THIS GAME, REMEMBER?
IF IT WEREN'T FOR ME, THIS GAME WOULDN'T WORK AT ALL!
WELL, IF THAT'S THE CASE...

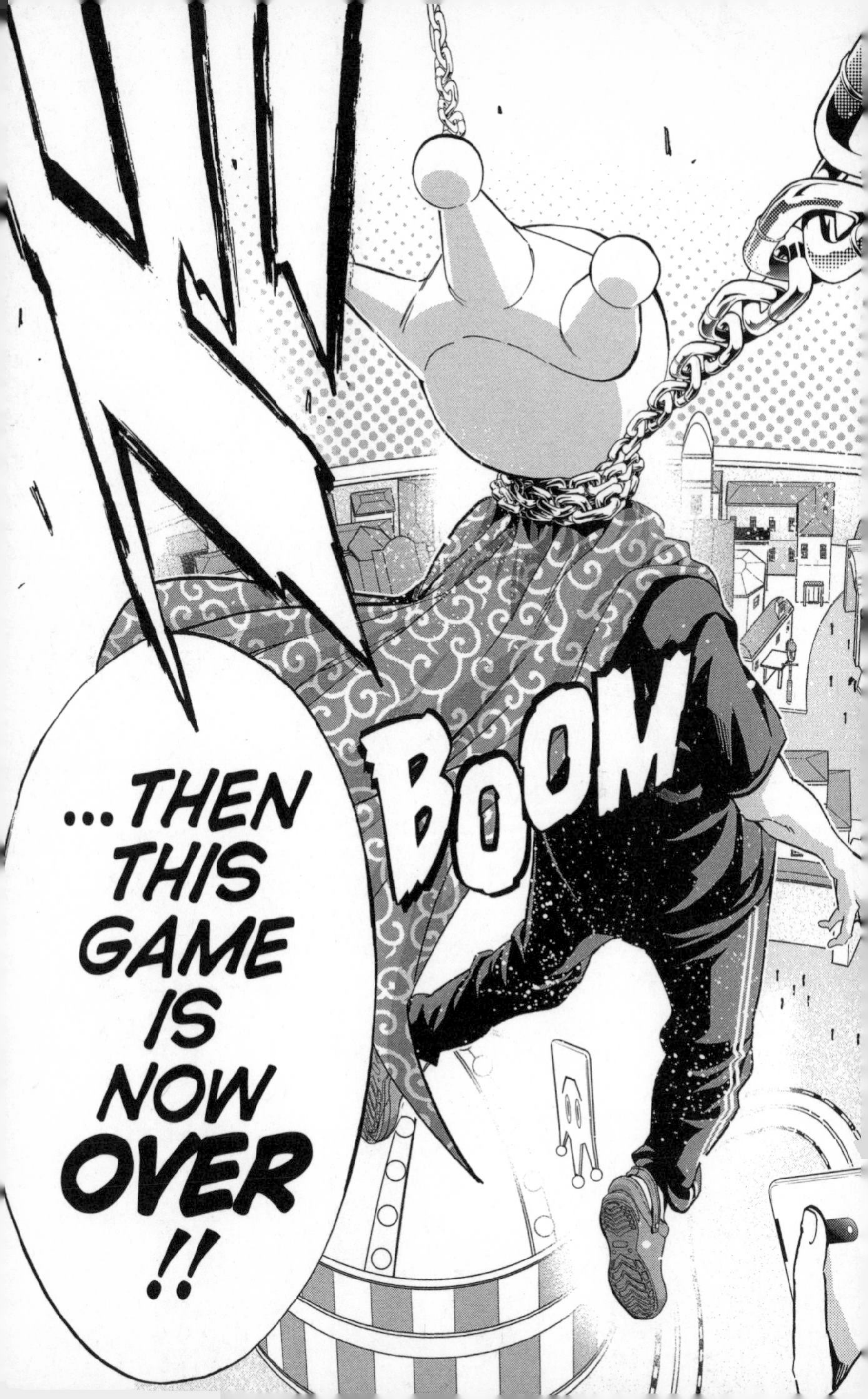
...THEN THIS GAME IS NOW OVER!!
BOOM

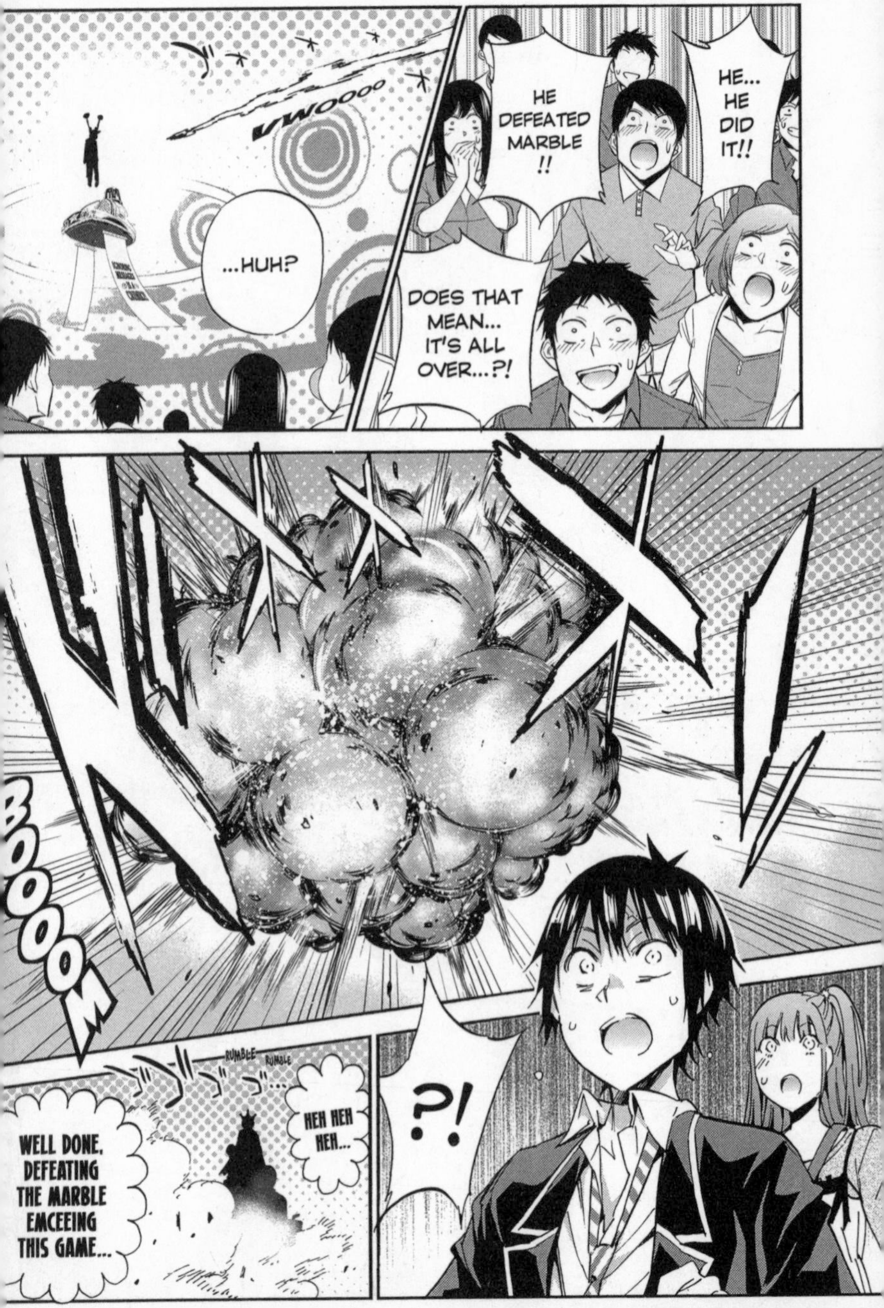
HE... HE DID IT!!
HE DEFEATED MARBLE !!
DOES THAT MEAN... IT'S ALL OVER...?!
VWOOOO
...HUH?
BOOOOOM
?!
RUMBLE
RUMBLE
HEH HEH HEH...
WELL DONE, DEFEATING THE MARBLE EMCEEING THIS GAME...

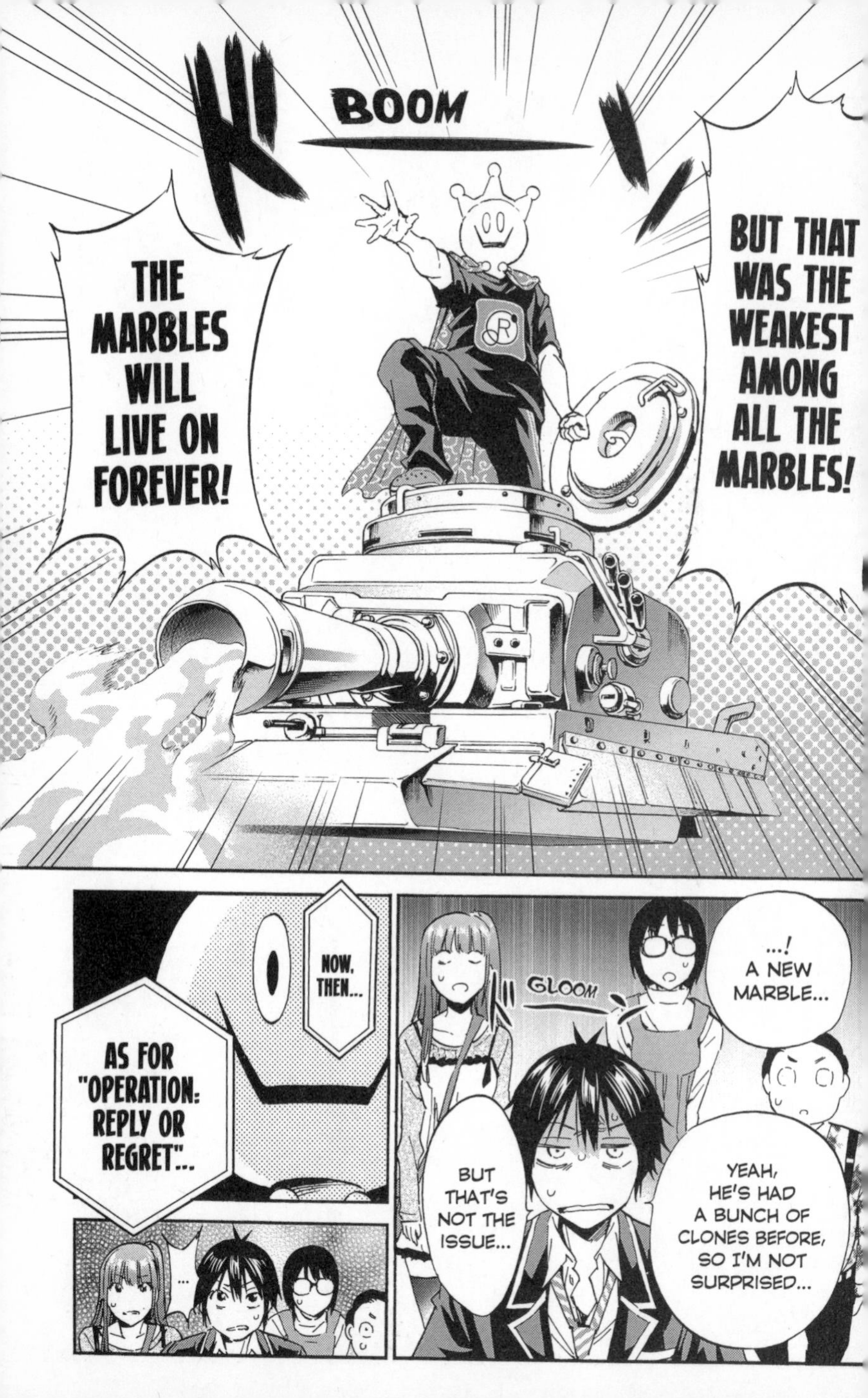
BOOM
BUT THAT WAS THE WEAKEST AMONG ALL THE MARBLES!
THE MARBLES WILL LIVE ON FOREVER!
...! A NEW MARBLE...
GLOOM
YEAH, HE'S HAD A BUNCH OF CLONES BEFORE, SO I'M NOT SURPRISED...
BUT THAT'S NOT THE ISSUE...
NOW, THEN...
AS FOR "OPERATION: REPLY OR REGRET"...
...

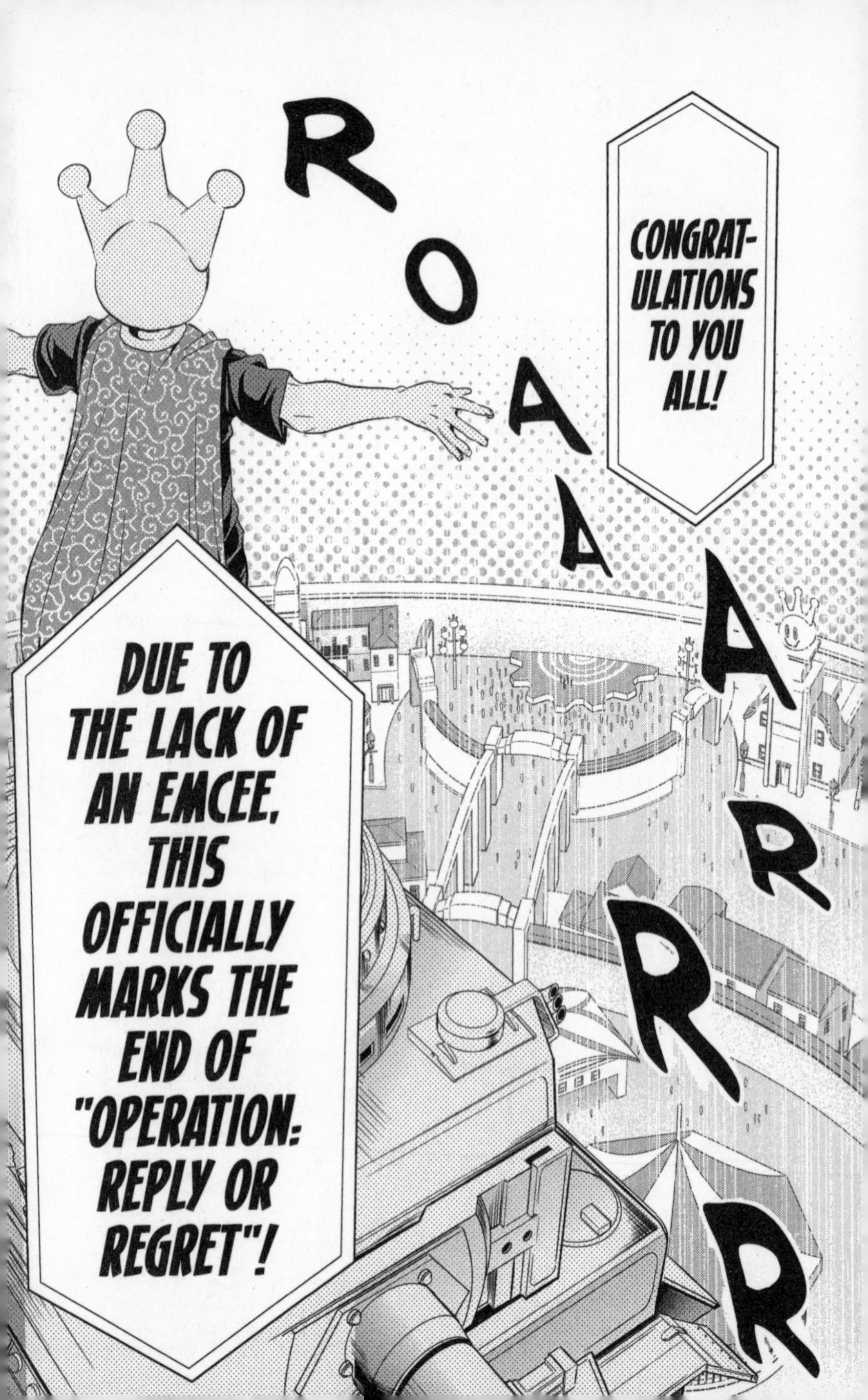
CONGRATULATIONS TO YOU ALL!
ROAAARRR
DUE TO THE LACK OF AN EMCEE, THIS OFFICIALLY MARKS THE END OF "OPERATION: REPLY OR REGRET"!

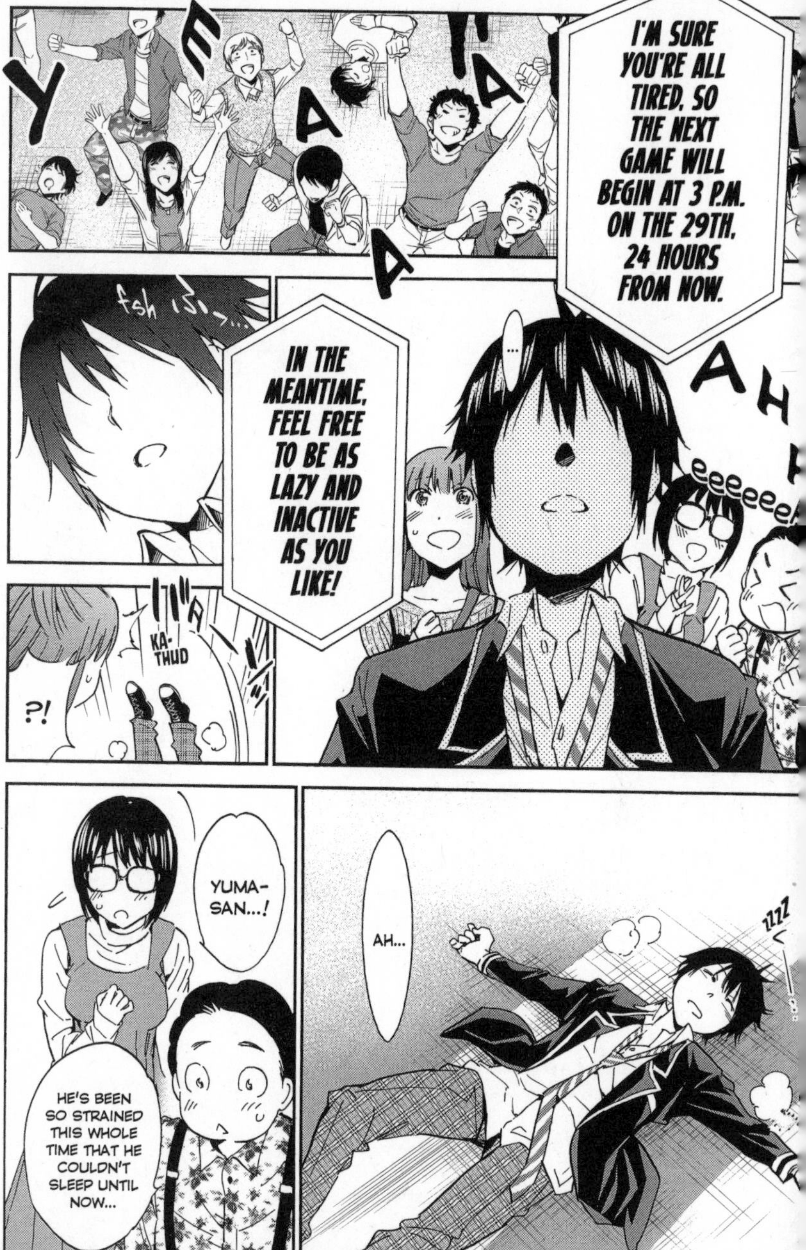
I'M SURE YOU'RE ALL TIRED, SO THE NEXT GAME WILL BEGIN AT 3 P.M. ON THE 29TH, 24 HOURS FROM NOW.
YEAAAA
...
IN THE MEANTIME, FEEL FREE TO BE AS LAZY AND INACTIVE AS YOU LIKE!
AHH
eeeeeee
fsh
KA-THUD
?!
AH...
zzzz
YUMA-SAN...!
HE'S BEEN SO STRAINED THIS WHOLE TIME THAT HE COULDN'T SLEEP UNTIL NOW...

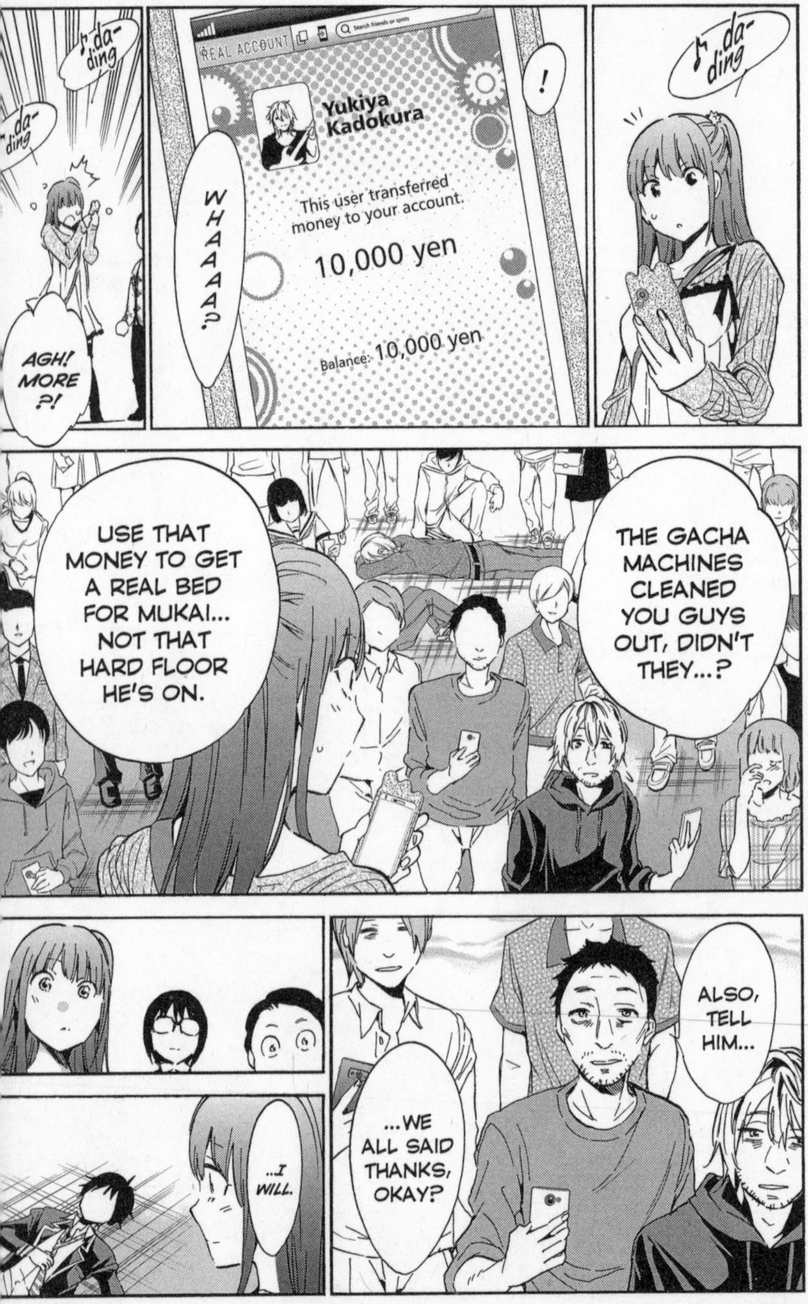
♪ da-ding
!
REAL ACCOUNT
Search friends or spots
Yukiya Kadokura
This user transferred money to your account.
10,000 yen
Balance: 10,000 yen
WHAAAAA?
♪ da-ding
da-ding
AGH! MORE ?!
THE GACHA MACHINES CLEANED YOU GUYS OUT, DIDN'T THEY...?
USE THAT MONEY TO GET A REAL BED FOR MUKAI... NOT THAT HARD FLOOR HE'S ON.
ALSO, TELL HIM...
...WE ALL SAID THANKS, OKAY?
...I WILL.

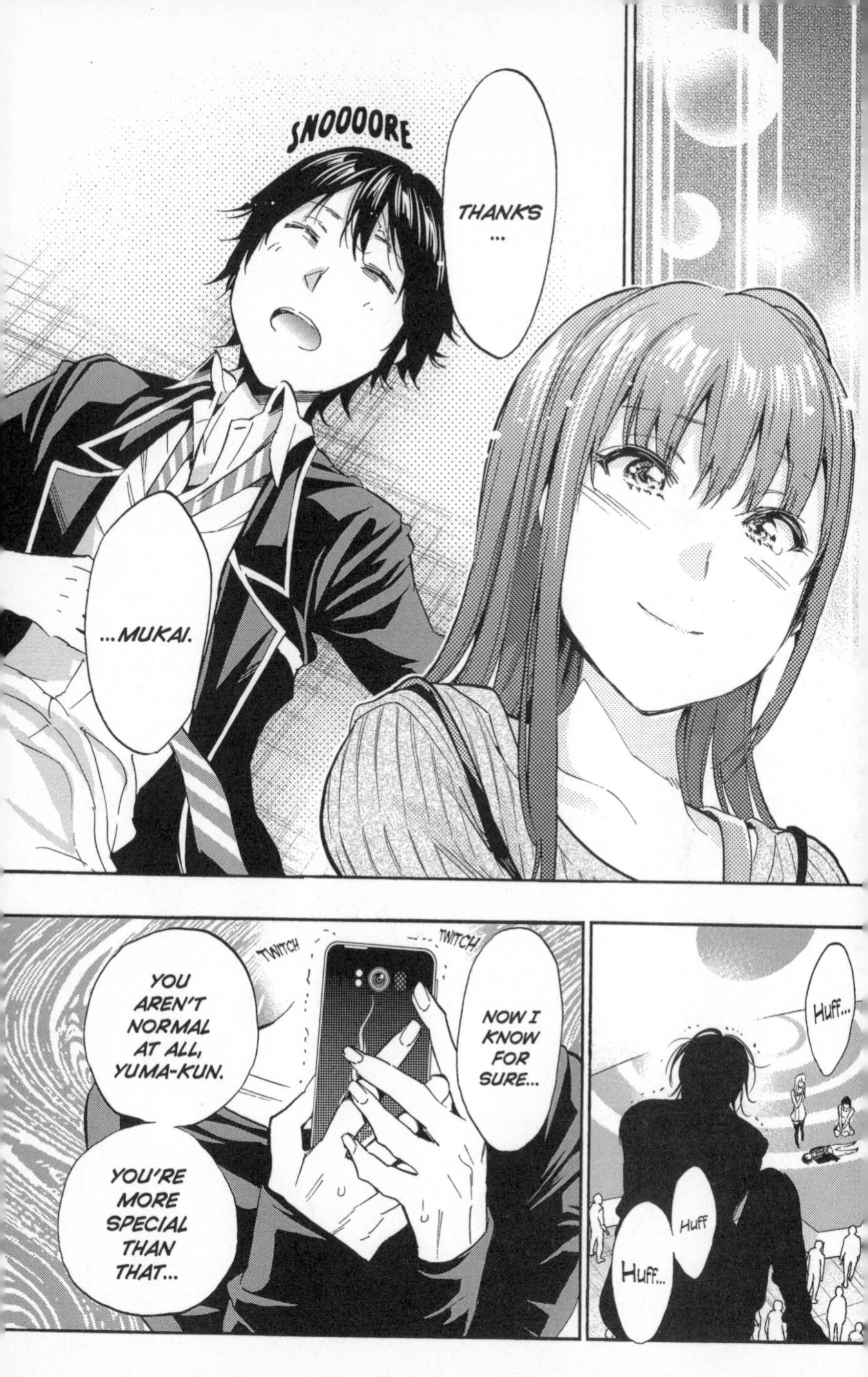
THANKS ...
SNOOOORE
...MUKAI.
Huff...
Huff
Huff...
TWITCH
NOW I KNOW FOR SURE...
TWITCH
YOU AREN'T NORMAL AT ALL, YUMA-KUN.
YOU'RE MORE SPECIAL THAN THAT...

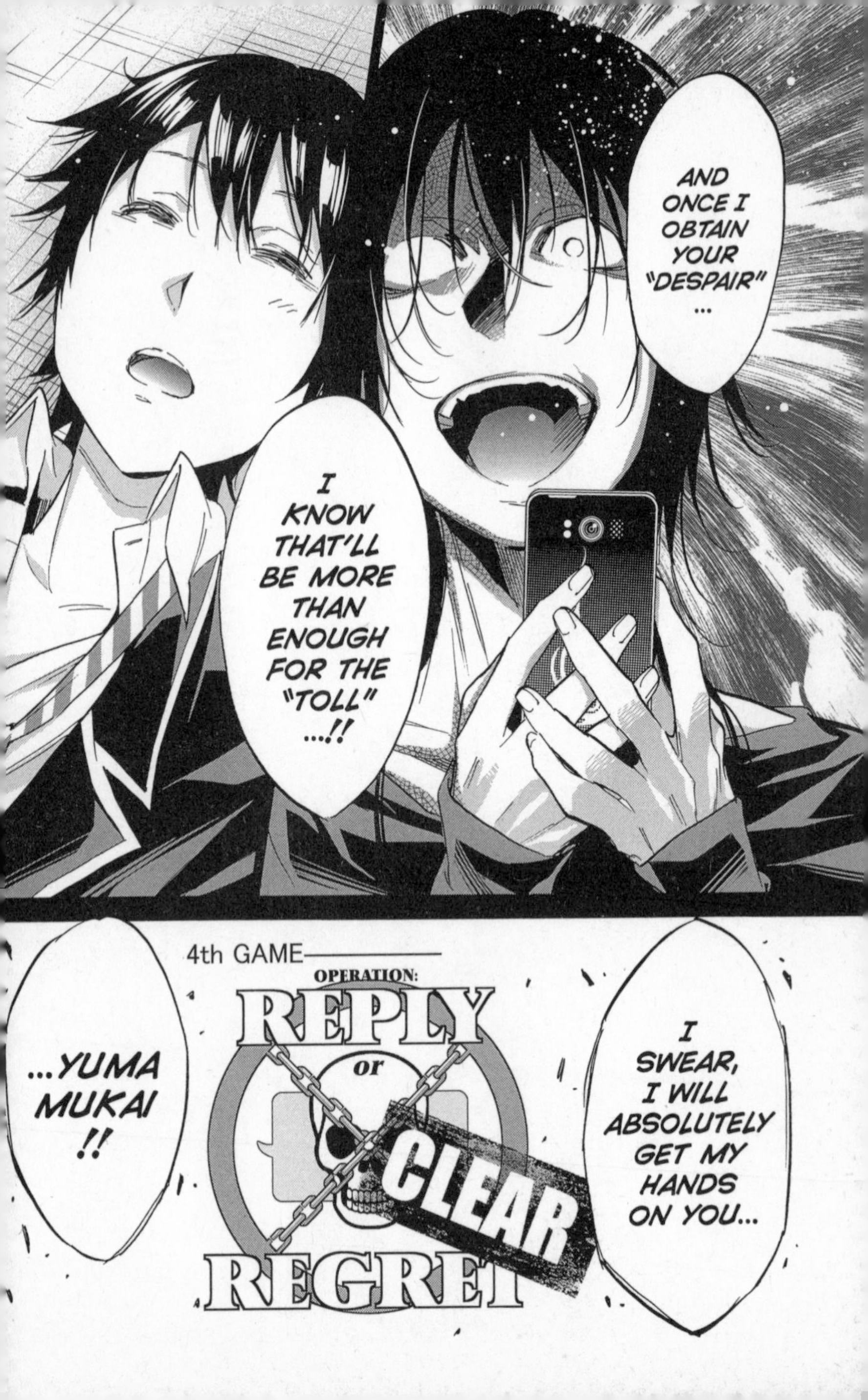
AND ONCE I OBTAIN YOUR "DESPAIR" ...
I KNOW THAT'LL BE MORE THAN ENOUGH FOR THE "TOLL" ...!!
I SWEAR, I WILL ABSOLUTELY GET MY HANDS ON YOU...
4th GAME——
OPERATION: REPLY or REGRET
CLEAR
...YUMA MUKAI !!

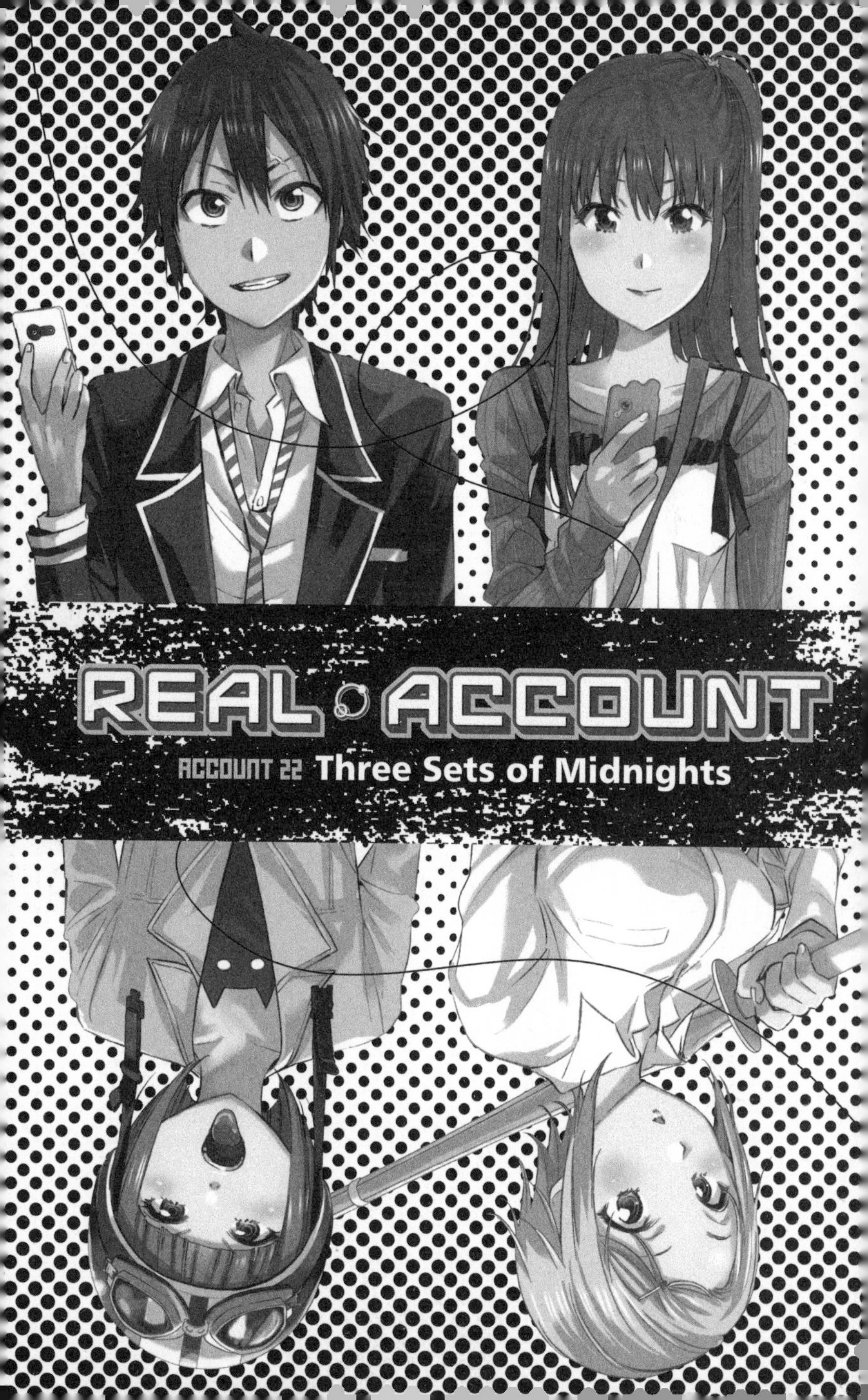
REAL ACCOUNT
ACCOUNT 22 Three Sets of Midnights

REAL ACCOUNT

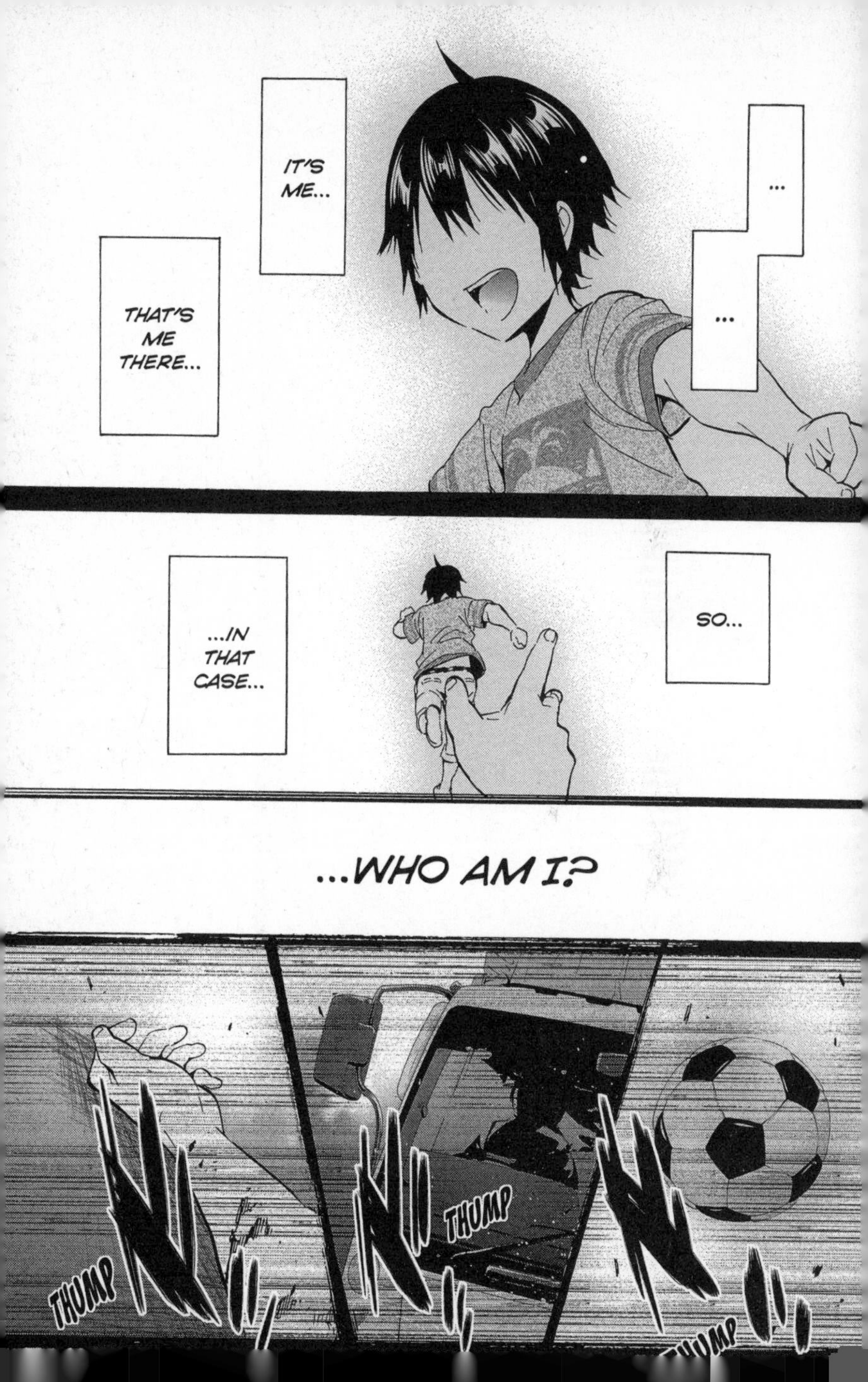
...
...
IT'S ME...
THAT'S ME THERE...
SO...
...IN THAT CASE...
...WHO AM I?
THUMP
THUMP
THUMP

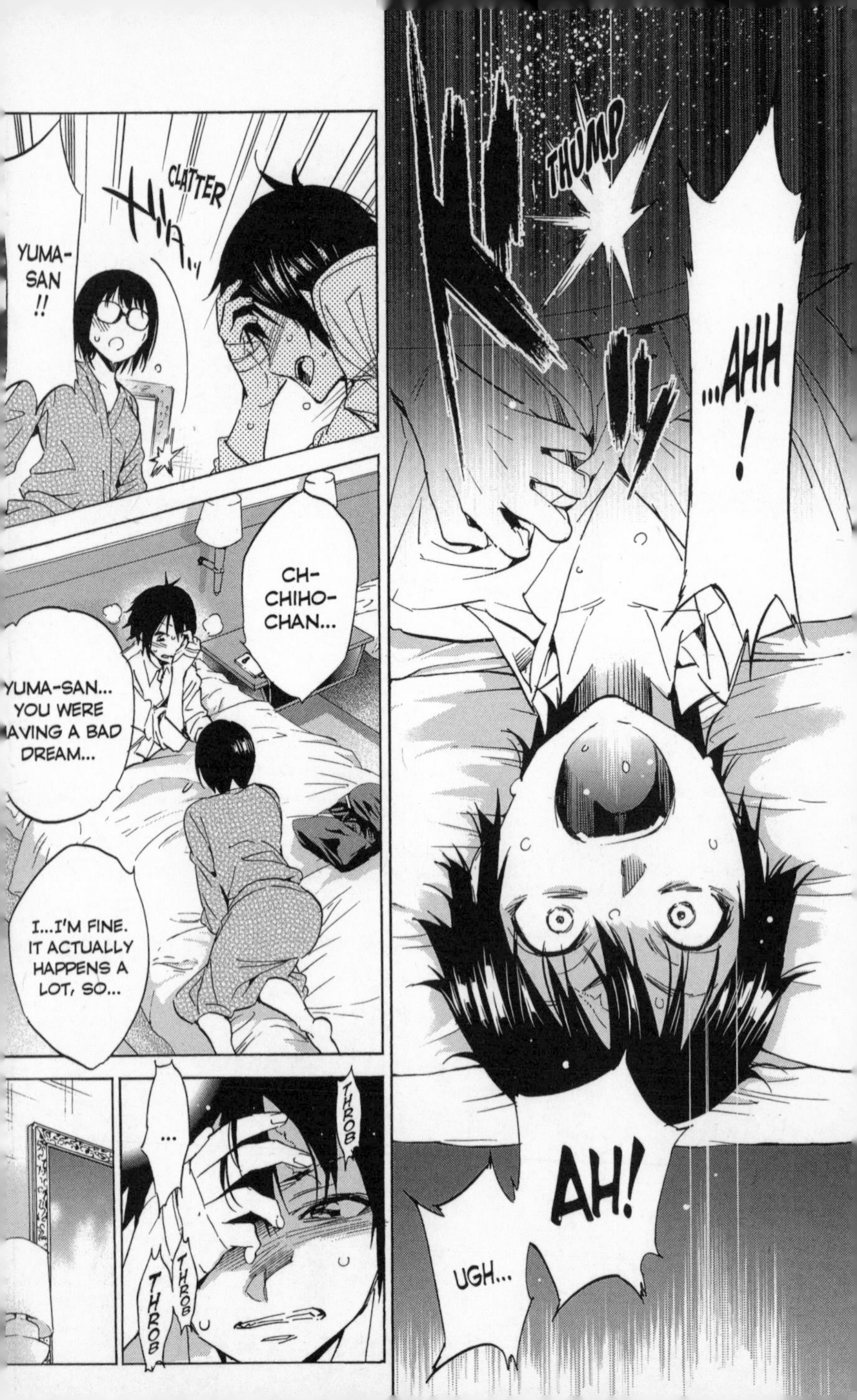
THUMP
...AHH!
AH!
UGH...
CLATTER
YUMA-SAN!!
CH-CHIHO-CHAN...
YUMA-SAN... YOU WERE AVING A BAD DREAM...
I...I'M FINE. IT ACTUALLY HAPPENS A LOT, SO...
...
THROB
THROB
THROB

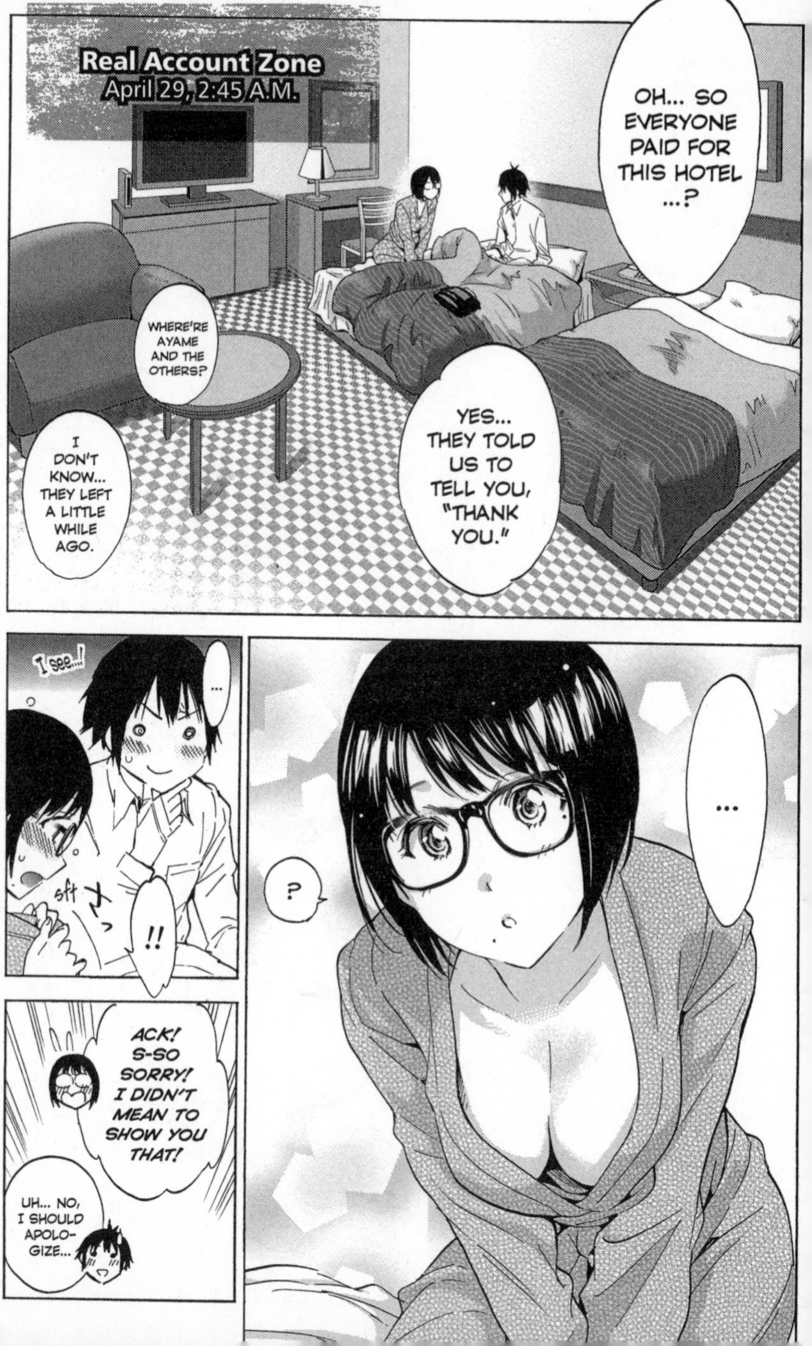
Real Account Zone
April 29, 2:45 A.M.
OH... SO EVERYONE PAID FOR THIS HOTEL ...?
YES... THEY TOLD US TO TELL YOU, "THANK YOU."
WHERE'RE AYAME AND THE OTHERS?
I DON'T KNOW... THEY LEFT A LITTLE WHILE AGO.
...
?
...
I see...!
sft
!!
ACK! S-SO SORRY! I DIDN'T MEAN TO SHOW YOU THAT!
UH... NO, I SHOULD APOLO-GIZE...

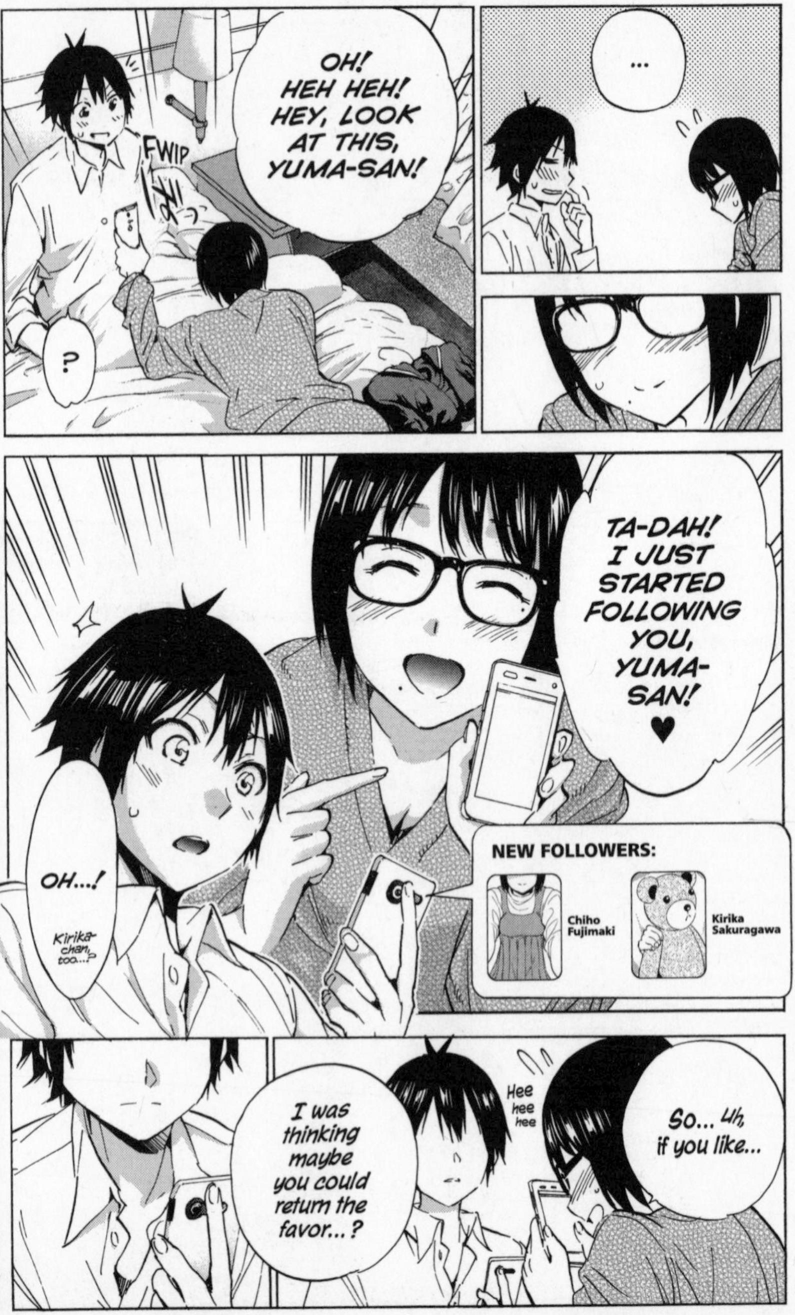
...
OH! HEH HEH! HEY, LOOK AT THIS, YUMA-SAN!
FWIP
?
TA-DAH! I JUST STARTED FOLLOWING YOU, YUMA-SAN! ♥
NEW FOLLOWERS:
Chiho Fujimaki
Kirika Sakuragawa
OH...!
Kirika-chan, too...?
So... uh, if you like...
Hee hee hee
I was thinking maybe you could return the favor...?

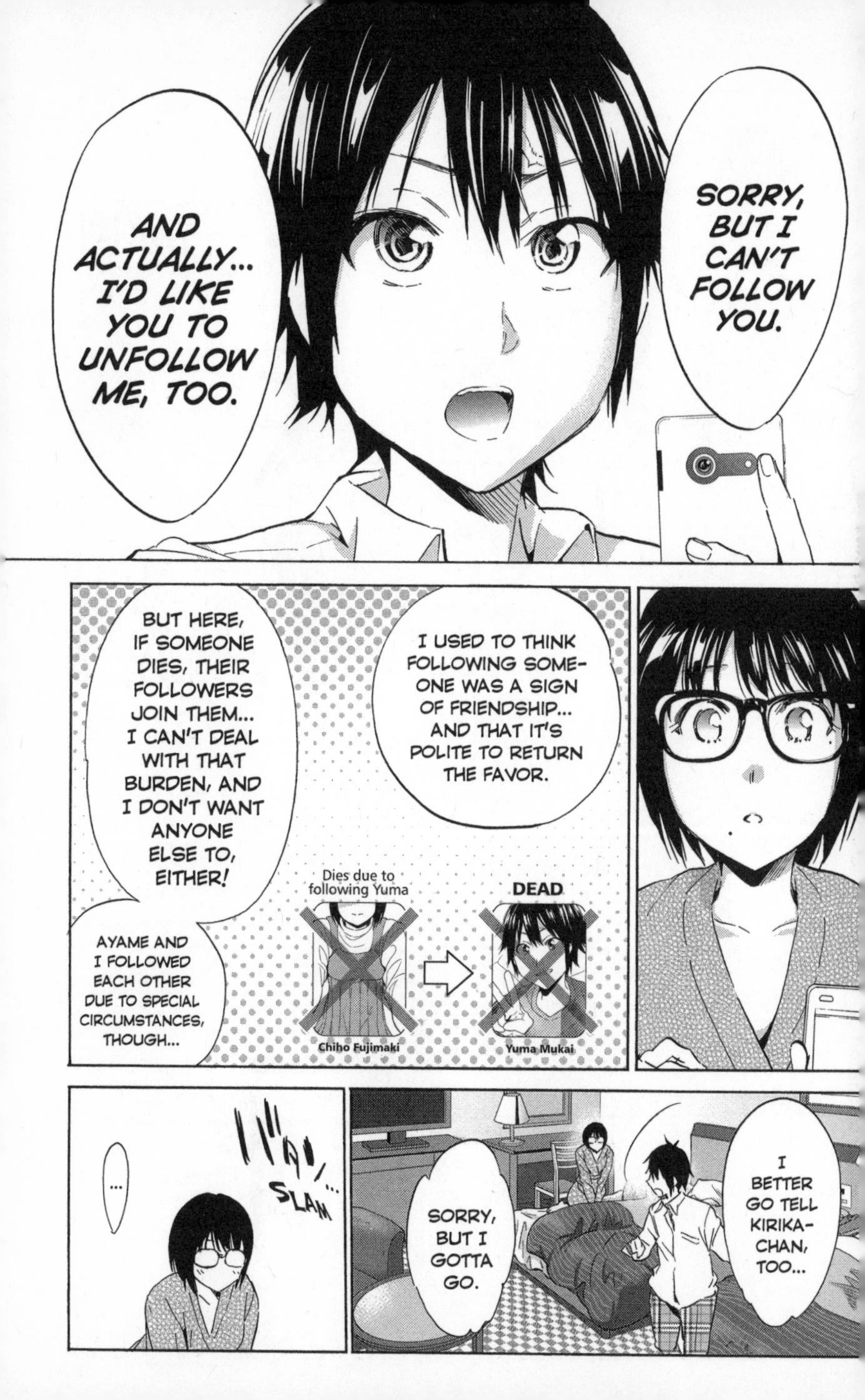
SORRY, BUT I CAN'T FOLLOW YOU.
AND ACTUALLY... I'D LIKE YOU TO UNFOLLOW ME, TOO.
I USED TO THINK FOLLOWING SOME-ONE WAS A SIGN OF FRIENDSHIP... AND THAT IT'S POLITE TO RETURN THE FAVOR.
BUT HERE, IF SOMEONE DIES, THEIR FOLLOWERS JOIN THEM... I CAN'T DEAL WITH THAT BURDEN, AND I DON'T WANT ANYONE ELSE TO, EITHER!
DEAD
Dies due to following Yuma
Yuma Mukai
Chiho Fujimaki
AYAME AND I FOLLOWED EACH OTHER DUE TO SPECIAL CIRCUMSTANCES, THOUGH...
I BETTER GO TELL KIRIKA-CHAN, TOO...
SORRY, BUT I GOTTA GO.
SLAM
...

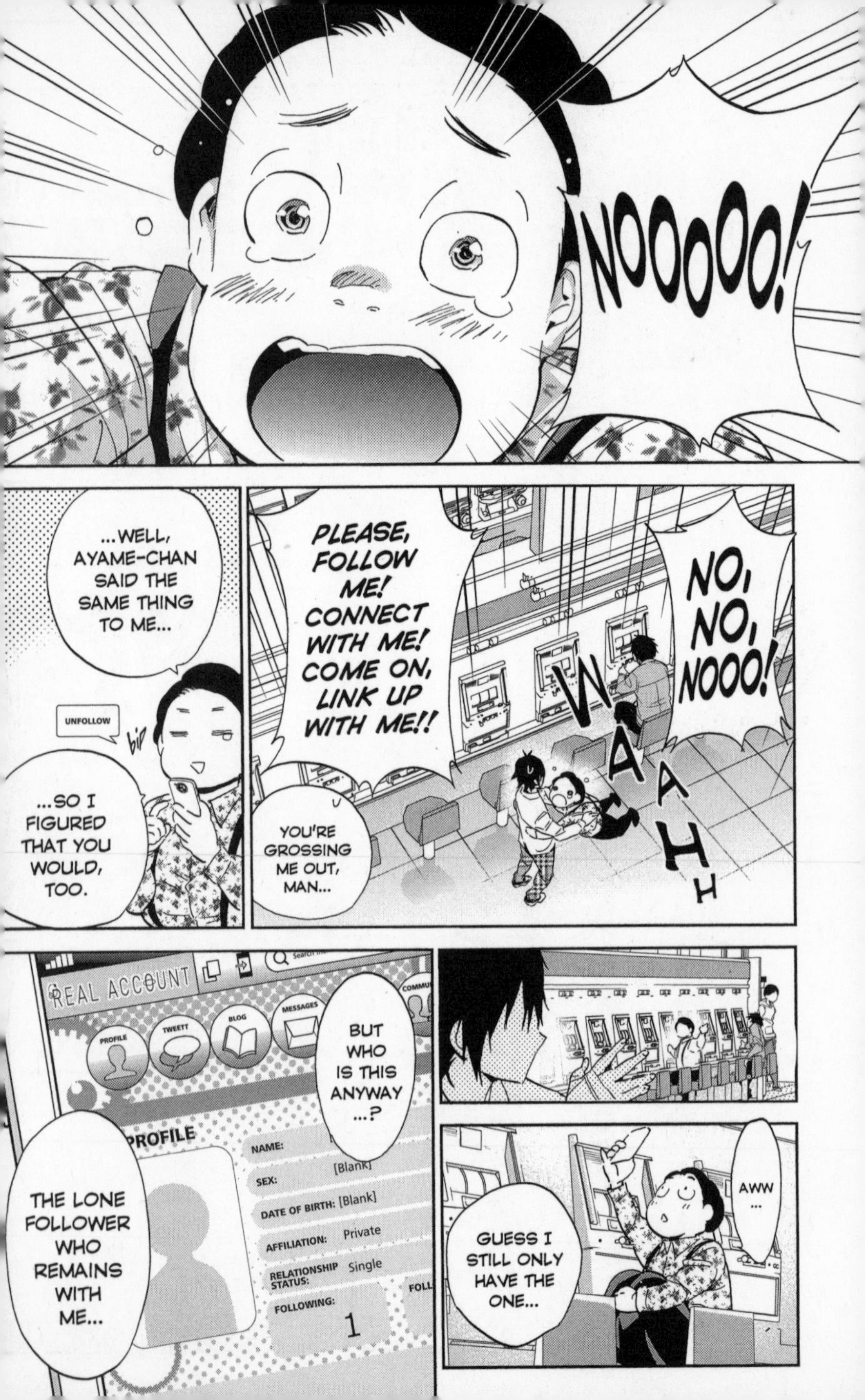
NOOOOO!
NO, NO, NOOO!
PLEASE, FOLLOW ME! CONNECT WITH ME! COME ON, LINK UP WITH ME!!
WAAHH
YOU'RE GROSSING ME OUT, MAN...
...WELL, AYAME-CHAN SAID THE SAME THING TO ME...
UNFOLLOW
bip
...SO I FIGURED THAT YOU WOULD, TOO.
AWW...
GUESS I STILL ONLY HAVE THE ONE...
REAL ACCOUNT
PROFILE
TWEETT
BLOG
MESSAGES
BUT WHO IS THIS ANYWAY...?
PROFILE
NAME:
SEX: [Blank]
DATE OF BIRTH: [Blank]
AFFILIATION: Private
RELATIONSHIP STATUS: Single
FOLLOWING: 1
THE LONE FOLLOWER WHO REMAINS WITH ME...

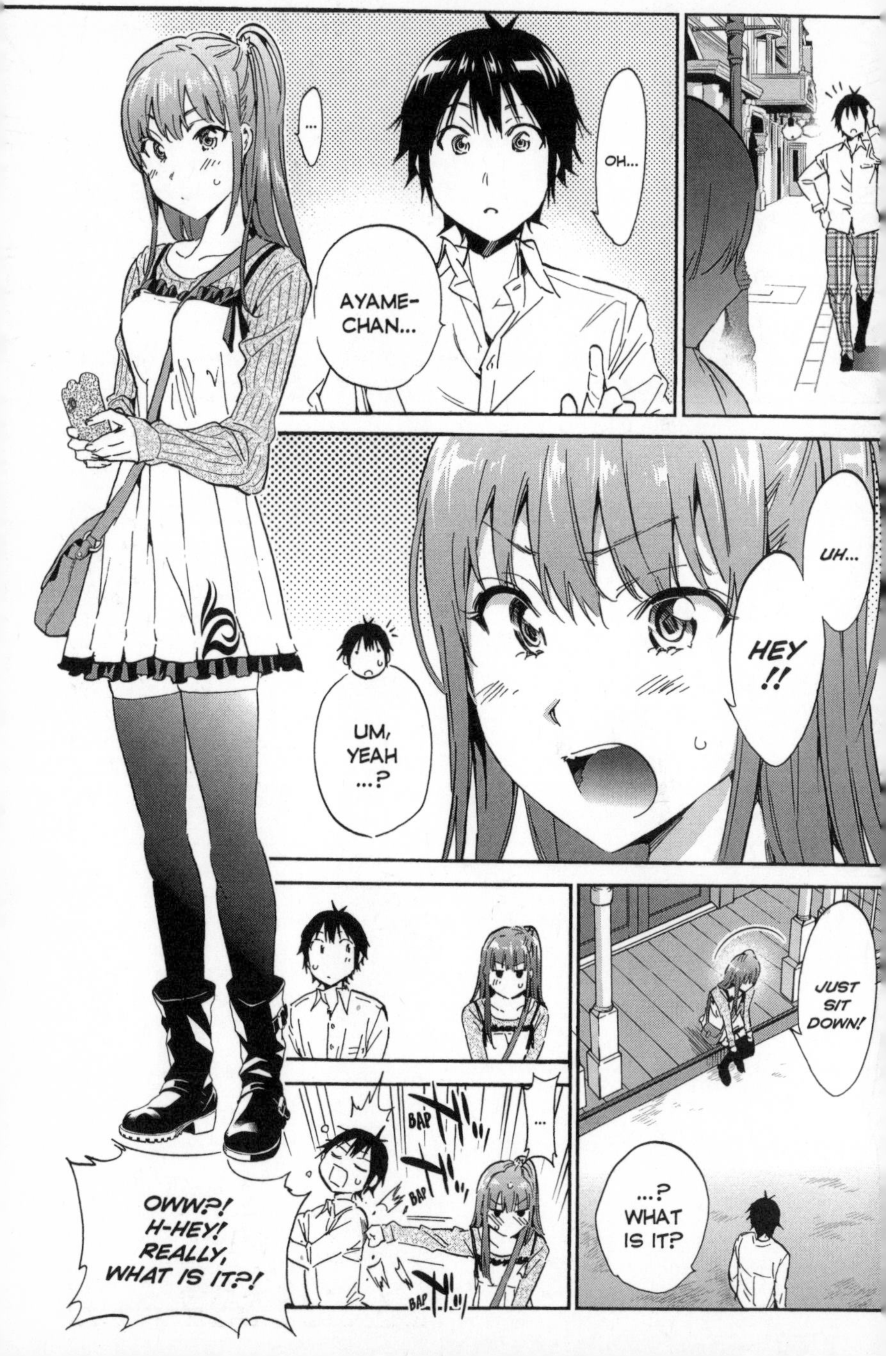
OH...
...
AYAME-CHAN...
UH...
HEY!!
UM, YEAH ...?
JUST SIT DOWN!
...? WHAT IS IT?
...
BAP
BAP
BAP
OWW?! H-HEY! REALLY, WHAT IS IT?!

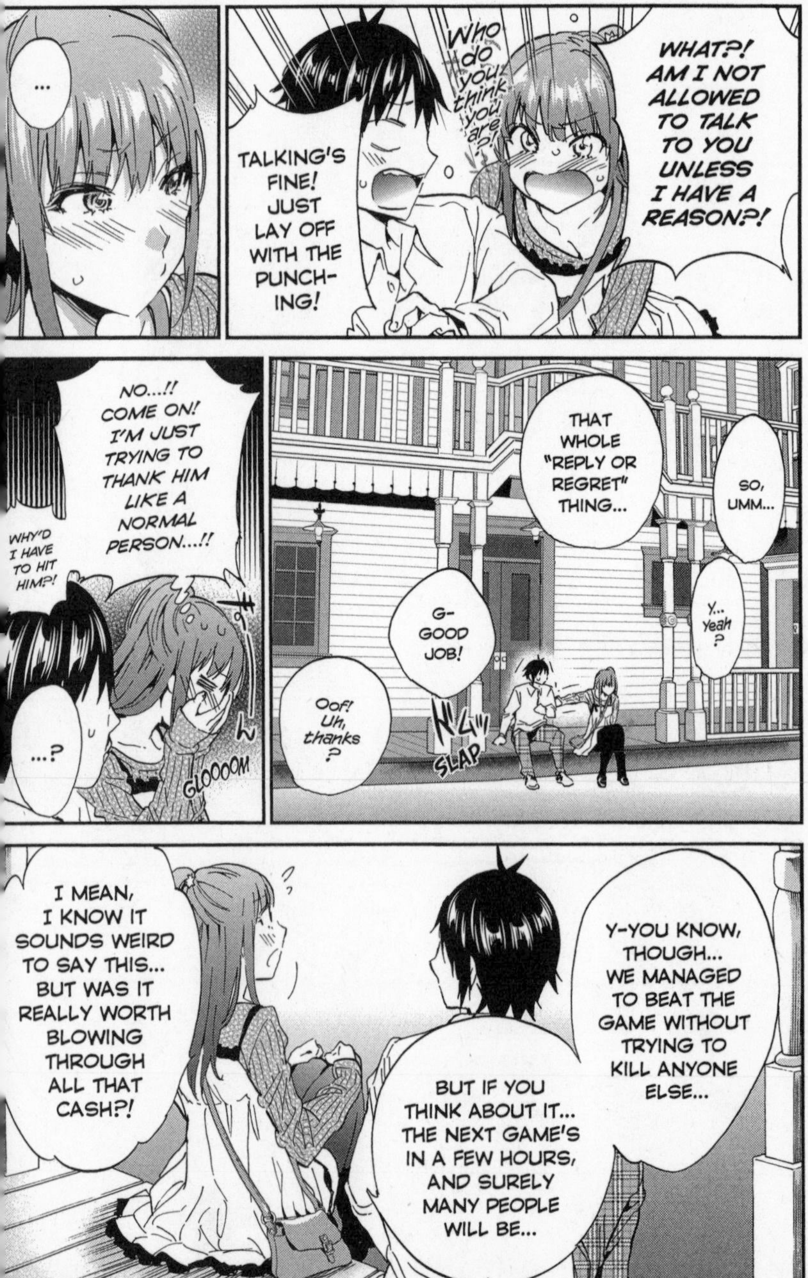
WHAT?! AM I NOT ALLOWED TO TALK TO YOU UNLESS I HAVE A REASON?!
Who do you think you are?!
TALKING'S FINE! JUST LAY OFF WITH THE PUNCH-ING!
...
SO, UMM...
THAT WHOLE "REPLY OR REGRET" THING...
Y... Yeah?
G-GOOD JOB!
SLAP
Oof! Uh, thanks?
NO...!! COME ON! I'M JUST TRYING TO THANK HIM LIKE A NORMAL PERSON...!!
WHY'D I HAVE TO HIT HIM?!
GLOOOOM
...?
Y-YOU KNOW, THOUGH... WE MANAGED TO BEAT THE GAME WITHOUT TRYING TO KILL ANYONE ELSE...
BUT IF YOU THINK ABOUT IT... THE NEXT GAME'S IN A FEW HOURS, AND SURELY MANY PEOPLE WILL BE...
I MEAN, I KNOW IT SOUNDS WEIRD TO SAY THIS... BUT WAS IT REALLY WORTH BLOWING THROUGH ALL THAT CASH?!

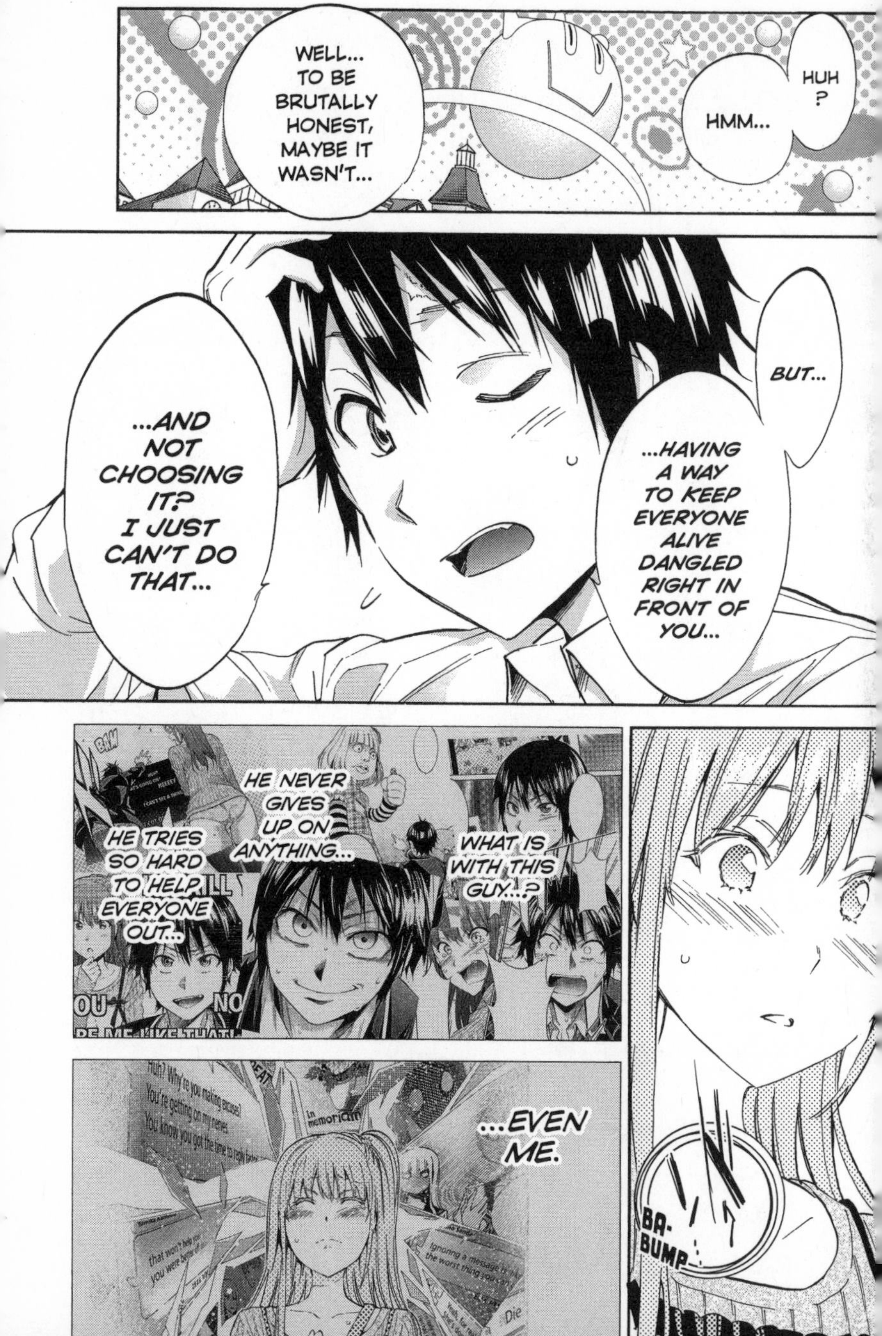
HUH?
HMM...
WELL... TO BE BRUTALLY HONEST, MAYBE IT WASN'T...
BUT...
...HAVING A WAY TO KEEP EVERYONE ALIVE DANGLED RIGHT IN FRONT OF YOU...
...AND NOT CHOOSING IT? I JUST CAN'T DO THAT...
BA-BUMP
HE NEVER GIVES UP ON ANYTHING...
WHAT IS WITH THIS GUY...?
HE TRIES SO HARD TO HELP EVERYONE OUT...
...EVEN ME.

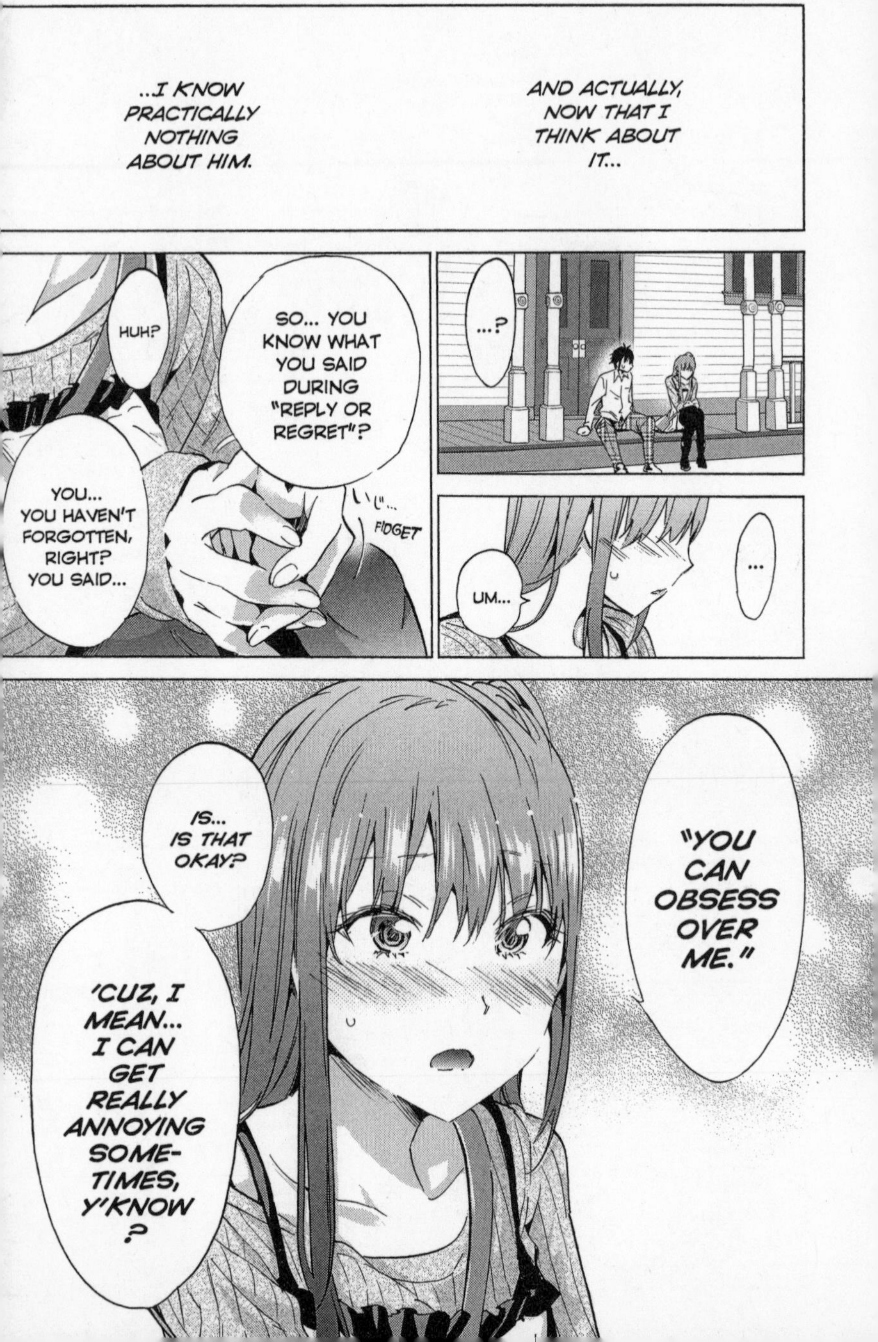
AND ACTUALLY, NOW THAT I THINK ABOUT IT...
...I KNOW PRACTICALLY NOTHING ABOUT HIM.
...?
...
UM...
SO... YOU KNOW WHAT YOU SAID DURING "REPLY OR REGRET"?
HUH?
FIDGET
YOU... YOU HAVEN'T FORGOTTEN, RIGHT? YOU SAID...
"YOU CAN OBSESS OVER ME."
IS... IS THAT OKAY?
'CUZ, I MEAN... I CAN GET REALLY ANNOYING SOME-TIMES, Y'KNOW?

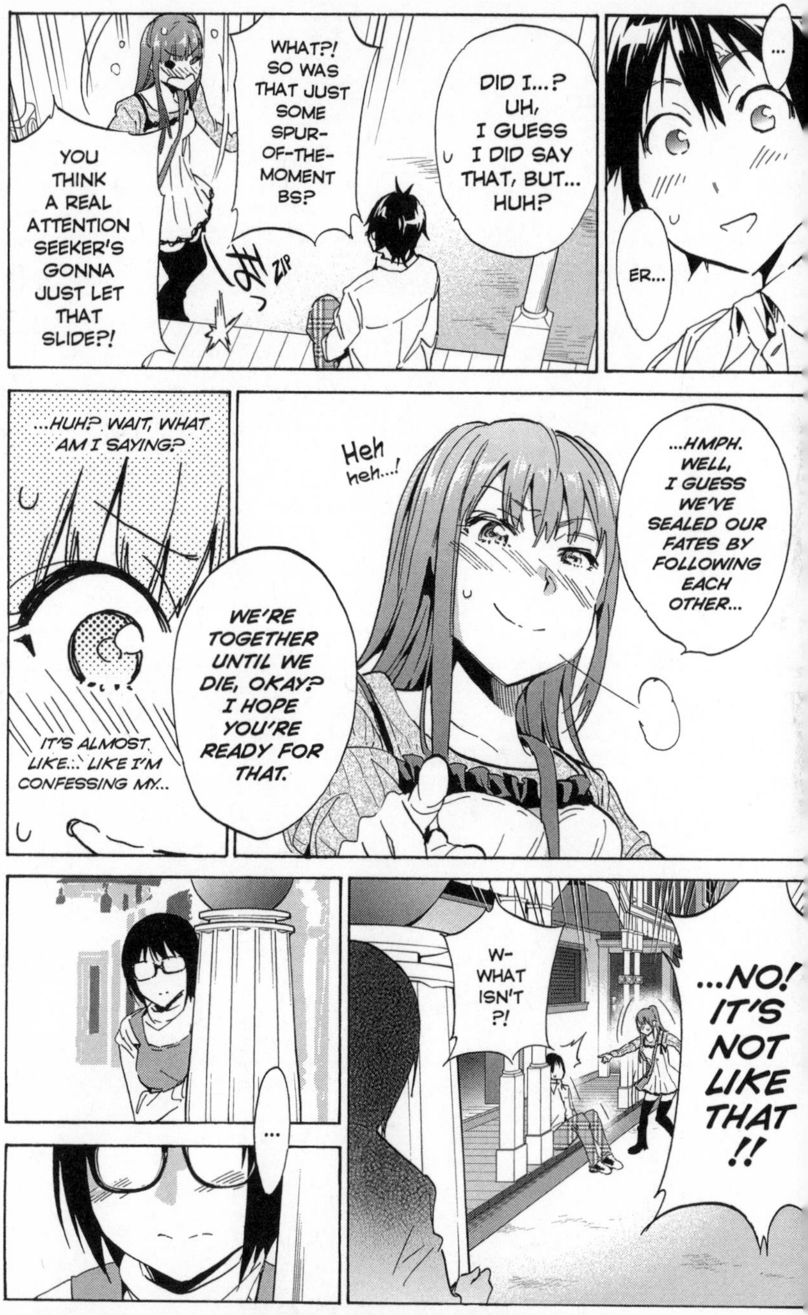
...
ER...
DID I...? UH, I GUESS I DID SAY THAT, BUT... HUH?
WHAT?! SO WAS THAT JUST SOME SPUR-OF-THE-MOMENT BS?
ZIP
YOU THINK A REAL ATTENTION SEEKER'S GONNA JUST LET THAT SLIDE?!
Heh heh...!
...HMPH. WELL, I GUESS WE'VE SEALED OUR FATES BY FOLLOWING EACH OTHER...
WE'RE TOGETHER UNTIL WE DIE, OKAY? I HOPE YOU'RE READY FOR THAT.
...HUH? WAIT, WHAT AM I SAYING?
IT'S ALMOST LIKE... LIKE I'M CONFESSING MY...
...NO! IT'S NOT LIKE THAT!!
W-WHAT ISN'T?!
...

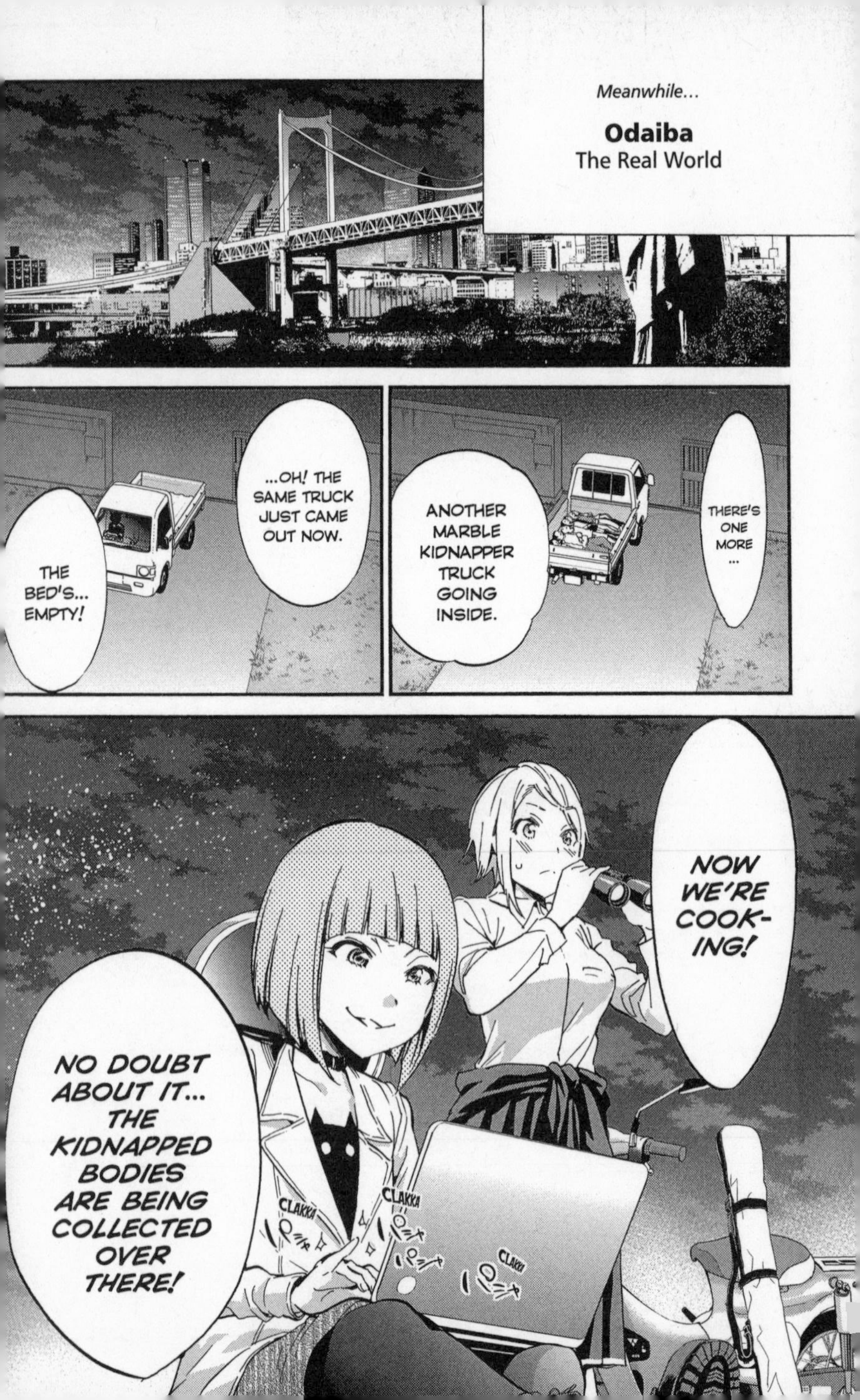
Meanwhile...
Odaiba
The Real World
THERE'S ONE MORE ...
ANOTHER MARBLE KIDNAPPER TRUCK GOING INSIDE.
...OH! THE SAME TRUCK JUST CAME OUT NOW.
THE BED'S... EMPTY!
NOW WE'RE COOK-ING!
NO DOUBT ABOUT IT... THE KIDNAPPED BODIES ARE BEING COLLECTED OVER THERE!
CLAKKA
CLAKKA
CLAKK

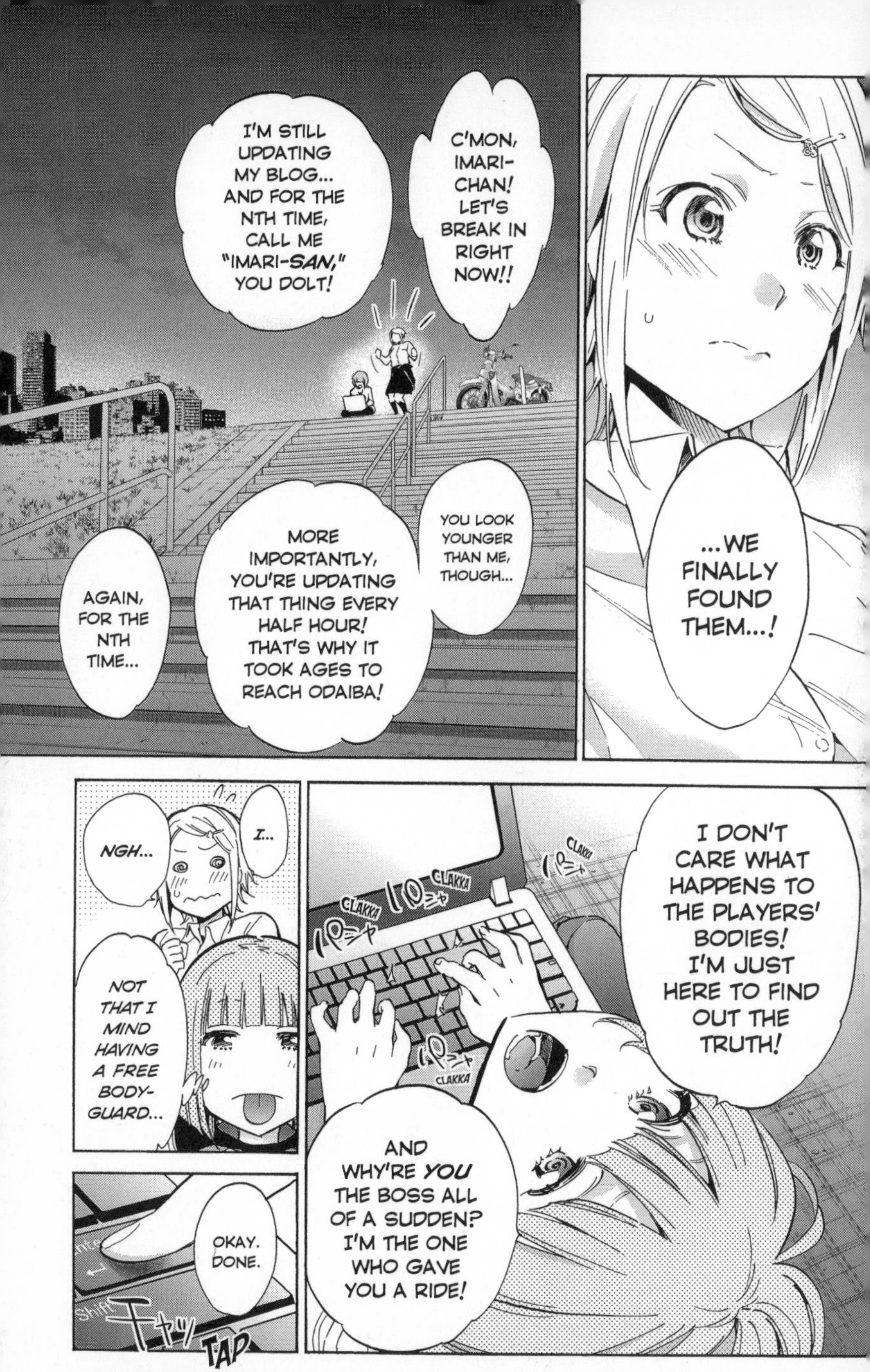
...WE FINALLY FOUND THEM...!
C'MON, IMARI-CHAN! LET'S BREAK IN RIGHT NOW!!
I'M STILL UPDATING MY BLOG... AND FOR THE NTH TIME, CALL ME "IMARI-*SAN*," YOU DOLT!
YOU LOOK YOUNGER THAN ME, THOUGH...
MORE IMPORTANTLY, YOU'RE UPDATING THAT THING EVERY HALF HOUR! THAT'S WHY IT TOOK AGES TO REACH ODAIBA!
AGAIN, FOR THE NTH TIME...
I DON'T CARE WHAT HAPPENS TO THE PLAYERS' BODIES! I'M JUST HERE TO FIND OUT THE TRUTH!
CLAKKA
CLAKKA
CLAKKA
CLAKKA
AND WHY'RE *YOU* THE BOSS ALL OF A SUDDEN? I'M THE ONE WHO GAVE YOU A RIDE!
I...
NGH...
NOT THAT I MIND HAVING A FREE BODY-GUARD...
OKAY. DONE.
TAP

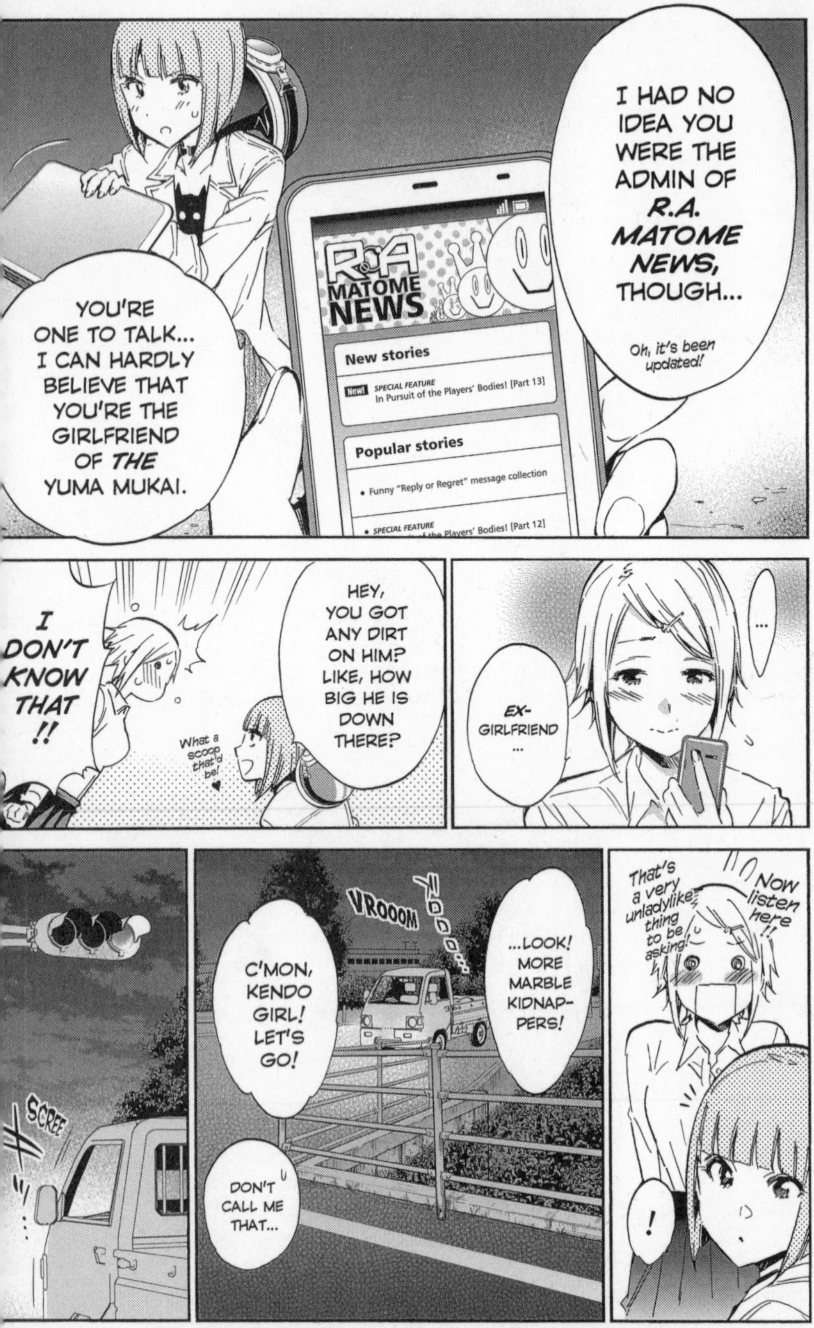
I HAD NO IDEA YOU WERE THE ADMIN OF *R.A. MATOME NEWS,* THOUGH...
Oh, it's been updated!
R.A MATOME NEWS
New stories
New! SPECIAL FEATURE In Pursuit of the Players' Bodies! [Part 13]
Popular stories
Funny "Reply or Regret" message collection
SPECIAL FEATURE the Players' Bodies! [Part 12]
YOU'RE ONE TO TALK... I CAN HARDLY BELIEVE THAT YOU'RE THE GIRLFRIEND OF *THE* YUMA MUKAI.
...
EX- GIRLFRIEND...
HEY, YOU GOT ANY DIRT ON HIM? LIKE, HOW BIG HE IS DOWN THERE?
What a scoop that'd be! ♥
I DON'T KNOW THAT!!
Now listen here!!
That's a very unladylike thing to be asking!
!
...LOOK! MORE MARBLE KIDNAP-PERS!
VROOOM
C'MON, KENDO GIRL! LET'S GO!
DON'T CALL ME THAT...
SCREE

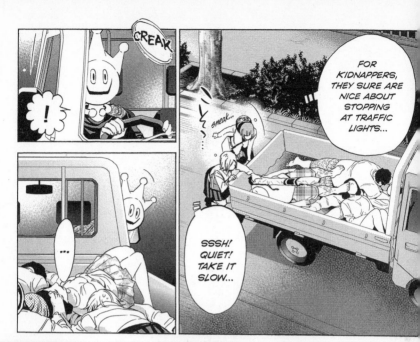

CREAK

!

...

FOR KIDNAPPERS, THEY SURE ARE NICE ABOUT STOPPING AT TRAFFIC LIGHTS...

sneak...

SSSH! QUIET! TAKE IT SLOW...

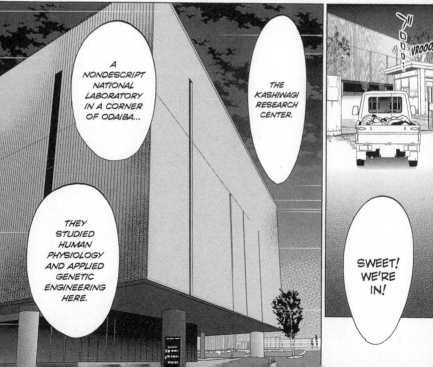

A NONDESCRIPT NATIONAL LABORATORY IN A CORNER OF ODAIBA...

THE KASHIWAGI RESEARCH CENTER.

THEY STUDIED HUMAN PHYSIOLOGY AND APPLIED GENETIC ENGINEERING HERE.

VROOOM

SWEET! WE'RE IN!

...HUH?
THAT'S THIS BUILDING. I JUST LOOKED IT UP.
FOUR YEARS AGO, THE HEAD RESEARCHER AND HER ASSISTANT DIED HERE IN AN ACCIDENT... THEY WERE HUSBAND AND WIFE.
Head researcher
Chitose Kashiwagi
Head research assistant
Shin Kashiwagi
THE REMAINING MEMBERS LEFT AFTER THAT, AND THIS BUILDING'S BEEN ABANDONED EVER SINCE.
...OR SO THEY THOUGHT.
FREIGHT ENTRANCE
BUT LOOK AT THAT. THE LIGHTS AND EVERYTHING ARE ON.
BEEP
BEEP
BEEP
CRUNCH
CRUNCH
CRUNCH
GRRRNN

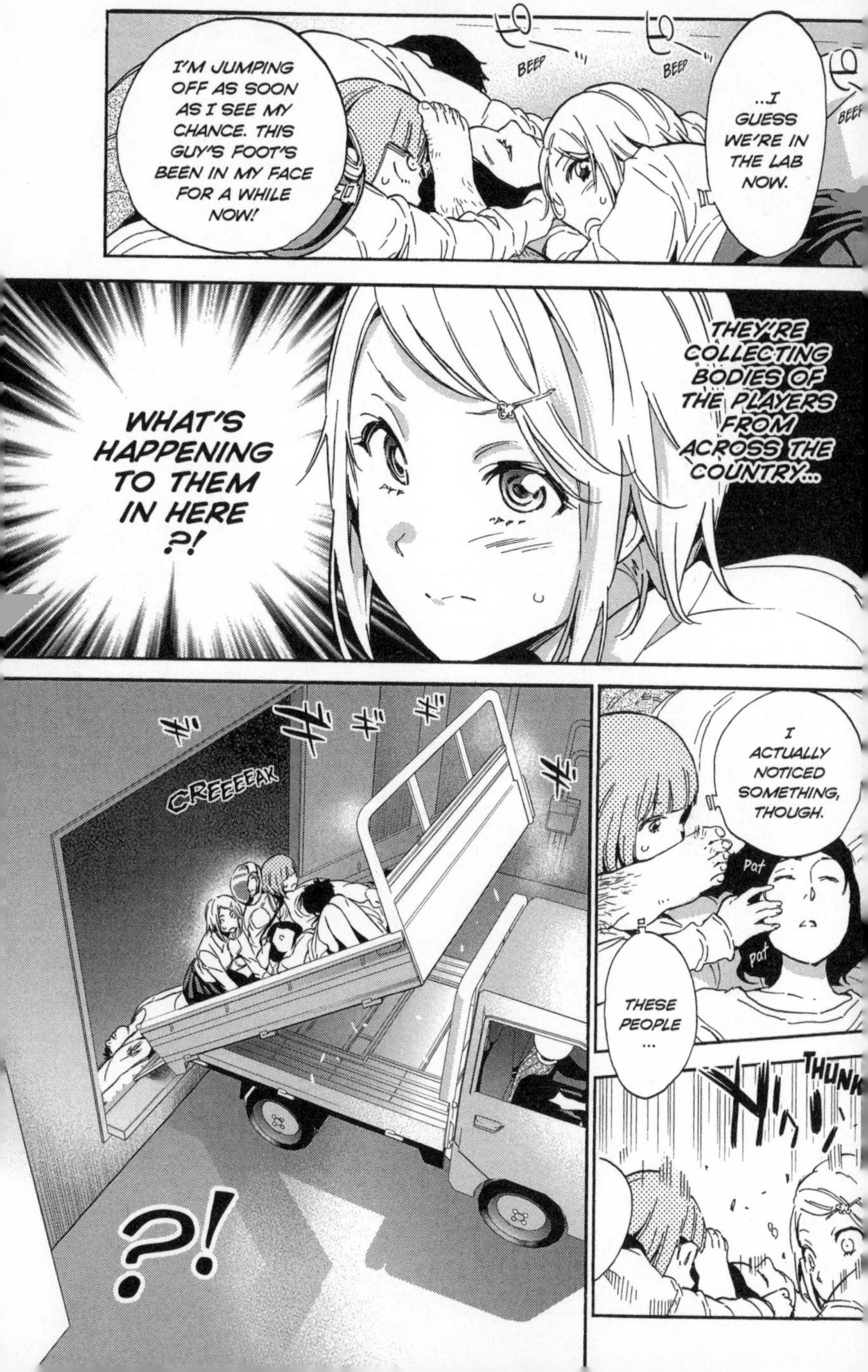
BEEP
...I GUESS WE'RE IN THE LAB NOW.
BEEP
BEEP
I'M JUMPING OFF AS SOON AS I SEE MY CHANCE. THIS GUY'S FOOT'S BEEN IN MY FACE FOR A WHILE NOW!
THEY'RE COLLECTING BODIES OF THE PLAYERS FROM ACROSS THE COUNTRY...
WHAT'S HAPPENING TO THEM IN HERE ?!
I ACTUALLY NOTICED SOMETHING, THOUGH.
Pat
Pat
THESE PEOPLE ...
THUNK
CREEEEAK
?!

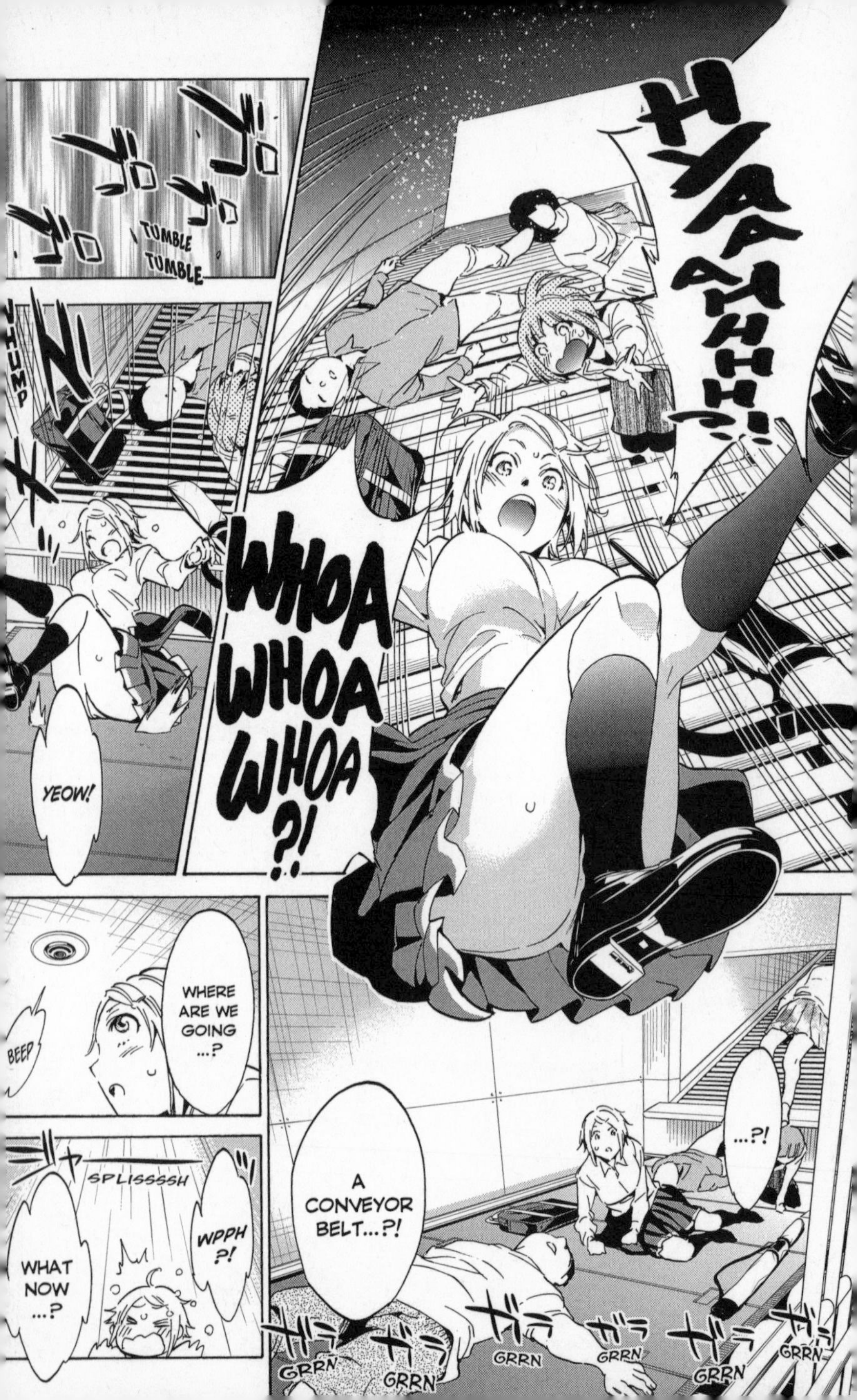
HYAAAAHHH?!!
WHOA WHOA WHOA?!
TUMBLE TUMBLE
THUMP
YEOW!
...?!
A CONVEYOR BELT...?!
GRRN
GRRN
GRRN
GRRN
GRRN
GRRN
WHERE ARE WE GOING ...?
BEEP
SPLISSSSH
WPPH?!
WHAT NOW ...?

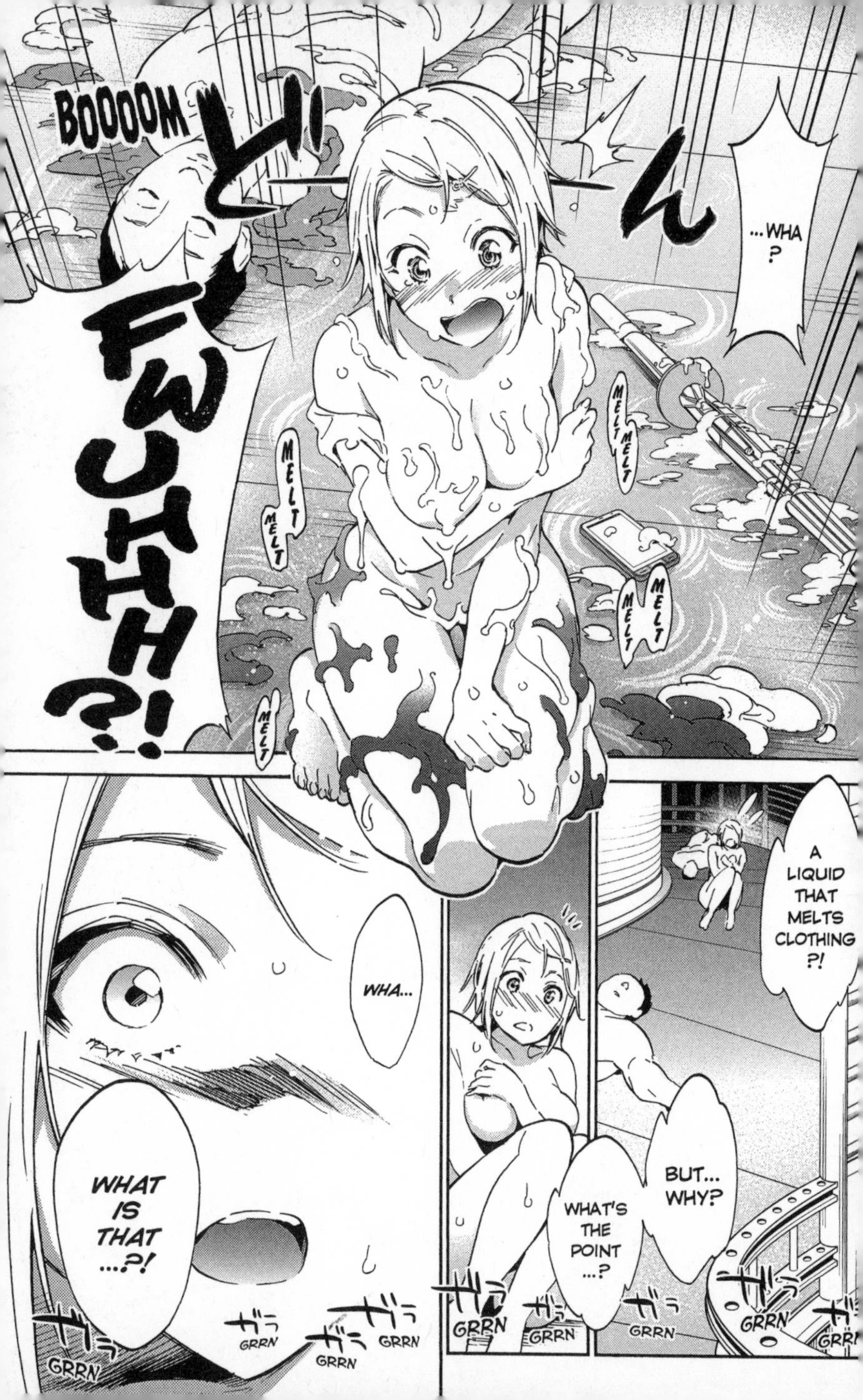
...WHA ?
MELT MELT
MELT MELT
MELT MELT
MELT
BOOOM
どん
FWUHHH?!
A LIQUID THAT MELTS CLOTHING ?!
BUT... WHY?
WHAT'S THE POINT ...?
ガラ GRRN
ガラ GRRN
ガラ GRRN
ガラ GRRN
WHA...
WHAT IS THAT ...?!
ガラ GRRN
ガラ GRRN
ガラ GRRN
ガラ GRRN

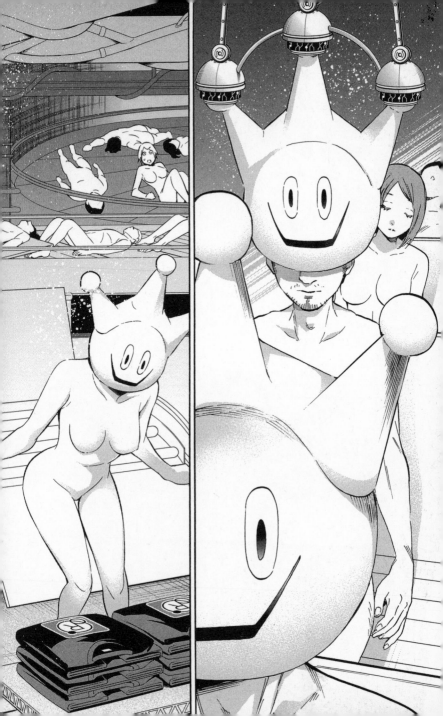

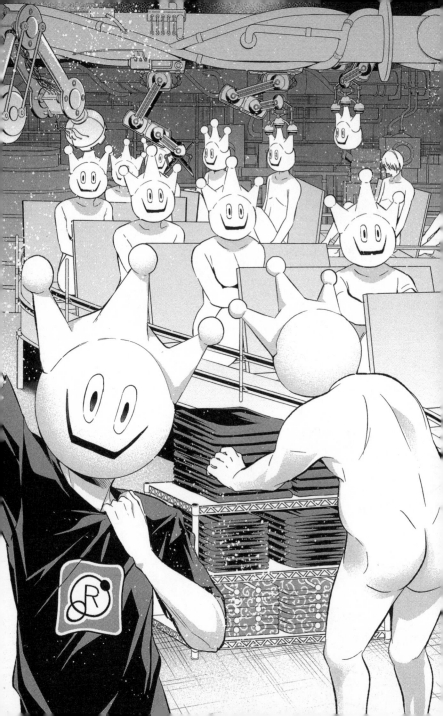

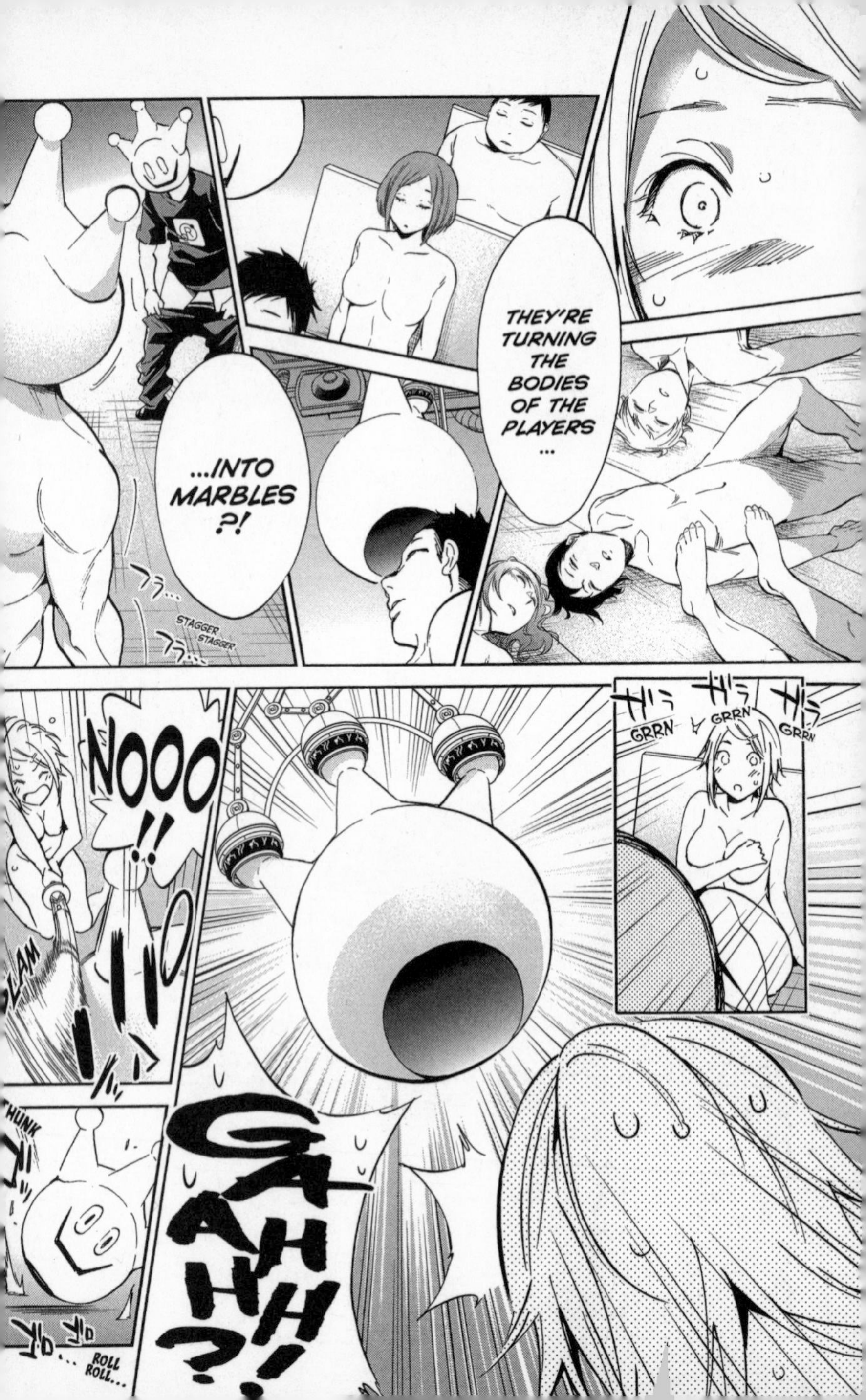
THEY'RE TURNING THE BODIES OF THE PLAYERS...
...INTO MARBLES?!
STAGGER STAGGER
GRRN GRRN GRRN
NOOO!!
SLAM
GAAHH?!
THUNK
ROLL ROLL...

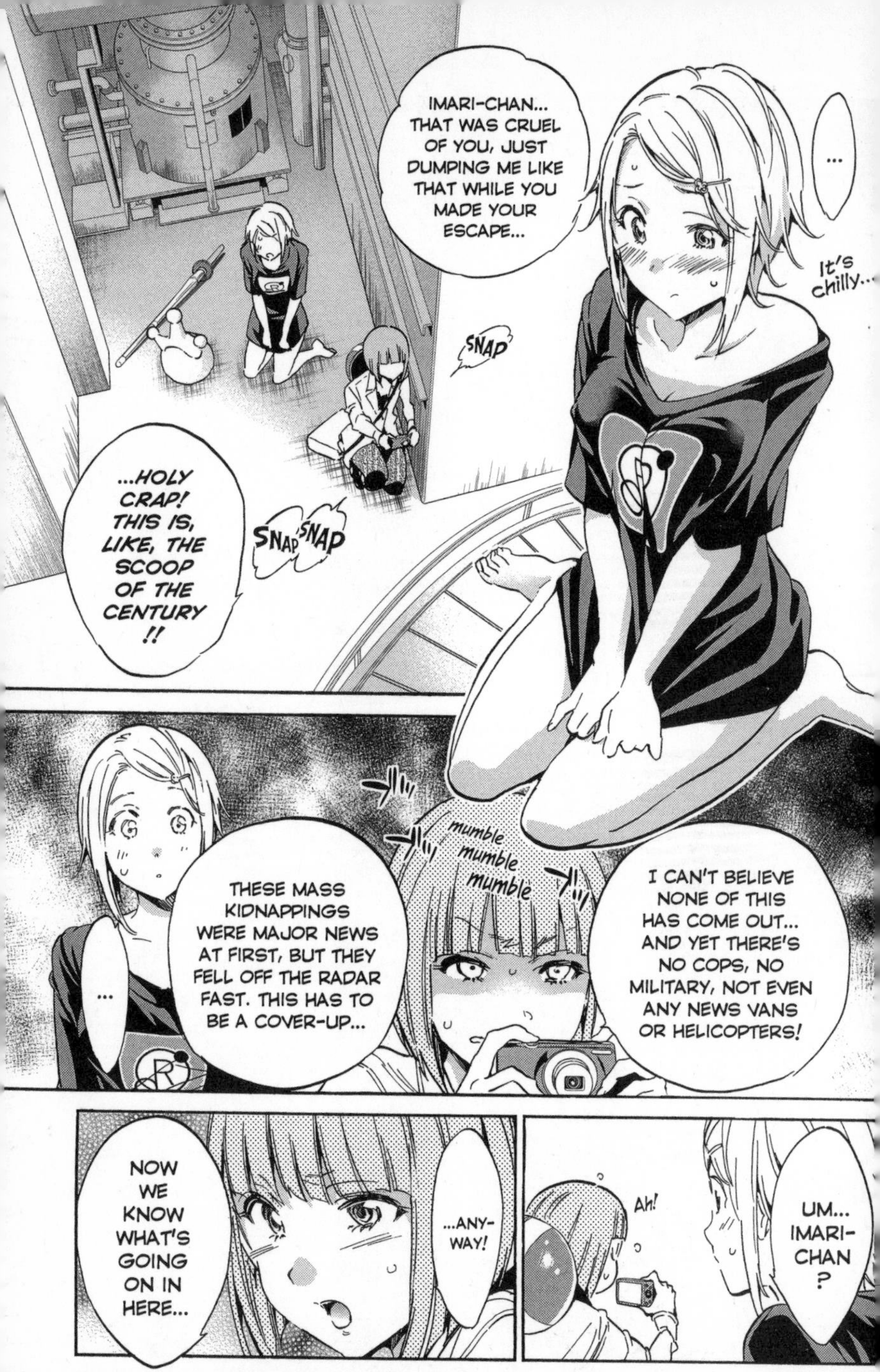
...
It's chilly...
IMARI-CHAN... THAT WAS CRUEL OF YOU, JUST DUMPING ME LIKE THAT WHILE YOU MADE YOUR ESCAPE...
SNAP
...HOLY CRAP! THIS IS, LIKE, THE SCOOP OF THE CENTURY!!
SNAP SNAP
mumble mumble mumble
I CAN'T BELIEVE NONE OF THIS HAS COME OUT... AND YET THERE'S NO COPS, NO MILITARY, NOT EVEN ANY NEWS VANS OR HELICOPTERS!
THESE MASS KIDNAPPINGS WERE MAJOR NEWS AT FIRST, BUT THEY FELL OFF THE RADAR FAST. THIS HAS TO BE A COVER-UP...
...
UM... IMARI-CHAN?
Ah!
...ANY-WAY!
NOW WE KNOW WHAT'S GOING ON IN HERE...

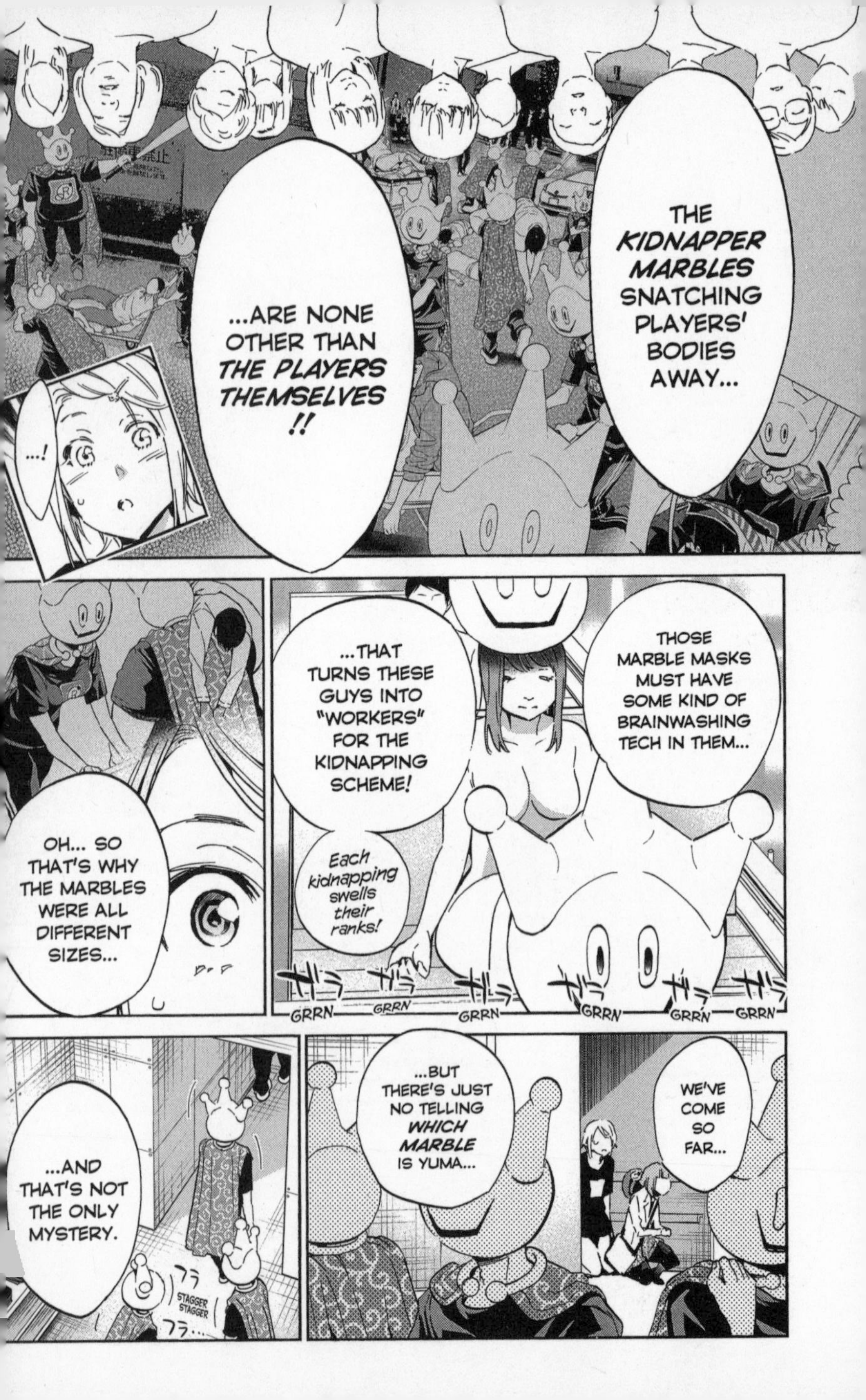
THE KIDNAPPER MARBLES SNATCHING PLAYERS' BODIES AWAY...
...ARE NONE OTHER THAN THE PLAYERS THEMSELVES !!
...!
THOSE MARBLE MASKS MUST HAVE SOME KIND OF BRAINWASHING TECH IN THEM...
...THAT TURNS THESE GUYS INTO "WORKERS" FOR THE KIDNAPPING SCHEME!
Each kidnapping swells their ranks!
GRRN GRRN GRRN GRRN GRRN GRRN
OH... SO THAT'S WHY THE MARBLES WERE ALL DIFFERENT SIZES...
WE'VE COME SO FAR...
...BUT THERE'S JUST NO TELLING WHICH MARBLE IS YUMA...
...AND THAT'S NOT THE ONLY MYSTERY.
STAGGER STAGGER

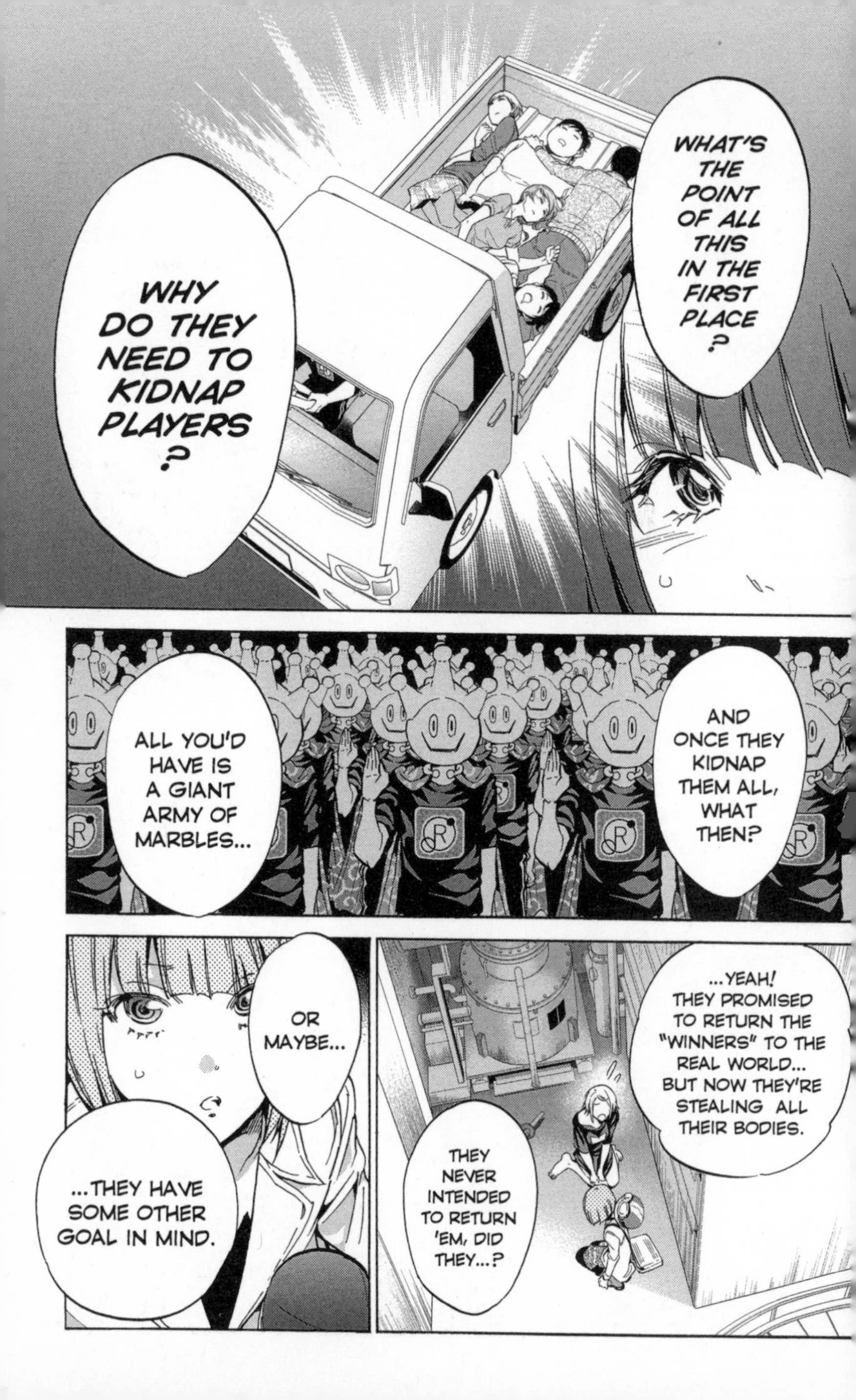
WHAT'S THE POINT OF ALL THIS IN THE FIRST PLACE?
WHY DO THEY NEED TO KIDNAP PLAYERS?
AND ONCE THEY KIDNAP THEM ALL, WHAT THEN?
ALL YOU'D HAVE IS A GIANT ARMY OF MARBLES...
...YEAH! THEY PROMISED TO RETURN THE "WINNERS" TO THE REAL WORLD... BUT NOW THEY'RE STEALING ALL THEIR BODIES.
THEY NEVER INTENDED TO RETURN 'EM, DID THEY...?
OR MAYBE...
...THEY HAVE SOME OTHER GOAL IN MIND.

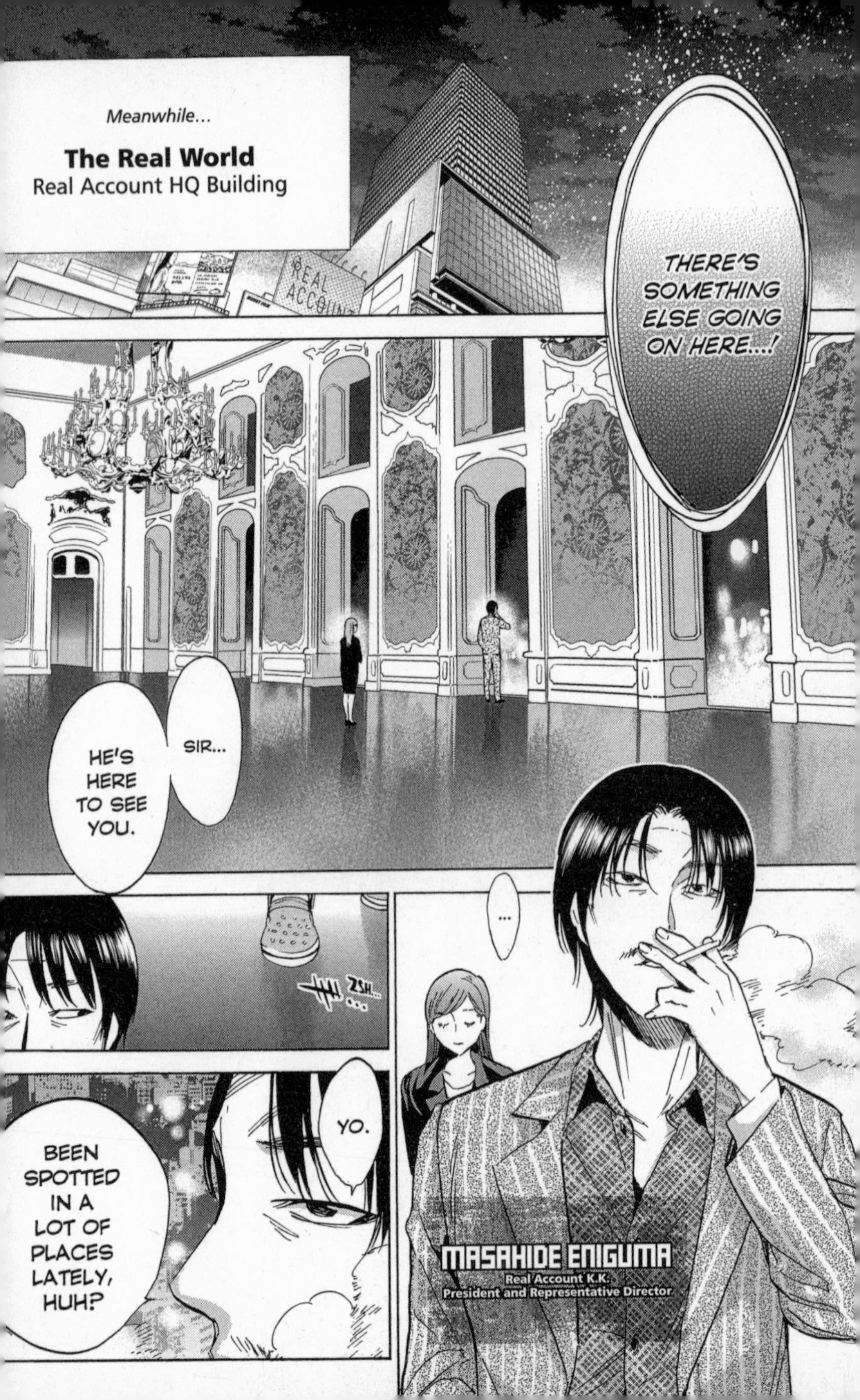
THERE'S SOMETHING ELSE GOING ON HERE...!
Meanwhile...
The Real World
Real Account HQ Building
SIR...
HE'S HERE TO SEE YOU.
...
MASAHIDE ENIGUMA
Real Account K.K.
President and Representative Director
ZSH...
YO.
BEEN SPOTTED IN A LOT OF PLACES LATELY, HUH?

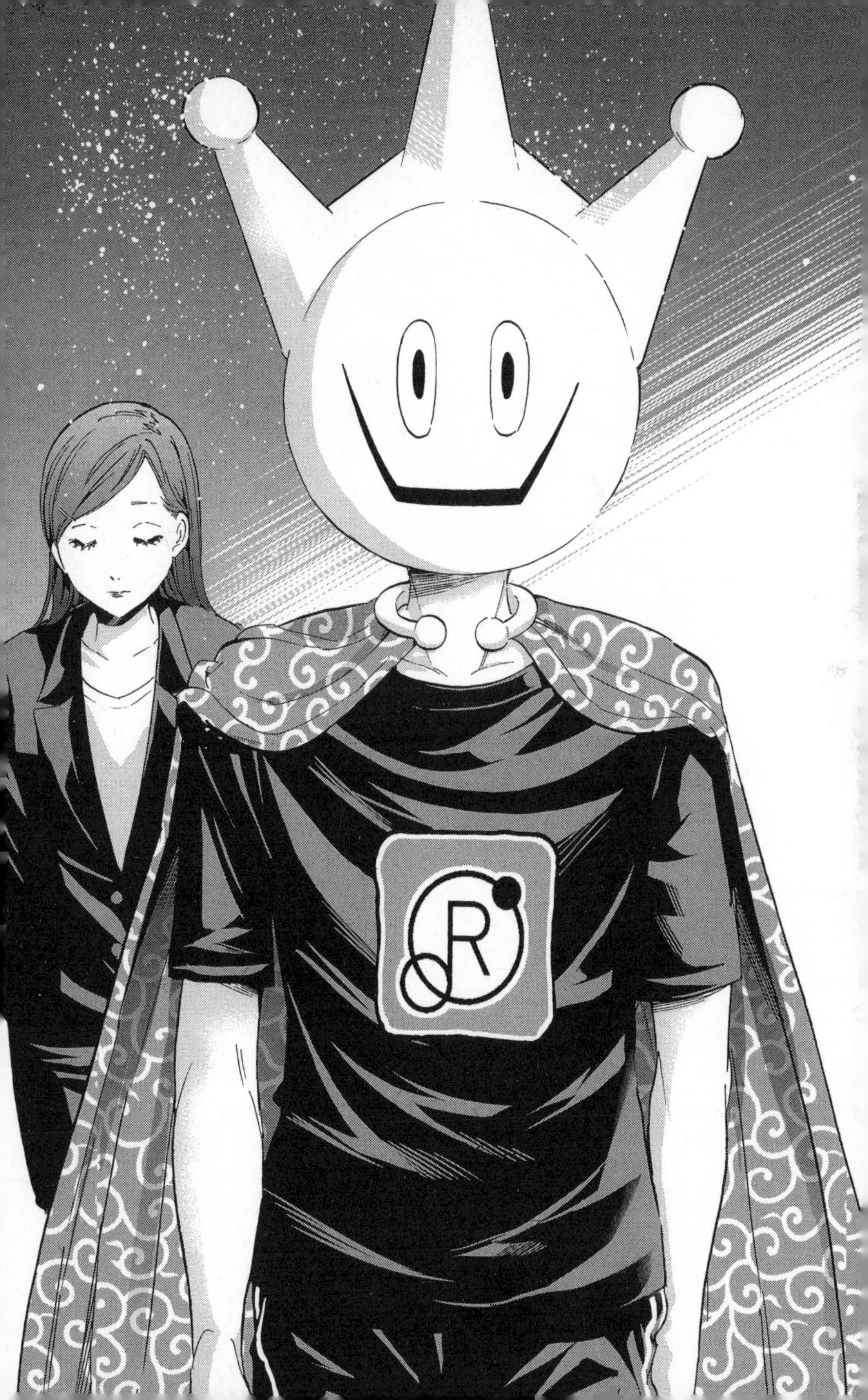

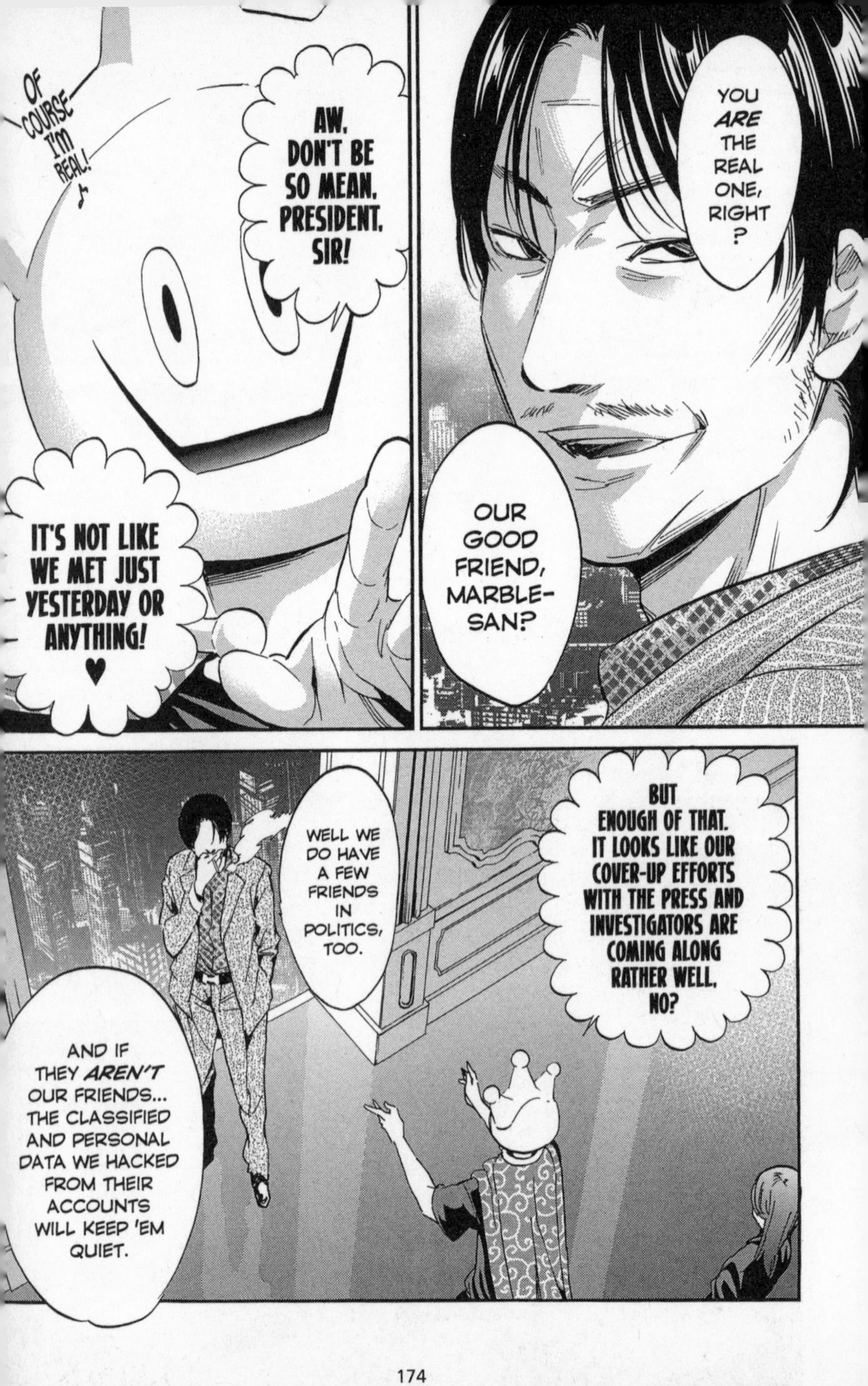
YOU *ARE* THE REAL ONE, RIGHT?
OUR GOOD FRIEND, MARBLE-SAN?
OF COURSE I'M REAL! ♪
AW, DON'T BE SO MEAN, PRESIDENT, SIR!
IT'S NOT LIKE WE MET JUST YESTERDAY OR ANYTHING! ♥
BUT ENOUGH OF THAT. IT LOOKS LIKE OUR COVER-UP EFFORTS WITH THE PRESS AND INVESTIGATORS ARE COMING ALONG RATHER WELL, NO?
WELL WE DO HAVE A FEW FRIENDS IN POLITICS, TOO.
AND IF THEY *AREN'T* OUR FRIENDS... THE CLASSIFIED AND PERSONAL DATA WE HACKED FROM THEIR ACCOUNTS WILL KEEP 'EM QUIET.

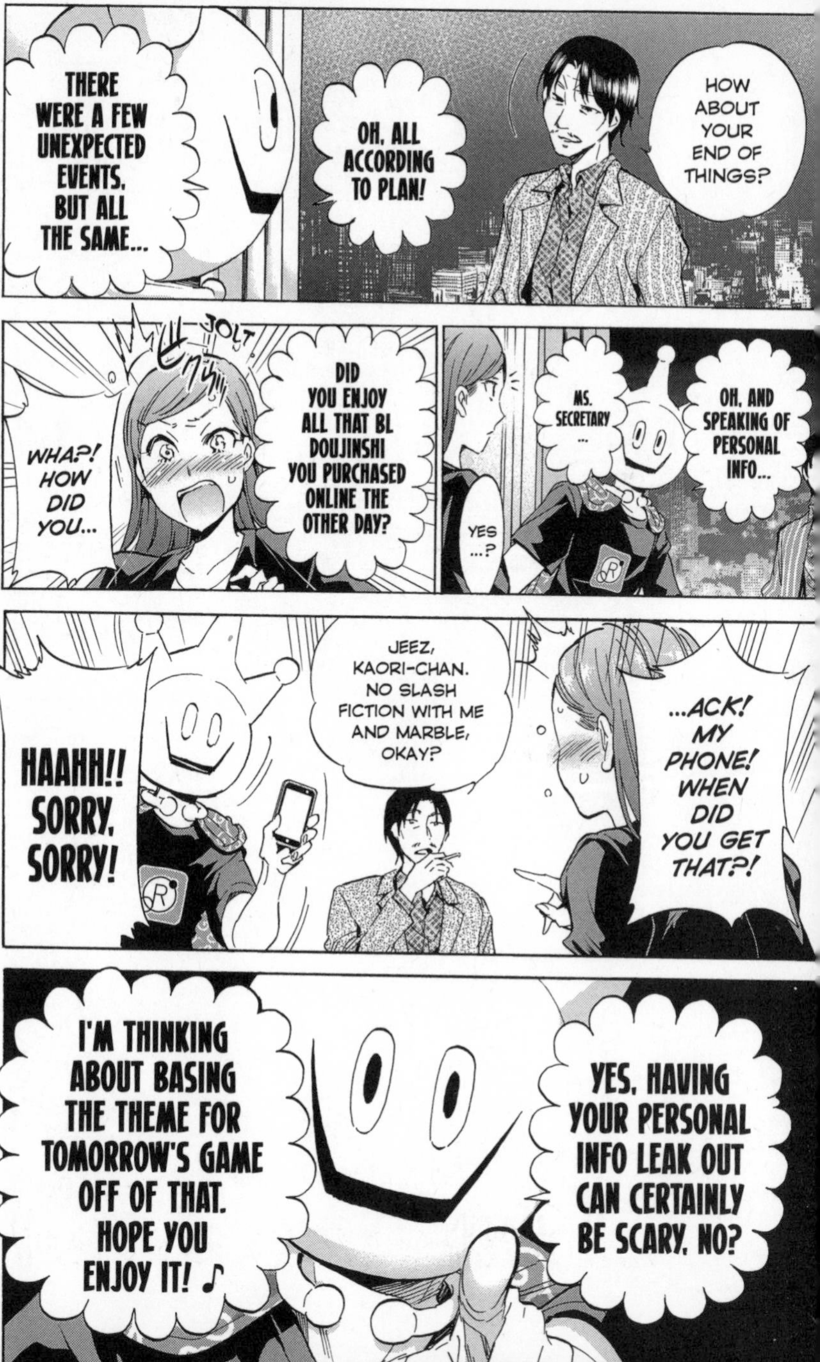
HOW ABOUT YOUR END OF THINGS?
OH, ALL ACCORDING TO PLAN!
THERE WERE A FEW UNEXPECTED EVENTS, BUT ALL THE SAME...
OH, AND SPEAKING OF PERSONAL INFO...
MS. SECRETARY ...
YES ...?
JOLT
DID YOU ENJOY ALL THAT BL DOUJINSHI YOU PURCHASED ONLINE THE OTHER DAY?
WHA?! HOW DID YOU...
...ACK! MY PHONE! WHEN DID YOU GET THAT?!
JEEZ, KAORI-CHAN. NO SLASH FICTION WITH ME AND MARBLE, OKAY?
HAAHH!! SORRY, SORRY!
YES, HAVING YOUR PERSONAL INFO LEAK OUT CAN CERTAINLY BE SCARY, NO?
I'M THINKING ABOUT BASING THE THEME FOR TOMORROW'S GAME OFF OF THAT. HOPE YOU ENJOY IT! ♪

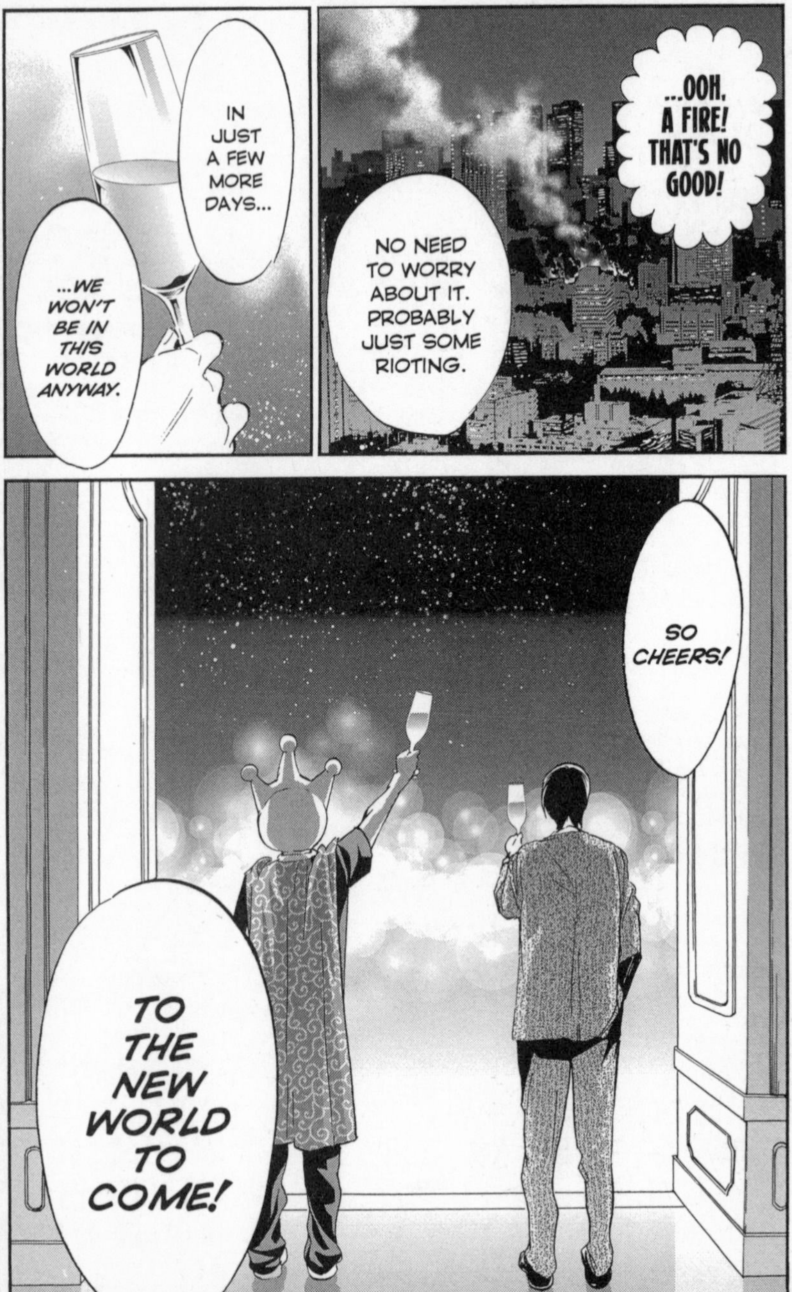
...OOH, A FIRE! THAT'S NO GOOD!
NO NEED TO WORRY ABOUT IT. PROBABLY JUST SOME RIOTING.
IN JUST A FEW MORE DAYS...
...WE WON'T BE IN THIS WORLD ANYWAY.
SO CHEERS!
TO THE NEW WORLD TO COME!
To be continued...

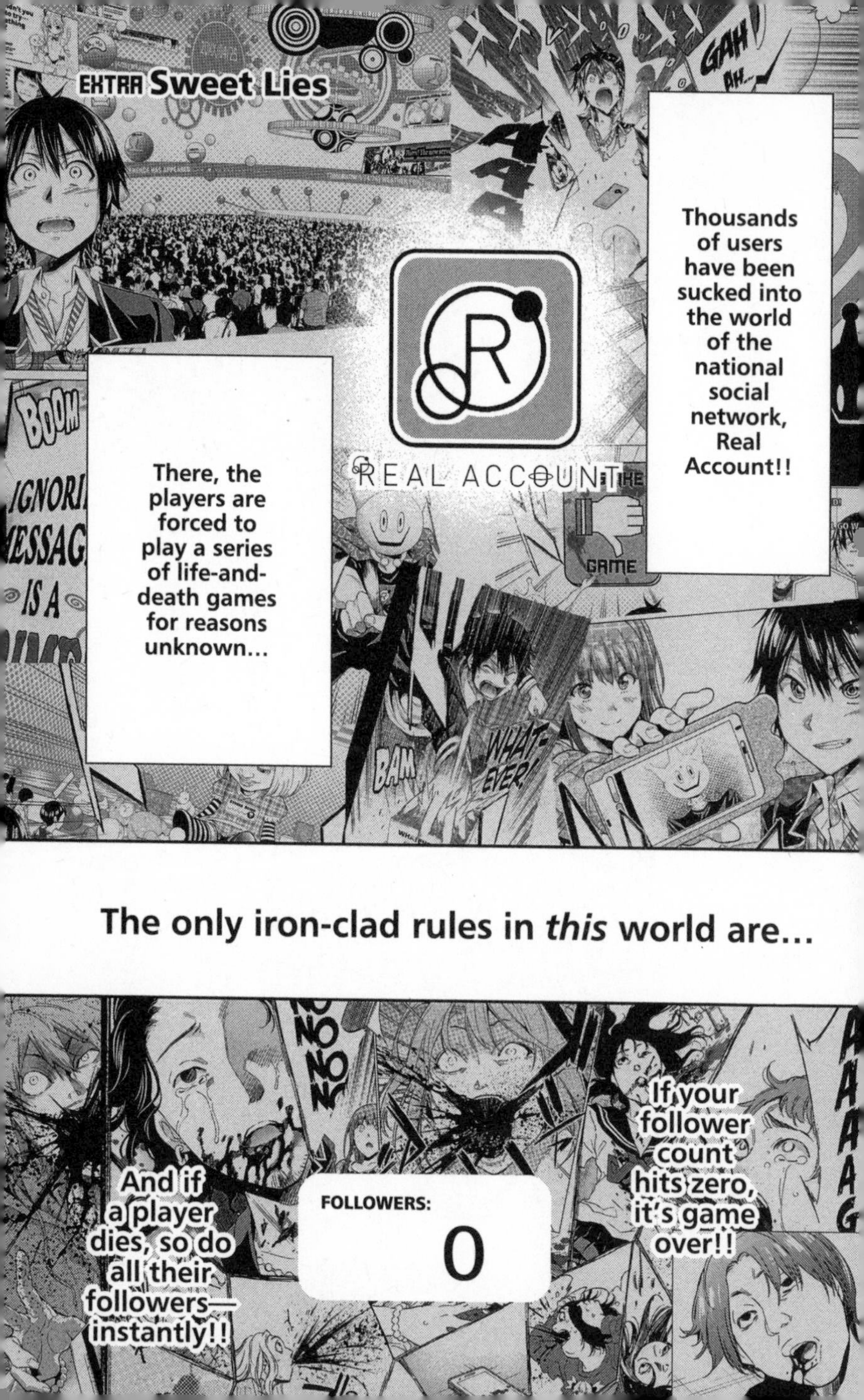
EXTRA Sweet Lies
GAH
AH...
Thousands of users have been sucked into the world of the national social network, Real Account!!
REAL ACCOUNT
GAME
There, the players are forced to play a series of life-and-death games for reasons unknown...
BOOM
WHAT-EVER!
BAM
The only iron-clad rules in *this* world are...
AAAAG
If your follower count hits zero, it's game over!!
NONONONO
FOLLOWERS:
0
And if a player dies, so do all their followers—instantly!!

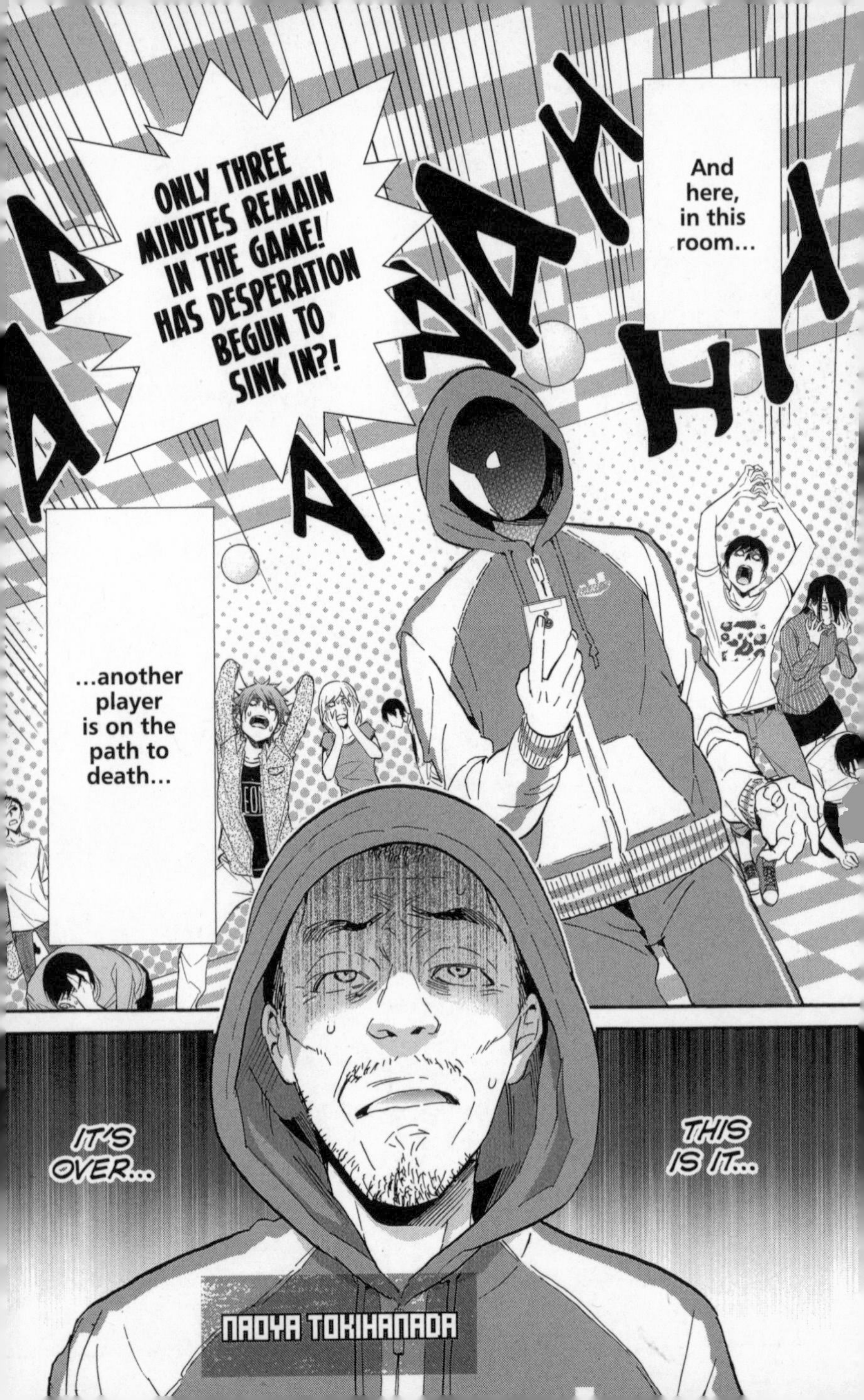
And here, in this room...
ONLY THREE MINUTES REMAIN IN THE GAME! HAS DESPERATION BEGUN TO SINK IN?!
...another player is on the path to death...
THIS IS IT...
IT'S OVER...
NAOYA TOKIHANADA

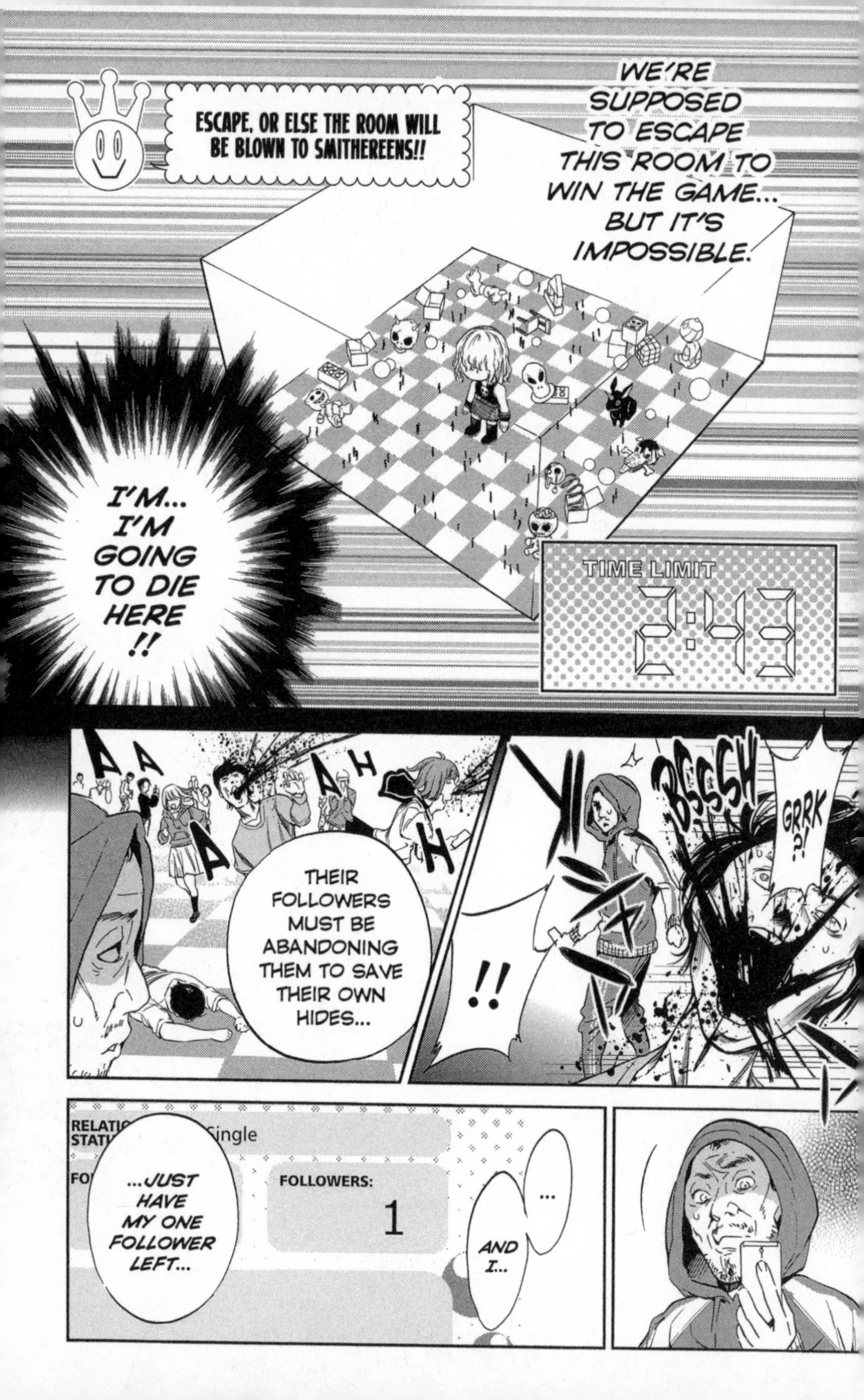
WE'RE SUPPOSED TO ESCAPE THIS ROOM TO WIN THE GAME... BUT IT'S IMPOSSIBLE.
ESCAPE, OR ELSE THE ROOM WILL BE BLOWN TO SMITHEREENS!!
TIME LIMIT
2:43
I'M... I'M GOING TO DIE HERE!!
BSSSH
GRRK?!
!!
THEIR FOLLOWERS MUST BE ABANDONING THEM TO SAVE THEIR OWN HIDES...
...
AND I...
FOLLOWERS:
1
Single
...JUST HAVE MY ONE FOLLOWER LEFT...

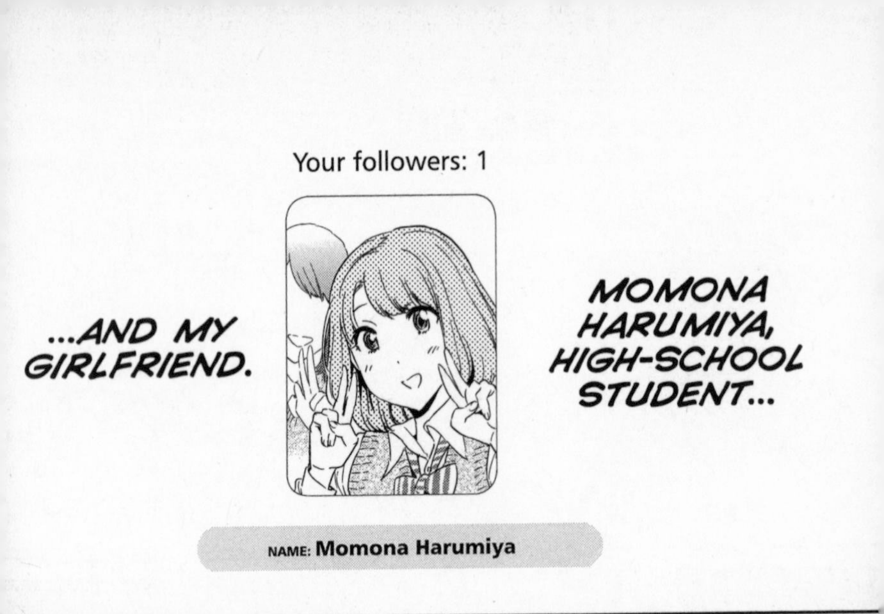
Your followers: 1
MOMONA HARUMIYA, HIGH-SCHOOL STUDENT...
...AND MY GIRLFRIEND.
NAME: Momona Harumiya

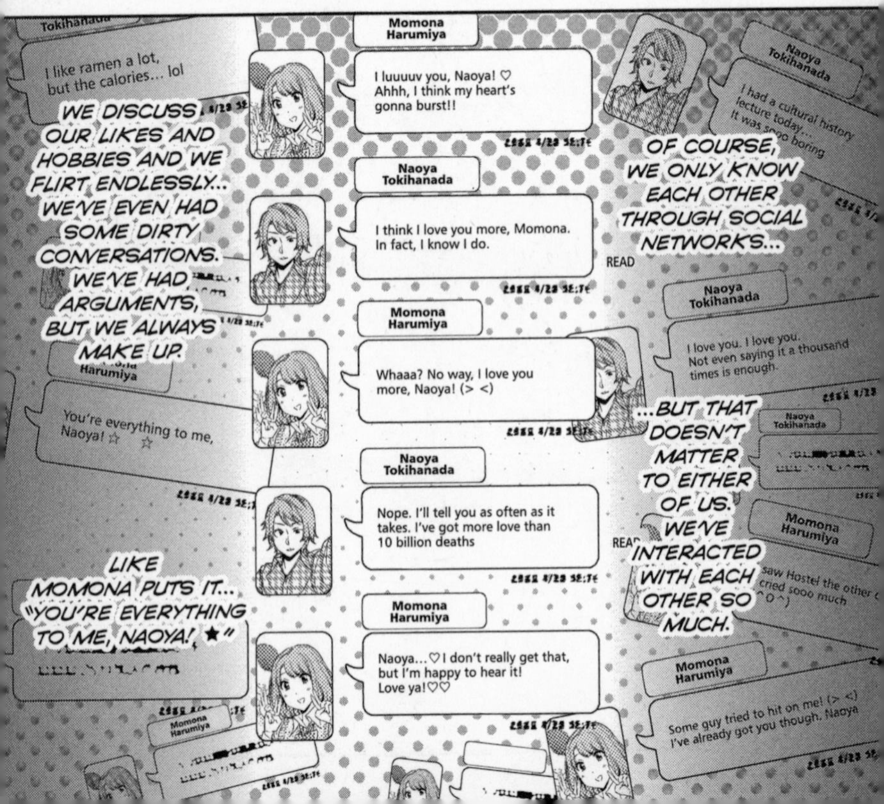
Naoya Tokihanada
I had a cultural history lecture today... It was sooo boring
OF COURSE, WE ONLY KNOW EACH OTHER THROUGH SOCIAL NETWORKS...
Momona Harumiya
I luuuuv you, Naoya! ♡ Ahhh, I think my heart's gonna burst!!
Naoya Tokihanada
I think I love you more, Momona. In fact, I know I do.
READ
Momona Harumiya
Whaaa? No way, I love you more, Naoya! (> <)
Naoya Tokihanada
Nope. I'll tell you as often as it takes. I've got more love than 10 billion deaths
Momona Harumiya
Naoya...♡ I don't really get that, but I'm happy to hear it! Love ya!♡♡
I like ramen a lot, but the calories... lol
WE DISCUSS OUR LIKES AND HOBBIES AND WE FLIRT ENDLESSLY... WE'VE EVEN HAD SOME DIRTY CONVERSATIONS. WE'VE HAD ARGUMENTS, BUT WE ALWAYS MAKE UP.
Harumiya
You're everything to me, Naoya! ☆ ☆
Naoya Tokihanada
I love you. I love you. Not even saying it a thousand times is enough.
...BUT THAT DOESN'T MATTER TO EITHER OF US. WE'VE INTERACTED WITH EACH OTHER SO MUCH.
Momona Harumiya
Momona Harumiya
Some guy tried to hit on me! (> <) I've already got you though, Naoya
LIKE MOMONA PUTS IT... "YOU'RE EVERYTHING TO ME, NAOYA! ★"

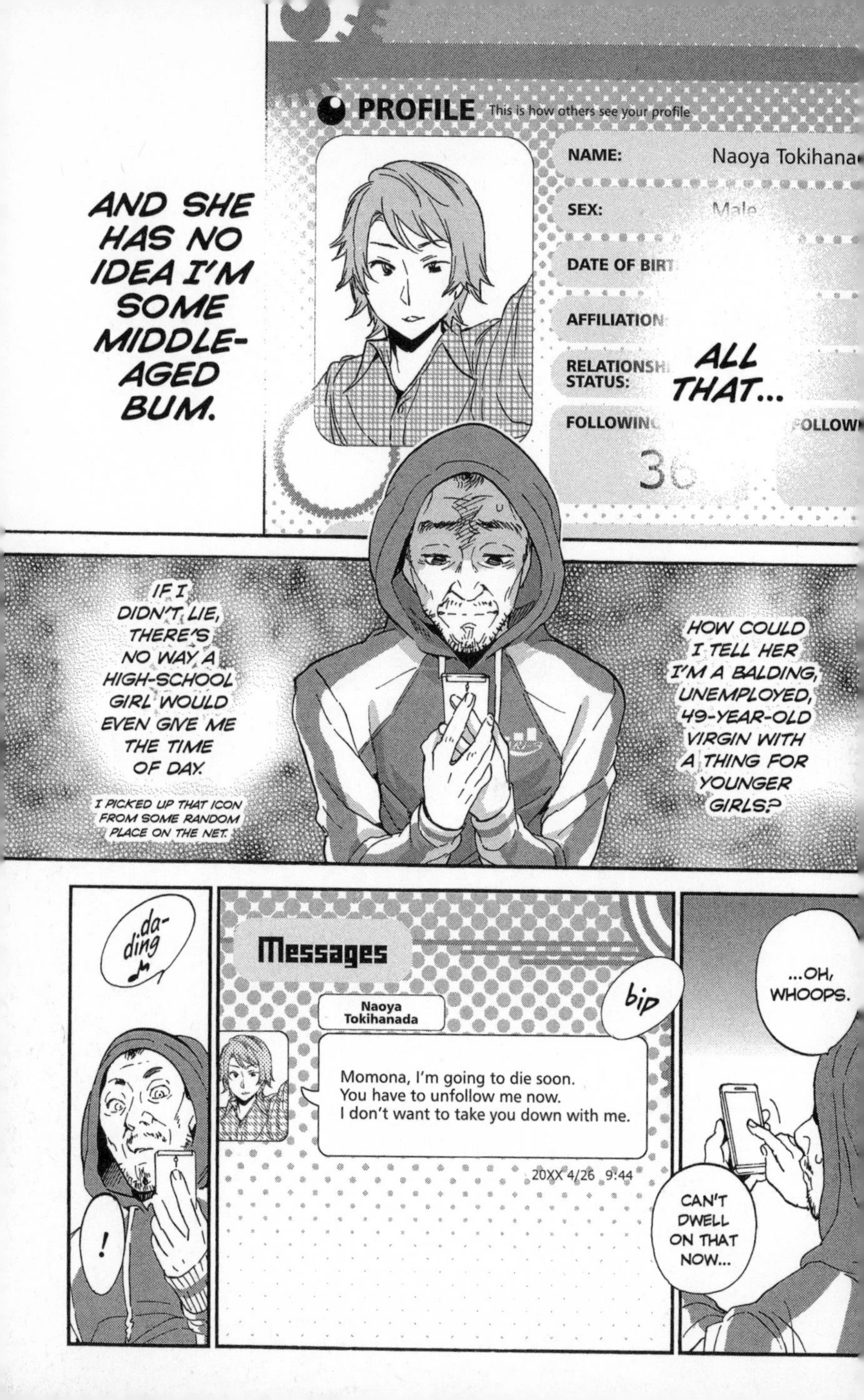
PROFILE This is how others see your profile
NAME: Naoya Tokihana
SEX: Male
DATE OF BIRT
AFFILIATION
RELATIONSH STATUS:
FOLLOWING
36
FOLLOW
ALL THAT...
AND SHE HAS NO IDEA I'M SOME MIDDLE-AGED BUM.
HOW COULD I TELL HER I'M A BALDING, UNEMPLOYED, 49-YEAR-OLD VIRGIN WITH A THING FOR YOUNGER GIRLS?
IF I DIDN'T LIE, THERE'S NO WAY A HIGH-SCHOOL GIRL WOULD EVEN GIVE ME THE TIME OF DAY.
I PICKED UP THAT ICON FROM SOME RANDOM PLACE ON THE NET.
...OH, WHOOPS.
CAN'T DWELL ON THAT NOW...
bip
Messages
Naoya Tokihanada
Momona, I'm going to die soon. You have to unfollow me now. I don't want to take you down with me.
20XX 4/26 9:44
da-ding
!

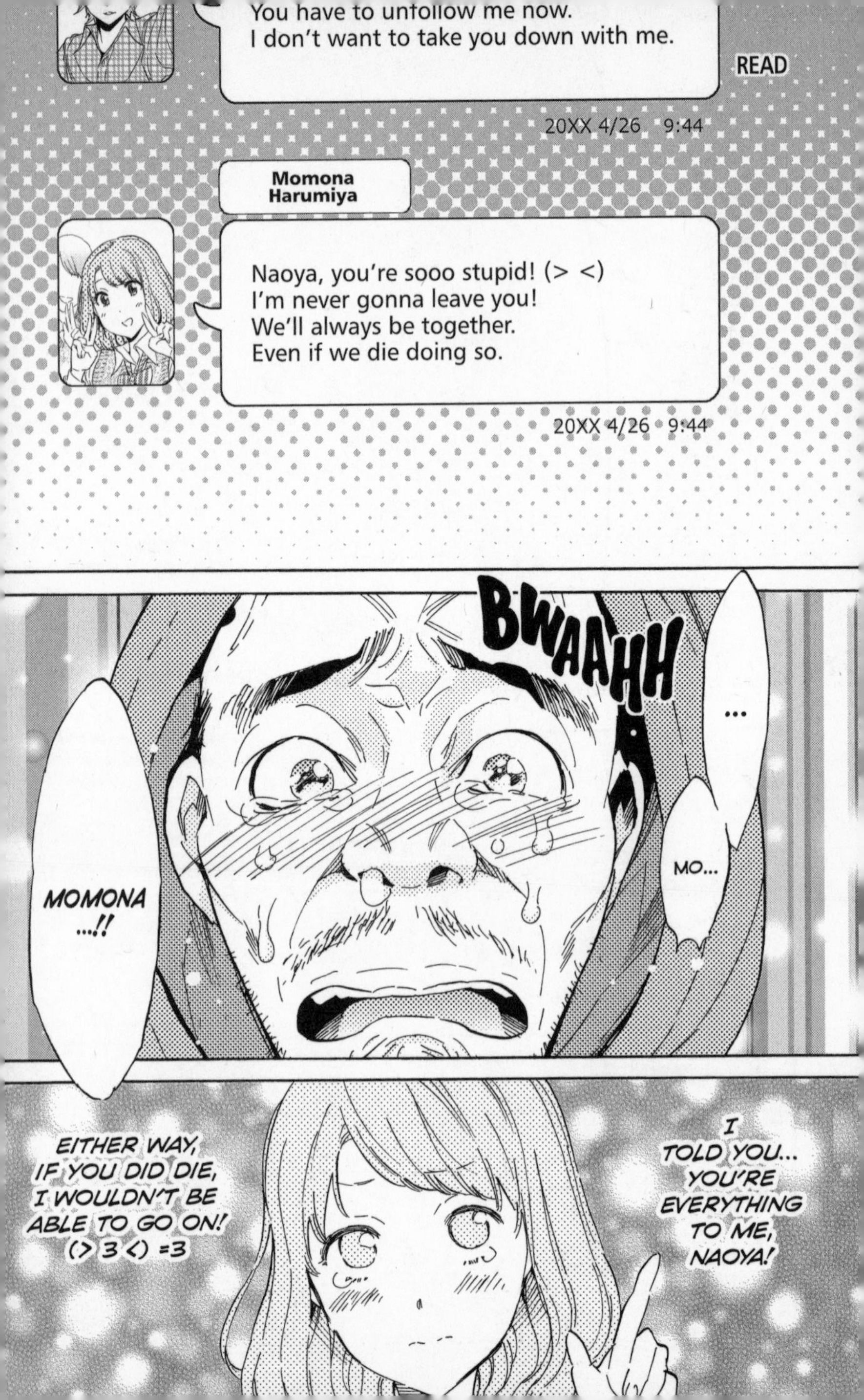
You have to unfollow me now.
I don't want to take you down with me.
READ
20XX 4/26 9:44
Momona Harumiya
Naoya, you're sooo stupid! (> <)
I'm never gonna leave you!
We'll always be together.
Even if we die doing so.
20XX 4/26 9:44
...
BWAAHH
MO...
MOMONA ...!!
I TOLD YOU... YOU'RE EVERYTHING TO ME, NAOYA!
EITHER WAY, IF YOU DID DIE, I WOULDN'T BE ABLE TO GO ON! (> 3 <) =3

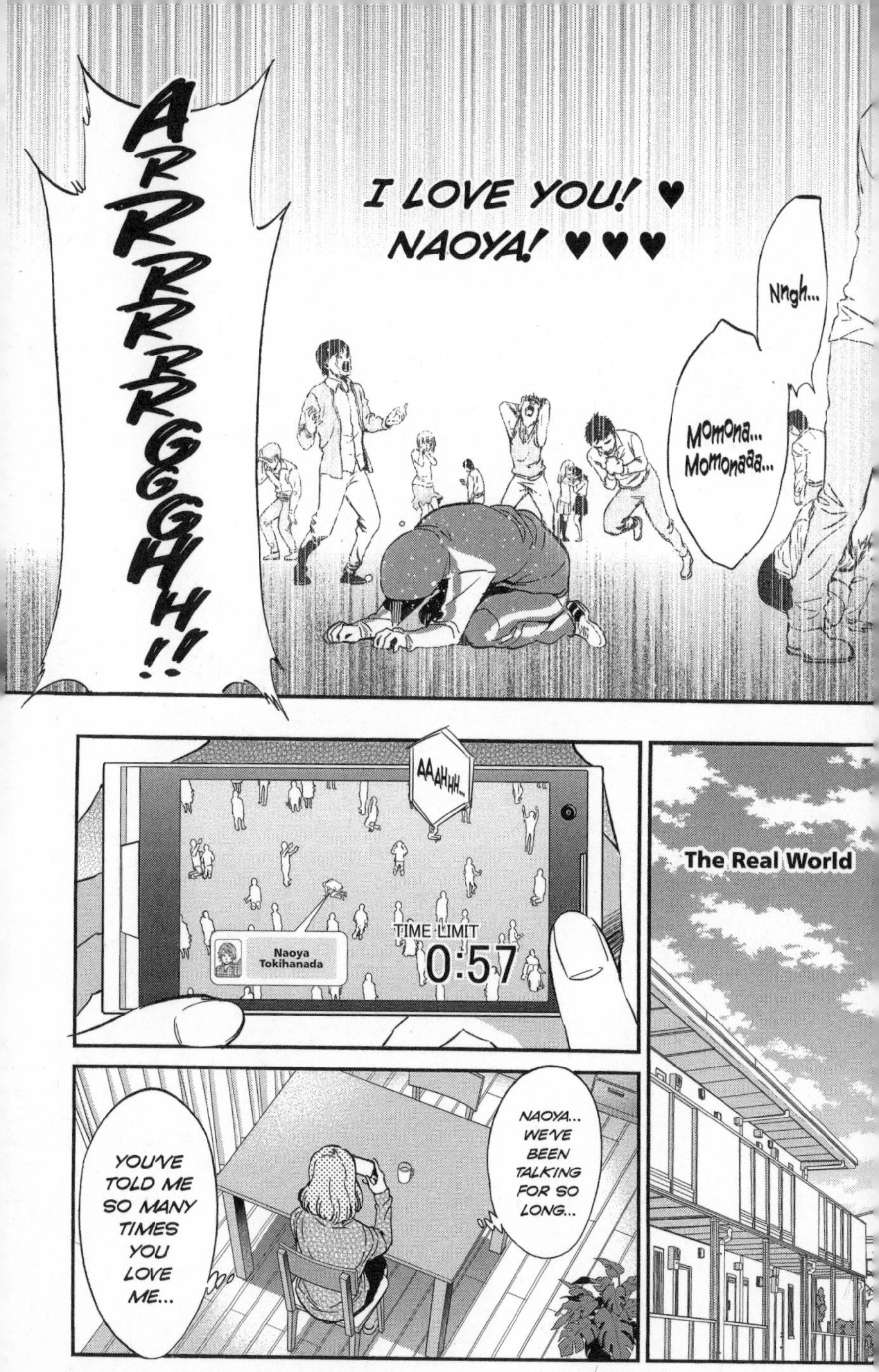
Nngh...
Momona... Momonaaa...
I LOVE YOU! ♥
NAOYA! ♥♥♥
ARRRRRRGGGHH!!
The Real World
AAAHHH...
Naoya Tokihanada
TIME LIMIT
0:57
NAOYA... WE'VE BEEN TALKING FOR SO LONG...
YOU'VE TOLD ME SO MANY TIMES YOU LOVE ME...

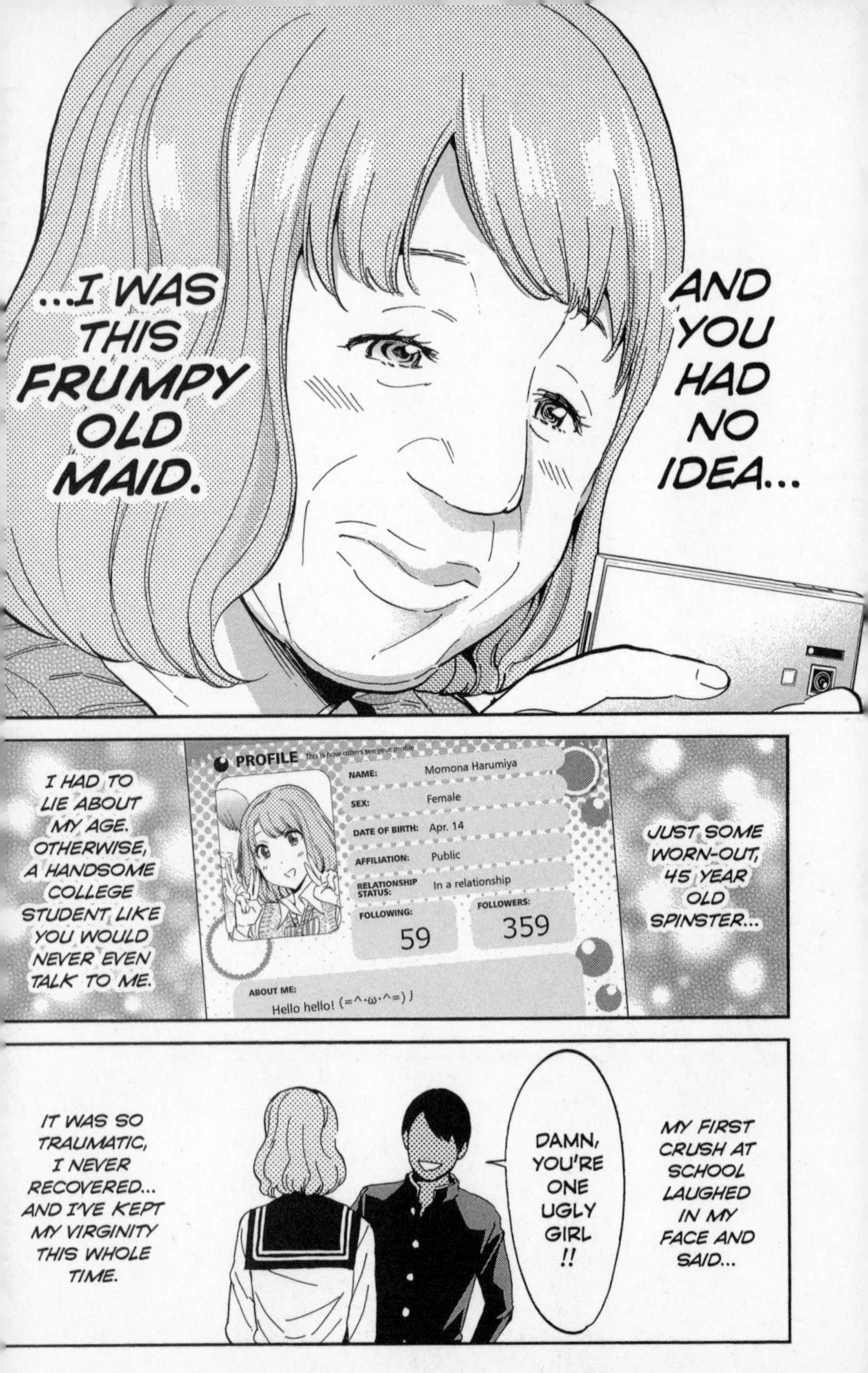
AND YOU HAD NO IDEA...
...I WAS THIS FRUMPY OLD MAID.
JUST SOME WORN-OUT, 45 YEAR OLD SPINSTER...
PROFILE This is how others see your profile
NAME: Momona Harumiya
SEX: Female
DATE OF BIRTH: Apr. 14
AFFILIATION: Public
RELATIONSHIP STATUS: In a relationship
FOLLOWING: 59
FOLLOWERS: 359
ABOUT ME: Hello hello! (=^･ω･^=)♪
I HAD TO LIE ABOUT MY AGE. OTHERWISE, A HANDSOME COLLEGE STUDENT LIKE YOU WOULD NEVER EVEN TALK TO ME.
MY FIRST CRUSH AT SCHOOL LAUGHED IN MY FACE AND SAID...
DAMN, YOU'RE ONE UGLY GIRL!!
IT WAS SO TRAUMATIC, I NEVER RECOVERED... AND I'VE KEPT MY VIRGINITY THIS WHOLE TIME.

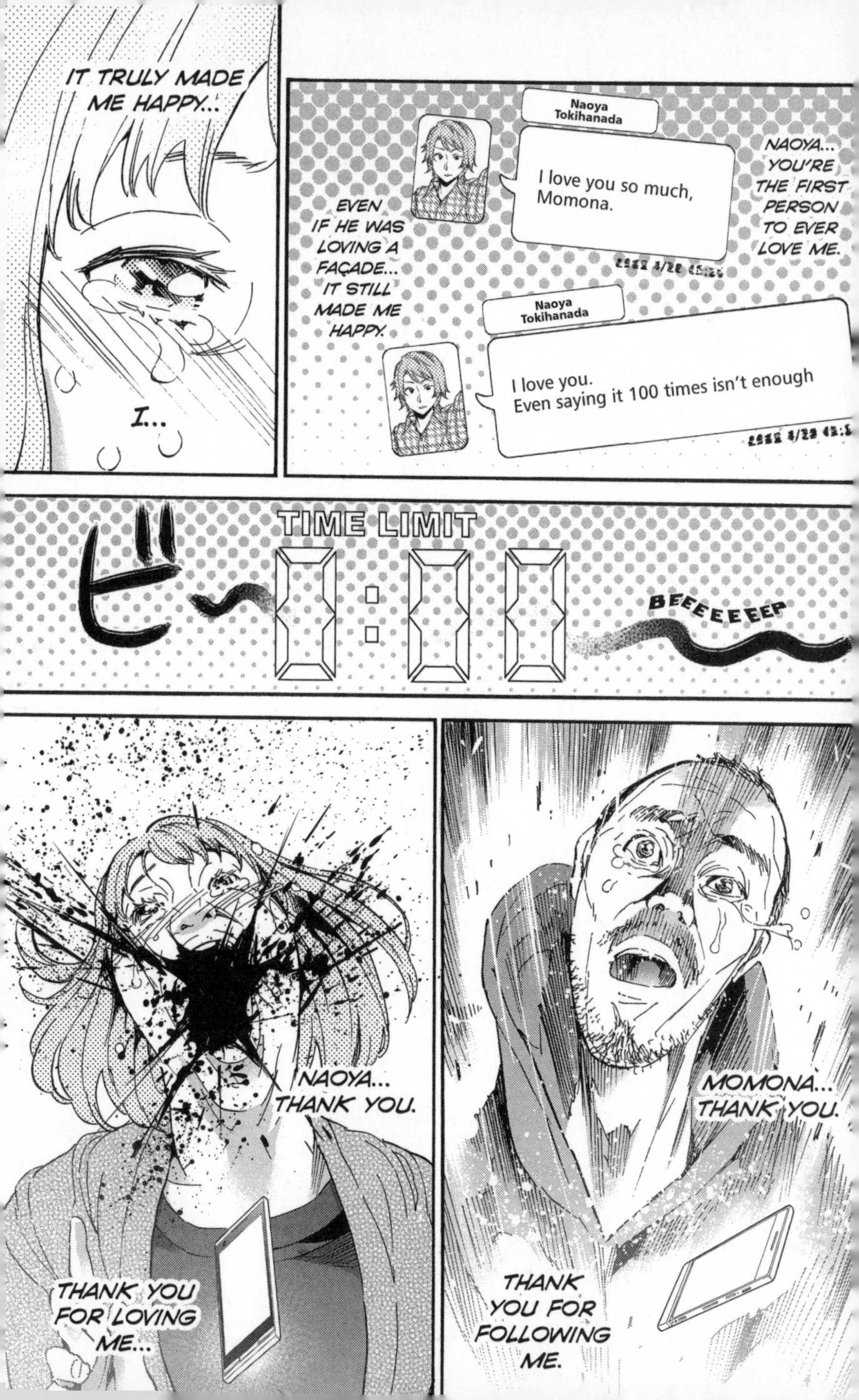
NAOYA... YOU'RE THE FIRST PERSON TO EVER LOVE ME.
Naoya Tokihanada
I love you so much, Momona.
EVEN IF HE WAS LOVING A FAÇADE... IT STILL MADE ME HAPPY.
Naoya Tokihanada
I love you.
Even saying it 100 times isn't enough
IT TRULY MADE ME HAPPY...
I...
TIME LIMIT
0:00
ビー
BEEEEEEEP
MOMONA... THANK YOU.
THANK YOU FOR FOLLOWING ME.
NAOYA... THANK YOU.
THANK YOU FOR LOVING ME...

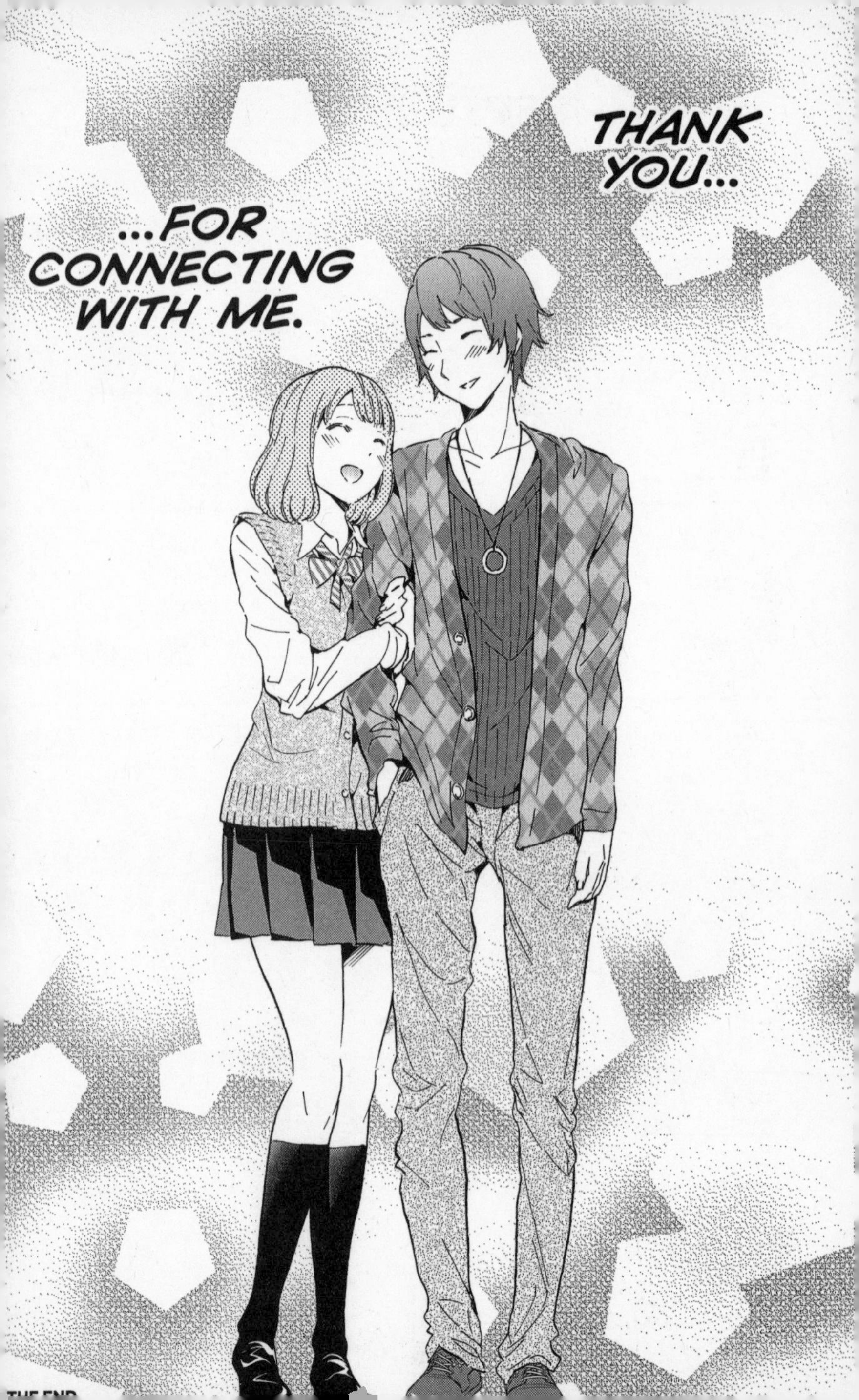
THANK YOU...
...FOR CONNECTING WITH ME.
THE END

OPERATION:

REPLY or REGRET STAMP COLLECTION

● 25 REGULAR STAMPS

(No. 01-15 rarity: [1 star], No. 16-25 rarity: [2 stars])

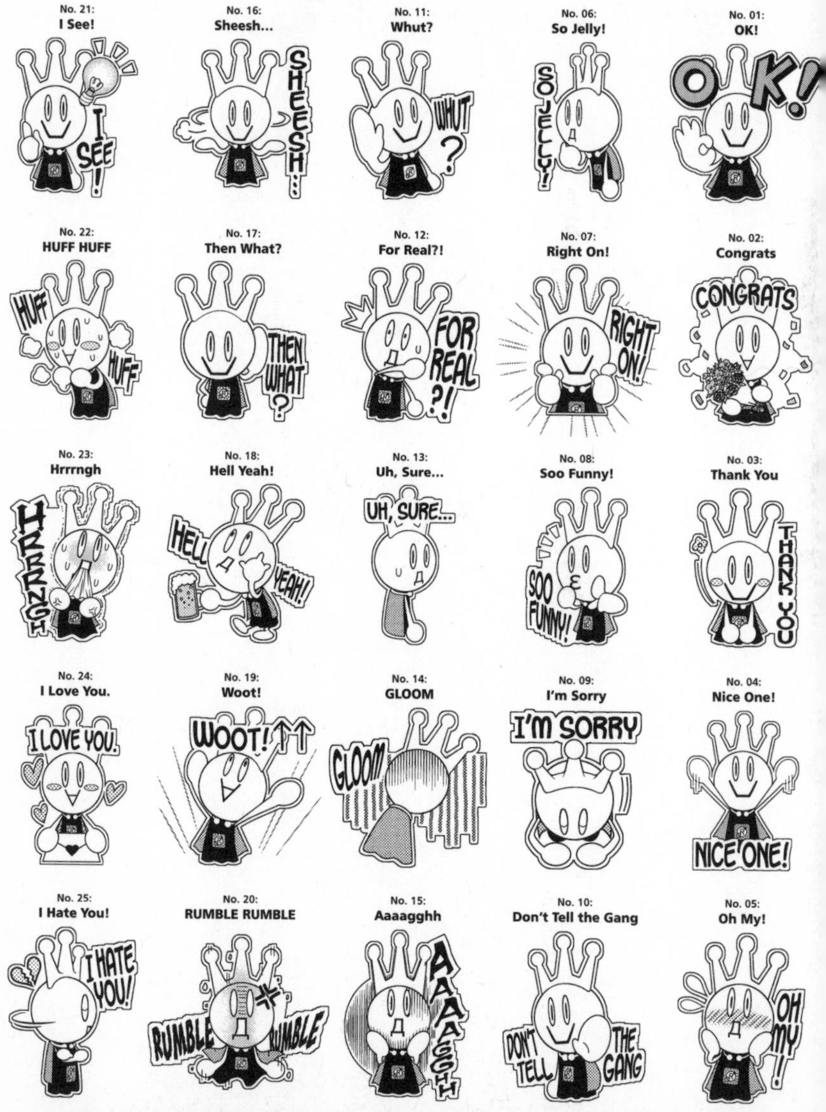

No. 01: OK!
OK!
No. 06: So Jelly!
SO JELLY!
No. 11: Whut?
WHUT ?
No. 16: Sheesh...
SHEESH...
No. 21: I See!
I SEE !
No. 02: Congrats
CONGRATS
No. 07: Right On!
RIGHT ON!
No. 12: For Real?!
FOR REAL ?!
No. 17: Then What?
THEN WHAT ?
No. 22: HUFF HUFF
HUFF HUFF
No. 03: Thank You
THANK YOU
No. 08: Soo Funny!
SOO FUNNY!
No. 13: Uh, Sure...
UH, SURE...
No. 18: Hell Yeah!
HELL YEAH!
No. 23: Hrrrngh
HRRRNGH
No. 04: Nice One!
NICE ONE!
No. 09: I'm Sorry
I'M SORRY
No. 14: GLOOM
GLOOM
No. 19: Woot!
WOOT!↑↑
No. 24: I Love You.
I LOVE YOU.
No. 05: Oh My!
OH MY!
No. 10: Don't Tell the Gang
DON'T TELL THE GANG
No. 15: Aaaagghh
AAAAGGHH
No. 20: RUMBLE RUMBLE
RUMBLE RUMBLE
No. 25: I Hate You!
I HATE YOU!

●20 EFFECT STAMPS

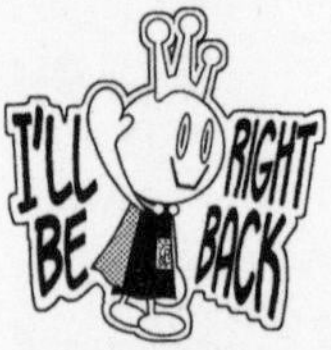
I'LL BE RIGHT BACK

No. 26:
I'll Be Right Back

Rarity: ★★

Send this stamp, and your turn won't come up again for 500 turns.

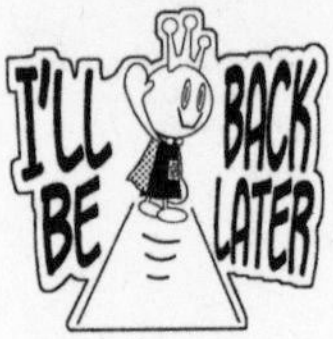
I'LL BE BACK LATER

No. 27:
I'll Be Back Later

Rarity: ★★★★

Send this stamp, and your turn won't come up again for 3000 turns.

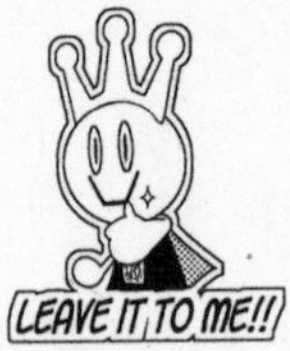
LEAVE IT TO ME!!

No. 28:
Leave It to Me!!

Rarity: ★★

For five hours after activation, any message meant for people in a three-meter radius will be sent to you instead.

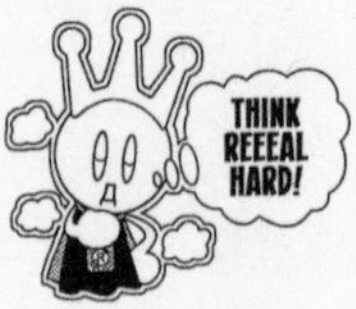
THINK REEEAL HARD!

No. 29:
Think Reeeal Hard!

Rarity: ★★★

Gives the recipient twice your remaining time.

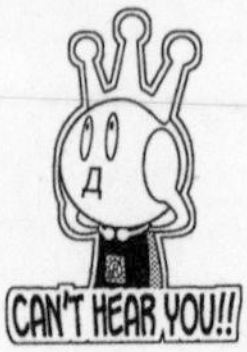
CAN'T HEAR YOU!!

No. 30:
Can't Hear You!!

Rarity: ★★★

Cancels any stamp effects placed upon you.

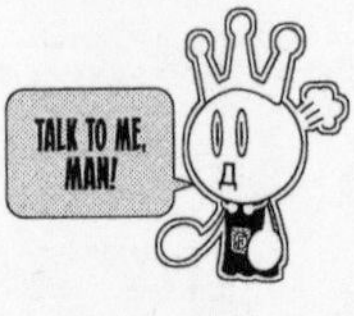
TALK TO ME, MAN!

No. 31:
Talk to Me, Man!

Rarity: ★★

Blocks the recipient from using stamps.

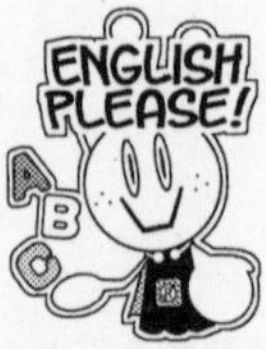
ENGLISH PLEASE!
A B C

No. 32:
English Please!

Rarity: ★★★

The recipient must send a reply in English.

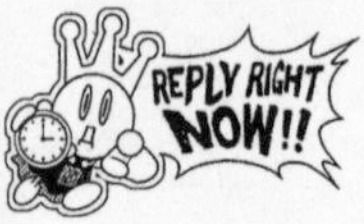
REPLY RIGHT NOW!!

No. 33:
Reply Right Now!!

Rarity: ★★★

Subtracts the time you didn't use from the recipient's clock.

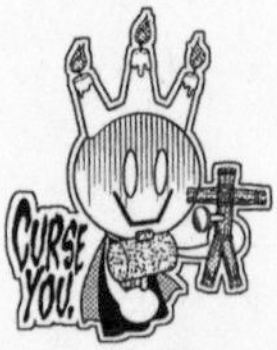
CURSE YOU.

No. 34:
Curse You.

Rarity: ★★★

For the next six hours, the recipient has a 666x-boosted chance of receiving a message.

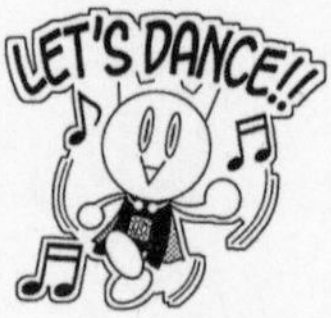
LET'S DANCE!!

No. 35:
Let's Dance!!

Rarity: ★★★

The recipient must shake their phone ten times before they can send a reply.

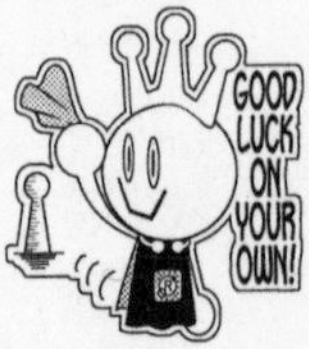
GOOD LUCK ON YOUR OWN!

No. 36:
Good Luck on Your Own!

Rarity: ★★★★

The recipient must be at least 10 meters away from all other players before they can send a reply.

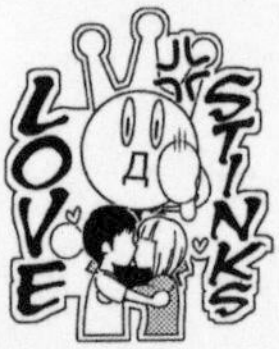
LOVE STINKS

No. 37:
Love Stinks!

Rarity: ★★★★

If the recipient's profile indicates they're in a relationship, they have only three seconds to send a reply.

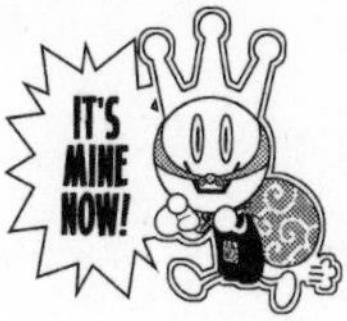
IT'S MINE NOW!

No. 38:
It's Mine Now!

Rarity: ★★★★★

After using, enter a stamp name in your remaining time to steal a stamp from the recipient.

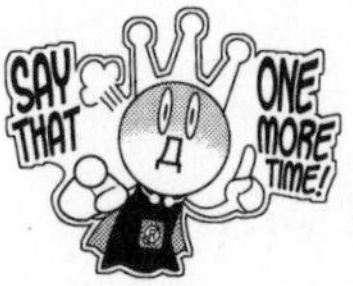
SAY THAT
ONE MORE TIME!

No. 39:
Say That One More Time!

Rarity: ★★★

Brings the chat back to the previous recipient.

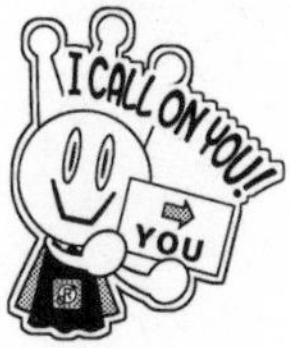
I CALL ON YOU!!
YOU

No. 40:
I Call on You!

Rarity: ★★★

After using, enter a person's name in your remaining time to send your message to them.

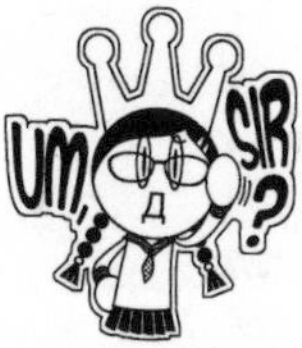
UM,
SIR?

No. 41:
Um, Sir?

Rarity: ★★

The recipient will always be male.

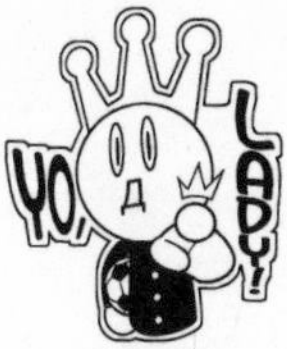
YO,
LADY!

No. 42:
Yo, Lady!

Rarity: ★★

The recipient will always be female.

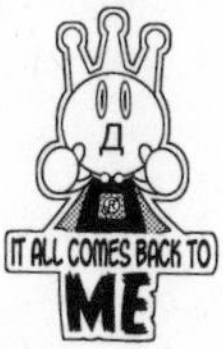
IT ALL COMES BACK TO
ME

No. 43:
It All Comes Back to ME

Rarity: ★★★

After using, you can then send two more messages, but your remaining time will not reset.

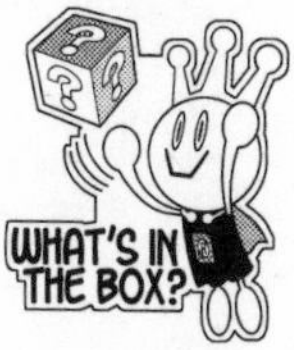
WHAT'S IN THE BOX?

No. 44:
What's in the Box?

Rarity: ★★★★★

Randomly turns into one of the other 44 stamps.

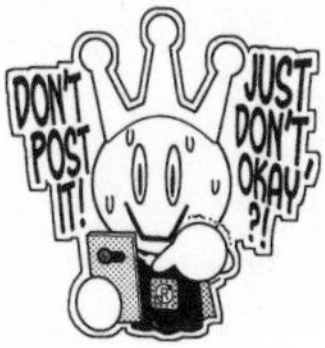
DON'T POST IT!
JUST DON'T, OKAY?!

No. 55:
Don't Post It! Just Don't, Okay?!

Rarity: ★★★★★

A mystery stamp. Sending triggers an unknown effect.

●1 SPECIAL STAMP

Awarded when you collect all 45 regular and effect stamps

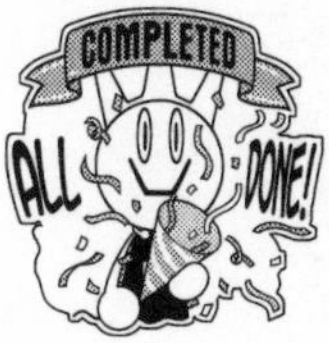
COMPLETED
ALL DONE!

Extra:
All Done!

Rarity: ★★★★★

Use this stamp, and Operation: Reply or Regret will immediately end for all players.

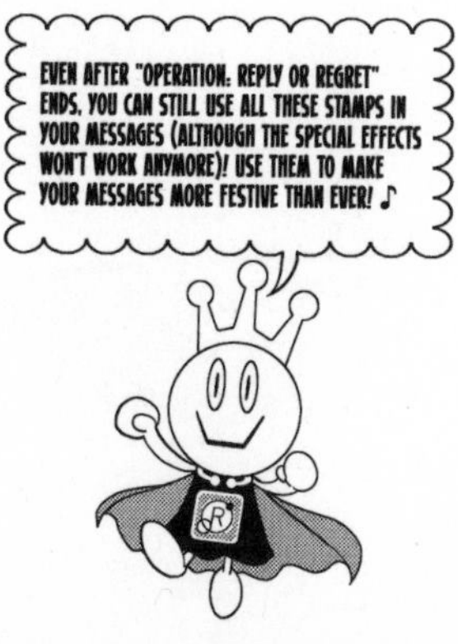
EVEN AFTER "OPERATION: REPLY OR REGRET" ENDS, YOU CAN STILL USE ALL THESE STAMPS IN YOUR MESSAGES (ALTHOUGH THE SPECIAL EFFECTS WON'T WORK ANYMORE)! USE THEM TO MAKE YOUR MESSAGES MORE FESTIVE THAN EVER! ♪

REAL ACCOUNT

Shizumu Watanabe   **Okushou**

STAFF
Shotaro Kunimoto
Iyo Mori
Yushi Takayama
Kazuki Ishihara
Minato Fuma

HELP STAFF
Yoneko Takamoto
Akoron
Mio Tsutsumi

EDITORS
Kazuhiko Otoguro
Sho Igarashi
Hideki Morooka
(Japanese GN)

JAPANESE COVER DESIGN
Tadashi Hisamochi
(HIVE)

Artist:
Shizumu Watanabe
Twitter account: @shizumukun

I'm a pretty negligent person, so I ignore people's texts all the time. If I ever joined a community where you'd get attacked for failing to reply... Just the thought of it is enough to send shivers down my spine. But I do believe that read receipts have a lot of wonderful uses, too.

Author:
Okushou
Twitter account: @okushou

You hear a lot about people winding up in the doghouse after their significant other reads through their phones, but I suppose a person's true personality really comes out in their bookmarks, doesn't it? Ladies: When peeking into your lover's phone, make sure to click on all the bookmarks that start with "x" or "fc" for me, all right? Have fun! (^ ^)

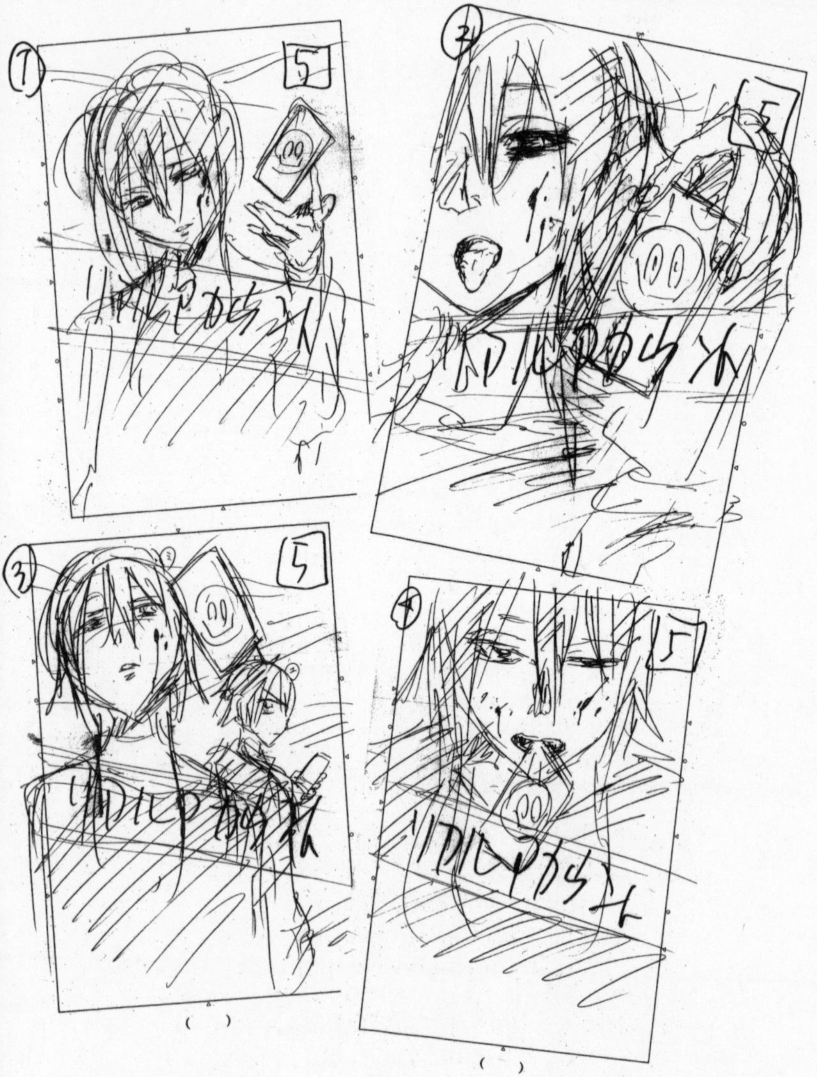

Four sketches for the Volume 5 cover. Sketch 2 was accepted.
My intention here was to provide a different atmosphere from before.

渡辺静

-Shizumu Watanabe

Rejected Cover Ideas #1

by Okushou

REAL ACCOUNT

STORY BY
OKUSHOU × ART BY
SHIZUMU
WATANABE

1

SNS TIME

SHONEN MAGAZINE COMICS

*This immediately got turned down by the designer... naturally, I suppose.

```
_ ʌ ʌ ʌ _
> I'm sorry! <
‾ ˅ ʌ ˅ ʌ ˅ ʌ ˅
```

Translation
Notes

PAGES 8 & 9

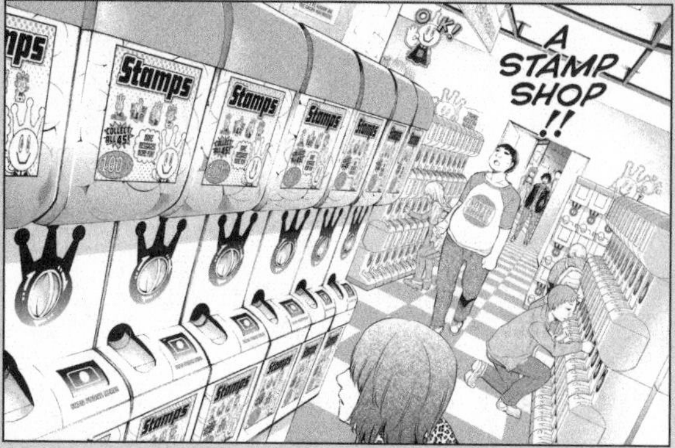
A STAMP SHOP !!
O K!
Stamps
Stamps
Stamps
COLLECT ALL 45!
100

GACHA-GACHA

Gacha-gacha or just *gacha* (also known as *gashapon* or *gachapon*) are vending machines that sell toys, figures, and other goods in capsules, usually for 100 to 500 yen per spin of the handle. Like the cheap toy vendors at US supermarkets, the exact toy you're given is random, driving users to spin multiple times per go to try and complete the whole set of whatever's on offer. Rooms like these, lined with long rows of *gacha* machines, are a common sight in places where otaku gather in Japan, such as Akihabara in Tokyo or Nihonbashi in Osaka. Secondhand shops may also sell whole *gacha* toy sets without any spinning required, although some rarer sets have serious collector value.

PAGE 41

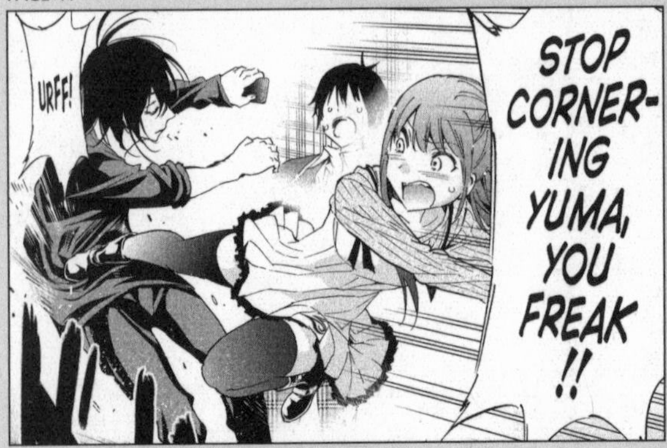
STOP CORNERING YUMA, YOU FREAK!!
URFF!

STOP CORNERING YUMA!

In the original Japanese, instead of "cornering," a specific term, *kabe-don,* was used. *Kabe-don,* [literally, wall slam] refers to a popular trope in romantic dramas and manga, where a man leans over a woman with her back against a wall, and slams his hand or hands on the wall. This creates a scene of heart-racing tension as the man's face is almost close enough to kiss the woman, and while in this position, the man may confess his love or ask the girl out on a date. In Real Account, Mizuki Kurashina is leaning over Yuma in the same fashion. Though it's unlikely that Mizuki intended to do this with any romantic undertones, it's not outside the realm of possibility that his infatuation with Yuma could go in such a direction.

PAGE 73

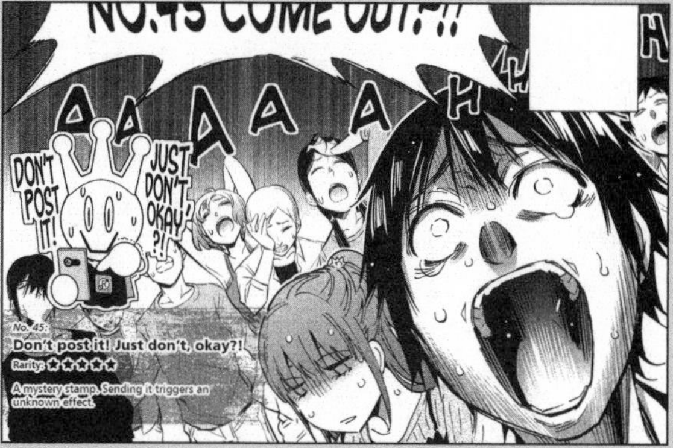
NO.45 COME OUT?!!
AAAAAAHHHH
DON'T POST IT!
JUST DON'T, OKAY?!
No. 45:
Don't post it! Just don't, okay?!
Rarity: ★★★★★
A mystery stamp. Sending it triggers an unknown effect.

DON'T POST IT! JUST DON'T, OKAY?!

This original Japanese translates to "Don't push, okay?! Absolutely do not push, okay?!" This comes from a Japanese meme that has its origins in a joke from a 90s comedy group called Dachou (Ostrich) Club. On a variety show called Super Jockey, there was a segment called the Nettou (hot water) Commercial, where participants would be able to promote whatever they want—the catch being that the amount of promotion time is equal to the amount of time they can stay almost fully submerged in a tub of hot water (at around 150°F). Dachou Club did a bit where one of the members held himself over the tub of hot water to cross over it without falling in and while slowly crossing, nervously looks back now and then to say, "Don't push, okay?! Absolutely do not push (me in), okay?" Naturally, he gets pushed and laughter ensues. In Real Account, because the stamps are pressed to post into a chat/message, the famous meme was used as a joke for the stamp.

PAGE 77

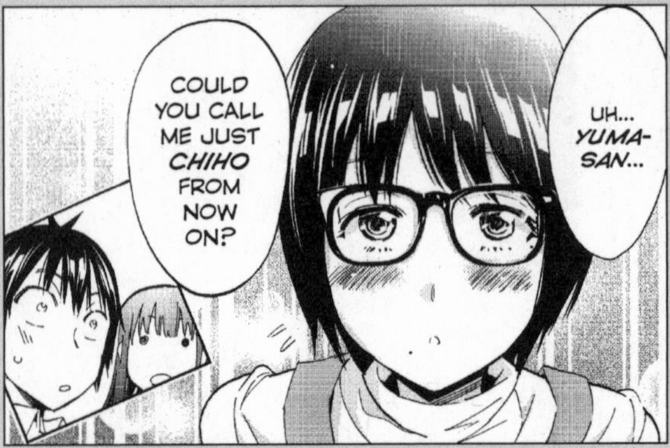
UH... YUMA-SAN...
COULD YOU CALL ME JUST CHIHO FROM NOW ON?

UH... YUMA-SAN...

It may not seem out of the ordinary for Chiho to call Yuma by his first name, but because it's formal to call people by their last names in Japan, Chiho's change signifies a change in their relationship. She now considers Yuma to be a close friend, or perhaps something more...

PAGE 109

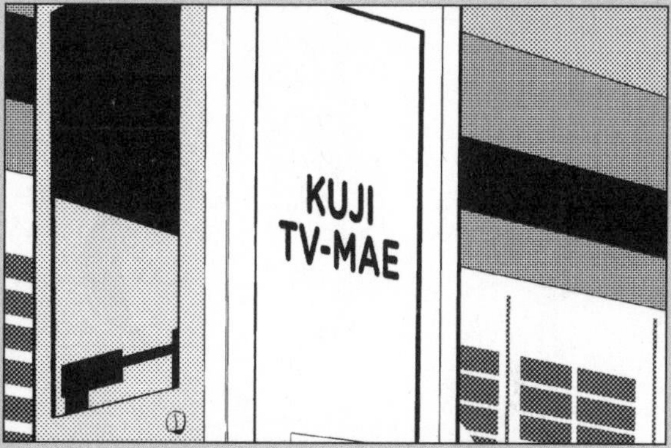
KUJI
TV-MAE

KUJI TV

Kuji TV is a play on Fuji TV, one of the five privately-owned stations serving the Kanto area of Japan, which includes metro Tokyo.

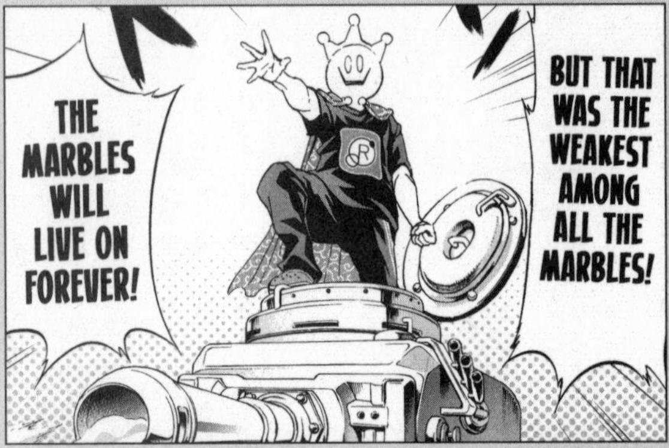
BUT THAT WAS THE WEAKEST AMONG ALL THE MARBLES!
THE MARBLES WILL LIVE ON FOREVER!

BUT THAT WAS THE WEAKEST AMONG ALL THE MARBLES! / THE MARBLES WILL LIVE ON FOREVER!

Both of these lines are well-known memes in Japanese culture. The "weakest among all" line is from a comic known as *Gag Manga Biyori*, parodying the tendency of action series to have the hero's sidekick say "You defeated the boss!" and the hero replying "Yes...but that was the weakest among the Four Emperors" or the like, in order to stretch out the story. The second comes from Shigeo Nagashima, a star Japanese baseball player who was in the Yomiuri Giants in the 1950s and 60s. At his retirement speech in 1974, he famously declared that the Giants "will live on forever." and then went on to prove it by leading the team to five Nippon Professional Baseball championships as their manager. He retired in 2001.

PAGE 175

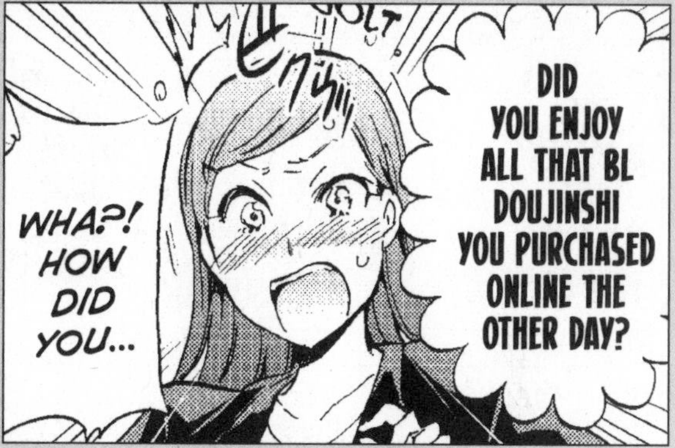
DID YOU ENJOY ALL THAT BL DOUJINSHI YOU PURCHASED ONLINE THE OTHER DAY?
WHA?! HOW DID YOU...

BL

BL, or "Boys' Love," is media genre featuring romantic encounters between men, usually created for a female audience. Media in this genre may also be called *shonen-ai* or *yaoi*, although the former term is slightly outdated and the latter tends to refer to more sexually explicit material. BL or *yaoi* indie comics (*doujinshi*) may also have stories featuring pairings between previously existing characters, which is similar to "slash" fanfiction.

ignificant other reads through t
phones, but I suppose a person's
personality really comes out in th
bookmarks, doesn't it? Ladies: W
peeking into your lover's phone,
ure to click on all the bookmark
tart with "x" or "fc" for me, all
Have fun! (^ ^)

BOOKMARKS THAT START WITH "X" OR "FC"

The implications of URLs starting with "x" should be obvious, but "fc" is short for FC2 Video, a Japanese site whose free "adult" section featured over 850,000 videos at the time of publication.

PAGE 193

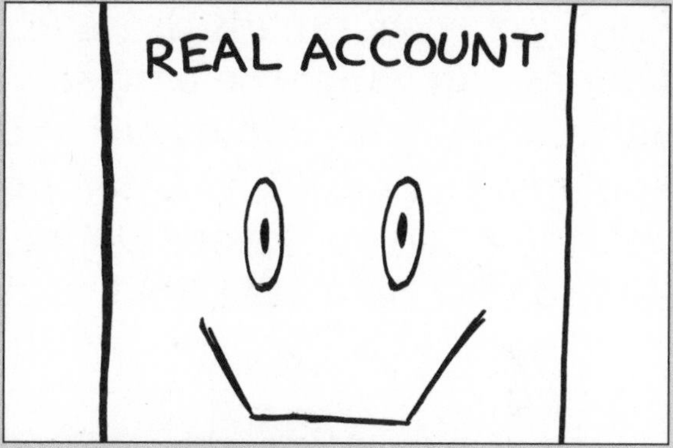
REAL ACCOUNT

REJECTED COVER IDEA 1

This cover is a parody of the cover from Volume 1 of *Assassination Classroom*, a manga series that ran in the rival magazine *Weekly Shonen Jump* from 2012 to 2016.

a Silent Voice

"The word heartwarming was made for manga like this." –Manga Bookshelf

"A harsh and biting social commentary... delivers in its depth of character and emotional strength." -Comics Bulletin

"A very powerful story about being different and the consequences of childhood bullying... Read it." –Anime News Network

Shoya is a bully. When Shoko, a girl who can't hear, enters his elementary school class, she becomes their favorite target, and Shoya and his friends goad each other into devising new tortures for her. But the children's cruelty goes too far. Shoko is forced to leave the school, and Shoya ends up shouldering all the blame. Six years later, the two meet again. Can Shoya make up for his past mistakes, or is it too late?

Available now in print and digitally!

INUYASHIKI

A superhero like none you've ever seen, from the creator of "Gantz"!

Ichiro Inuyashiki is down on his luck. He looks much older than his 58 years, his children despise him, and his wife thinks he's a useless coward. So when he's diagnosed with stomach cancer and given three months to live, it seems the only one who'll miss him is his dog.

Then a blinding light fills the sky, and the old man is killed... only to wake up later in a body he almost recognizes as his own. Can it be that Ichiro Inuyashiki is no longer human?

Comes in extra-large editions with color pages!

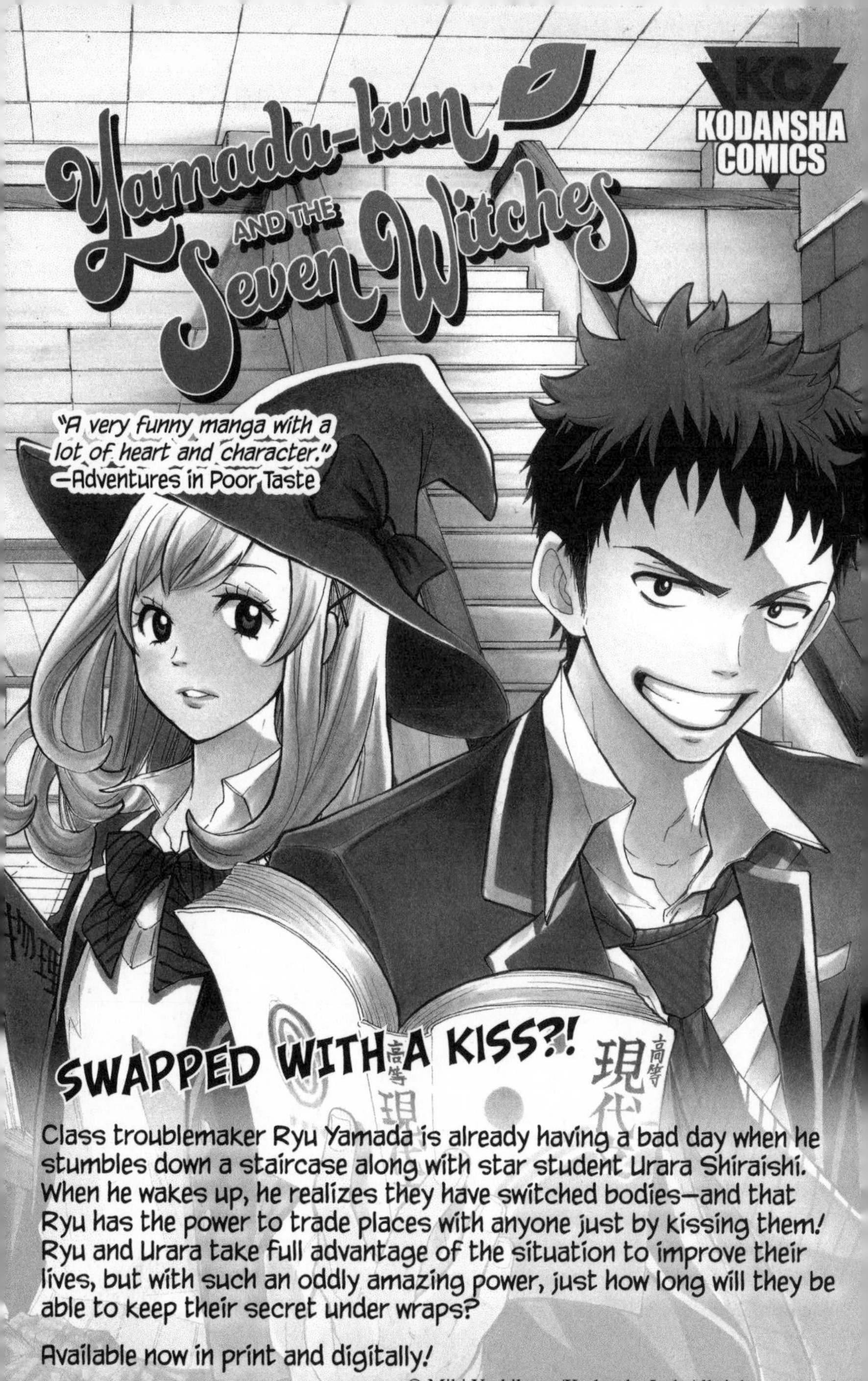
Yamada-kun AND THE Seven Witches
KODANSHA COMICS
"A very funny manga with a lot of heart and character."
—Adventures in Poor Taste
SWAPPED WITH A KISS?!
Class troublemaker Ryu Yamada is already having a bad day when he stumbles down a staircase along with star student Urara Shiraishi. When he wakes up, he realizes they have switched bodies—and that Ryu has the power to trade places with anyone just by kissing them! Ryu and Urara take full advantage of the situation to improve their lives, but with such an oddly amazing power, just how long will they be able to keep their secret under wraps?
Available now in print and digitally!

Real Account volume 5 is a work of fiction. Names, characters, places, and incidents are the products of the author's imagination or are used fictitiously. Any resemblance to actual events, locales, or persons, living or dead, is entirely coincidental.

A Kodansha Comics Trade Paperback Original.

Published in the United States by Kodansha Comics,
an imprint of Kodansha USA Publishing, LLC, New York.

Publication rights for this English edition arranged through Kodansha Ltd., Tokyo.

First published in Japan in 2015 by Kodansha Ltd., Tokyo, as *Real Account* volume 5.

ISBN 978-1-63236-306-0

Printed in the United States of America.

www.kodanshacomics.com

9 8 7 6 5 4 3 2 1

Translation: Kevin Gifford
Lettering: Evan Hayden
Editing: Ajani Oloye
Kodansha Comics edition cover design: Phil Balsman